Sky-map-calendar (Astronomicum
Caesareum, Ingolstadt, 1540, Petrus
Apianus, Metropolitan Museum of Art.
Photo courtesy of Linda Hall Library.)

THAT LONELY GAME

Melville, *Mardi,* and the Almanac

MAXINE MOORE

WITH A FOREWORD BY HENNIG COHEN

UNIVERSITY OF MISSOURI PRESS, 1975

Dedicated to the memory of HAROLD PAYNE STEWART

Copyright © 1975 by
The Curators of the University of Missouri
Library of Congress Catalog Card Number 75–8578
Printed and bound in the United States of America
University of Missouri Press, Columbia, Missouri 65201

Library of Congress Cataloging in Publication Data

Moore, Maxine, 1927–
 That lonely game.

 (University of Missouri studies; 63)
 Bibliography: p.
 Includes index.
 1. Melville, Herman, 1819–1891. Mardi. I.
Title. II. Series: University of Missouri—Columbia.
University of Missouri studies; 63.
PS2384.M33M66   818′.3′07   75–8578
ISBN 0–8262–0175–X

Acknowledgments

In pursuing this quest through *Mardi* I have found myself indebted to more people than can be listed here. Among these, certainly, are the many scholars whose works are mentioned in notes, bibliography, and appendixes, but especially Professor Merrell R. Davis. His detailed study of *Mardi* provided a wealth of material on which to build, even as his conclusions inspired the urge to argue that resulted in this book.

I am grateful also to Professors Edwin Eigner, Floyd Horowitz, Elizabeth Schultz, and Robert M. Smith for their help and encouragement, and to Professor Hennig Cohen for valuable critiques, cogent questions, and scholarly acceptance.

In addition, I deeply appreciate help and materials received from The American Antiquarian Society, the Department of Geography at the University of Missouri —Kansas City, the R. A. Long Planetarium of the Kansas City Museum of History and Science, Rodale Press, U.S. Playing Card Company, The Library of Congress, Linda Hall Library, and Ms. Helen Bennett of the library at the University of Missouri—Kansas City.

For invaluable help in production I am deeply indebted to Bessie Clare Stewart, who listened patiently and perceptively as I labored to work out the problems and who gave creative and critical suggestions for both riddle and composition; also to Selma Dreiseszun, proofreader extraordinaire, and to Camillie Lester, patient typist.

And finally, I would offer heartfelt thanks to Francis Harry Moore, and to Frances, Rebecca, Miranda, and Patricia Moore for their patience, support, forebearance, and devotion during the four years this work was in progress.

Preface

Tho' somewhat unusual for a donor, I must beg to apologize
for making you the accompanying present of "Mardi." But
no one who knows your library can doubt, that such a choice
conservatory of exotics & other rare things in literature, after
being long enjoyed by yourself, must, to a later posterity, be
preserved intact by a place in it for a plant, which tho' now
unblown (emblematically, the leaves, you perceive, are uncut) may
possibly—by some miracle, that is—flower like the aloe, a hundred
years hence—or not flower at all, which is more likely by far for
some aloes never flower.

> .   .   .   .   .   .

The leaves, I repeat, are uncut—let them remain so—and let
me supplementaryly hint, that a bit of old parchment (from some
old Arabic M.S.S. on Astrology) tied round each volume, &
sealed on the back with a Sphynx, & never to be broken till
the aloe flowers—would not be an unsuitable device for the
bookbinders of "Mardi."

Herman Melville to Evert Duyckinck.
From Eleanor Melville Metcalf,
Cycle and Epicycle (Cambridge, Massachusetts, 1953)

Egyptian horoscope

The subject of this book is the astrological riddle of
Melville's aloe-bound book of *Mardi, and a Voyage Thither.* In the
initial stages of my study, I had planned to limit the work to an
exploration of the astronomical dating system, without attempting
either interpretation or judgment. As research progressed,
however, the implications spread like Uhia's girth or Maramma's
banyan tree, and the dating system proved to be only an entrance
into a far greater substructure of *Mardi.*

Melville's repeated emphasis on the riddling nature of *Mardi,*
his tendency to present and then drop lines of imagery, and his
constant allusions to games all combined to suggest that *Mardi*
was designed less as a literary work than as a riddle game, and in
this study I have approached the book from that perspective. My
aim has been to allow Melville's imagery to have its way, and to
follow it wherever it leads. The surprising rather than the
expected result has been the discovery of a unity in *Mardi* that is
anything but evident in a more conventional literary study.

M. M.   Kansas City, Missouri, February, 1975

Foreword by Hennig Cohen

Melville's novels from *Typee* (1846) to *Moby Dick* (1851) are
circular in form, abound in images of circularity, and have
first-person narrators who describe retrospectively the maturing
effect of adventurous, meaningful voyages. *Mardi* is no exception.
Melville's relatively unpretentious first novel, *Typee,* is the
narrative of a "land-sick" young sailor on a whaleship beguiled
by the prospect of life in a South Sea island paradise. He jumps
ship to enjoy freedom from the restraints of civilization, to enjoy
the physical ease and free play of the instincts, but learns that the
instincts have their inconsistencies, and he circles back to
civilization, his hands red with blood. *Omoo* (1848) continues the
same narrative and, though more casual, is similarly structured.
Rescued by another whaleship, with an inept captain and an
unruly crew that eventually refuses duty, the narrator is jailed in
Tahiti until he drifts away to become a beachcomber. The
"impulse" to go "to sea once more" is compelling, however, and
he signs "for the coming cruise" on a whaleship appropriately
named the *Leviathan,* again completing the circle. *Mardi* (1849)
begins aboard a whaleship in the Pacific, the narrator a
disgruntled young seaman brooding on the possibility of
desertion. Its circularity and the initiation experience of the
narrator are fully considered in Maxine Moore's book. *Redburn*
(1849), subtitled *His First Voyage,* is the recollection of a
round-trip cruise of a "sailor boy" on a packet between New
York and Liverpool remembered years later by a mature
narrator. *White-Jacket* (1850) is a first-person narrative of an
"ordinary seaman" serving on an American man-of-war, returning
to its home port from the Pacific around Cape Horn, and
approaching maturity along the way. And *Moby Dick* (1851) is
the "circumnavigating" voyage of a greenhorn whaler, once
more a retrospective first-person narrative of initiation.

Portrait of Herman Melville circa 1846
by Asa W. Twitchell (Courtesy Berkshire
Atheneum, Pittsfield, Massachusetts)

Yet if these novels are circular in that the situation at the
end is a return to the beginning and that as retrospective
narratives they are a return from the present to the past, they are
also open ended, and this establishes the prospect of breaking out
of the circle. Ambivalently, the potential for linear progress
co-exists with the circumscription of cyclic recurrence. Bearing

directly westward in the open sea, Taji enters the Archipelago of
Mardi. It lies within a reef-encircled lagoon, and the shape of the
lagoon determines the further itinerary of Taji and his
companions. By the end of their travels "the circuit's done"
(p. 638). The round of the seasons has turned from spring to
autumn, and the voyagers are only a day's sail from their point of
departure. When Taji, who poses as "A Gentleman from the
Sun" (Chapter 54), envisions himself transcending the
Archipelago, his track in the firmament is still circular. In fantasy
he "wheels through the Ecliptic; threading Cancer, Leo, Pisces,
and Aquarius . . ." (p. 556). But Taji's ultimate direction is
beyond "the circumvallating reef" (p. 654). He turns the prow
of his shallop into an "outlet in the outer reef," where it is
carried forward "by the racing tide." Such linear progress is at
odds with the circular configuration of reefs and ecliptics, but
Mardi embraces both. For *Mardi*'s essence is ambivalence.

Taji's visit to Juam produces an illustrative episode. Juam,
ruled by the handsome prisoner-king, Donjalolo, is "one of the
largest islands" of the Mardian Archipelago and one of the first
and most extensively explored by Taji and his entourage
(Chapters 71–85). Its political system, the curious resolution of a
fratricidal dynastic struggle, requires the king to be confined to
the cliff-encompassed glen of Willamilla. For this reason
Donjalolo must depend upon "special agents" and "observers" to
satisfy his curiosity about the physical details of his realm. These
observers supply information that, taken together, is ambivalent.
One of them reports that the coral reef on the isle of Rafona is
red. His coadjutor counters that it is white. Each exhibits a
specimen of coral to sustain his report. Donjalolo dashes both
specimens to the ground, crying out:

> Oh mighty Oro [God]! Truth dwells in her fountains; which every one
> must drink for himself. For me, vain all hopes of ever knowing Mardi.
> Better know nothing than be deceived. (P. 250)

He departs leaving behind "a storm of vociferations." This is not
simply a statement on the subjectivity of knowledge, or the
limitations of knowing. When logically presented, factual
information, though in itself valid, may lead to illogical situations.
It happens that Babbalanja, Taji's philosophic companion, has also
visited the coral reef. He knows that in "various places it is of

various hues" and hence both observers "are wrong, and both
are right" (p. 250). Looking back, then, at Donjalolo's peculiar
conclusion—to know nothing is better than to be deceived—is to
become infected by the suspicion that to know anything, at least
in terms of common logic, *is* to be deceived. Somewhere nearby
the Confidence Man lurks.

Mardi is a "world of the mind" (p. 557), but to comprehend
it common logic is inadequate. Mardi, like mankind, is composed
of inconsistencies by its very nature. Man, Melville implies, has
been taught to rationalize in absolute and mutually exclusive
terms: yes and no, either and or, right and wrong, male and
female, love and hate, life and death, past and present, fact and
fiction. These dichotomies may be resolved in favor of one term
or the other, or mediated, or balanced in a tension, creative or
destructive. But despite this emphasis on rationalization, man, at
bottom, is composed of contradictory states, simultaneous and
unresolved, and they shape his being. The same in *Mardi.*

The importance of Melville's concern with what he saw as
the reality of living in a world of inconsistencies may be
corroborated by his response to a now little remembered dispute
within the legal profession, the so-called "codification
controversy." The issue was whether the English tradition of
common law, adopted by state legislatures after the Revolution,
should be superseded by state "codes." The common law was
unwritten, derived from precedent court decisions. Codified law
would be the accumulated decisions digested and systematized
into a consistent body of rules which would have statutory force
and apply broadly to cases brought before the court. The
common law procedure was to treat each case individually and to
seek prior decisions and apply them on an ad hoc basis. If this
seems remote from *Mardi* or from Melville's interests and
ordinary experiences, two matters should be remembered.

The first is the coral reef "of various hues" on the isle of
Rafona. The procedure at the court of King Donjalolo is essentially
judicial. The opposing parties present their arguments and exhibits.
In his judicial role, Donjalolo decides that second-hand evidence
does not hold up in court. Melville is enunciating in legal
terms a philosophical question that for him had literary
implications. Legal equivocation, inherent in the

common law process, was tacit recognition of the inconsistencies of the human condition. As a writer who sought to record the facts of life in the fullest sense, Melville was attracted to the parallel. His concern with this and other profound implications of the law and his exploitation of its complex literary possibilities begins in *Mardi,* is conspicuous in *White-Jacket,* subtle but vital in *Moby Dick.* It abounds elsewhere, and it culminates in *Billy Budd.* The second matter, for which an abundance of external information exists (compared, for example, with Melville's knowledge of astrology), is the fact of Melville's association with lawyers and legal thinking. It must be summarized barely. His family: Uncle Peter Gansevoort, surrogate father, the Albany judge; Lemuel Shaw, justice of the Massachusetts Supreme Court, father-in-law; Allen Melville and Gansevoort Melville, his brothers, both lawyers; close associates Cornelius Mathews, New York friend and sometimes Pittsfield resident, a lawyer before he became a writer notable for his satiric treatment of the legal system; Evert Duyckinck, his New York literary sponsor; David Dudley Field, another New York friend and Berkshire neighbor, the most prominent advocate of codification. There were others. Duyckinck's liberal, nationalistic journal, *The Literary World,* to which Melville contributed, was reflecting a contemporary interest when it published articles on the codification controversy and other legal questions. Unlike Evert Duyckinck and Field, however, Melville did not think well of codification. After all, it was scarcely consistent with the possibility that conflicting evidence might be equally valid, that coral reefs might be "of various hues," or that a personality might consist of diverse and contrary elements.

If *Mardi* contains contradictions and inconsistencies, so does Taji. One way of seeing him is as an inclusive, composite entity. While still a nameless sailor on the whaling ship *Arcturion,* he affirms pantheistically that "All things form one whole" (p. 12). In a subsequent dream–vision he rhapsodizes, "In me, many worthies recline, and converse" (p. 367). This concept is particularized in Taji's travelling companions—King Media, the philosopher Babbalanja, the historian Mohi, the poet Yoomy. Taji, in a way, is a composite of them all, their internal diversities included.

As they travel through Mardi, Babbalanja's role becomes increasingly significant. He inclines toward the serenity of center, attracted by the inner light, "the one Shekinah" (p. 636). Taji thrusts outward into the "realm of shades" (p. 654). Adept in "logic and conic sections" but a self-styled "lunatic" subject to mystical visions and possessed of a devil, Babbalanja has his own reasons for exploring Mardi and his own inconsistencies. King Media calls him to account:

> "How many theories have you? . . . You are inconsistent."
> "And for that very reason, my lord, *not* consistent; for the sum of my inconsistencies make up my consistency. And to be consistent to one's self, is often to be inconsistent in Mardi. Common consistency implies unchangeableness; but much of the wisdom here below lives in a state of transition." (P. 459)

Reason? Babbalanja responds with a "Shark-Syllogism" (p. 564). He is "inconsistent" for the word literally means *"not consistent,"* and he is *"not* consistent" because he consists of the sum of diverse, illogical, and contradictory elements. But this sum is his "consistency," the density and viscosity of the mass that is the man. At the same time, his "consistency" resides in the paradox that the seemingly discordant elements that compose this mass may be perceived as harmonious if seen from a certain viewpoint, situated presumably some distance above; meanwhile "here below," his "consistency" is the existential fact of his holding together. "Common consistency" requires fixed, logical, circumspect definitions and is an uncommon commodity in Mardi. To grasp this insight, Melville seems to imply, one must in fact discard common logical consistency, which is common as it exists "here below" mainly in the sense that it is ordinary and crude, though it may well be extraordinary and refined above.

The definition of "consistency" is not mere wordplay, a minor "riddle game," nor youthful extravagance, in Melville's phrase to his English publisher, John Murray, "a longing to plume my pinions." It is an incipient statement of the literary theory that underlies *Mardi* and the subsequent novels. Melville was moving toward a theory of structure (cf. the "shady talk" on literary "plans," p. 559) and characterization that culminates in one of his rare discussions of his craft. In *The Confidence-Man*

(1857), his last novel, three chapters (14, 33, and 44) on the craft of fiction occur as digressions, and they are presented in a voice that approximates Melville's own. Unlike *Mardi,* in which he is trying out literary ideas but distancing himself by putting them into Babbalanja's mouth, the voice in *The Confidence-Man,* though necessarily fictive, is authorial. Melville is less concerned with decorum than with *"what is."* In Chapter 14, engagingly titled "Worth the consideration of those to whom it may prove worth considering," the Confidence Man lays bare the ambivalent psychodynamics of a merchant, whose character, the authorial voice asserts, "may be thought inconsistent." The authorial voice agrees that the reader has the right to expect "in the depiction of any character, its consistency should be preserved"; yet the writer must be faithful to fact, so he asks, "is it not a fact that, in real life, a consistent character is a *rara avis?"* This is Babbalanja all over again. It follows that readers may be perplexed by inconsistent characters but they cannot complain of "their untrueness." One therefore must conclude "That fiction, where every character can, by reason of its consistency, be comprehended at a glance, either exhibits but sections of character, making them appear for wholes, or else is very untrue to reality; while, on the other hand, that author who draws a character, even though to common view incongruous in its parts, as the flying-squirrel, and, at different periods, as much at variance with itself as the butterfly is with the caterpillar from which it changes, may yet, in so doing, be not false but faithful to the facts." A fictional character, then, is a composite of disparate structural components, like a rodent with wings, and characteristically is at one moment a creeping worm and at another an airy butterfly. Implicitly, the larger structure of the novel is likewise a composite. This incongruity of the "common view" remarked in *The Confidence-Man* is comparable with the "common consistency" noted by Babbalanja. The end result, the narrative voice informs us, is that we may look to fiction "for more reality, than real life itself can show" (Chapter 33).

Something further follows from this masquerade. In *The Confidence-Man* a transcendental logician, Mark Winsome, is tasked for his logical inconsistencies. He defends himself by claiming a consistency with, in Emerson's phrase, the "natural

facts." His analogy is to the changing levels of the natural
landscape as seen by a passanger on a canal boat moving through
the locks:

> In a philosophical view, consistency is a certain level at all times,
> maintained in the thoughts of one's mind. But, since nature is nearly all
> hill and dale, how can one keep naturally advancing in knowledge
> without submitting to the natural inequalities in the progress? Advance
> into knowledge is just like advance upon the grand Erie canal, where,
> from the character of the country, change of level is inevitable; you are
> locked up and locked down with perpetual inconsistencies. . . . (Chapter 36)

Locked up and locked down indeed. Babbalanja, who can argue
like a confidence man, adopts the guise of a logician to convey
the proposition that "consistency" in Mardi works against itself. It
is both the tight circle of an absolute system and the openness of
diverse vectors that break out of the circle.

Babbalanja's tactic is consistent with Maxine Moore's
explication of the structure and meaning of *Mardi*—that in *Mardi*
Melville establishes a logically calculated circular design based on
an elaborately extended astrological conceit, not to reach but to
avoid a conclusion. The strength of Moore's position depends
largely on two factors: first, whether her astrological "riddle
game" is applicable extensively and at all important points;
second, whether the widely held opinion, which Moore shares,
that Melville took a dim view of the possibility of achieving
absolute knowledge, at least "here below," applies precisely in
this instance. (I am putting aside questions of detail, such as the
extent of Melville's knowledge of astrology, tarot cards, *The
American Almanac,* Captain Cook's voyages, and the equatorial
Neptune initiation, about which I would like to have more
external evidence and more corroboration from his other
writings.) My own opinion is that in *Mardi* Melville is attempting
something more complicated. He is not setting up a debate
between the relativism of Babbalanja and the absolutism of Taji.
Nor does he establish them as mutually qualifying oppositions in
order to make a statement about epistemological limitations.
Rather, he is stating that the World of Mardi is a composite that
can include ambivalent elements such as absolutes and relatives,
closed circles and open endedness, fugle-fi and fugle-fo.

From a practical point of view, open endedness permitted

THE

AMERICAN ALMANAC

AND

REPOSITORY

OF

USEFUL KNOWLEDGE,

FOR THE YEAR

1845.

BOSTON:
PUBLISHED BY JAMES MUNROE & Co.
1844.

Melville to slide easily from *Typee* into *Omoo*. In the preface he explains that *Omoo* "begins where 'Typee' concludes." It ends with the narrator once more aboard a whaling ship, "Crowding all sail . . . the breeze freshening" and "the wide Pacific" ahead. The momentum makes another sequel seem inevitable.

Omoo was published in London by John Murray in May 1847 and in New York the following month. On March 31 Melville wrote hopefully to Murray that *Omoo* and *Typee* might well "assist each other," in which case he would "follow it up by something else, immediately." He had published that month in the *Literary World* a review of two nautical books, J. Ross Browne's *Etchings of a Whaling Cruise* and John Codman's *Sailors' Life and Sailors' Yarns,* and, as was his custom when he had a book germinating, he was buying titles that might prove useful. Among them were Thomas Jacob's *Scenes, Incidents, and Adventures in the Pacific Ocean,* Benjamin Morrell's *Voyages . . . to the South Sea,* J. N. Reynold's *Voyage of the . . . Frigate Potomac,* Charles Darwin's *Journal of . . . the Voyage of H. M. S. Beagle,* and Charles Wilkes' *United States Exploring Expedition,* a set that included a volume of charts of the Pacific. By June 19 Melville had a book sufficiently in the offing to reply "in confidence" to "friendly overtures" from Richard Bentley, who would eventually publish the English edition of *Mardi,* that he would be interested in knowing "in what value you hold a new work of South Sea adventure, by me, occupying entirely fresh ground."

Domestic affairs during the summer of 1847 diverted Melville from the business of writing. On August 4 he married Elizabeth Shaw, daughter of a family friend, Chief Justice Lemuel Shaw of Massachusetts to whom he had dedicated *Typee,* and he moved from Lansingburgh, New York, to New York City, where he and his wife shared a residence with his brother, Allen, a Wall Street lawyer, also newly wed, and their mother and four sisters. He wrote John Murray on October 29 expressing gratification for the reception of *Omoo,* informing him of the interest of "a house in London concerning . . . a third book," and reporting that he was "engaged upon another book of South Sea Adventure (continued from, tho' wholly independent of, Omoo)—The new work will enter into scenes altogether new. . . ."

In his preface to *Mardi* Melville described *Typee* and *Omoo* as

"narratives of voyages in the Pacific. . . ." He had been called upon to defend their factuality. His third book, he stated, was a "romance of Polynesian adventure," and he added testily that it now remained to be seen whether his "fiction" would be mistaken for fact. This was never a problem, but the preface, by emphasizing the distinction, may have encouraged the persistent notion that there is a notable change of direction within the work. What appears to be a factual "narrative" of a nameless young whaleman boldly setting off with a single companion in an open boat for a voyage of a thousand miles seems to shift to "wild," episodic "romance" when he kills the wicked priest to rescue the maiden, assumes a name, claims descent from the sun god, and sails into the Archipelago of Mardi, a constellation of isles as allegorical as it is romantic. The shift is usually explained through what is known of the history of *Mardi*'s composition. However, a literary discussion near the end of the voyage should be kept in mind. King Abrazza complains that the great Mardian masterpiece, the bard Lombardo's *Koztanza,* "lacks cohesion; it is wild, unconnected, all episode" to which Babbalanja replies, "so is Mardi . . ." (p. 597). The effect of using both the name of the archipelago and the book is to interject the possibility that the facts of composition are consonant with Melville's philosophy of composition.

Early on Melville may have considered a whaling narrative along the lines of Browne's *Etchings of a Whaling Cruise.* Given the open ending of *Omoo,* an account of a whaling voyage would follow logically. After all, most of Melville's years before the mast had been spent on whalers, and when he came to draw upon his maritime adventures for *Typee* and *Omoo,* he begins on whalers but does not exploit the whaling experience. In *Mardi,* his nameless sailor deserts the starry *Arcturion,* not the greasy *Leviathan,* and his avowed purpose is to avoid the arctic whaling grounds. So much, then, for conjectures about *Mardi* in its initial stage. What we know is that Melville did not produce a manuscript "immediately" after nor "continued from" *Omoo,* and it is not about whaling, a topic he saved for another day.

By January 1, 1848, he expressed his concern to Murray "that after producing two books on the South Seas, the subject must necessarily become somewhat barren of novelty."

Therefore, he had hit upon the idea of "new attractions . . . romantic, whimsical & poetic. . . ." He added, but crossed out, "& its [*sic*] authentic." One suspects that Melville was trying to justify to himself and to a publisher who declined fiction changes of direction he had seriously in mind. By March 25 the novel was clearly in a second stage. On that date he wrote Murray about his commitment to a "downright . . . 'Romance of Polynesian Adventure.' " He explained that "proceeding in my narrative of *facts* I began to feel . . . irked, cramped & fettered" and besides, it was best to follow one's *"instinct"* for "instincts are prophetic, & better than acquired wisdom— . . ." He would have been more reasonable to have followed the success of the two factual narratives with a third and logically should have overcome his sense of being irked and cramped, but at this point Melville seems to have been of one mind with Babbalanja in regard to consistency and logic. Babbalanja's literary discussions are again pertinent. When King Abrazza objects that "the unities . . . are wholly wanting" in Lombardo's *Koztanza,* Babbalanja counters that Lombardo refused to be fettered by the traditional bonds of unity: "though Lombardo abandoned all monitors from without; he retained one autocrat within—his crowned and sceptered instinct. And what, if he pulled down one gross world, and ransacked the etherial spheres, to build something of his own —a composite! . . ." (p. 597). Upon which, directing his remarks toward Babbalanja's effusions, King Media comments, "Incoherent again!" The kings object to what they recognize as subversive doctrine, for Lombardo acknowledges no external kingship, political or literary, and creates a unity composed of ambivalencies, "a composite." King Media's choice of words is more apt than he could appreciate. Lombardo's unity is not coherent in the conventional sense. Nor, do I believe, was Melville's.

Melville's changed direction in the novel had its counterpart in his reading, and his reading and writing seem to have fed on each other. He now added to the accounts of voyages that dominate the record of his book buying and borrowing works that may fairly be called "romantic, whimsical & poetic." For example, in January and February, he bought Coleridge's *Biographia Literaria,* Burton's *Anatomy of Melancholy,* unidentified editions of Shakespeare and Montaigne, and probably James

Macpherson's *Fingal*. He joined the New York Society Library in
January and borrowed Bougainville's *Voyage Round the World* but
also David Hartley's *Observations on Man*, important for its
influence on romantic literary theory. From Evert Duyckinck he
borrowed volumes of Rabelais and Sir Thomas Browne. This was
heavy fare, and how well he digested it remains an open
question.

Another open question is the place of his bride, Elizabeth
(Lizzie, Lily? Yillah?), beneath the surface of a novel that had
turned in a "romantic" direction. To what extent did he identify
her with the water sprite in la Motte Fouqué's romantic novel,
Undine, which Melville borrowed on Judge Shaw's membership
card from the Boston Athenaeum on March 19, 1847? Did they
read it together during their engagement? Yillah resembles
Undine, as she also has qualities in common with romantic
heroines in Shelley's *Alastor*, Byron's *The Island*, and Keats'
Endymion, and his *Lamia*, for that matter, and other contrasting
figures such as Duessa and Fidessa in Spenser's *Faerie Queene*, who
apparently form part of the ambivalent composite, Yillah–Hautia.

On May 5, 1848, Elizabeth wrote to her stepmother in
Boston telling her that "The book is done now . . . and the copy
for the press is in far progress" and on June 6 she reported that
she was "nearly through—shall finish this week" making a clean
copy of the manuscript for the printer. It was not until November
11, however, that Melville received a preliminary agreement
from Harper & Brothers to publish *Mardi*. A week later the
Literary World announced that Melville was "putting to press a
new work." Finally, on January 27, 1849, Melville's sister
Augusta wrote Lizzie, who was visiting the Shaws in Boston, that
"The last proof sheets are through. 'Mardi's' a book!"

Between June and November the book had gone into a third
stage. Merrell R. Davis has shown that the bulk of Chapters
145–169, referring to the real world and contemporary events
rather than the imaginary world, were inserted into the
manuscript at a late stage. He documents allusions to the effects
of the 1848 revolutions in France (Franko) and in Europe
generally (Porpheero), to the Chartists' march on Parliament in
England (Dominora), and American political conventions and the
California Gold Rush (Vivenza) which could not have been made
until a period between April and October 1848. Melville's

summer reading is also reflected in material inserted at the third stage of the manuscript. On June 22 he bought Carey's translation of Dante's *The Vision; or Hell, Purgatory, and Paradise*, which may have been the inspiration for Babbalanja's vision of ascending with an angel into the heavens above *Mardi* (Chapter 188) and which is likely the source for the grim title "L'Ultima sera" (Chapter 185), in Carey's translation, "the fartherest gloom," that immediately precedes the landing at Serenia. Perhaps Chapter 180 on Lombardo's method of composition is an outgrowth of Melville's late alterations, an attempt to explain how Melville himself set about his work: "When Lombardo set about his work, he knew not what it would become," Babbalanja informs us. "He did not build himself in with plans; he wrote right on; and so doing, got deeper and deeper into himself; and like a resolute traveller, plunging through baffling woods, at last was rewarded for his toils" (p. 595). If Melville is, as it seems, referring to his own method of composition, his statement is consistent with the history of *Mardi* as we know it. He does indeed appear to have been unrestrained by plans, to have written right on, to have got deeper into himself, and in the end, one hopes, to have had his reward. Confusion occurs because, though *Mardi* is topical and allegorical at specific points, though fixed referents and contemporary allusions can be identified, the novel remains organic and symbolic. Allegories are built with plans. They are rationalizations. Symbolic romances tend to grow. The argument that Melville had a plan, astrological or otherwise, and applied it consistently from the beginning, is counter to the evidence discovered prior to Moore's star-gazings. The watcher of the skies must have good luck and sharp eyes; but new planets do, on rare occasions, swim into our ken, a fact that Moore makes the most of.

If Moore is given to wild surmises about the discovery of the planet Neptune by Adams and Leverrier in 1846, she scants the explorations of the planet Earth by Taji and his fellow explorers. She agrees that this section of some twenty-five chapters, which we have been led to believe were added by Melville at the third stage of composition deals mainly with contemporary affairs "explicated thoroughly by others" (see pp. 205–6). She asserts that these chapters are "an integral part of the total metaphor, maintaining chronology throughout." Perhaps she is right and

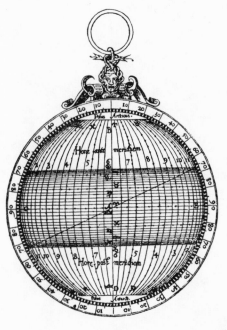

Astrolabe

Melville, through happy coincidence and clever patchwork, tailors the material added at the last stage so that it fits the astrological pattern planned from the beginning. This is a lot to ask, and something that he did not fully achieve in *Moby Dick,* for example, which also underwent a shift in direction during the process of composition. So a question remains: Could Melville have built upon a plan established when he first set about his work which could accommodate events yet to take place, events that his prophetic instincts or astrological evidence, for that matter, could have scarcely foretold?

Melville's plan, according to Moore, was the "riddle game," provoked by Murray's irksome insistence on factual documentation of the authenticity of *Typee* and *Omoo* to allay the doubts of British readers that a common sailor could display such literary talent. A look at the nautical background of Murray's problem shows that it was genuine enough and complicated. There remained a residual class bias against sailor narratives that was dramatized in the *Wager* controversy of a century before. In 1740 the storeship *Wager,* attached to the celebrated Anson Expedition, was wrecked off Cape Horn. Of the handful of survivors, half of them, led by the ship's gunner and carpenter, managed to make their way back to England after they had rebelled against an incompetent commander who appeared to be leading them to certain destruction. They were charged with mutiny but cleared themselves because the gunner and carpenter had the temerity to publish a narrative relating the events and the mitigating circumstances. Such publication by common sailors was unprecedented. It was the prerogative of their betters. Melville refers to the shipwreck, the controversial narratives, and to Richard Henry Dana in his description of rounding the Horn in *White-Jacket.* The popularity of Dana's *Two Years Before the Mast* (1840) shows that class consciousness, this time partly in an affirmative way, was still a factor after a hundred years, even in the United States. The operative forces were ambivalent. They included the covert appeal that Dana was, after all, a gentleman assuming a temporary role—the Harvard student slumming. Melville was by calling a common sailor and nothing else. He may have been proud of this but his thoughts sometimes went in another direction. In *Omoo* the narrator takes the trouble to inform us that he was the only educated member of the crew, and in *Mardi* the narrator's literary allusions identify him to the other sailors as somewhat uncommon. In short, not just the narratives of American sailors but those of British sailors as well were traditionally suspect. Conversely, in America and England, a sailor's narrative like Dana's and its many imitators, had a certain appeal because, genuine or not, the hand that bore inkstains also had been stained in the tar bucket.

If sailor narratives on both sides of the water were viewed askance, then why was the riddle game a "stated challenge to British readers" (p. 7) *only?* What about American readers— likewise infected with snobbery (though of an inverted kind), for all of their Jacksonian talk? Even if the challenge was aimed exclusively at the British, does this rule out the possibility that an American reader could not confront it? In fact, for an American to solve a riddle directed against the British would be piquant. Other questions are provoked. Was this a public challenge to which an answer could be expected at all? If so, Melville must have felt chagrin that, insofar as we know, he got none. Perhaps it was a more private game. But public or private, did he share his secret with anyone? His family, the Duyckincks, or others of the nationalist Young America group? There is no evidence that he did. Melville was a popular author, newly married and in need of yams. Would he alienate the book-buying Englishmen by making them the butt of his riddle game? Despite his exasperation with Murray's requests for authenticating documents, he was tender in his treatment of the British. Vide Dominora and King Bello. Finally, was the provocation so great that Melville, assuming it was his practice to build himself in with plans, would have made his riddle game the master plan for the whole of *Mardi?*

I think not. I think it is a little game Melville is playing for his own amusement. It is one facet, and an intriguing facet, of a rich and busy book. It is one more riddle that Melville expected to remain unanswered. The Melville corpus is packed with such insolvable problems, riddles, puzzles, enigmas, labyrinths, mazes, hieroglyphics, mysteries of virtue and iniquity, inscrutable questions, fathomless depths. They serve various purposes, but a prime reason for their prevalence is his abiding interest in epistemological problems. This applies to the riddle game Moore has discovered in *Mardi.* I agree that it functions as a riposte to

Murray, though on a more modest scale, but I think at the same
time it carries the motif of the epistemological quest. Seen as a
composite, *Mardi* can contain these ambivalent elements.
Babbalanja ranges the Archipelago unsuccessfully seeking ultimate
knowledge. He learns, through the grace of Alma, "In all things
mysterious, to seek no more, but rest content with knowing
naught but Love" (p. 633). Taji pursues the epistemological
quest "over the endless sea." The professed object of his search,
and for him and the reader the principal unsolved riddle, is the
composite figure, Yillah–Hautia. This ambivalent composite
symbolizes ultimate and absolute knowledge, which is not to deny
it may also represent *any* transcendent ideal, for example, a
balance of spiritual and physical love or of head and heart; and
does not exclude recognition that the quest transforms the
character of the quester.

Yillah–Hautia personifies a riddle unsolved for Melville until
the end of his life. The year he died, he published a brief poem,
"The Marchioness of Brinvilliers," in which she appears, as
Moore might say, in another avatar. The poem describes a
painting of a strangely beautiful woman:

> He toned the sprightly beam of morning
>   With twilight meek of tender eve.
> Brightness interfused with softness,
>   Light and shade did weave:
> And gave to candor equal place
> With mystery starred in open skies;
> And floating all in sweetness, made
>   Her fathomless mild eyes.

The strangeness of her beauty is not simply because we learn that
her appearance is at odds with her character. The artist as maker
has created a portrait that is a composite of ambivalent qualities.
He mingles the light of the morning with the shade of evening,
sprightliness with meekness, brightness with softness, and candor
with a mystery suggesting the spaciousness of the starry heavens.
His figure seems to float in an aura of sweetness that is
concentrated in her "fathomless mild eyes." She is the original
woman, the tender Eve created by God, who proffers poisonous
fruit—Yillah–Hautia. She is, historically, the Marquise de
Brinvilliers, a woman of delicate beauty, a confessed poisoner
executed in Paris in 1676. The portrait, a composite of

ambivalence, becomes even more ambivalent in its historical
context. Melville chose his words carefully. "Tone," according to
Ruskin's *Modern Painters* (1843), which Melville read when he
visited the Shaws in the summer of 1848 and later owned, meant
the "relation of the colours of the shadows to the colours of the
light, so that they may be felt at once to be merely different
degrees of the same light." In other words, when juxtaposed, the
colors comprising light and shadow give the impression that the
light and shadow are different in degree rather than in kind,
though actually they differ in kind as "Light and shade" differ in
kind. But the elements of which the portrait is composed are not,
in each case, in an equipoise of difference. "Brightness" is not
the polar opposite of "softness"; "candor" and "mystery" are not
precisely antonyms; and these qualities are not fused, i.e.,
integrated, but "interfused." They pervade or permeate the
painting, the painter weaving them into its fabric in such a way
that they contribute to the whole without losing their separate
identities.

Long before, in *Moby Dick,* Melville transformed the
meaning of the word *mild,* loading it with ominous connotations
through repeated association with calm seas that signal, literally
and figuratively, disastrous storms. Hautia is introduced as "an
inscrutable incognito." Her face is muffled, but it reveals a
solitary "fathomless eye" (pp. 186, 646). In the last chapter, she
gazes at Taji with "her fixed eyes" as he demands an answer to
the mystery of Yillah, "the mystery I die to fathom" (p. 652).
She dismisses him with the words, "Go, go,—slay thyself . . ."
(p. 653).

The mystery of Yillah–Hautia entices him to his death but at
the same time its power keeps him alive. Clinically, his condition
might be described as partial death. Recognized as a composite
figure, Taji can contain a multitude of inconsistencies and
ambivalencies. He consists of the qualities personified by
Yillah–Hautia and by Babbalanja, Yoomy, Mohi, and King
Media. He moves in both lines and circles. He is both alive and
dead. His pursuit of Yillah–Hautia leads him out of the circular
Mardian lagoon, through the strait, and in a linear direction
"over the endless sea," but lines that extend long enough turn on
themselves, and Taji circles back to his beginning, his endless end
his starting point, to tell the story of his suicidal quest.

I hope I have made clear my respect for Maxine Moore's remarkable argument. I find it fascinating, but I do not rest easy with it. To make the basis of my reservations available for evaluation, I have outlined my own reading of *Mardi.* Moore argues for synthesis. I argue for ambivalence. Ambivalence may explain, but it may be as threatening to the work of art (hence the flaws in *Mardi*?) as to the human personality, and this is why efforts to confront it are so attractive.

I cannot agree that *Mardi,* or any Melville novel, is a code to be broken, and decoded will yield a unitary, categorical meaning. Nor that *Mardi* is "a masterpiece of synthesis" (p. 242) informed by a "riddle game." Melville's method of composition I take to be organic and symbolic, and rather haphazard, too. But it was also consistent with his definition of reality. This definition recognized that man and his works are irrational composites. A mind like Melville's could encompass a composite sufficiently ample to embrace Moore's tight, logical argument for synthesis and my own impression of richness but discursiveness, a plan that was charted and chartless.

A Note on Sources

For factual information on the composition and publication history of *Mardi,* I am indebted to Merrell R. Davis, *Melville's* Mardi: *A Chartless Voyage* (New Haven: Yale University Press, 1952); Jay Leyda, *The Melville Log: A Documentary Life of Herman Melville* (New York: Gordian Press, Inc., 1969); the "Historical Note" by Elizabeth Foster to the Northwestern-Newberry Edition of *Mardi* (1970); and *The Letters of Herman Melville* (New Haven: Yale University Press, 1960) edited by Merrell R. Davis and William H. Gilman. Davis' monograph remains basic to all subsequent commentary on *Mardi,* including my own, and has not been seriously challenged until Maxine Moore promulgated her heretical opinions. In formulating my own views of *Mardi* I found particularly stimulating John Seelye, *Melville: The Ironic Diagram* (Evanston: Northwestern University Press, 1970); William B. Dillingham, *An Artist in the Rigging: The Early Work of Herman Melville* (Athens: University of Georgia Press, 1972); Edwin S. Shneidman, *Deaths of Man* (Baltimore: Penguin Books, Inc., 1973); Nathalia Wright, "The Head and the Heart in Melville's *Mardi,*" PMLA, 66 (1951), 351–62, and "Form as Function in Melville," *ibid.,* 67 (1952), 330–40; Priscilla A. Zirker, "The Anson-Squadron Narratives: A Modern View," *The Mariner's Mirror,* 51 (1965), 321–41; and Jill McKinney, "Herman Melville and the Law," Dissertation, University of Pennsylvania, 1975.

Contents

Introduction

"Why, what trash is all this!" exclaimed one of the reviewers of Herman Melville's third book, *Mardi, and A Voyage Thither,* upon its publication in March, 1849.[1] "Puerile!" "Crazy!" "Puzzling!" "Disorderly!" "Foggy!" "Absurd!" "Tedious!" "Offensive!" "Disgusting!" "Grotesque!" "A failure!" cried others—discouraging comments indeed for any author, especially when accompanied by financial as well as critical and popular failure for the work. Modern criticism has been kinder and far more perceptive. Many sensitive scholars have attempted to plumb the depths of *Mardi,* and because of their researches and insights, the book has gained in stature, taking its place as an important transitional work—a bridge across the stylistic chasm that separates *Moby Dick* from the relatively uncomplicated *Typee* and *Omoo.*

Even so, numerous critical problems arise from *Mardi*'s eccentricities to plague and intrigue the modern Melville scholar. Did Melville begin the work with one intention and finish with another, having changed his plan in midstory? Did he become so engrossed in his philosophical meanderings that he lost track of his narrative voice? Did he, illogically, permit his first-person narrator to commit suicide? Are these and other inconsistencies to be attributed to the expansive abandon of an overenthusiastic author who is, to quote a critic, "feeling his oats"?[2]

It is natural to approach *Mardi* solely as a literary work, but there is textual evidence that Melville may have intended to create something quite different: a complex and highly structured riddle-game to be played at and solved by the reader—not hurriedly in one reading, but after hours upon days, perhaps weeks upon months, of patient rereading, researching, tracing of clues, rummaging through literature, poring over maps, calendars, and almanacs, and calculating with logs, sines, compasses, and retractors. Such an intention, or even such a hope, would seem to indicate an arrogant intellectual conceit—or confidence—on the part of an author who was, after all, presenting a mere third book. The evidence reveals, however, that both provocation and tradition played roles in the composition of this elaborate riddle. In the context of *Mardi,* the devices of image, symbol, and

1. Herman Melville, *Mardi, and A Voyage Thither* (Evanston and Chicago, 1970). All page references in this book are to the Northwestern-Newberry Edition. The quotation from Melville's reviewer appeared in *Blackwood's Edinburgh Magazine* (August 1849). Jay Leyda, in *The Melville Log,* cites it as one of a number of derogatory comments (I, 292–311). See also Hugh W. Hetherington, *Melville's Reviewers, British and American, 1846–1891.*

2. "To borrow an expression from the stable, Mr. Melville 'feels his oats.' He has been overfed with praise. . . . He is 'somebody.' " Park Benjamin, *Southern Literary Messenger* (April 1849), from *The Melville Log.* Merrell R. Davis, *Melville's* Mardi, *A Chartless Voyage,* pp. 45 f., discusses the possibility that Melville gradually changed his plans as the composition of *Mardi* proceeded. See Tyrus Hillway, "Taji's Abdication in Herman Melville's *Mardi,*" *American Literature,* 16 (November 1944), 204–7, regarding the narrator's suicide, and also William B. Dillingham, *An Artist in the Rigging,* p. 117, regarding both suicide and loss of narrative voice.

structure serve not only the author's literary purposes but also as clues to the puzzles he propounds. They carry not merely a double but a multiple burden of significance, any one of which may be chosen, to the reader's satisfaction, as the basis for his riddle-game with the author.

The purpose of this study then is to accept Melville's challenge to "play Mardi," in order to discover the hidden messages that may be derived from the book's obscurities. Melville provides several approaches through which the reader may engage in the metaphorical game, though all seem to lead ultimately to the stellar myth that points toward the discovery of new worlds. Although I have chosen to "play Mardi" by delving directly into the stellar myth, relating characters and their movements to the zodiac and to the planetary motions, I indicate also the possibilities of other routes into the game. Figures of the Tarot, along with the progressive avatars of Vishnu, move through the heavily textured story, while the ploys of Pinochle, Hearts, Cribbage, and Pitch provide still other avenues. My emphasis, however, is on the metaphor of Time and its corollary, the zodiacal significance of characters and events.

The first objective in applying astro-mythology to *Mardi* is to date the events in the story, utilizing those navigational aids that *Mardi*'s narrator, Taji, either lacks or spurns: a map of the Pacific Ocean, an atlas of the heavens and a sky-map-calendar, and a specific almanac. Pursuant to the imagery clues, the characters must be identified with an appropriate planet or star and placed at the start precisely on the zodiac according to an exact date— December 24, 1845—and then followed with the help of the almanac through the ensuing ten months. By this device, the reading of *Mardi* reveals a tumultuous undertow of unexpected metaphors and meanings, linked together by one hidden and subtle figure—Neptune.[3]

3. This work was on its way to press when I had the pleasure of reading Professor Viola Sachs, *La Contre-Bible de Melville: Moby-Dick dé Chiffré*. Mouton Éditeur, Paris, La Haye, 1975. Sachs has taken a numerological approach to *Moby Dick*, based on Cabalistic numerology, and has, I believe, demonstrated her position thoroughly and well.

Part I: The Games

I. Neptune and Albion

The Provocation

Not long ago, having published two narratives of voyages in the Pacific, which, in many quarters, were received with incredulity, the thought occurred to me, of indeed writing a romance of Polynesian adventure, and publishing it as such; to see whether, the fiction might not, possibly, be received for a verity: in some degree the reverse of my previous experience.   —Preface to *Mardi*

In 1847, after the successful reception of his first two novels, *Typee* and *Omoo*, Melville received word from his English publisher, John Murray, confirming what many reviews had already indicated: British readers could not believe these charming books to have been written by an American common sailor.[1] Piqued by Murray's request for proof that he had indeed been to sea, Melville replied on March 25, 1848, in a jovial though decidedly indignant tone:

1. Jay Leyda, *The Melville Log*, p. 263. Subsequent references to this work will be provided in the text.

> Will you continue, Mr. Murray, to treat me as from the Land of Shadows—persisting in carrying on this mysterious correspondence with an imputed shade, that under the fanciful appellation of Herman Melville still practices upon your honest credulity?—Have a care, I pray, lest while thus parleying with a ghost you fall upon some horrible evil, peradventure sell your soul ere you are aware.
>
> .   .   .   .
>
> By the way, you ask again for "documentary evidence" of my having been in the South Seas, wherewithall to convince the unbelievers—Bless my soul, Sir, will you Britons not credit that an American can be a gentleman, and have read the Waverly Novels, tho every digit may have been in the tar bucket?—You make miracles of what are commonplaces to us.—I will give no evidence —Truth is mighty & will prevail—& shall & must.

In this same letter, Melville announced his change of plan in regard to *Mardi:*

> To be blunt: the work I shall next publish will be downright & out a "Romance of Polynesian Adventure"—but why this? The truth is, Sir, that the reiterated imputation of being a romancer in disguise has at last pricked me into showing those who may take any interest in the matter, that a *real* romance of mine is no Typee or Omoo, & is made of different stuff altogether. This I confess has been the main inducement in altering my plans.

Here Melville indicates that one of his primary conscious motivations for changing his approach to *Mardi* is to answer that challenge—indeed to counterchallenge those who would not "credit his tale." Nor shall his counterchallenge be an ordinary one. He continues: "My romance I assure you is no dish water nor its model borrowed from the Circulating Library. It is something new I assure you, & original if nothing more." This would seem a strange promise for Melville to make regarding a book that is on the surface merely another variation of the age-old quest motif—especially one so determinedly and frankly derivative. Few authors have filched so much from so many sources in a single work; if *Mardi* is as original as Melville claims here, it must be so on some basis other than the obvious one.

> It opens like a true narrative—like Omoo for example, on ship board—the romance & poetry of the thing thence grow continuly [*sic*], till it becomes a story wild enough I assure you & with a meaning too.

It is apparent from this description that both the simplicity of the opening and the wildness of the ending are already planned at this early stage and that this progression is quite intentional. By no means need Melville's change of intention be connected to the change in tone that occurs in *Mardi*. We might notice also that he claims a meaning for the romance—not *meaning* or *meanings*, but *a meaning*.

Murray rejected *Mardi* because it was not his policy to publish fiction or romance. Instead, Richard Bentley published the book, and its poor reception was immediately apparent. On June 5, 1849, Melville wrote to Bentley:

> The critics on your side of the water seem to have fired quite a broadside into "Mardi"; but it was not altogether unexpected. . . . And I can not but think that its having been brought out in England in the ordinary novel form must have led to the disappointment of many readers, who would have been better pleased with it, perhaps had they taken it in the first place for what it really is. (*Log,* 306)

But what is it? and what does Melville mean by the "ordinary novel form"? Certainly *Mardi* contains elements of the epic romance, including the poetic language; nevertheless, we are compelled to suspect that Melville would have preferred his work to be couched in a form as unique as its highly "original" content. In any case, he had reason to insist that not a single word be altered or corrected, a requirement that gives rise to speculation over the need for such precision.[2]

Taken together, these factors form an intriguing pattern. Melville, irked by British incredulity regarding the intellectual potential of the American common man, composes a work that he considers to be extraordinarily original—a work that is unsuited to the ordinary novel form—as a directly stated challenge to British readers. It is not difficult to understand his motive for perpetrating such literary mischief. Through their skepticism his English critics, he believed, had impuned not only his personal integrity but also the entire concept of American democracy. In England, the figure of the "gentleman sailor," even in its Renaissance heyday, was confined to the nobility—to such knights-errant as Sir Walter Raleigh and other sea-going courtiers. That an American common sailor could aspire to intellectual achievements appeared unlikely to the caste-minded Briton of the period, hence Melville's insistence on the "commonplace" nature of American versatility. Accurately or not, he protested in essence that the American intellectual was thoroughly capable of hard physical labor and that the American laborer was equally capable of producing a work of art at the drop of a top block. As to his personal annoyance, it was reported by Philarete Chasles of Paris that "his family, who know that the adventures related by him are *genuine,* are not flattered by the eulogisms bestowed on Mr. Herman Melville's imagination at the expense of his morality" (*Log,* 300). By posing a riddle laden with literary clues, Melville could put these British skeptics to the test, to see whether and how well they could cope with American ingenuity aroused.

2. Merrell R. Davis, *Melville's* Mardi, *A Chartless Voyage.* p. 96, notes that Melville had experienced problems with changes made by editors in earlier works.

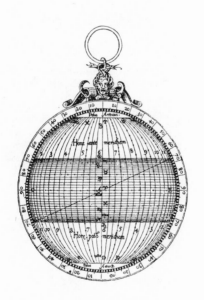

The Fall of Adams: 1846

Yea, with uttermost reverence, as to human understanding, increase of dominion seems increase of power; and day by day new planets are being added to elder-born Saturns.—*Mardi,* 229–30

To poke a riddle at the English was all very well, but what if some astute British scholar, with flying Union Jack, promptly solved the riddle? Where then would be Melville's revenge? To achieve the magnitude and universality obviously intended in *Mardi,* Melville had need of a universal theme and an appropriate myth to embody it. At the same time, the solution to his riddle, when found, should be as exasperating to the British as possible. To fulfill both of these requirements, Melville utilized the myth of Adam, but with a new twist.[3] Because of its puckish function in the metaphorical structure of *Mardi,* the story of the fall of the English mathematician, John Couch Adams, deserves a brief review.[4]

In 1781, Sir William Herschel discovered the first new planet in the history of astronomy. Originally named "Herschel" after its discoverer and by some called "Georgius Sidus" after King George, the planet gradually assumed the mythological name of "Uranus," for the elder high god of the heavens. In the eighteen-forties all three names were still in use.[5] Because of the eccentric orbital behavior of Uranus, it was postulated even at the time of its discovery that another planet might exist at a still greater distance, exerting its gravitational pull to effect the orbital wobble of Uranus. There interest in the new planet rested until early in 1846, when the British Royal Astronomer, Sir George Airy, received a letter from Adams, a young Cambridge scholar, who stated that he proposed to compute the location of the hypothetical planet, partly in order to revalidate Newton's law of gravity and Bode's law of orbital distances. Adams requested any assistance and information available on the subject. About the same time, coincidentally, Sir George received from a French mathematician, Urbain Jean Joseph Leverrier, a similar proposal and request. Throughout the ensuing months, Sir George corresponded with both men, transmitting information between them, until September, 1846, when he departed for a holiday. By now, Adams had arrived at a coordinate that later proved correct. Desiring to channel his findings through the Royal Astronomical Society so as to share the credit with that august body, he posted his figures to Sir George. His letter lay unopened on the vacant desk. About mid-September, Leverrier also arrived at the sought-after answer and, practical man that he was, took immediate action. He sent his computations to a German astronomer and instructed him to focus his telescope according to

3. Taji has not received much attention as an Adam figure, though Melville's use of the myth of Adam in other works, notably *Moby Dick,* has been well discussed by, among others, Richard W. B. Lewis in *The American Adam: Innocence, Tragedy, and Tradition in the Nineteenth Century,* pp. 127–55.

4. *Monthly Notices of the Royal Astronomical Society,* Vol. 7 (London, 1847). This volume contains Sir George Airy's account of the search for Neptune, with correspondence from Adams and Leverrier.

5. For example, *The Farmer's Almanack,* by Robert B. Thomas; specifically Number 54, for 1846.

them. The astronomer obliged, then waited a few days for the equinoctial clouds to dissipate. On the first clear night, September 24, 1846, he sighted Neptune, perched in the arm of Aquarius overhanging the fish tail of Capricorn.

When Sir George returned from his holiday the discovery of Neptune was a *fait accompli,* and Adams's letter, with prior information, lay unopened on his desk. The Frenchman had won by a fluke, Adams was crestfallen, and the Royal Astronomer embarrassed. Sir George published the Adams-Airy-Leverrier correspondence in the *Monthly Notices of the Royal Astronomical Society* and awarded to Leverrier a medal commemorating the discovery. The Frenchman was immortalized, having been accorded nominal credit for the accomplishment, but Adams's share in the discovery did not go unrewarded. He received a duplicate medal.

For his riddle to cause maximal irritation to his British critics, Melville charted the voyage through *Mardi* to coincide with the mathematical quest for the new world, Neptune. Thus, solution of the riddle would reveal a satirical play on a major blow to British scientific prestige. The moral issues involved in this situation provided Melville with symbolic and allegorical significance far transcending his playful vengeance, and he takes full advantage of the possibilities in his study of cosmic justice. The Adams who "fell" because of a mere circumstance could quite readily be seen as a figure of that earlier Adam, who also was felled by a fluke. His attempt to "do the right thing" operated against him, while his competitor, unhampered by loyalty to the Royal Society and giving not a sou for good sportsmanship, raced like the proverbial tortoise over the finish line. And Melville, of course, would be the first to notice that the winner's fine Frank name translates as "truth."

In a word, the key to the riddle of *Mardi* is "Neptune." But Neptune is only the key, for from this recognition of the hidden god as source of the figures in the story and controller of their movements springs a multitude of related metaphors. These carry Melville's deeper and more serious explorations as he sends his questing characters through the Mardi Isles in search of "new worlds of the mind."

II. The Application

And what, if he pulled down one gross world, and ransacked the
etherial spheres, to build something of his own—a composite:—
what then?   —*Mardi,* 597

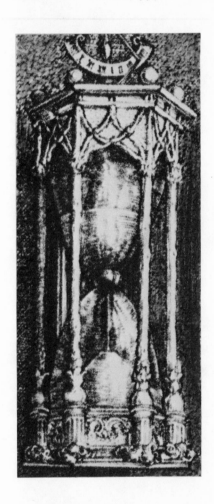

1. Edward H. Rosenberry, *Melville
and the Comic Spirit* (Cambridge, Mass.,
1955), finds twenty-nine puns in *Mardi,*
including such word-play as "eschews his
chew." In light of the stellar metaphor,
the pun count more nearly approaches
twenty-nine per chapter, not to speak of
image play and structural puns that
pervade the book.

In order to reap full benefit from the rich texture of *Mardi,*
the reader must become aware of various metaphorical systems
that underlie the surface plot. Indeed, this plot seems all too
superficial and derivative to warrant the excessive verbiage
expended upon it by Melville unless some substructure does
exist. The density and sequence of the imagery, the capacity of
words, phrases, and lines to sustain multiple meanings, cannot be
fully appreciated except in terms of the metaphor of Time, that
is, of the specific dating of the events of *Mardi* leading up to the
discovery of Neptune. In turn, the dating derives from the clues
presented through Melville's adaptation of the stellar myth. The
parallels drawn between the actions of the characters and the
positions of the planets during the year 1846 provide the first
step toward recognition of the structural order of the book. The
temporal symbolism in turn reveals an astonishing tapestry of
interlocking themes, synthesized by Melville into a complex but
unified whole. Astrological and astronomical lore—so widely
divergent and at odds—are yoked together to perform as a
dynamic unit; Pythagorean number symbolism is wedded to
Euclidian geometry to "square the circle" of planetary orbits, and
both blend into the modern "proving out" of Newton and Bode;
the Arthurian quest for the Grail and the ancient folk custom of
shipboard initiation are linked to the ten Avatars of Vishnu
through the device of a game of cards. Each strand of metaphor,
by the use of pivotal puns with multiple meanings, is carried
complete throughout the book.[1] Thus, to explicate the imagery of
astronomical chronology requires line-by-line interpretation, while
those same lines may be cited as evidence for other full-scale
metaphors and symbol systems.

Hints, stated clues, and open announcements of the riddling
nature of *Mardi* abound in every chapter. That the metaphor of
Time has remained so long obscure may be attributed in part to

that same problem Melville deplored—the ever-widening disparity between the scholar and the sailor. Even in his own day, the tar-stained intellectual was not so commonplace as Melville would have his British readers believe. The weakness of *Mardi*— as well as its fascination—lies in its plethora of obscure and esoteric references and in the metaphysical synthesis of diverse and eccentric elements.

*   *   *

Mardi, Melville's third book, derives its name from the third day, Tuesday, the third month, March, and the third planet, Mars. It is a book of Mardi Gras Carnival, based on the Pythagorean triad by which diversity and unity combine to form harmony, the Euclidian "fat three," or *pi* (3.1416 or 3 1/7), by which all circles may be measured, and Bode's progression of three by which orbital distance may be reckoned.[2]

From this motif Melville constructs his three levels of credibility. The device might be likened to the undertow principle: surface waves moving toward the shore; a cross-hatch of conflicting currents barely visible just underneath; and below it all, a powerful hidden undertow leading back out to what Hawthorne called "depths that force a man to swim for his life."[3] The narration of the hero, Taji, demonstrates the three levels of credibility. On the surface, the information Taji provides seems true and reasonable, and his depiction of himself is acceptable. A deeper look, however, reveals Taji as the traditional rogue hero, cunning and deceitful, who justifies to himself the theft of a whaleboat and cleverly victimizes his devoted but rather stupid old chummy.[4] In rescuing a maiden during the course of his voyage, he commits murder and sacrilege, and he then sets himself forth as a demigod. On this second level the character becomes richer and more complex, embodying a wealth of ambiguous symbolism; at the same time, however, inconsistency, confusion, and vagueness creep into the characterization, and the critic is forced to impute the flaw to Melville.

To reach the third level of credibility, the reader must check Taji's statements thoroughly, whereupon he will find that the

2. Euclid's forty-seventh postulate establishes *pi* as 3.1416, or 3 1/7. Bode's law provides a formula by which orbital distances may be calculated: $D = 0.3 (2) (n-1) + 0.4$, where D = distance and n is the number of the planet outward from the sun. The formula proved valid for all planets except Mercury. Later, Neptune proved to be still another planet for which the formula did not work. Thus Bode's law joined Buffon's cosmogony as an exploded error of science.

3. In a letter to Evert Duyckinck, Hawthorne wrote, " 'Mardi' is a rich book, with depths here and there that compel a man to swim for his life. It is so good that one scarcely pardons the writer for not having brooded long over it, so as to make it a great deal better" (*Log,* p. 391).

4. See Bruce Franklin's "Introduction" to the Capricorn edition of *Mardi* (New York, 1964) for an excellent discussion of Taji as rogue hero.

The Hevelius sky-map
Northern Hemisphere

Southern Hemisphere

character's capacity for error exceeds the normal. Though Taji's voice rings with experience and expertise in nautical matters, the facts he provides are consistently incorrect when checked against maps and almanacs. Further, Taji persists in his errors; he repeats them to the point of comedy. The reader eventually realizes that nothing Taji says can be believed. He is actually an ignorant, bumbling landlubber who knows nothing at all about the sea, the sky, or the principles of navigational astronomy. Since Taji is the narrator, and his "facts" are blatantly incorrect, how then can the reader arrive at the accurate computations required for the dating system? Here the ingenuity of Melville's method comes into play, for Taji's lies and errors in regard to one matter become truths when applied to another. For example: Taji intends to deceive the maiden Yillah by falsely claiming to be a demigod; because the astronomical imagery reveals him as a figure of the planet-god Saturn, however, he is truly a demigod. Again, at the outset of the narrative Taji reports that he sailed from Ravavai, just north of the Tropic of Capricorn, whereas Ravavai is just south of that line; on the other hand, at the beginning of the *Arcturion's* voyage his planet, Saturn, is in the constellation Sagittarius in a position just north of the winter solstice in the *sign* of Capricorn. Thus Taji's earth-related errors prove to be celestial truths when seen from that perspective.

As his figure of Time and Authority, Melville utilizes an almanac, but here again the reader must be wary, for Melville will permit no authority to go unchallenged. The guide selected is *The American Almanac,* beginning with December of the 1845 issue and continuing through October of 1846.[5] Needless to say, these issues do not include information on the position of the undiscovered planet Neptune, and therefore they are guilty of error by omission through ignorance. The December, 1845, calendar page contains a misprint that places Jupiter in Capricorn when he is actually in Pisces: a second error, this one of commission through carelessness. And finally, on December 21, the *Almanac* reports that "Sun enters Capricorn, Winter begins," when Sol is actually located in Sagittarius: a third error, which represents those committed by following unquestioned and outdated tradition. Nevertheless, the same page on which the latter two errors appear contains the means by which they can be corrected. Only the absence of Neptune remains uncorrected,

THE

AMERICAN ALMANAC

AND

REPOSITORY

OF

USEFUL KNOWLEDGE,

FOR THE YEAR

1845.

BOSTON:
PUBLISHED BY JAMES MUNROE & Co.
1844.

5. *The American Almanac* (Boston, 1844 and 1845), issues for 1845 and 1846. See Appendix for reproduction of calendar pages.

and the *Almanac* provides a planet that, though spurious, fills that
place. Here again we find illustrated the three levels of
credibility, for the *Almanac* is seemingly correct at face value,
false upon first investigation, but precisely true when approached
from the standpoint of judicious interpretation.

The challenge set forth by the British skeptics gives rise to
one of the central purposes of *Mardi,* that is, to demonstrate
man's capacity for straining at the truth yet easily swallowing
dromedaries of falsehood. Throughout *Mardi* the star Arcturus
recurs as a symbol of the exposure of error. As stated in the
preface to the magazine *Arcturus,* edited by Melville's friend
Evert Duyckinck, it is "a star that shines high and brightly, and
looks down with a keen glance on the errors, follies, and
mal-practices of men."[6] Taking as one example Sir Thomas
Browne's explosion of Vulgar Errors while "hugging to his breast
all the mysteries of the Pentateuch," Melville presents instance
upon instance of error, miscalculation, misnomer, incorrect
classification, ridiculous theory, misinterpretation of lore and
tradition, superstition, and falsehood, all manfully swallowed and
disgorged like ambergris by one of the most consistently mistaken
narrators in literary history. Only when he lies, or thinks he lies,
does Taji approach truth. For each error that Taji accepts as
truth, Melville juxtaposes the reality for contrast, thereby
challenging the reader to distinguish between them. For example,
in Chapter 13, Taji sets about delivering a learned dissertation on
the *Chondropterygii,* or sharks, taking his information from the
German naturalists Müller and Henle. The "heathenish" word
itself means "cartilage-wing" and could hardly refer accurately to
any member of the *Elasmobranchae* except possibly the ray fish. At
the end of his scientific description Taji tells of a flying fish that
had inadvertently leaped into his boat. After removing one of its
wings, he spreads it out to dry, noting later the fine traceries in
the parchmentlike wing that bear resemblance to the veins of a
leaf. By this juxtaposition Melville demonstrates that the shark
has been mislabeled while the true "cartilage-wing" is the flying
fish. Notably, Taji remains unaware of the discrepancy and
continues to credit the misnomer.

In keeping with his concept of credibility as existing in
layers, Melville presents authority in layers ranging from the
utterly wrong narrator through the human author and his guide,

6. Gordon Mills, "The Significance of
'Arcturus' in *Mardi,*" *American Literature*
(May 1942), 158–61. This note proposes
that the name of the ship is derived from
Duyckinck's publication of that title, and
that *Mardi*'s function is to expose the
errors of the world, an argument I find
quite convincing.

The "Aisles" of Mardi

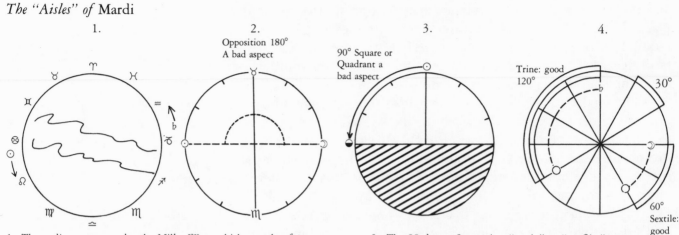

1   The zodiac, cross-cut by the Milky Way, which stretches from Gemini (II) to Sagittarius (♐). Planets run counterclockwise. Sol (☉) is shown transiting from Cancer to Leo on east side, and Saturn (♄) from Capricorn to Aquarius on west side.   2. Shown in opposition are Taurus and Scorpio on the north-south poles, and Sol and Luna on the east-west poles.

3. The 90-degree Square is a "strain" or "conflict" aspect. In *Mardi*, a planet squared to Sol is sinking into the night sky, and thus into death and/or metamorphosis.
4. The Trines and Sextiles are beneficial aspects that form harmonious "chords" in the "music of the spheres."

the *Almanac* with the stars it represents, to the ultimate Authority who guides the stars. As Taji misleads the reader, Melville the author misleads Taji. The author's authority, the *Almanac,* is especially selected because of the gross error that it in turn displays. As noted, Taji's characterization is so constructed that, through judicious interpretation on the part of the reader, it can be made to yield truth; by the same token, if Taji were able to interpret correctly the motions of the Sun, symbol for his author, he too could achieve understanding. At the top of this hierarchy stands the figure of God—a misleading AUTHOR to all creatures who fail to gaze beyond the obvious or to peer beneath the veil of established authority so as to interpret Him judiciously. Thus, the almanac stands as metaphor for the Bible insofar as each presents celestial truth through a human, error-prone medium.

It is but another step to connect this theme of misleading authority with that of authorship itself. Another major element in *Mardi* is the quest for the sources of artistic creativity.[7] For this function Melville utilizes his metaphor of solar mythology to suggest two prime sources of art: first, the author's preparation for writing by compilation, assimilation, and digestion of the works of other writers; second, the mysterious force of

7. Melville's reiterated quest for the sources of art has been dealt with by, among others, James E. Miller, Jr., "Melville's Quest in Life and Art," *South Atlantic Quarterly,* 58 (Autumn 1959), 587–602. In "The Complex Figures in Melville's Carpet," *Arizona Quarterly,* 15 (Autumn 1959), 197–210, Miller discusses Taji's movement from the position of Young Seeker to that of Masked Man.

inspiration, pictured as an unknown power that uses the author as a mere amanuensis. By using the zodiac and invoking the astrological aspects, Melville humorously treats the first element as a digestive process: The planets move around the zodiac and through the animal constellations as a yam moves through a yellow lion. The second appears as a sexual process that occurs when planets are in opposition either to other planets or to important fixed stars.[8] Melville also makes use of the sperm whale imagery to illustrate the fertility of the creative imagination, as hinted at in his Preface: "This thought was the germ of others, which have resulted in Mardi." It is from this metaphor that much of *Mardi*'s hidden ribaldry stems, for Melville's nautical experiences apparently left him with a hearty delight in the naughty. For his imagery of compilation, he puts to a second use the same catalogue of authors that also serves the motif of error. These authors become the meat of the cannibalistic artist-in-training.

Having drawn God into the structure of *Mardi,* Melville delves into the problem of predestination, the fall of Adam, responsibility, and afterlife. To develop the concept of fixed fate, he calls into play a multitude of illustrative factors, drawing especially on those occult arts that purport to predict the future. Astrological imagery, his most versatile tool, permeates the book, assisted by the various fortune-telling card decks that constitute another of the major metaphors to be explored in this study. In addition, we encounter phrenology, numerology, "palm" reading, and even a variation on tea-leaf reading.

The idea of fixed fate participates in the basic structure of *Mardi,* since Taji's every move is charted in accordance with the stars as shown in the almanac. One interpretation of Taji's alleged "chartless voyage" extends the chartlessness to Melville, while another postulates that Melville extends it to God.[9] As the extraordinary structure of *Mardi* unfolds, however, Taji's voyage appears to be thoroughly charted, and this hint of destiny raises the problem of cosmic injustice as it applies to Adam and his descendants and, by extension, to Cain, Judas, and Satan. Having already brought a deck of cards into play to illustrate the concept of the fixed future, Melville combines three great playing-card packs to work out the problem of predestination and responsibility: the well-known Pinochle pack, the ancient Tarot,

8. The aspects will be discussed in later chapters, but it might be noted at this point that Melville's use of the opposition rather than the conjunction for his sexual imagery arises from a necessary distribution of use. The conjunctions designate actual meetings and exchanges, while the oppositions form corridors through which planetary or stellar influences may pass. These influences are often presented as marriages. During the quest, the *isles* of Mardi form *aisles.*

9. I refer here to Davis's work, cited above, and to that of Lawrance Thompson, *Melville's Quarrel with God.*

and the medallion-shaped Hindu–Persian Avatar cards. The major trumps of the Tarot represent the progress of the Fool (our Joker) through the twenty-one steps of experience, while the Avatar deck depicts the ten reincarnations of Vishnu, lowest of which is Matsyavatara, the blue fish–man. Melville equates this half-and-half figure to that of Capricorn the goat–fish and thence to Saturn, the halved planet that represents Taji. The parallel to Satan (and to the *Cobali,* or "Blue Devils" of Burton, to be discussed later) is readily apparent, since in Hebrew legend Satan is associated with the figure of Leviathan, and in Dante's *Inferno* he is pictured as half encased in ice. By way of this synthesis, Melville presents man as a fallen god, once a Nob (Jack of trumps), but now shorn of memory and steeped in ignorance, who must in a ritual manner pass through the steps of experience to achieve the next avatar. This concept will receive further attention as I deal with the related metaphors of Mardi Gras and Crossing the Line.

Melville stresses that in *Mardi* there is a search for "new worlds of the mind." For this purpose he puts his compilation of authors to the yoke a third time. He travels through the ages, tracing the history of man's concept of God and of the relationships between church and state, idealism and materialism, faith and science. The episode of Annatoo and Samoa on the *Parki* illustrates one stage of this progress, with Samoa as the beleagured State wedded to the Church Militant, locked in material rivalry and blind faith, a mass of amputations. This struggle is, however, only one of numerous forays, for another of the metaphorical strands in *Mardi* is that of exploration and discovery. The names and feats of famous explorers recur throughout the book, and it is important to note Melville's contention that all daring explorers of time, space, or ideas are God's noblemen, regardless of the truth or falsehood of their conclusions.[10] The only question to be asked is whether they dare to leave the shallows and dive deep. So important is this metaphor to the story that the figures of great explorers are hidden characters in *Mardi.* Annatoo represents Captain Cook, for example, while Samoa personifies the great explorer of inner and outer space, Dante. Such unlikely images as these are among *Mardi*'s surprises.

10. After hearing Emerson lecture, Melville expressed disagreement with his ideas but admiration for his ability to dive deep (*The Melville Log*, 292).

Houses, Exaltations and Depressions

Planet	Solar house	Lunar house	Exaltation	Depression
Sol	Leo	———	Aries	Libra
Luna	———	Cancer	Taurus	Scorpio
Mars	Scorpio	Aries	Capricornus	Cancer
Mercurius	Virgo	Gemini	Virgo	Pisces
Iuppiter	Sagittarius	Pisces	Cancer	Capricornus
Venus	Libra	Taurus	Pisces	Virgo
Saturnus	Capricornus	Aquarius	Libra	Aries

The Manilian and Ptolemaic Systems

	Guardian deity	
Sign	Manilian system	Ptolemaic system
1. Aries	Pallas	Mars
2. Taurus	Venus	Venus
3. Gemini	Apollo	Mercurius
4. Cancer	Mercurius	Luna
5. Leo	Iuppiter and Iuno	Sol
6. Virgo	Ceres	Mercurius
7. Libra	Vulcan	Venus
8. Scorpio	Mars	Mars
9. Sagittarius	Diana	Iuppiter
10. Capricornus	Vesta	Saturnus
11. Aquarius	Iuno and Iuppiter	Saturnus
12. Pisces	Neptunus	Iuppiter

As noted, one of *Mardi*'s prime functions is to correct errors, and one of its most elaborate metaphors involves astrology, which, with the discovery of Neptune, was embarrassingly in need of immediate correction. A vast cosmic subplot exists in hiding here, designed to create a stellar mythology modernized to include the newly discovered planet Neptune. The challenge offered to the reader, for which all these other elements serve as clues, is to compute the dates of the actions in *Mardi* so as to discover Neptune, symbol of new worlds, and to fit him into the scheme of things. Neptune must of necessity become ruler of the constellation and the sign of Pisces, a realm already controlled by his brother Jupiter, who, during this particular year of 1845, has

11. The figure of Neptune was not new to astrology. Though he is excluded by Ptolemy in the *Tetrabiblos*, he has a place in the system of Manilius, who allotted an Olympian guardian to each of the twelve signs. Here Neptune is the guardian deity of Pisces, while Jupiter and Juno jointly rule Leo and Aquarius, a marriage of oppositions as described in Note 8. See A. E. Housman's analysis of Manilius (Vol. 2, Cambridge, 1937, Introduction, p. xvi) and other sources. See page 18.

occupied Pisces and is about to pass into Aries, despite the notation in *The American Almanac* that he is in Capricorn.[11] How is Neptune to acquire half rulership over Pisces? Fortunately, a precedent had been established when, in 1781, the planet Uranus was discovered and eventually placed by astrologers on the throne of Aquarius, formerly ruled by Saturn alone. Now Neptune has three possibilities: He could usurp Pisces' throne by force—but he is not located in the constellation Pisces; he could bring in an assassin, which is what he apparently does; he could co-rule with Jupiter after the manner of Saturn and Uranus, or of Hello and Piko, and this is what he actually does, ceremoniously dethroning Jupiter through a ritual murder that provides him with a deed to half of Pisces—and Taji is the self-styled author of that deed.

This mythical context places Taji in a position analogous to that of Judas. In murdering Aleema the Priest—the Jupiter figure—Taji commits what seems to him to be a murder, although his cause, the rescue of a maiden, seems to justify the act—unless his motivation is purely a selfish one. If on the other hand he has been brought to this time and place by a god in disguise—Jarl–Neptune—to participate unknowingly in an essential ritual, is Taji guilty?

The answer to this question lies in the riddle of *Mardi*'s dating and is inherent in the book's title. The murder of Aleema occurs on Shrove Tuesday—a fact known to Jarl, the keeper of the almanac, but not to Taji. The following day begins the Lenten period. Is Taji to be condemned for an act that carries out a design planned by the gods, or is he to be full shriven by the powers that drive him? This problem of cosmic justice, posed on behalf of Taji, Satan, Cain, Judas, Adam, and all mankind, underlies the riddle of *Mardi*.

*   *   *

Would Melville trouble himself to construct such an elaborate and obscure riddle merely to indulge in a mischievous revenge on his readers? According to his own comments about a mariner's knowledge of the heavens, to him comparatively little trouble would be involved. As a sailor he should be well acquainted with the movements of the stars and the hieroglyphics of the almanac, so effort in these matters would be minimal. His experience as a mariner could have qualified him also as a "forecastle astrologer," with at least the rudiments of celestial navigation, and he would have listened to the folklore, myths, and superstitions of sailors from all over the world. He relates in *Redburn* his exposure to the secrets of astrology and dream interpretation by way of the small pamphlet, *Napoleon's Dream Book,* first published in 1843, which contained information about Napoleon's interest in the Tarot cards.[12] It is not shown in his collected correspondence that Melville ever described in detail the information he had acquired on shipboard, yet his works reveal his knowledge of a wide range of sailors' lore.

Upon his return to the life of a landsman, he began to read in all areas, and his studies continuously expanded as his concern with composition grew. During the early stages of *Mardi,* he abruptly increased his research—reading and rereading, buying and borrowing a wide variety of books, attending lectures, and synthesizing art, science, and literature into a complex mythology of his own.[13] At the same time, he began to function as a self-critic, analyzing and judging certain trends in his own earlier writing. His two rather straightforward books of sea adventure were characterized by an apparently natural tendency to fall into an episodic pattern—a pattern that moves into *Mardi* on a conscious and intentional basis, now raised from a tendency to a technique. His heroes—nameless, incognito, inclined to "jump ship" at the turn of a whim—were in each case associated with a "chummy"—the jovial Toby or the saturnine Dr. Long Ghost. Even in these earlier works the heroes leaned toward the picaresque: generally subject to circumstance, easily influenced, but nonetheless resourceful and clever. *Mardi*'s Taji seems remarkably similar to the adventurous Typee and Omoo, but when fully exposed he bears a stronger resemblance to *Omoo*'s Dr. Long Ghost, skillfully blended with Manfred, Dante's and Milton's Satans, Don Quixote, Parsifal, and the consummate, blindfolded Fool.[14] These are just a few of the characteristics Melville apparently recognized in his earlier creations as being useful in *Mardi,* his first production as a fully conscious artist.

12. During this period there was a spate of Napoleon dream books by various authors. The most likely candidate, however, was a popular volume by Mme Camille LeNormand, or Marie Adelaide LeNormand, published in 1843. It contained interpretations of Napoleon's dreams, astrological instructions and ephemerides, and Tarot card fortune-telling techniques. In *Redburn,* Chapter 18, Melville refers to a Bonaparte dream book, "with a red cover, marked all over with astrological signs and ciphers, and purporting to be a full and complete treatise on the art of Divination; so that the most simple sailor could teach it to himself." He states further that "the magic of it lay in the interpretation of dreams," and that the problems were to be cast by means of a set of tables at the end of the pamphlet, something like those at the end of Bowditch's *American Practical Navigator.* It is apparent from this reference that Melville had been exposed both to astrology and to dream interpretation; hence his extensive use of dreams in *Mardi.*

13. The valuable researches of Merton M. Sealts, Jr., *Melville's Reading,* along with those of Leyda and Davis, reveal Melville's prolific reading during this period.

14. See Henry F. Pommer, *Milton and Melville;* Joseph J. Morgan, Jr., "Pierre and Manfred: Melville's Study of the Byronic Hero," *Papers on English Language and Literature,* I (1965), 230–40; and A. F. Beringause, "Melville and Chrétien de Troyes," *American Notes and Queries,* 2 (1963), 20–21, among others. Also, in regard to Jarl's use of the oar as almanac, see Luther S. Mansfield, "Some Patterns from Melville's 'Loom of Time,'" *Essays on Determinism in American Literature,* 33 (1965), 19–35.

As Melville entered a new phase of life in his marriage to Elizabeth Shaw, the contrasts between his domestic present and his adventurous past must have merged and coalesced into a pattern that enhanced the vivid past. The world of propriety, gentility, responsibility, and restriction stood at the opposite pole from the life and the sexual mores of a whaleship three years at sea, peopled by rough, deprived men of all races, cultures, and temperaments. This undercurrent also affects *Mardi,* the first of a long series of stories and poems built around a sexual metaphor. "Before a full developed man," states Mardi's logician, Babbalanja, "Mardi would fall down and worship" (593). It must be noted that the Mardi Islands are remarkably lacking in such men. With the exception of Aleema the Priest, not one major male character has fathered a child, and many are mutilated in one way or another. Though ostensibly the quest is for Yillah the Maiden, on another level the primary quest is for the Father, for the "whole man," and for the source of artistic potency—the great sperm from the brain that enlightens the world (3).[15]

The riddle form of *Mardi* potentially serves to enrich the book by permitting reader participation. The high irony inherent in the almanac metaphor lies in the reader's knowledge of Taji's ignorance. When Taji cries out, "Oh, reader, list, I have chartless voyaged," the reader who has been listing from the almanac knows that Taji is charted, mapped, predestined, and predictable down to the hour, degree, minute, and second. Without this knowledge, the reader is all too liable to take Taji at face value and to accept Taji's own self-estimate, thereby losing a good portion of the wit, psychological satire, and rich humor within the work. The almanac riddle places the reader in the author's line of sight, able to view the narrator's past and future as they extend far beyond the confines of the immediate story.

In utilizing the riddle genre, Melville calls upon an ancient literary tradition that is most often confined to short poetry, such as the Medieval Riddle group of the *Exeter Book* and the Latin riddles attributed to Symphosius, Aldhelm, Eusebius, and others. The sixteenth-century prophetic astrological riddle-poems of Nostradamus provide a more recent and familiar case in point.[16]

The astrological tradition in literature derives from such honored names as Chaucer, Spenser, and the Renaissance

15. Melville's use of sexual and phallic imagery to express artistic creativity has been discussed by, among others, D. H. Lawrence in *Studies in Classic American Literature* (New York, 1923), and Leslie Fiedler in *Love and Death in the American Novel.* Particularly helpful because of its broad coverage of ideas is Robert Shulman, "The Serious Function of Melville's Phallic Jokes," *American Literature,* 33 (May 1961), 179–94. Needless to say, these works are more concerned with *Moby Dick* than with *Mardi.*

16. See the Introduction to *The Exeter Book,* George Philip Krapp and Elliott van Kirk Dobbie, eds., pp. lxvi–lxvii.

playwrights. It is probable that Melville borrowed in large part from the techniques wielded by Spenser in *The Faerie Queene*, as he has been shown to have used Spenser's allegorical motifs.[17] The astrological and numerological significances of the characters in both works are strikingly similar, and Melville's use of the solar myth and the symbolism of seasons is well in keeping with the Renaissance mode.[18] Johnstone Parr has demonstrated Marlowe's use of a horoscope in constructing his tragedy of humors, *Tamberlaine the Great,* and while Melville's approach to astrology constitutes a departure from natal horoscope techniques, he is in his own way as precise as Marlowe.[19]

Though solidly rooted in literary tradition, *Mardi* must remain unique by its very complexity—a potpourri of metaphor unequaled, I believe, in the history of letters.

17. Melville's use of Spenser has been discussed by Nathalia Wright in "A Note on Melville's Use of Spenser: Hautia and the Bower of Bliss," *American Literature,* 24 (March 1952), 83–85.

18. See Alastair Fowler, *Spenser and the Numbers of Time,* for a full-scale discussion of Spenser's extensive use of numerology and astrology.

19. Johnstone Parr, *"Tamburlaine's Malady" and Other Essays on Astrology in Elizabethan Drama,* contains helpful material on the Renaissance concept of astrology and humors.

III. The Almanac Metaphor

Ptolemy, Copernicus, and the Almanac Metaphor

Foul anchors, skewered hearts, almanacs, Burton-blocks, love verses, links of cable, Kings of Clubs; and divers mystic diagrams in chalk, drawn by old Finnish mariners, in casting horoscopes and prophecies. Your old tars are all Daniels. —*Mardi*, 64

The stellar imagery in *Mardi* is so pronounced that one might wonder why no astronomer or astrologer has recognized the metaphor over the past century. Today, as in Melville's day, the two fields are in distinct opposition to each other, and Melville takes full advantage of the rift in order to further his riddle of error. His system in *Mardi* stands midway between the two, partaking of both but complying fully with neither; instead, the imagery is based on what we might call "almanac astronomy" or "forecastle astrology"—probably the reason for his metaphor remaining unperceived. Since both astronomer and astrologer tend to be dogmatically knowledgeable, each in his own field, this combination, which is neither fish nor fowl, would be difficult for either to recognize or acknowledge as a system. On the other hand, Melville's approach might be seen as a synthesis of and a correction to both. Before proceeding into *Mardi*'s almanac metaphor, I shall discuss some of the special problems that result from Melville's method.

Astrology maintains four major conventions that to the scientific astronomer constitute gross error. First, there is the basic dichotomy between the ancient Ptolemaic stellar hypothesis and the modern Copernican theory. As *Mardi*'s logician Babbalanja explains,

> The astronomers maintain that Mardi moves round the sun; which I, who never formally investigated the matter for myself, can by no means credit; unless, plainly seeing one thing, I blindly believe another. Yet even thus blindly does all Mardi subscribe to an astronomical system, which not one in fifty thousand can astronomically prove. And not many centuries back, my lord, all Mardi did equally subscribe to an astronomical system, precisely the reverse of that which they now believe. But the mass of

Mardians have not as much reason to believe the first system, as
the exploded one; for all who have eyes must assuredly see, that
the sun seems to move, and that Mardi seems a fixture, eternally
here. (P. 455)

Astrologers, who are often competent amateur astronomers, know
full well that the earth moves around the sun; nevertheless, the
elder art ignores this fact and postulates a geocentric system after
the Ptolemaic mode. Astrology is not alone in holding to this
formal error, for nautical navigation also ignores Copernicus and
adheres to the outmoded hypothesis. The reasons are simple: It is
easier to compute, and it works. In this instance, then, the
sophisticated mariner achieves practical and effective truth by
holding fast to error.

It has long been known to those who study the heavens that
the sun reaches its position over the earth's equinoctial point
slightly earlier each year, creating the problem known as
"precession of the equinoxes." In ancient times, the constellation
Leo marked the period of the summer solstice; then, as the sun
continued to fall behind this point, the constellation Cancer
became the summer sign.[1] In order to determine a fixed center
for their computations, astrologers ceased to consider precession
and affixed the zodiac signs to the four cardinal changes of
season. As a result, Cancer remains the summer solstice, even
though the sun is now in Gemini on solstice day. It follows that

1. The book I have found most
informative on the historical aspects of
astrology is Rupert Gleadow, *The Origin of
the Zodiac* (New York: Atheneum
Publishers, 1969). His discussion of the
zodiac and the constellations includes the
evolution of the figures of the zodiac from
antiquity and explains the problem of
precession as it resulted in a double
zodiac. See especially Gleadow, p. 147.

Precession of the Equinoxes

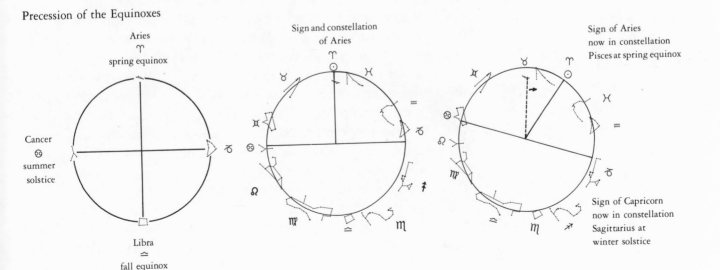

the planets are also displaced, since they must retain their precise angular distance from Sol in order to provide those all-important astrological aspects that separate planetary influences into "good" and "evil." In this regard, the mariner is forced to side with the astronomer. The position of Sol in the constellation is of little concern to the sailor, for when he can see Sol he cannot see the stars. For his nocturnal navigation, however, he must recognize the planets in their "real" location in the constellations, and he must also know the angular measure of planets to the sun. Here the sailor finds effective truth in a half-truth: Let the sun precess as it will, the planets must be accurately placed to meet his navigational requirements.

Further, since the astrologer has divorced the signs from the constellations, he provides himself with a neat and tidy heaven consisting of twelve signs of exactly thirty degrees each, thereby greatly facilitating his computations. The constellations themselves are not so precise. They vary in length from the mere twelve degrees or so of the four cardinal constellations to a sprawling fifty-some degrees of divine Virgo. To the astronomer, the ancient mythic figures of the constellations are a convenient nuisance, but there they are—well established and too well charted to change without total disruption. In this area, despite the changes in attitudes brought by the Age of Enlightenment and the mild but supercilious disapproval of such observers as Sir William Herschel, discoverer of Uranus, the astronomers tolerate the old sky gods and their animals, which provide handy boundaries and known reference points for stellar topography. Even so, the astronomer holds to a measuring system that deals in degrees from the vernal equinox and does not relate his computations to the constellations. The sailor of necessity follows the astronomer's system of measurement, but imposes upon it the astrological concept of stellar influence. This use of astrology, to the scientific astronomer, constitutes sheer superstition. In this area the astrologers, among themselves, either disagree or equivocate, for some believe that the stars cause events on earth; others claim that the stars only reveal events; still others straddle the fence with compromise: "The stars incline, but do not impel." The astronomers to all these reply, "Balderdash!" Here, however, the sailor abandons science and opts for the signs and

Mythological zodiac (top) and configurations of constellations.

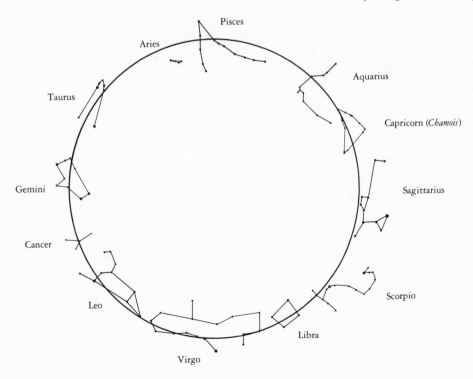

Astronomy and Astrology

The signs, planets, and elements listed here will assist the reader
in following the calendar pages of the *Almanac*.

Mark	Sign	Element	Characteristic
♈	Aries	Fire	Impulsive, courageous, childish, temperamental
♉	Taurus	Earth	Stubborn, kind, luxurious, patient, enrageable
♊	Gemini	Air	Restless, versatile, mischievous, clever
♋	Cancer	Water	Sensitive, changeable, moody, feminine; memory
♌	Leo	Fire	Proud, authoritative, masculine, generous
♍	Virgo	Earth	Exact, intelligent, chaste, critical, quick
♎	Libra	Air	Just, artistic, honest, discriminating
♏	Scorpio	Water	Passionate, sensual, mystic, cruel, deep, subtle
♐	Sagittarius	Fire	Candid, impatient, generous, nature-loving
♑	Capricorn	Earth	Ambitious, tenacious, melancholy, shrewd, selfish
♒	Aquarius	Air	Idealistic, honest, solitary, intellectual
♓	Pisces	Water	Subtle, tricky, feminine, dreamy, sensitive, treacherous, but also devoted and mystical

Mark	Planet	Rules	Characteristic
☉	Sol	* ♌	Honorable, powerful, vital, fortunate, beneficent
☽	Luna	♋	Female, emotional, mutable, fickle
☿	Mercury	♊ ♍	Versatile, literate, tricky, restless
♀	Venus	♉ ♎	Affectionate, loving of children, lucky; "the Lesser Fortune"
♂	Mars	♈ ♏	Courageous, enthusiastic; wounds, war, violence
♃	Jupiter	♓ ♐	Religious, law, power, ritual, travel; "the Greater Fortune"
♄	Saturn	♑ ♒	Selfish, dishonest; hard work, earth, and mines
♅	Uranus	♒	Intellectuality, eccentricity, sudden change
♆	Neptune	♓	Mysticism, dreams, fraud, drunkenness, death

*Cf. horseshoe on mast behind doubloon in *Moby-Dick*.

portents. Taji is nearly correct when he comments, "All your old tars are Daniels." Like the early stargazers of ancient Babylon, the mariner keeps a close and interpretive eye on the heavens, using the celestial bodies both as early-warning system and as cosmic clock. One of Taji's more definite errors may be found in his declaration that "forecastle chronology is ever vague and defective"; it is neither.

The astronomer computes from direct telescopic observation, star catalogues, and the laws of physics. The astrologer computes from ephemerides prepared especially for his needs. The sailor relies on eye, instrument, and almanac, and the almanac is a hypocritical blend of science and lore.

Like the astrologer, the almanac reports the sun in the *sign* at the seasonal changes four times each year. Thus, when the almanac states, "Sun enters Capricorn, Winter begins," Sol is only about halfway through Sagittarius. Like the astrologer, the almanac reports the aspects: that is, "Jupiter conjunct Sol" or

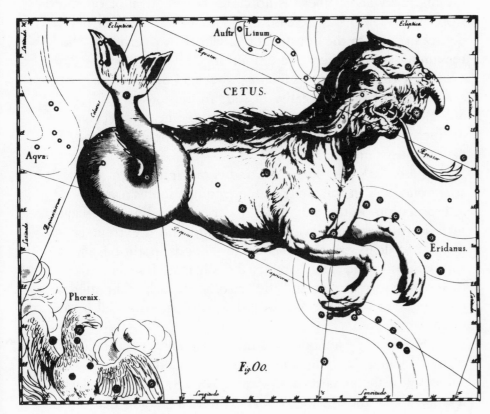

Cetus the Whale

2. The constellation Cetus the Whale, a large stelleration just south of the ecliptic at the Pisces sector, is connected with Leviathan both mythologically and nautically. It is considered malefic, partly because its configuration resembles that of the Great Bear, thereby confusing sailors and causing them to sail off course. Like Satan, Cetus misleads man to his downfall. Though south of the ecliptic, Cetus is adjacent to the north celestial pole marked by the zodiacal constellation Aries. For full mythological treatment, see Gertrude Jobes and James Jobes, *Outer Space*.

"Saturn square Sol." But like the astronomer, it places the planet in the constellation—not the sign. As a result, a *greenhorn* who tries to read an almanac can become thoroughly confused in his attempt to "square" Saturn in Pisces to Sol in Capricorn. In short, the reader who approaches the almanac in ignorance is faced with some appalling problems in interpretation. The sailor who does so can be fatally misled, in mistaking Cetus the Whale for the Great Bear, a common error among inexperienced mariners.[2] Nevertheless, the book is practical, expedient, and in its own way accurate—the "old Daniel's" best friend.

Like the almanac, Melville's solar myth contains elements of both astrology and astronomy. Although he utilizes the astrological and mythological symbolism of the zodiac figures, he positions Sol and the planets in their true locations in the zodiac, not in the signs. In this respect he follows the almanac and also conforms to the sailor's practice of noting the position of the planets simply by looking at them in the night sky—if they are in the night sky and if there is no cloud cover. A sailor on watch from sundown to sunrise can, if sober, see about three hundred degrees of sky as the constellations wheel by overhead. The remaining sixty degrees are hidden in the "sunglade" of dawn or evening twilight. As the sun rises, the stars dim, and the mariner can no longer see the reality of stars in the too-strong light of Sol. Because Sol's light quenches the stars, he can deceive the inexperienced tar who does not have the proper reverence for nautical instruments.

These are some of the contradictions inherent in nautical astronomy and in the almanac that require sophisticated interpretation on the part of an experienced sailor. The landsman, such as Taji betrays himself to be, would find it extremely difficult to deal with the practical falsehoods, traditions, and ambiguities of the sailor's bible, the almanac. For the same reason, the astronomer and the astrologer, each committed to a pure and consistent system, would see no pattern at all in *Mardi*'s stellar imagery.

One other factor obscures the metaphor for the modern reader. Even as Melville was writing *Mardi,* the prestige and authority of the almanac was waning. In 1877, Melville lamented the passing of the almanac era and the imagination that once graced the pages of these useful books.[3] Since then, the almanac has been relegated to the realm of the quaint, and it no longer serves as a bridge between astronomy and astrology. Also, the emphasis on the planet Neptune that is central in *Mardi* has little relevance today, since few readers can cite offhand the year of his discovery. In 1849, when *Mardi* was published, the planet was still newsworthy. In fact, Melville acquired the nickname "Neptune," and retained it for many years, despite his closer astrological relationship to old Sol, the misleading pilot.[4]

*   *   *

To claim *The American Almanac* as Melville's specific guide from among the hundreds of almanacs then published and without any statement from Melville to that effect, might be judged a considerable risk. For that reason, it would be well to examine the circumstantial evidence on which I base this claim.

Because of Melville's reiteration of the "riddling" elements of *Mardi,* it may be that he expected someone to try to solve the riddle, though he was very quickly disenchanted on that score. With such a naive and overenthusiastic expectation, however, it stands to reason that he would have selected an almanac that enjoyed a large and general circulation. The nautical almanacs published by the Greenwich Observatory in England and the United States Naval Observatory in this country were by far the most elaborate and accurate and were in use on most if not all ships. They did not, however, circulate widely among the general public. The many popular almanacs, such as *The Farmer's, The Albany Almanac*—both of which Melville knew—and the other similar ones published in Massachusetts and New York, contained very little astronomical information. *The American Almanac,* on the other hand, enjoyed broad general circulation and presented a great deal of astronomical matter. According to Richard Anders of the American Antiquarian Society, it was "really a book-length compendium [with] by far the most astronomical information of any almanac of this period, enough to function as a nautical almanac, and is certainly the only one a seaman would be drawn

3. Melville's interest in almanacs is revealed retroactively in a letter to Abraham Lansing, January 20, 1877: "By the way,—the almanac—I should have been sorry to have forgotten it—That venerable almanac, which bears witness to the old times when some imagination yet lingered in this sort of publication. I relish looking over it mightily. It has set me to getting from Boston a similar almanac which still continues to be published there" (*Log,* II, 756). In Merton M. Sealts, Jr., *Melville's Reading: A Check-list of Books Owned and Borrowed,* 83, No. 388, this copy is identified as *The (Old) Farmer's Almanack* for 1877. The gift almanac is suggested to be *Webster's Calendar: or, The Albany Almanac,* in listing No. 553.

4. Cornelius Mathews, in "Several Days in Berkshire," *Literary World,* August 24, 1850, referred to Melville as "New Neptune," and he is last associated with the sea-god by Robert Buchanan, in August, 1885. See *Log,* I, 383, and II, 792.

28

1846. DECEMBER, twelfth Month.

Astronomical Calculations.

☉ Declination. Days.	d.	m	Days.	d.	m.	Days.	d.	m.	Days.	d.	m.	Days.	d.	m.
1	21	S.48	7	22	37	13	23	9	19	23	25	25	23	24
2	21	57	8	22	43	14	23	13	20	23	26	26	23	23
3	22	.6	9	22	49	15	23	17	21	23	27	27	23	20
4	22	10	10	22	55	16	23	19	22	23	27	28	23	18
5	22	22	11	23	0	17	23	22	23	23	26	29	23	14
6	22	30	12	23	5	18	23	24	24	23	26	30	23	11

○ Full Moon, 2d day, 6h. 2m. evening.
☾ Last Quarter, 10th day, 4h. 32m. evening.
● New Moon, 18th day, 7h. 58m. evening.
☽ First Quarter, 25th day, 1h. 52m. morning.

D. M.	D. W.	☉ r.	☉ s.	L. D. h. m.	DAY'S DEC. h.m.	☉ F.	● A.	F.SEA. h. m.	●'s PLACE.	● r. s.	● SOU. h. m.
1	Tuesd.	7 26	5	9 8	5 58	11	13	10 40	neck	5 25	11 10
2	Wedn.	7 27	5	9 6	6 0	10	○	11 23	arms	○ ris.	morn.
3	Thurs.	7 28	5	9 4	6 2	10	15	morn.	arms	5 32	0 4
4	Friday	7 28	5	9 4	6 2	10	16	0 13	breast	6 19	0 58
5	Satur.	7 29	5	9 2	6 4	9	17	0 50	breast	7 16	1 50
6	*SUN.*	7 30	5	9 0	6 6	9	18	1 20	heart	8 19	2 40
7	Mond.	7 30	5	9 0	6 6	8	19	2 7	heart	9 5	3 37
8	Tuesd.	7 31	5	8 58	6 8	8	20	3 43	heart	10 14	4 13
9	Wedn.	7 32	5	8 56	6 10	7	21	3 26	belly	11 11	4 56
10	Thurs.	7 32	5	8 56	6 10	7	22	4 9	belly	morn.	5 39
11	Friday	7 32	5	8 56	6 10	7	23	5 1	reins	0 18	6 21
12	Satur.	7 32	5	8 56	6 10	6	24	6 4	reins	1 7	7 4
13	*SUN.*	7 32	5	8 56	6 10	6	25	7 13	reins	2 3	7 48
14	Mond.	7 33	5	8 54	6 12	5	26	8 22	secrets	3 5	8 34
15	Tuesd.	7 33	5	8 54	6 12	5	27	9 12	secrets	4 7	9 22
16	Wedn.	7 33	5	8 54	6 12	4	28	9 54	thighs	5 9	10 14
17	Thurs.	7 33	5	8 54	6 12	4	29	10 39	thighs	6 14	11 9
18	Friday	7 33	5	8 54	6 12	3	●	11 36	knees	☽ sets	eve 6
19	Satur.	7 33	5	8 54	6 12	3	1	11 24	knees	5 18	0 4
20	*SUN.*	7 33	5	8 54	inc.	2	2	eve 44	legs	6 11	1 2
21	Mond.	7 33	5	8 54	0 0	2	3	1 38	legs	7 20	2 58
22	Tuesd.	7 33	5	8 54	0 0	1	4	2 18	legs	9 30	3 53
23	Wedn.	7 33	5	8 54	0 0	1	5	3 4	feet	10 41	4 46
24	Thurs.	7 33	5	8 54	0 0	0	6	4 35	feet	11 52	5 38
25	Friday	7 33	5	8 54	0 0	S.	7	5 29	head	morn.	6 29
26	Satur.	7 33	5	8 54	0 0	0	8	6 30	head	1 1	7 20
27	*SUN.*	7 33	5	8 54	0 0	1	9	7 41	neck	2 12	8 11
28	Mond.	7 33	5	8 54	0 2	2	10	8 44	neck	3 44	9 4
29	Tuesd.	7 32	5	8 56	0 2	2	11	9 40	arms	4 19	9 56
30	Wedn.	7 32	5	8 56	0 2	3	12	10 39	arms	5 11	10 49
31	Thurs.	7 32	5	8 56	0 2	3	13	11 25	breast	5 52	11 41

29

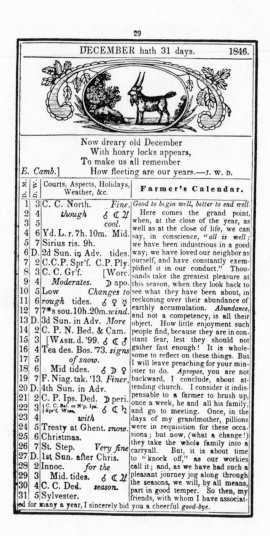

DECEMBER hath 31 days. 1846.

Now dreary old December
With hoary locks appears,
To make us all remember
E. Camb.] How fleeting are our years.—J. W. D.

D. M.	D. W.	Courts, Aspects, Holidays, Weather, &c.
1	3	C. C. North. *Fine,*
2	4	*though* ☌ ☾ ♃
3	5	*cool.*
4	6	Yd. L. r. 7h. 10m. Mid.
5	7	Sirius ris. 9h.
6	D.	2d Sun. in Adv. tides.
7	2	C.C.P. Spr'f. C.P. Ply.
8	3	C. C. Gr'f. [Worc.
9	4	*Moderates.* ☽ apo.
10	5	Low *Changes to*
11	6	*rough* tides. ☌ ♀ ☿
12	7	7*s sou. 10h. 20m. *wind.*
13	D.	3d Sun. in Adv. *More*
14	2	C. P. N. Bed. & Cam.
15	3	[Wash. d. '99. ☌ ☾ ♂
16	4	Tea des. Bos. '73. *signs*
17	5	*of snow.*
18	6	Mid tides. ☌ ☽ ♀
19	7	F. Niag. tak. '13. *Finer,*
20	D.	4th Sun. in Adv.
21	2	C. P. Ips. Ded. ☽ peri.
22	3	{C. C. Sal. or N'p. Ips. {Spr'f. Wos. ☌ ☾ ♄
23	4	*with*
24	5	Treaty at Ghent. *snow.*
25	6	Christmas.
26	7	St. Step. *Very fine*
27	D.	1st Sun. after Chris.
28	2	Innoc. *for the*
29	3	Mid. tides. ☌ ☾ ♃
30	4	C. C. Ded. *season.*
31	5	Sylvester.

Farmer's Calendar.

Good to begin well, better to end well.

Here comes the grand point, when, at the close of the year, as well as at the close of life, we can say, in conscience, "*all is well*; we have been industrious in a good way; we have loved our neighbor as ourself, and have constantly exemplified it in our conduct." Thousands take the greatest pleasure at this season, when they look back to see what they have been about, in reckoning over their abundance of earthly accumulation. *Abundance*, and not a competency, is all their object. How little enjoyment such people find, because they are in constant fear, lest they should not gather fast enough! It is wholesome to reflect on these things. But I will leave preaching for your minister to do. *Apropos*, you are not backward, I conclude, about attending church. I consider it indispensable to a farmer to brush up, once a week, he and all his family, and go to meeting. Once, in the days of my grandmother, pillions were in requisition for these occasions; but now, (what a change!) they take the whole family into a carryall. But, it is about time to "knock off," as our workies call it; and, as we have had such a pleasant journey jog along through the seasons, we will, by all means, part in good temper. So then, my friends, with whom I have associated for many a year, I sincerely bid you a cheerful *good-bye*.

Pages from the 1845 issue of the *Farmer's Almanac* (courtesy of the publishers of *The Old Farmer's Almanac,* Rodale Press, Emmaus, Pa.).

to for practical purposes."[5] Therefore, this book, which contains information on weather, railroad schedules, crops, business trends, and so forth, would have provided the broadest circulation, which suited Melville's purposes. Published yearly, almanacs were offered for sale on newsstands and in book stores, and were not available by subscription. Therefore, no records of subscribers are available.

It was the practice of most families to keep their almanacs over the years, since they served as handy references. Births, deaths, and other vital family statistics were entered by many families on the margins of the calendar pages of the almanacs, pending eventual formal entry into the family Bible.[6] Thus, though *Mardi* was written from 1847 to 1849, Melville could reasonably expect readers to have on hand their 1845 and 1846 almanacs. Most of the popular almanacs were in pamphlet form, but *The American Almanac* was a sturdy book that a thrifty householder would judge easier to keep than to throw away. For this reason, it is to this day fairly common to find full sets of the *American* in major libraries.

In his later work, *Moby Dick* (Chapter 99, "The Doubloon"), Stubb, in attempting to interpret the horoscope on the coin, goes below to get his "Massachusetts almanac"; *The American Almanac* was published in Boston. Anders states that "when Melville speaks of a 'Massachusetts almanac,' it sounds as though he meant the best-known one or the one most identified with the state. That would seem to suggest either the Farmer's or the American."

Finally, there is the Jupiter error, which Melville emphasizes in his characterization of Jarl, as will be discussed at length in a later chapter. An examination of the leading Massachusetts and New York almanacs for 1845 reveals that the error occurs only in the *American,* and it is apparently a misprint. The other almanacs, which contain far fewer entries, either make no mention of Jupiter at all or else note only the end of his retrograde period on December 26. If it can be established then that Melville utilized the Jupiter error in his imagery, the *American* becomes a certain choice as the author's reference book.

5. Richard Anders of the American Antiquarian Society maintains a large collection of American almanacs of the nineteenth century. Subsequent to a helpful correspondence in August, 1971, Mr. Anders personally aided me during my visit to the society's collection in 1973 to examine their almanacs and atlases.

6. See example on page 32.

Sol   Be thou, old pilot, our guide!   —*Mardi*, 229–30

There is no character in *Mardi* who represents Sol, though each one in turn displays a solar identity. It would seem, then, that Sol signifies the creative power of the author, Melville: creator, vitalizer, animator, and deceiver of his creatures. Because August 1 is his birth date, Melville's "sun sign" is Leo the Lion; the planetary ruler of that sign is Sol. Hence, both the lion and the sun symbolize the power and the presence of the author, who participates as a silent character in *Mardi*.

In treating Sol as a planetary body, the celestial illuminator that moves on the author's behalf through the zodiac and in passing the other planets provides them with life and light, Melville adheres to the Ptolemaic system of astronomy, thereby committing himself as well as his characters to an "error." On the other hand, navigational astronomy has always followed Ptolemy's system, and still does. By equating his own ruling planet Sol to the creative power of the author, Melville pictures the creative force as content to work with a practical error and to circumscribe Earth, even though it is in fact the central force around which our world revolves.

But both Sol and the author have the power to deceive or mislead the unwary: Sol because his light hides the stars and because the almanac does not reveal his true position, the author because he deals in fiction and yields his truths in a "merry and mythical way" (369). If, as *Mardi*'s poet Yoomy eventually points out, the questers leave Odo in the spring, we may be sure that, even without the astronomical dating system, the escape of the *Chamois* takes place in winter, when Sol is well to the south. Taji disdains nautical instruments but instead cavalierly invokes Sol, "Be thou, old pilot, our guide!" Day by day, as the year moves toward spring, Sol moves northward from the Tropic of Capricorn toward the Equator, luring Taji so far to the north that he is caught unaware in the easterly currents.

Taji is not alone in his inability to comprehend his creator. King Media of Odo slights Sol by honoring the errant narrator with both the idol and the title that rightfully belong to the springtime sun. As the "saturnine" narrator is entertained in Media's temple, the "garish sun" lingers without "like some lackey in waiting" (172). Moreover, the narrator is surprised by Media's "unaffected indifference" to his amazing voyage from the sun and, indeed, "his indifference to the sun itself" (176). For his error in judgment, and for his failure of justice, Media undergoes a metamorphosis and eventually faces sedition.

By involving himself as a solar figure of deceptive authority without actually appearing either as narrator or as character, Melville allows for both consistency and flexibility in point of view. The progress of Sol around the zodiac places him in contact with each of the planets for a certain period and enables the solar author to animate and speak through various characters without abandoning the narratorship of Taji. Insofar as Taji is represented by two planets—Saturn in Capricorn-Aquarius and Uranus in Pisces—Taji's dominance as narrator continues during Sol's passage from Sagittarius through Aries—December through March. But these slow planets cannot follow Sol around the sky, so those characters represented by the small, swift planets dominate the latter portion of the story while Saturn–Uranus–Taji is deprived of the solar power during the summer transit. At the end of the quest, as Sol passes through Libra into the winter sky, Taji again, though briefly, regains his dominance.

Melville's technique relates somewhat to that of Henry Fielding, who in *Tom Jones* repeatedly steps into the story and asserts his complete control over circumstance and character. Even so, Fielding's omnipotent and omniscient intrusive author stands apart from his story, while Melville as the Sol figure participates subtly without intrusion. In this capacity, Melville establishes a symbolic ratio: as Melville the author is to Taji, so God the Author is to mankind.

In addition to his role in Melville's "comedy of error," Sol also serves the theme of the process of creativity and the growth of the artist. In dealing with this vital theme of the growth of creativity in the artist, Melville explores four stages or aspects of

progression: experience, influence, inspiration, and motivation—
all of which are brought into focus in Chapter 180 during the
dramatic dialogue on the island of King Abrazza. Taji's progress
from ignorant and irresponsible sailor to artist–narrator is
paralleled by the passage of Sol from that section of the zodiac
called the "Celestial Sea" (Capricorn, Aquarius, and Pisces) to
the sign that symbolizes both the fall of the year and the
harmony of esthetics—Libra, House of Venus. To illustrate the
aspect of experience, Melville uses the metaphor of initiation,
with imagery of knighthood, of the Eleusinian Mysteries, and,
hidden in the riddle of Neptune, the nautical ritual of Crossing
the Line. To show how the author assimilates influences, both
consciously and unconsciously, Melville permeates *Mardi* with
allusions to food and drink, cannibalism, digestion, and such
digestive ills as dyspepsia. Inspiration is dealt with in terms of
possession by devils, of melancholia, and, in Babbalanja's
discourse, of artists used by a higher power as amanuenses.
Though these are major essentials to artistry, they are not
enough, for some force must spur the artist to muster his creative
energy and take action. One such motivation is described as "the
necessity of bestirring himself to procure his yams" (592).
Another, however, involves the revenge factor, around which the
plot of *Mardi* revolves and which Melville declares to be the
motive-power for the writing of *Mardi.*

In Babbalanja's discussion of art and artists, he portrays the
artist-potential as a yellow lion (593), languid and dreaming, but
at last roused to fury. In the zodiac, Leo the Lion is the
constellation and sign ruled by Sol and associated with Melville's
birth-month of August. On August 1, Sol enters the head (in
some sky-map drawings, the open mouth) of Leo and becomes, in
Babbalanja's words, "the live coal" on the lips of the author
(599). Positioned exactly at the front paw of Leo, Sol might well
be referred to when Babbalanja says of the yellow lion that "his
paw had stopped a rolling world" (593). Thus Sol becomes a
burning yam as he moves through the Lion, causing divine
heartburn and creative dyspepsia, in a graphic and abrasive
description of the author at work.

In this revealing section Melville stresses not only the agony of the artist striving to digest and organize his compilations but the intense loneliness as well. Creativity is shown as a solitary game: in fact, a game of Solitaire. By this means, Melville combines his solar myth with the "lonely game" of literary Sol wherein an author predestines the fate of his creatures by the stars and by the fall of the cards.

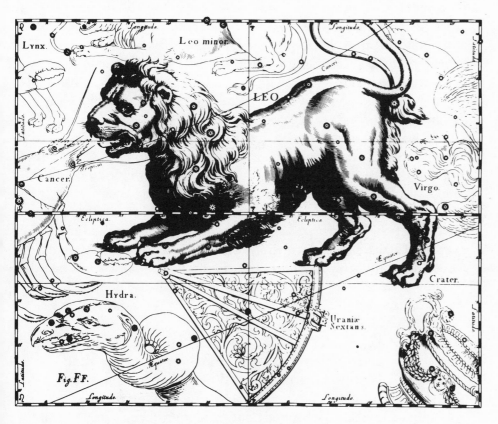

The summer quadrant of the zodiac, including Cancer, Leo, and Virgo. At lower right is the constellation Crater, interpreted as a Grail figure (traced from Hevelius, 1690).

The Mardi Holidays

Time, which is the solver of all riddles, will solve "Mardi!"
—Herman Melville to Lemuel Shaw, April 23, 1849[7]

7. *Log*, I, 300. In a letter dated April 23, 1849, Melville wrote to his father-in-law, Lemuel Shaw: "I see that Mardi has been cut into by the London Atheneum, and also burnt by the common hangman in the Boston Post. However the London Examiner & Literary Gazette; & other papers this side of the water have done differently. These attacks are matters of course, and are essential to the building up of any permanent reputation—if such should ever prove to be mine—'There's nothing in it!' cried the dunce, when he threw down the 47th problem of the 1st Book of Euclid—'There's nothing in it—' ——Thus with the posed critic. But Time, which is the solver of all riddles, will solve 'Mardi!' "

8. Melville's use of the solar myth has been explored by, among others: H. Bruce Franklin in *The Wake of the Gods: Melville's Mythology,* as well as in his "Introduction" to the Capricorn *Mardi.* William B. Dillingham, in *An Artist in the Rigging: The Early Work of Herman Melville,* pp. 112–16, has noted the quest in *Mardi* as a voyage through the zodiac and has dealt with it in a summary though perceptive manner, finding no special significance in the metaphor.

The progress of Sol through the constellations of the zodiac, accompanied by seven known planets plus one incognito, forms a vast cosmic calendar by which the dates may be followed precisely through that portion of the year covered by *Mardi.* A detailed study of Melville's chronometrics will demonstrate the dating system, but it might be helpful first to preview those high points of the action that acquire their significance through their relationship to the calendar of holidays.[8]

The time period covers a little more than ten months—the nine-month gestation period for Neptune, an additional month for the disposition of Taji and the year's final religious holiday—and can be roughly divided into three parts: the establishment of the metaphor, which includes a backward look at the three-year voyage of the *Arcturion,* Chapters 1 through 8; the holiday period, Christmas to Ascension, during which the planets are active in conjunctions, realigning themselves from a winterside cluster of transits to a summerside processional, Chapters 9 through 65; and the quests, Chapters 66 to the end. Although the precise dates must be garnered from the all-pervasive astronomical imagery, Melville does include, later in the book, some overt though generalized information about the time element. In addition, certain crucial events are accompanied by imagery relating to specific holidays. The imagery is inserted so casually as to seem incidental, but its significance is revealed by the chronological order in which it appears.

The escape of Taji and Jarl from the *Arcturion* is marked by references to the Nativity, and the genealogy of Jarl, like that of Christ, is traced back to Adam. The association of the escape with the Yuletide season is reinforced by Taji's geographical coordinates, which place the *Arcturion* near Christmas Island. Related imagery that arises from this opening scene includes conception, birth, and initiation.

The encounter between Taji's party and that of Aleema the Priest is preceded by imagery of costuming, disguise, procession, and Communion, identifying the occasion with the season of Mardi Gras carnival. Because this action gives rise to the title metaphor, it will be discussed fully in a later chapter.

Immediately after the Fray—Taji's encounter with Aleema's party, in which Taji stabs Aleema the Priest and absconds with the maiden Yillah—imagery of remorse and guilt and relinquishment tokens the Lenten season. In keeping with the

MOVABLE FESTIVALS OF THE CHURCH, IN 1846.

Septuagesima Sunday,	Feb. 9th	Rogation Sunday,	May 17th
Quinq. or Shrove do.	" 22d	Ascen. Day, or Holy Th.	" 21st
Ash Wed. Lent begins,	" 25th	Whitsunday or Pentecost,	" 31st
Mid Lent Sunday,	Mar. 1st	Trinity Sunday,	June 7th
Palm do	Apr. 5th	Corpus Christi Day,	" 11th
Easter do	" 12th	Fête Dieu,	
Low do	" 19th	Advent Sunday,	Nov. 29th

JEWISH CALENDAR.

[The anniversaries marked with an asterisk (*) are to be strictly observed.]

Year. Names of the Months.

5606	Thebet begins	. . . .	Dec. 30, 1845.
"	" 10th	Fast for the Siege of Jerusalem	Jan. 8, 1846.
"	Sebat begins	. . . .	Jan. 28, "
"	Adar begins	. . . .	Feb. 27, "
"	" 11th	Fast of Esther . . .	Mar. 9, "
"	" 14th	*Purim	" 12, "
"	" 15th	Schuscan Purim . . .	" 13, "
"	Nisan begins	. . . . .	" 28, "
"	" 15th	*Beginning of the Passover .	Apr. 12, "
"	" 16th	*Second Feast, or Morrow of the Passover	" 12, "
"	" 21st	*Seventh Feast . . .	" 17, "
"	" 22d	*End of the Passover .	" 18, "
"	Ijar begins	. . . . . .	" 27, "
"	" 18th	Lag Beomer	May 14, "
"	Sivan begins	. . . . . .	" 26, "
"	" 6th	*Feast of Weeks or Pentecost .	" 31, "
"	" 7th	*Second Feast . . .	June 1, "
"	Thammus begins	. . . . .	" 25, "
"	" 17th	Fast for the taking of the Temple	July 11, "
"	Ab begins	. . . .	" 24, "
"	" 9th	*Fast for the burning of the Temple	Aug. 9, "
"	Elul begins	. . . .	" 23, ".
5607	Tisri begins	*Feast for the New Year	Sept. 21, "
"	" 2d	*Second Feast for the New Year	" 22, "
"	" 4th	Fast of Gedaljah,	" 24, "
"	" 10th	*Fast of the Reconciliation or Atonement	" 30, "
"	" 15th	*Feast of the Huts or Tabernacles	Oct. 5, "

1*

Year. Names of the Months.

5607	Tisri	16th	*Second Feast of the Huts	.	Oct. 6, 1846.
"	"	21st	Feast of Palms or Branches		" 11, "
"	"	22d	*End of the Hut, or Congregation Feast	" 12, "
"	"	23d	*Rejoicing for the discovery of the Law	" 13, "
"	Marchesvan begins				" 21, "
"	Chisleu begins		. . . .	Nov. 19 "
"	"	25th	Consecration of the Temple	.	Dec. 13, "
"	Thebet begins		. . . . . .	" 19, "
"	"	10th	Fast for the Siege of Jerusalem	" 28, "
"	Sebat begins		. . . . . .	Jan. 17, 1847.

The Jewish year generally contains 354 days, or 12 lunations of the Moon, but, in a cycle of 19 years, an intercalary month (Veadar) is 7 times introduced, for the purpose of rendering the average duration of the year quite or nearly correct.

MAHOMETAN CALENDAR.

Year. Names of the Months.

1261	Muharrem begins	. . . .	Dec. 30, 1845.
"	Saphar	"	. . . . . .	Jan. 30, 1846.
"	Rabia I.	"	. . . . . .	Feb. 28, "
"	Rabia II.	"	. . . . . .	Mar. 30, "
"	Jomadhi I.	"	. . . . . .	April 28, "
"	Jomadhi II.	"	. . . . . .	May 28, "
"	Redjeb	"	. . . . . .	June 26, "
"	Chaban	"	. . . . . .	July 26, "
"	Ramadan	"	(Month of Fasting)	Aug. 24, "
"	Schewall	"	(Bairam) . . .	Sept. 23, "
"	Dsu'l-kadah	"	. . . . . .	Oct. 22, "
"	Dsu'l-hejjah	"	. . . . . .	Nov. 21, "
1262	Muharrem	"	. . . . . .	Dec. 20, "

The Mahometan Era dates from the flight of Mahomet to Medina, July 16th, A. D. 622.

The Mahometan year is purely lunar; it consists of 12 synodical periods of the Moon, or of 354 days, 19 times in a cycle of 30 years, and 11 times of 355 days. The average length of this year is therefore $354\frac{11}{30}$ days, which differs only *thirty-three seconds* from the truth; a degree of exactness that only could have been attained by a long series of observations. But as no allowance is made for the excess of 11 days in the length of a tropical year over the time of 12 revolutions of the Moon, it is obvious that in about 33 years, the above months will correspond to every season and every part of the Gregorian year.

Pages from *The American Almanac*, 1846, listing holidays for major religions.

spirit of sacrifice, Samoa the Navigator gives up the baubles that adorn his nose and ear, and it is disclosed that Jarl bears on his arm a tattoo of Christ crucified.

The party reaches the Mardi Islands on March 2 and departs from Odo on March 29, according to the astronomical reckoning. The disappearance of Yillah coincides with Purim, or the Feast of Lots, on March 12 (Adar 14). Late in the book, Melville provides some assurance that we are dealing with the correct season by reporting through the poet Yoomy that the quest had begun in the spring (617). The Isle of Odo represents the month of March, the meridian, and the spring equinox at "o degrees o."

Easter is celebrated on Donjalolo's Isle of Juam, with the feast of twenty-five kings. Until they attend this banquet, Taji and his party have abstained from meat in accordance with Lenten tradition.

Jarl's departure from the story and his subsequently reported death (along with that of Samoa) occur in late May on the "Capricorn Island" of Borabolla. This period coincides with the celebration of Ascension on May 20 and involves Jarl in two ways. As *Mardi*'s Christ figure, Jarl leaves the story near the day that Christ ascended to Heaven; as the Neptune figure, representative of the sea, Jarl may be seen as the "He-bride" of the Doges, central to the Venetian custom of the Espousal of the Adriatic on Ascension Day. Thus, the double image of funeral and wedding marks the questers' visit to Mondoldo. It should be noted that the reappearance of the Avengers, the sons of Aleema, is contemporaneous with the disappearance of Jarl.

The trip to Dominora follows hard on the heels of a casual mention of "high midsummer noon" and "meridian sun" (432) and "Greenwich" (443), which together identify the period of the summer solstice, June 21. In the passage by Porpheero, the "eruption" in Franko figures the bloody uprising against the Second Republic of France on June 23, 1848, while a brief mention of the Jubilee day in Vivenza (525) suggests the passage through the month of July.

August has no official holiday, but it begins with a day significant to Melville—his birthday. The passage of his ruling planet, Sol, through his constellation Leo is devoted to the search for new worlds of the mind, which culminates in the lengthy drama-form discussion of authorship on the Isle of King Abrazza.

As the questers leave Abrazza's Isle of Bonavona, we are told that the harvest moon has risen, marking the month of September. On the Isle of Serenia one quest comes to an end— that of the logician Babbalanja. After months of agonized computation, during which he gleans knowledge, information, and experience from his fellow questers as well as from persons and events encountered during the voyage, Babbalanja reaps the harvest of his labors. His celestial vision occurs on September 24, 1846, the date on which the planet Neptune was discovered.

Although Babbalanja has reaped the fruits of the harvest moon, Taji still cries, "I am the hunter, that never rests! the hunter without a home!"—and the hunter's moon heralds the month of October, according to the *Almanac.* On into October Taji pursues his memory of Yillah, ironically revealed by the astronomical imagery as the figure of the fickle, mutable Luna.

Guided by the Duessa-like Hautia and goaded by the Avenger sons of Aleema, Taji unwillingly arrives at the last isle, Hautia's Flozella-a-Nina. Here, without awareness or volition, Taji takes Communion and is lured into a baptismal plunge. On the midnight of October 29, Taji declares himself a "spirit's phantom's phantom," flitting like a ghost along the beach of Flozella. As he speeds away in the shallop, still convoyed by his three specters, he performs the final saving act of self-renunciation: "I am my own soul's emperor; and my first act is abdication!" On the eastern horizon, red Arcturus, newly risen, heralds the stormy autumn sunrise, and the morning is that of All Saints' Eve, or Hallowe'en.

*   *   *

The importance of the metaphor of Time lies in its revelation of the ritual nature of Taji's passage through Mardi. Here is no chartless voyage, but a vast and highly structured processional that Taji cannot recognize because he keeps no almanac and never knows what day it is. His escape from the *Arcturion* has been, not a willful act or venial sin, but a providential deliverance on the morning of the Nativity. When, after arriving on Mardi, haunted by guilt for the stabbing of Aleema the Priest, he cries, "Am I a murderer, stars?" the reader of the stars recognizes a carnival ritual in which Taji has served as "Goat." Finally, Hautia's pursuit, which Taji interprets as her wicked treachery, is revealed as her participation in his ultimate salvation.

The interminable arguments on predestination and man's responsibility, so fascinating to Babbalanja throughout the quest, resolve themselves in the metaphor of Time. As he strains for an answer to his theological enigma, Babbalanja proposes the full range of "vulgar errors" by which man has attempted to justify this harsh doctrine. The question, to be sure, is never resolved on a verbal level; instead, it is buried in the structure of the novel. The reader who voyages chartless through *Mardi* can perceive Taji, as he sees himself, to be a damned soul, while one who assumes a "supralunar" perspective and obtains "a glimpse of what we are from the Belts of Jupiter and the Moons of Saturn" (577) recognizes in Taji's rites of passage an initiatory function. That escape from the *Arcturion,* though rife with imagery of birth, may be understood instead as a mere preliminary "ejaculation," with Taji as a homunculus "jack" struggling toward fulfillment in baptismal immersion and new life. To arrive at his deepest aim, Taji, like all questers, must dive deep, and this he does on Flozella-a-Nina (note that *niña* is the Spanish word for *child*).

If Babbalanja is to be identified with Leverrier, searching for and finding a new world, Taji stands as the fallen astronomer Adams. It is essential to recall here that Adams, though regarded as a failure, was first to begin the search for the new planet and first to arrive at a solution. Just as he received a duplicate medal for his achievement, albeit in the nature of a consolation prize, so also does Taji become the sperm: Through his immersion and self-renunciation he finds—or founds—a new life, and *Mardi* becomes, among other things, a resounding epithalamion.

IV. The Geography of Mardi

> At all events, the thing seemed feasible enough, notwithstanding old Jarl's superstitious reverence for nautical instruments, and the philosophical objections which might have been urged by a pedantic disciple of Mercator. —*Mardi*, 18

The critical view of Taji as the errant narrator stems primarily from his dubious morality. To ascertain the full nature and extent of Taji's errors it is necessary to consult a chart or map of the Pacific, preferably a globe that shows the direction of winds and currents in the equatorial regions. Taji's geography, though stated in fairly precise terms, is faulty in the extreme. Moreover, the type and the consistency of the mistakes are such that collectively they take on a significant pattern.

Taji states that the *Arcturion* had sailed from Ravavai, "not very far northward from the tropic of Capricorn, or very far westward from Pitcairn's Island, where the mutineers of the Bounty settled" (3). According to the chart, Ravavai lies south, not north, of the tropic line, at a distance of 31.61 miles, throwing Taji about 62 miles off in his north–south estimate.[1] Since he uses the same term "not very far" in relation to Pitcairn, we might expect that island to be not more than one or two hundred miles distant. Actually, Pitcairn is 823 miles from Ravavai. This, Taji's first error, amounts to little more than an inaccuracy, easily attributable to Melville. Following the currents shown on the globe, the *Arcturion* sails far to the southeast, encountering no islands until she swings northward to pass Mas Afuero, off the coast of Chile. The currents begin to sweep in a westerly direction near the Tropic of Capricorn, so the *Arcturion* would cut across toward the Equator fairly well south of the Galápagos Islands. Taji describes the voyage:

> In good time making the desired longitude upon the equator, a few leagues west of the Gallipagos, we spent several weeks chassezing across the Line, to and fro, in unavailing search for our prey. . . . So, day after day, daily; and week after week, weekly, we traversed the self-same longitudinal intersection of the self-same Line; till we were almost ready to swear that we felt the ship strike every time her keel crossed that imaginary locality.
>
> At length, dead before the equatorial breeze, we threaded our

1. Information on distances in the Pacific was provided by the Department of Geography at the University of Missouri—Kansas City.

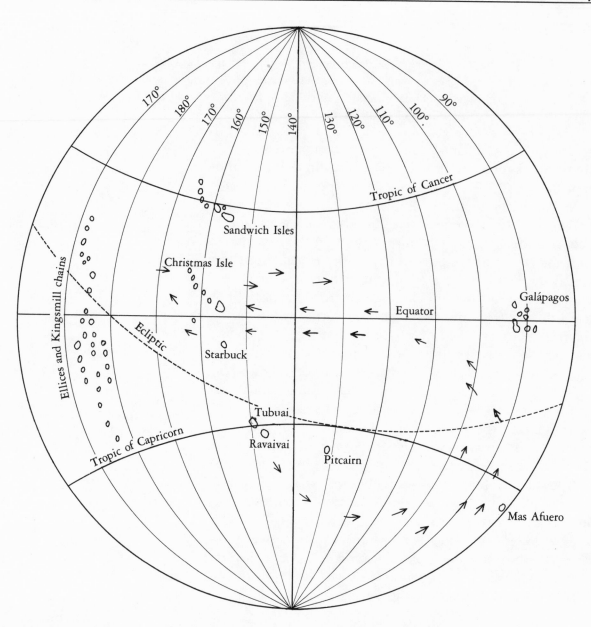

The Pacific currents. Melville's own globe would have
provided approximately the same information
on location of islands and directions of currents.

way straight along the very Line itself. Westward sailing; peering right, and peering left, but seeing naught. (P. 4)

By his use of the word *Line,* Taji indicates that the *Arcturion* is sailing back and forth across the Equator. Any old tar reading *Mardi* might wonder why this narrator, after such emphasis, has not reported a visitation from Neptune—a traditional occurrence on ships crossing the Equator with novice sailors aboard. And Taji has stated that several islanders joined the crew at Ravavai. Since Taji began his journey under a false impression of locality, he might still be miscalculating. If so, he is south of the Equator by as much as 62 miles, repeatedly approaching it and receding from it, but never crossing it.

"At the time I now write of, we must have been something more than sixty degrees to the west of the Gallipagos. And having attained a desirable longitude, we were standing northward," writes Taji, and then continues with a statement that he reiterates five times with variations: "But due west, though distant a thousand miles, stretched north and south an almost endless Archipelago. . . . Ellice's group; then, the Kingsmill isles; then, the Radack and Mulgrave clusters" (11). Of these islands, the Kingsmill group is nearest the Equator, and all the islands mentioned are not 1,000 but 3,000 miles to the west of the *Arcturion*'s position. When Taji chats with Jarl atop the foremast, he repeats that the islands he seeks are "a thousand miles and no less" distant (17), adding that "no known land lay between us and the place we desired to reach" (18). Again Taji is wrong, for, according to his coordinates, the *Arcturion* is 160 miles south and 480 miles east of Christmas Island, discovered December 4, 1777, by Captain Cook. By her northwesterly heading, the *Arcturion* is in direct line with this reef-ringed island.

After Taji unsuccessfully petitions the captain to put him ashore, he climbs to the masthead one evening. "Where we were then," he reports, "was perhaps the most unfrequented and least known portion of these seas" (7). Gazing into the sunset, that is, toward the southwest, he muses:

To and fro, and all over the towers of this Nineveh in the sky, flew troops of birds. Watching them long, one crossed my sight, flew through a low arch, and was lost to view. My spirit must have sailed in with it; for directly, as in a trance, came upon me the cadence of mild billows laving a beach of shells, the waving of

POLYNESIA

Longitude East 160 of Greenwich.

Maria Lazara I.

Gaspar I.

Cooper I.

Gord K.

Washington I.

Manuel Rodriquez

Marquesas

Nuuhiva

SANDWICH Is.

Hawaii

Maui Is.

Oahu

Tauai

Nihau

Necker I.

Birds I.

Gardner I.

Allen I.

Lisianski I.

Yurk I.

Banks I.

Patrocinio I.

Lacker I.

Massachusetts I.

Maria Lazara I.

Volcano I.

I. Sebastian Lobos

Gaudalupe Tres Colunas

Grampus I.

Mears I.

Dolores I.

Jardines

Pajaro

Lamira

Desierta

Low I.

Washington I.

Fanning I.

Christmas I.

Malden I.

Johnson I.

Wake I.

Jarvis I.

Sarah

Starbuck I.

Palmyra I.

Penrhyn I.

Caroline I.

Flint I.

Equator

Kingsmills Groupe

Scarborough Reefs

Aranue I.

Matuua

Tahite

Georgian

Society Is.

Austral Is.

Tubuai

Rivarua

Rapa or
High I.

Four towns
Bapa

Scilly

Bolabola

Huaheine

Harvey Is.

Mauti

Mitiaki

Navigators Is.

FRIENDLY
ISLANDS

FIJI ISLANDS

Tongataboo

NEW
HEBRIDES

New Caledonia

Norfolk I.

Howe I.

Middleton I.

Sandwich I.

Chatham I.

NEW ZEALAND

North Cape

Bay of Plenty

Cook's Strait

Banks

Van Diemens Land

Hobart Town

Bass's Strait

Port Jackson or Botany Bay

Port Philip

Spencer G.

AUSTRALIA

TERRA

Gulf of Carpentaria

Torres Strait

NEW GUINEA

PAPUA

New Ireland

New Britain

Louisiade Archip.

Bougainville I.

Solomon Is.

Isabel I.

Admiralty Is.

CAROLINE ISLANDS

Yap

Pelew Is.

St. Andrew

Anna I.

Egoi I.

Farewellap

Radack Ch.

Ralick Ch.

Mariana or Ladrone Is.

Guaham

Tinian

Anatxan

Assumption I.

Bonin Is.

boughs, and the voices of maidens, and the lulled beatings of my own dissolved heart, all blended together. (P. 8)

To the experienced sailor, the sight of certain types of birds is one sign of nearby land and the sound of billows on shells indicates close proximity. Though this vague description seems to refer to a dream-beach strewn with the usual mollusc shells, it would be well to note that Christmas Island is inhabited only by shellback tortoises, while the surrounding waters teem with sharks.

Taji, of course, imputes his own ignorance to Jarl as he says, "For geography, in which sailors should be adepts, since they are forever turning over and over the great globe of globes, poor Jarl was deplorably lacking" (13). As grounds for this statement Taji gives the fact that Jarl knows nothing about land nor about other worlds: "He weened not of them; yet full as much as Chrysostom" (13). With this punning reference, Melville again confirms the Christmas imagery, since Saint John Chrysostom had denounced the Magi for coming openly to Bethlehem in their quest for the infant Jesus, on the grounds that, since they were astrologers, they should have known that their visit would bring the birth to the attention of Herod. The point here is that Taji thinks of geography in terms of land only, and not in terms of water, for to him, water has no geography. Ironically, he imputes his own ignorance of time and place to the man he himself describes as the oldest and most experienced tar on board the *Arcturion.*

After the escape, Taji and Jarl occupy the whaleboat *Chamois* for sixteen days before boarding a ghostly brigantine, the *Parki.* On the eighth day after the escape, a calm falls, lasting a full four days. As a breeze stirs the *Chamois* again to motion on the thirteenth day, Taji reports a flight of sea fowls. The following day he states that Jarl has carved fourteen notches on the loom and that no tern, noddy, or reef bird could be seen. Yet, when they board the *Parki* two days later, Annatoo and Samoa state that they had sighted islands nearby.

Taji subsequently estimates that the encounter with the *Parki* occurs two hundred leagues—about six hundred miles—west of the location of the *Arcturion* at the time they left her, thereby placing the *Parki* a short distance west of Christmas Island. Here

(From Ellis, *Polynesian Researches,* Vol. I, p. xvii.)

Jarl informs Taji that the *Parki* appears to be drifting toward the north, but Taji disregards the warning, assuming an equatorial position because he cannot see the polar constellations either to the north or to the south. Referring to the globe, the reader will find that just west of Christmas Island the currents take a swing toward the north and continue in that direction for about ten degrees before meeting an easterly current.

Taji, of course, never reaches the great chain of islands to the west. The *Parki* follows the currents that circle the Line Islands—of which Christmas Island is the southernmost—and sinks at a point to the east of Christmas. Nothing more is said of direction until, after the encounter with Aleema and his party, the *Chamois* moves south. Both the evidence of the globe and the names of the Mardi islands indicate that Taji reaches the Society group, not Ellice's or Kingsmill. Certainly the quest that follows the loss of Yillah is a voyage through society, and far be it from Melville not to avail himself of such a felicitous coincidence.

It is the geographical pattern that establishes Taji as an utterly errant and ignorant wayfarer. By the same device, Jarl is shown to be invariably correct, and this must be remembered when, on land in Mardi, he appears to be wrong. By providing these seemingly precise coordinates and by stressing so frequently Taji's lack of and contempt for the nautical instruments so revered by Jarl, Melville invites investigation of Taji's geography, for this is the easiest way into the metaphor. Even those who know nothing of the heavens can detect Taji's error simply by consulting and interpreting the charts that map the Pacific. It would be natural enough to assume that Melville is incorrect and careless, but to do so would be to repeat Taji's error as he imputes ignorance to old Jarl.

Just as the stellar imagery shows Taji to be at the mercy of the forces of fate, so the geographical device reveals that he must follow the currents wherever they lead, especially since he has neither the knowledge by which to interpret them nor the industry to overcome them.

The position of the *Arcturion* in relation to Christmas Island supports the stellar imagery that dates the beginning of Taji and Jarl's adventure at December 24. In addition, it gives rise to two other metaphors to be discussed further, the image of Captain Cook and that of the shipboard initiation ritual, Crossing the Line.

V. Crossing the Line

> With his long tangled hair and harpoon, he looked like the
> sea-god, that boards ships, for the first time crossing the Equator. —*Mardi*, 127

The divergence between Taji's self-image and our judgment of him continues to widen as we realize him to be, not cleverly evil, but pitiably ignorant, suffering always the consequences of his failure to recognize and interpret correctly. In his pride he assumes the posture of one who knows all and attempts to persuade his audience to accept his estimate of himself and regard him as a swashbuckling knight-errant of Manfredian stature. Taji's ambiguous description also renders a false image of Jarl, whether we see him as the loyal and sincerely devoted old chummy or as the dull-witted victim of Taji's cleverness. Once recognized as the figure of Neptune, however, Jarl is perceived as deep, subtle, moody, capable of cruelty and violence yet basically without malice, a personification of the ocean itself. Taji fails to recognize the sea god, for he shares the error of the *Almanac*, thus mistaking his chummy for a jovial uncle.

Mardi is the only book in which Melville specifically mentions the ritual of shipboard initiation, though initiatory metaphors have been noted in both *Redburn* and *White Jacket*.[1] It is not known whether he himself ever underwent the ritual, since he never describes it and since the records of the ship in which he first crossed the Equator are not available. Even if the captain of the *Acushnet* had been one of the many captains who would not permit the crew to indulge in the ancient ritual, we may rest assured that Melville had access to more than adequate details from his shipmates. Mentions of and descriptions of the ritual appear in many books and journals available to Melville.[2]

In the *Journals* of Captain Cook, the ritual of "ducking" received frequent mention.[3] Richard Henry Dana, Jr., expressed relief upon crossing the Equator that he could call himself "a son of Neptune" without "the disagreeable initiation which so many have to go through" and could claim "full powers to play tricks on others."[4] Francis Allyn Olmsted was also spared the indignities of the ritual, but he provides a lengthy description of hazing practices that Melville quite probably read, since his

1. James E. Miller, Jr., "*Redburn* and *White-Jacket*: Initiation and Baptism," *Nineteenth-Century Fiction*, 13 (1959), 273–93.

2. The works cited throughout this chapter contain more details of the custom of initiation in the nineteenth century.

3. *The Journals of Captain James Cook on His Voyages of Discovery, 1776–1780*, III, Parts I and II, ed. J. C. Beaglehold. At each crossing of the Equator by ships that carried novice sailors, Cook recorded a ducking. Dr. Anderson's objection is recorded on p. 743, in his journal entry for Sept. 1, 1776.

4. R. H. Dana, Jr., *Two Years Before the Mast* (New York, 1909), p. 24.

Neptune (from the sculpture by Adam in the Louvre, Paris).

Incidents of a Whaling Voyage is considered a possible source for some of the material in *Omoo*.[5] According to one account:

> That diverting marine saturnalia which, within living memory, always took place on Crossing the Line, when a vessel had "boys" on board who were passing from the north to the south latitudes, or vice versa, for the first time, was nothing more than a burlesque of certain religious observances of the ancient mariners as they sailed out of the Mediterranean past the "Pillars of Hercules" into the broad Atlantic. In their time the exploration of that vast watery waste was supposed to be attended with peculiar dangers, which could only be averted by invocations to Neptune, the god of the sea, in much the same manner as they were accustomed to invoke him in their temples on the 3rd of December, the day set apart for a festival in honor of Neptune and Minerva.

Thus it became customary for Neptune to board ships in company with his wife, Amphitrite, and the royal court.[6]

The ceremony varied from ship to ship, but certain elements appear to have been fairly constant. Traditionally, the hazing of the "greenhorn" sailor begins a week or so before the scheduled Crossing of the Line, while the boarding by Neptune and his retinue takes place on the eve of crossing. As that crucial eve approaches, the "boy" is subjected to all manner of indignities that increase his fears and arouse his nervousness. He is sent aloft to the masthead to look for the "line" drawn on the sea or to watch for the appearance of Neptune's light. In the early chapters of *Mardi* we find Taji suffering a severe case of nerves during a calm and revealing an ever-increasing obsession with the Line. His ascent to the masthead may represent such a vigil, and on his second visit, he encounters Jarl.

It is customary for the role of Neptune to be assumed by the oldest and most experienced hand on board, which, on the *Arcturion,* would have been Jarl, according to Taji's description of his age and seamanship.

Obnoxious or unpopular sailors receive an extra portion of hazing when ships cross the Line, and Taji makes it clear that his shipmates are not precisely to his mind. We may assume the probability that the feelings are mutual. According to his own

5. Francis Allyn Olmsted, *Incidents of a Whaling Voyage* (Rutland, Vermont, and Tokyo, Japan, 1969), Chapter V, 69–73. Charles Roberts Anderson, in *Melville in the South Seas,* p. 93, notes that Olmsted's book may have been Melville's source for an incident in *Typee,* but subsequently (p. 218), sees Olmsted's work as more probably a corroboration for an incident in *Omoo.*

6. Leopold Wagner, *Manners, Customs, and Observances,* William Heinemann, London: 1894, p. 34.

description he is "exclusive," arrogant, lazy, and tricky. He makes impossible demands of the captain; he becomes frantic during a calm; and upon his decision to leave the ship, he displays the poor judgment to confide his intention to the ship's old Neptune.

Taji's description of his relationship to Jarl permits two interpretations in addition to the obvious one of loyal friendship. There is something insinuatingly erotic about Taji's imputation of effeminate characteristics to Jarl. Such terms as *laundress* and *sempstress, old maid* and *old wife,* even the visual pun on Jarl's homeland—"the constellated Hebrides," all combine into what could be construed as implied homosexuality. On the other hand, we might examine more closely the services rendered by Jarl. Having complained of monotony and boredom, Taji reports, "There were other things, also, tending to make my lot on shipboard very hard to be borne" (5). Then, however, he returns to the discussion of monotony and boredom without further elucidation. Having also declared that there was no soul a magnet to his, Taji claims that Jarl "cleaved" unto him, pouring needle and thread into the frightful gashes that agonized Taji's "hapless nether integuments" (15). He fails to explain how his integuments became gashed and agonized, but if Jarl's needle and thread were to be construed as a harpoon and line, Taji's comments might be less cryptic. He mentions that Jarl called his integuments "ducks," the name used by all experienced seamen for their heavy, canvaslike trousers, but also the term used to denote the roughest part of the initiation. "Nor," continues Taji, "could I even wrest from thy willful hands my very shirt, when once thou hadst it steaming in an unsavory pickle in thy capacious vat, a decapitated cask." The implication becomes even stronger here that Taji is being subjected to some rather strenuous hazing, as Jarl soaks his shirt in boiling pickle-juice. Note also the ambiguous sentence structure as Taji draws a distinction between "chummy the simple" and "chummy the cunning," who at mealtimes was last at the "kids" when their unfortunate partners were high upon the spars. "Now I ask you, Jarl," wheedles Taji, "whether I was ever chummy the cunning!" By now we begin to suspect that the answer is a resounding "No!" Taji continues: "Many's the good lump of 'duff' for which I was indebted to my

Viking's good care of me." The word *duff* refers to a type of
pudding served on shipboard, but it also means *lump of coal* or
decayed vegetable matter, and we are reminded of the custom of
feeding some unsavory, ill-smelling mess to the initiate, which
frequently sends him scuttling to the rail. In the words of
Olmsted, if while being interviewed by Neptune the initiate
becomes too communicative, "a *stopper* is introduced by one of
his majesty's attendants, consisting of the most disgusting
materials that can be collected together."[7] Notably also, in
sea-parlance, *duff* means a hearty clout.

7. Olmsted, *Whaling Voyage.* p. 71.

   As part of the hazing tradition, the initiate is expected to do
homage to Neptune, and we see Taji repeatedly referring to Jarl
in terms of royalty, devoting, in fact, an entire chapter to singing
paeans to Jarl, linking him with royalty throughout time and
space while in the same breath claiming kinship to him. The
chapter is entitled "A King for a Comrade," and Taji begins by
likening Jarl to a Norseman, descendant of Vikings. This is not
enough, so Taji calls him a "descendant of Heroes and kings."
He then extends his titles to King Alfred, Homer, and King
Noah. Still not enough; so Taji goes on to monarchs and sages,
angels and archangels, hierarchies of seraphs and thrones and
principalities in the zodiac. This last image we must bear in mind
when Babbalanja "discovers Neptune" on Serenia through his
vision of angels and archangels. Having linked Jarl with the "sons
of God" who did verily wed the irresistible daughters of Eve,
Taji reminds someone—anyone—that "the shades that roam
throughout space; the nations and families, flocks and folds of the
earth; one and all, brothers in essence—oh, be we then brothers
indeed!" A far cry, this, from his previous claim to exclusiveness,
and after this cry, he soars off almost hysterically into the zodiac.
Settling down at last, he tells of Jarl's lack of geography and then
comes forth with a most self-contradictory and ironic statement:
"Ah Jarl! An honest, earnest wight; so true and simple, that the
secret operations of thy soul were more inscrutable than the
subtle workings of Spinoza's" (13).

   "This much be said of the Skyeman; for he was exceedingly
taciturn, and but seldom will speak for himself." The picture now
grows of a silent, secretive, and subtle old tar, a cosmopolitan,
who demands and receives the adulation of the greenhorn. But
Taji is not one to admit that he is undergoing indignities. Instead,

he must leave the impression that Jarl is proffering adulation to him.

> Now, higher sympathies apart, for Jarl I had a wonderful liking; for he loved me; from the first had cleaved to me.
> It is sometimes the case, that an old mariner like him will conceive a very strong attachment for some young sailor, his shipmate; an attachment so devoted, as to be wholly inexplicable, unless originating in that heart-loneliness which overtakes most seamen as they grow aged; impelling them to fasten upon some chance object of regard. But however it was, my Viking, thy unbidden affection was the noblest homage ever paid me. And frankly, I am more inclined to think well of myself, as in some way deserving thy devotion, than from the rounded compliments of more cultivated minds. (Pp. 13–14)

The hint of homosexuality here is offset by the image of Jarl's harpoon, cleaving, attached inexplicably, fastened, and affixed to the "chance object" that is Taji's "ducks." It should also be noted that Taji's insinuations about old mariners and young shipmates do not directly refer to Jarl but to some hypothetical old mariner, leaving the uncautious reader to jump to conclusions. Taji prefers to think well of himself because of Jarl's special "sharp" attention as contrasted to the "rounded" compliments of others. It is interesting that Taji uses the word *blunt* three times in connection with Jarl and that much later in the book Media pointedly uses the same term to describe the arrows of the Avengers, though they have already pierced Taji's arm and drawn blood. We are to find that the "needling" of Taji does not end with his escape from the *Arcturion,* for Jarl, one way or another, keeps his promise to follow Taji through thick and thin.

At sea in the *Chamois,* Taji "would fain have built an altar to Neptune" (29). Nevertheless, his hazing continues, along with his insinuations. He would have the reader believe that he spent most of his time lounging under the canopy in the stern; but Jarl "during the day voluntarily remained exposed at the helm" almost two hours to Taji's one, and the steering rudder (not properly called a helm in a whaleboat, according to Melville's own description in *Moby Dick,* Chapter LIII) is in the stern of the boat where the canopy has been stretched. Taji also describes himself hooting, posturing, and cavorting in the boat while the Viking "stared hard" at the tragicomic performance.

When Neptune's party boarded any ship, the entire entourage was painted with yellow spots to simulate some amphibious creature, according to Capt. Frederick Marryat.[8] Only after the *Chamois* is afloat do we learn that Jarl is "masked by a visor of japanning, dotted all over with freckles, so intensely yellow, and symmetrically circular, that they seemed scorched there by a burning glass" (33–34). After the sinking of the *Parki,* much later, Taji notes Jarl's resemblance to the sea god "that boards ships, for the first time crossing the Equator." Notably, their companion Samoa is also spotted like a "tawny leopard, though his spots were all in one place" (127).[9]

It would seem, then, that when Taji escapes from the *Arcturion* he takes with him—or is taken by—the ship's Neptune, who is bent on completing the initiation of the greenhorn. The hazing has been thorough and severe, but two major initiatory steps remain to be taken: the piercing of Taji's ear (as Samoa's ear is pierced), and the ducking, or keelhauling. The accomplishment of these two symbolic functions are the matter of the remainder of the book. Taji's ear must be pierced in order that he may hear and, hearing, understand. Step by step he is led through the various modes of experience and, on the quest voyage, subjected to the degrees of philosophy in all fields. His function throughout the quest is to listen and interpet. But the primary objective is to cause Taji to "dive deep," to delve below the shallow surface of things, to find and evaluate the "self."

The ritual of ducking could be accomplished in either of two ways—or both—depending on the policy of the captain and the location of the ship. According to Olmsted, the victim sits on a board stretched across a large tub of salt water. He is given a trumpet of tin, "which he raises to his mouth and thunders forth, 'Neptune a-hoy!'" whereupon one of Neptune's attendants throws a bucket of salt water into the mouth of the trumpet, pushing the "greeny" backward into the tub, headfirst. The victim "scrambles out of the tub, almost strangled to death, with a most natural horror of the arcana of Neptune."[10] Olmsted

8. Capt. Frederick Marryat, 1792–1848, was the author of numerous books of nautical adventure, extremely popular among young boys. In Chapter 4 of *Typee,* Melville mentions "some long-haired, bare-necked youths who, forced by the united influences of Captain Marryatt and hard times, embark at Nantucket . . . oftentimes return very respectable middle-aged gentlemen." It is probable, then, that Melville had read Marryat's works, possibly the story "Frank Mildmay" among them. This story contains an elaborate description of shipboard initiation. Marryat's description is used in *Curiosities of Popular Customs,* ed., William S. Walsh, pp. 310–11.

9. The "burning glass" is a lens often used by campers and others to start fires. The association with the lens of a telescope follows readily. After Neptune was discovered, an American astronomer found that, months earlier, he had had the planet in his telescope and had taken photographs of it, not realizing that he had recorded on his plates a potential route to immortality. Also, during the period that Saturn and Neptune were in conjunction, there were no doubt many lenses trained on the hidden planet as they attempted to focus on Saturn.

10. Olmsted, *Whaling Voyage,* p. 70.

11. Olmsted, *Whaling Voyage*, p. 71.

12. A. B. C. Whipple, *Yankee Whalers in the South Seas*, Doubleday & Company, Inc. (Garden City, N.Y., 1954), 156–57.

13. In a term paper written for an American literature class, Michael P. Adams, an ex-Navy man intrigued by the suggestion of an initiation ritual in *Mardi*, researched the possibility for himself. He especially noted the three colors associated with Neptune from mythology: red, symbolizing the father's powers; blue, for the mother element; and yellow, denoting the child or new birth. To the last symbol Adams relates the custom of painting yellow spots on Neptune and his court. He also associates the color symbols with Taji's first mast-watch, noting that as Taji gazes toward the "yellow Moorish sun," he is symbolically facing the Pillars of Hercules.

For a true understanding of the image, more facts must here be introduced. The island of Gibraltar is one of the "Pillars of Hercules" and the other is Mount Acho, which lies directly south of Gibraltar on the northern coast of Morocco. Thus the Pillars of Hercules flank the Straits of Gibraltar and Melville has symbolically transported the Arcturion from a position in the Pacific, where it is about to bear north and cross the Equator, to a position in the Mediterranean Sea where it is about to sail through the Pillars of Hercules. The Arcturion, through Melville's symbolism, is sailing directly into the very origin of the ceremony of Crossing the Line. The color imagery of the "yellow Moorish sun" recalls that, associated with Neptune, yellow represents the child or new birth, and the very idea of the ritual is that a "youngster" is given a "new birth" as a "tar."

describes the keelhauling as the "grand finale which gives him an indisputable claim to the title of seaman." With a rope around his body, "he is thrown overboard to be drawn under the ship and hauled up on the other side."[11] A variant description has the victim "tied arm and leg to two ropes, tossed over the bow, and yanked under water the full length of the ship's keel before being hauled, more dead than alive, over the taffrail to be dropped like a sopping rag on the deck."[12] Certainly, keelhauling could be fatal in shark-infested waters such as those surrounding Christmas Island, but Taji's nature is such that only a deep dive will do. Therefore, he is removed from the *Arcturion* and taken to other waters; en route, he must be educated in geography, astronomy, mathematics, logic, comparative religion, natural history, and a host of other subjects. And after that, the deep water. If Taji is indeed undergoing an initiation without his knowledge, if his actions are completely controlled by a determined sea god intent on teaching the arrogant jack a lesson in seamanship, then Taji's willfulness is as much self-delusion as his knowledge of marine geography. Taji fears the depths because of the sharks that may be lurking there—especially the great white shark with the mild demeanor. He sees on the *Parki*'s log an illustration of a man whose "nether integuments" have been devoured by a shark, but he fails to recognize that the combination of man and fish forms the *Matsyavatar*—a symbol of reincarnation. In the end, Taji, the greenhorn pollywog, is lured to the depths by Hautia, who completes the ritual begun by Jarl, and Taji becomes a Shellback in spite of himself.[13]

VI. The Playing-Card Metaphors

> But suffice it to say, that it had gone abroad among the
> Arcturion's crew, that at some indefinite period of my
> career, I had been a "nob." —*Mardi,* 14

Chess has been utilized by many authors as a structural
device, and the Tarot has inspired some few, but it is doubtful
that any writer has worked so extensively and skillfully with a
metaphor of playing cards as Melville. The card imagery scattered
throughout *Mardi* with seeming carelessness is by no means as
casual as it appears, for it serves not only as auxiliary to the
astrological metaphor but also as an independent entry into the
riddle for readers unable to begin directly with the stellar
imagery. Though incomplete in itself, the card system is essential
to a full interpretation of the solar myth and can lead into it by
way of an established tradition of card symbolism. The text of
Mardi reveals Melville's acquaintance, not only with the regular
packs of fifty-two or the Pinochle forty-eight, but with the
European Tarot, widely used as a gaming deck during the
eighteenth and nineteenth centuries. In addition, there is strong
evidence that he also knew the round, medallionlike
Hindu–Persian Avatar cards used for the game of Ganjifa.[1] The
card imagery bears on the theme of fixed fate and predictable
future, but Melville makes deeper use of the three decks, each
one fulfilling a specific symbolic and structural function relating to
the metaphor of Time.[2]

The game of Sol, or Solitaire, is any game played by one
man against the cards themselves, and Melville plays at four
games simultaneously in *Mardi*. Taji the lubber plays the
groundling games of Cribbage and Hearts, while the author
engages him without his knowledge in the nautical games of
Pitch and Pinochle. To follow the plays, the reader must first
identify each character with his proper card. While Melville
provides adequate imagery for this purpose, the easiest route into
the metaphor is through the astrological equivalents traditionally
associated with the cards.

Diamonds, represented in the Tarot by Pentacles or Coins,
stand for the element of Earth, the cardinal sign Capricorn and

1. Melville's knowledge of the ten
avatars of Vishnu is demonstrated in
Chapter 55 of *Moby Dick:* "The Hindu
whale referred to, occurs in a separate
department of the wall, depicting the
incarnation of Vishnu in the form of
leviathan, learnedly known as the Matse
Avatar." Although Melville here refers to
temple wall carvings, he mentions
"shields, medallions, cups, and coins" as
sources for "the oldest Hindoo, Egyptian,
and Grecian sculptures." The Hindu
Ganjifa cards are round, medallionlike
pieces of wood or ivory.

That Melville had adequate
opportunity to acquaint himself with these
cards is indicated by his description in
Redburn, Chapter 34, of a visit aboard an
Indian ship and a conversation with a
Lascar sailor.

For further information about card
decks of the nineteenth century, see
Catherine Perry Hargrave, *A History of
Playing Cards and A Bibliography of Cards
and Gaming,* and Hennig Cohen,
"Melville's Copy of Broughton's 'Popular
Poetry of the Hindoos,'" *Papers of the
Bibliographical Society of America,* 61
(1967), 266–67.

2. This study of the card imagery is
far from complete. Only enough is
presented here to demonstrate its presence
and, to a limited extent, its use primarily
as it helps to establish the seasonal
symbolism. The game metaphor can be
carried much further than indicated here,
and the Tarot imagery, too, is far more
extensive. A full study of the card
imagery, however, must await a separate
study.

Tarot No. VIII, Justice as Libra.

hence the planet Saturn, the season of winter, and the character Taji.

Clubs, the Tarot Wands or Staves, equate to Fire, the cardinal sign Aries and hence the planet Mars, the season of spring, and the character Media.

Hearts, the Tarot Cups, Flagons, or Grails, represent Water, the cardinal sign Cancer and hence the Moon, the season of summer, and the character Yillah; and

Spades, the Tarot Swords, equate to the element of Air, the cardinal sign Libra and hence the planet Venus, the season of fall, and the character Hautia.

Obviously, Taji as a common sailor-boy is the Jack of Diamonds; Media and Hautia, as monarchs, are the King of Clubs and the Queen of Spades. Yillah, as the Una-like figure, serves as the Ace of Hearts. The other characters, when shown in their proper astrological signs, may also be placed in the deck.

Jarl, as Neptune, ruler-to-be of the watery sign Pisces, is a Heart. We might be inclined to identify him as a Jack, but Taji—sarcastically—informs us that Jarl is a Viking, and that he is indeed a monarch. Jarl, then, is identified as the King of Hearts. As the ninth planet, he may also be seen as the "dix," or nine, of the summer trumps.

Aleema, as Jupiter, is the soon-to-be-deposed ruler of Pisces and the undisputed ruler of the fire-sign Sagittarius; hence he is a Club—as evidenced also by the imagery of clubs and staves associated with him. As Jupiter, his number is five, so that in the game of Pitch he is the "Pedro." In Pinochle, combined with his five sons, he is the Ten—a card that outranks all but the Ace.

Samoa is identified as the fixed star Aldebaran, alpha star of the earthy constellation Taurus and hence, like Taji, a Diamond. With such emphasis placed on his extraordinarily bright eye and his one arm, we may equate him to the Ace.

Annatoo represents the fixed star Antares in the watery sign of Scorpio. Since Taji contemptuously calls her "Queen Annatoo," we may take him at his word and dub her the Queen of Hearts.

The captain of the *Arcturion* would necessarily be associated with the constellation Boötes, the stelleration of which is shaped like a great, lopsided diamond in the sky, its southernmost star, Arcturus, pointing toward the Earth-sign of Virgo. Since Taji compares him to Caesar, the captain may be identified as the King of Diamonds.

*　　*　　*

Taji alludes to the landsman's game of Cribbage when he informs us that he had been considered a "Nob," for this is the name given to the Jack of the opening-lead suit in this game invented by Sir John Suckling.[3] Certainly the terms *crib* and *suckling* fit well into the imagery of Christmas and birth that characterizes the opening section of *Mardi*. For future reference, we might note at this point that another name for Cribbage is "Noddy," meaning *fool*.

That yet another game is in progress is evidenced when Taji calls his captain a "trump, [who] stands on no quarterdeck dignity" (5). There are no trumps in cribbage, so we must look for a game in which a trump suit is established by "calling trumps." This specification, along with the opening emphasis on darkness, tar, and oil, suggests the sailors' favorite, Pitch, which Melville in *Redburn* refers to as "High-Low-Jack-Game." Since the King of Diamonds is led and Diamonds are trumps, Taji is no longer the Nob but is instead the Jack of Trumps. Unpopular as he is, Taji, having annoyed the captain, is about to be "ruffed," and when he leaves the *Arcturion*, he "takes" the King of Hearts, Jarl.

Running concurrently with Pitch as a metaphor, but not developed until the *Parki* episode, is the game of Pinochle, or "Binnacle." Whereas Pitch represents the initiatory function, Pinochle forwards the figure one step by symbolizing the position of the sailor "man" at the ship's binnacle compass—a position that can be occupied only by an experienced seaman with a proper reverence for nautical instruments, not by a sailor "boy." We have noted that in Pitch the trump suit is called, while in

3. In *Redburn*, Chapter 54, Melville writes: "Now, one of the favorite pursuits of sailors during a dog-watch below at sea is cards; and though they do not understand whist, cribbage, and games of that kidney, yet they are adepts at what is called '*High-low-Jack-and-the-game*,' which name, indeed, has a Jackish and nautical flavor."

Pinochle the first card "turned up" from the stack establishes the trump suit. On the double deck (110) of the *Parki,* as Taji and Jarl prepare to sup from the Bread-barge, a new trump is established as the King of Clubs "turns up" among the various images carved on the box: "Foul anchors, skewered hearts, almanacs, Burton-blocks, love verses, links of cable, Kings of Clubs; and divers mystic diagrams in chalk, drawn by old Finnish mariners, in casting horoscopes and prophecies. Your old tars are all Daniels" (64). Here the King of Clubs is turned up, and although "skewered hearts" are mentioned first, no specific card is named. Since we later meet Media, the King of Clubs, it is significant that the image of Belshazzar is introduced here as Taji notes that "like Belshazzar, my royal Viking ate with great fear and trembling." Media will subsequently be likened to "Belshazzar on the Bench." The skewered hearts represent the martial figure of Annatoo, whose "skewer" is soon to be broken.

The *Parki,* then, bears the Ace and Jack of Diamonds in Samoa and Taji, and the King and Queen of Hearts in Jarl and Annatoo. Their card symbols account for the attraction between Annatoo and Jarl, who score a "common marriage" meld in Pinochle. The Queen of Hearts is sloughed as the *Parki* sinks, while a Jack, King, and Ace proceed to a meeting with Aleema.

Aleema, the Five of Clubs, and his five sons (and there are only five sons—not fifteen as Taji later implies) form a black Pedro—the fives of Clubs and Spades—in Pitch, since Aleema is a Club and the sons are of the Air sign Gemini and are therefore Spades. In Pinochle, Aleema's group comprises the Ten of Clubs and is for the time being the high trumps, unless Sol–Melville, the Ace of Clubs, is in the hand. The Ace of Hearts, Yillah, is "in the hole," and will not be drawn until Aleema the Ten of Clubs is ruffed.

As Yillah relates her story, she tells of a white bird with a black bill, a gift from Aleema. After staying with Yillah for a while, the bird flies away and Yillah cries out after it, "Lil! Lil! Come back, leave me not, blest soul of the maidens" (157). This cryptic incident receives no further elucidation and appears to be another of Melville's dangling images. The name "Lil," however, is another card term—a nickname for the Queen of Spades, or

Black Lady, in the game of Hearts, and as he meets Yillah, Taji
begins to play, on his own, another landsman's game. The object
of the game of Hearts is to reduce one's own score; hence, the
low scorer wins. To achieve low score, the player must not be
caught with Lil, the Black Lady, in his hand. Yillah's bird had a
"bill, jet black, and eyes like stars," and Melville elsewhere uses
the word *bill* to denote *sword* (517). Thus, the reference to the
Queen of Spades is accompanied by imagery possibly relating to a
"Jet bill," or "black sword," the Tarot equivalent to the suit of
Spades. Yillah's story continues:

> And every morning it flew from its nest, and fluttered and
> chirped; and sailed to and fro; and blithely sang; and brushed
> Yillah's cheek till she woke. Then came to her hand: and Yillah,
> looking earnestly in its eyes, saw strange faces there; and said to
> herself as she gazed—"These are two souls, not one."
>
> But at last, going forth into the groves with the bird, it
> suddenly flew from her side, and perched in a bough; and
> throwing back its white downy throat, there gushed from its bill a
> clear warbling jet, like a little fountain in air. (Pp. 156–57)

For a second time the words *bill* and *jet* are associated, this time
in association with *air,* the element symbolized by the suits of
Swords and Spades. And as Lil flies into Yillah's hand, she sees
"strange faces [and] two souls, not one," as though she were
gazing at the two faces of the reversible card marked by the
Queen of Spades. The Black Lady comes first to Yillah's hand,
but is passed on. The imagery that identifies Queen Hautia with
the planet Venus and the sign of Libra imposes on her also the
identity of the Queen of Spades and raises the possibility that her
relationship with Yillah is less malignant than Taji's account
would imply. Unless the white bird with the jet bill is merely a
dangling image, utterly without purpose, we may be able to see
the Lil as guardian to Yillah. When at last Taji's game of Hearts
is lost as he finds himself possessed by the dark lady, Hautia, it
should be recalled that in the nautical game the Jack of Diamonds
and the Queen of Spades together form the Pinochle, or Binnacle
—the compass by which Taji can get his bearings.

In Odo, Media, the King of Clubs, reigns as high trump. In this play, the Ace of Hearts is sloughed as Yillah disappears. Was she taken by the Ten of Clubs, Aleema, or by the Queen of Spades, Hautia, or did she take a trick herself? It is possible that she was taken by the Ace of trumps. Since Sol is ruler of the Fire sign Leo, he would be a Club and certainly the high card in the suit. Yillah as the lunar figure disappears at the full of the moon, so we might well interpret this play in terms of solar domination as the sun approaches the spring equinox.

An interesting play occurs on the Isle of Juam, at a breakfast where, in addition to the usual settings around the well-laden table, there is the "empty hemisphere of a small nut, the purpose of which was a problem." Taji describes Jarl's reaction:

> Now, King Jarl scorned to admit the slightest degree of under-breeding in the matter of polite feeding. So nothing was a problem to him. At once reminded of the morsel of Arva-root in his mouth, a substitute for another sort of sedative then unattainable, he was instantly illuminated concerning the purpose of the nut; and very complacently introduced each to the other; in the innocence of his ignorance making no doubt that he had acquitted himself with discretion; the little hemisphere plainly being intended as a place of temporary deposit for the Arva of the guests. (P. 246)

According to Taji the guests are astounded—especially Samoa. But we read of "King Jarl, meanwhile, looking at all present with the utmost serenity. At length, one of the horrified attendants, using two sticks for a forceps, disappeared with the obnoxious nut, upon which, the meal proceeded." The attendant disappears and is not seen again for many days. Taji supposes that "he had embarked for some distant strand; there, to bury out of sight the abomination with which he was freighted." Now, for this faux pas, Babbalanja takes Jarl roundly to task, lecturing him on the importance of the conventions of good manners:

> "Moreover, Jarl," he added, "in essence, conventionalities are but mimickings, at which monkeys succeed best. Hence, when you find yourself at a loss in these matters, wait patiently, and mark

what the other monkeys do: and then follow suit. And by so
doing, you will gain a vast reputation as an accomplished ape."
(P. 246)

Two significant matters should be noted in connection with this
incident. First, Jarl, playing by the rules of Pinochle, is not
obliged to follow suit. Second, regal cosmopolite that he is, Jarl is
doing precisely the right thing in relation to the customs
prevailing in the Society and Sandwich Islands. Having read his
Ellis, Melville is fully acquainted with the Polynesian practice of
disposing secretly of such personal items as hair, fingernails, and
spittle in order to obviate their being used as instruments of
black magic.[4] Island monarchs do exactly as Jarl has done, and a
servant carries away the issue to bury or drown it. Jarl alone has
had the worldly experience to know what to do with the Arva
and the nut.

    On the Isle of Mondoldo, the King of Hearts and the Ace of
Diamonds are sloughed, and as the canoes sail into the month of
June, a new trump is called. Babbalanja, having just introduced a
new "diabolical theory," quotes the old philosopher Bardianna to
support his contention. "Faith!" cries Media, "though sometimes
a bore, your old Bardianna is a trump" (317). Since this
long-dead philosopher actually constitutes one half of Babbalanja
—the other half being the devil, Azzageddi—it becomes
necessary to discover Bardianna's suit. With the summer season
approaching, we know that the appropriate suit is Hearts, and the
astrological relationship is confirmed through the name
"Bar-Diana," or "Son of the Moon." As a lunar figure,
Bardianna represents the watery sign of Cancer and the summer
season. The imagery throughout the summer section of the quest
is filled with cups, flagons, and hearts and is readily identifiable to
the card-conscious reader.

    Hearts are trumps, then, as Media's canoes pursue the quest
into summer. The Greenwich passage to Earth provides the next
step in the education of the Jack, once he learns the art of the
finesse on Tapparia (413). After the return to Mardi, the fall of
the year is signaled by the fall of the singing bowsman and by a
long and melancholy discussion of death and graves. No trump is

4. William Ellis, *Polynesian Researches*,
II, 229: "The use of the portable spittoon
by the Sandwich Island chiefs, in which
the saliva was carefully deposited, carried
by a confidential servant, and buried every
morning . . . originated in their dread of
sorcery." References to Ellis abound in
Mardi, as noted by Merrell R. Davis,
Melville's Mardi: *A Chartless Voyage*, p. 29
and elsewhere. David Jaffe, "Some
Sources of Melville's *Mardi*," *American
Literature*, 9 (March 1937), 56–59.

mentioned, but by now we are expected to recognize the transition from the "farewell to cups" at the supper of Abrazza to the imagery of death and spades and "last trumpets" that heralds the fall of the year as well as the fall of man. On Serenia, Babbalanja makes his great discovery; his card, the Ten of Hearts, is played, and he "takes" the dix, or Nine of Hearts, with his discovery of the "ninth sphere," represented by the planet Neptune. Then Taji the Jack moves on to his final confrontation with the Queen of Spades.

The suit of Diamonds serves to represent the soul or self of Taji, and the opening imagery of *Mardi* shows Taji's initial quest as a search for "true coin of the realm" in any form available, be it Cachalot, mining interests, investment with interest, or, preferably, that hardest of all forms of black carbon, the diamond.[5] Even though he attributes this interest in money to Jarl, his own predilection is easy to detect:

> Sounded on the chest lid, the dollars rang clear as convent bells. These were put aside by Jarl; the sight of substantial dollars doing away, for the nonce, with his superstitious misgivings. True to his kingship, he loved true coin; though abroad on the sea, and no land but dollarless dominions around, all this silver was worthless as charcoal or diamonds. Nearly one and the same thing, say the chemists; but tell that to the marines, say the illiterate Jews and the jewelers. Go, buy a house, or a ship, if you can, with your charcoal! Yea, all the woods in Canada charred down to cinders would not be worth the one famed Brazilian diamond, though no bigger than the egg of a carrier pigeon. Ah! but these chemists are liars, and Sir Humphrey Davy a cheat. Many's the poor devil they've deluded into the charcoal business, who otherwise might have made his fortune with a mattock. (P. 60)

Here it can be seen that, regardless of his philosophical attitude toward the subject when he first brings it up, Taji soon works himself into a revelation of his own taste for diamonds.[6] Taji may thus be seen as "seeking his own soul" and in the process growing harder and icier each day. After the appearance of Yillah, however, Taji begins a new pursuit, turning his attention from the diamond "self" to the rose pearl, Yillah. At last, he is induced by the promise of pearls to dive into Hautia's pool. In

5. See Nathalia Wright, "The Head and the Heart in Melville's *Mardi*," *PMLA*, 66 (June 1951), 351–62; also Merlin Bowen, *The Long Encounter: Self and Experience in the Writings of Herman Melville.*

6. The imagery of mining permeates *Mardi* and stands as both corollary and contrast to that of diving. In each instance the depths are explored. In earth the landsman digs for diamonds, while in water the seaman dives for pearls. The devils of *Mardi*, with whom Taji must claim some kinship, derive from Burton's

the "diamond depths" he is forced to relinquish soul and heart, and he returns empty-handed. His act of self-renunciation lends support to the truth of his subsequent act of abdication.

*   *   *

In addition to the familiar deck of fifty-two cards, Melville makes use of the Tarot pack, particularly the twenty-two cards of the Greater Trumps.[7] The playing cards of the Tarot differ from the ordinary deck in having fourteen cards per suit, including the Page, Knight, Queen, King, and Ace, bringing the total to fifty-six. The modern Jack is the descendant, not of the Knight but of the Page or Knave, for the Knight has been omitted. The Tarot then provides an extra figure, which enables Melville to follow through with his initiation metaphor by allowing his Jack to raise his position from Knave to Knight. The opening imagery of *Mardi* makes it quite clear that Taji prefers to be identified as a Knight. Our awareness of his ignorance, however, enables us to place him as a mere Page to the older hands on deck. If he completes his initiation, he can raise his status from Knave of Diamonds to Knight of Stars (Pentacles or Coins, pictured as a five-pointed star enclosed in a circle).

The Tarot suits provide alternative images by which the characters may be identified. The suit of Clubs, for instance, appears in the Tarot as staves or wands—hence, scepters as well as spears and arrows and all other shafts may connote the suit of Clubs. Most important, however, is the frequent use of the imagery of Cups, or Urns, to identify the "heart" characters— particularly Jarl and Yillah—for Yillah is to serve as a Grail figure while Jarl, as Neptune, represents the vast urn that holds all lost sailors.

The twenty-two trumps of the Tarot serve a separate and distinct function in *Mardi*, permitting anyone acquainted with this ancient fortune-telling pack to read Taji's future each step of the way as the specific card is called. More significantly still, the trump identifies the function of the character, situation, or event

dissertation on the various types of devils that cause dyspepsia and madness: "Subterranean devils are as common as the rest, and do as much harm. Claus Magnus, *lib 6, cap. 19,* makes six kinds of them; some bigger, some less. These (saith Munster) are commonly seen about mines of metals, and are some of them noxious; some again do no harm. Georgius Agricola in his book *de subterraneis animantibus, cap. 37,* reckons two more notable kinds of them, which he calls 'Getuli and Cobali,' both 'are clothed after the manner of metal-men, and will many times imitate their works.' Their office, as Pictorius and Paracelsus think, 'is to keep treasure in the earth, that it be not all at once revealed' " (Robert Burton, *Anatomy of Melancholy,* p. 126). Here Burton bears directly on Melville's concept of the narrator as persona, disguising the true thought of the author. As Babbalanja expresses it, "The profoundest, frankest ponderers always reserve a vast deal of precious thought for their own private behoof" (*Mardi,* 511). Note the pun on the devil's "behoof." He continues: "And this unpleasant vibration is ever consequent upon striking a new vein of ideas in the soul. As with buried treasures, the ground over them sounds strange and hollow." Thus Babbalanja's "Azzageddi" may be linked to the "Cobali," or "blue devil," as well as to Taji.

Burton provides still another mode by which Melville may support his metaphor of narrator reigning as viceroy for the author: "Thus the devil reigns, and in a thousand several shapes, 'as a roaring lion still seeks whom he may devour,' 1 Pet. v." *Anatomy,* pp. 126–27.

7. See p. 167 for additional illustration of Tarot trumps.

The Tarot Cards

The Tarot cards shown on these pages are from decks with which Melville could have been familiar. The Tarot of Marseilles is the most likely choice on two counts: The Fool, shown on p. 67, is characterized by the torn trousers that augment the image of Taji's "agonized nether integuments." Further, the deck was a popular one and was designed for an English-speaking player. Cards 0-V and VII-XXI are shown on the page at the top.

0	The Fool (Le Mat)	Folly. Thoughtlessness. Lack of discipline. Delirium. Frenzy. Unrestrained excess.
		Inverted: A halt in progress.
I	Magician, or Juggler (See "Il Bagattel" on p. 88)	Self-confidence. Will power. Skill. Initiative. Creativity. Originality. Craft.
		Inverted: The above delayed.
II	High Priestess	Wisdom. Serenity. Judgment. Common Sense.
		Inverted: The above delayed.
III	Empress	Action. Development. Progress. Fertility.
		Inverted: Delay of an inevitable event.
IV	Emperor	Realization. Accomplishment. Worldly power. Wealth. Authority. Endurance.
		Inverted: Loss of wealth or authority.
V	Hierophant (Pope); also Jupiter	Mercy. Kindness. Good advice. Inspiration. Alliance. Humility. Compassion. Servitude.
		Inverted: A delayed project.
VI	Lovers	Love. Beauty. Attraction. Perfection. Harmony. Unanimity.
		Inverted: Separation.
VII	Chariot	War. Vengeance. Difficulty. Trouble. Victory. Triumph. Conquest.
		Inverted: Bad news.
VIII	Justice	Equity. Reasonableness. Balance. Virtue. Honor. Virginity.
		Inverted: Loss. Unjust condemnation.
IX	Hermit	Prudence. Withdrawal. Caution. Solitude.
		Inverted: Delay.
X	Wheel of Fortune	Destiny. Luck. Future. Necessity.
		Inverted: Difficult but inevitable change.
XI	Strength (Force)	Courage. Energy. Resolution. Defiance.
		Inverted: Overcome by events or people.
XII	Hanged Man	Sacrifice. Surrender. Abandonment. Renunciation. Transition.
		Inverted: Possible success in plan of sentimental nature, but doubtful success without enjoyment of pleasure. Also: Lack of frankness. Hidden plan. Hypocrisy.
XIII	Death	Sudden change. Destruction. Loss. Failure.
		Inverted: Illness.
XIV	Temperance	Patience. Moderation. Reflection. Friendship.
		Inverted: Fickleness annulled.
XV	Devil	Violence. Fatality. Fate. Bondage. Disaster.
		Inverted: Evil action. Harmful effects.
XVI	Falling Tower	Disruption. Adversity. Misery. Deception. Unexpected event. Ruin. Setback. Bankruptcy.
		Inverted: Downfall.
XVII	Star	Hope. Satisfaction. Bright prospects. Insight.
		Inverted: Harmony broken.
XVIII	Moon	Caution. Danger. Scandal. Error. Deception. Disillusionment.
		Inverted: Uneasy conscience.
XIX	Sun	Triumph. Success. Accomplishment. Contentment.
		Inverted: The above delayed.
XX	World	Completion. Perfection. Synthesis. Success. Ultimate change.

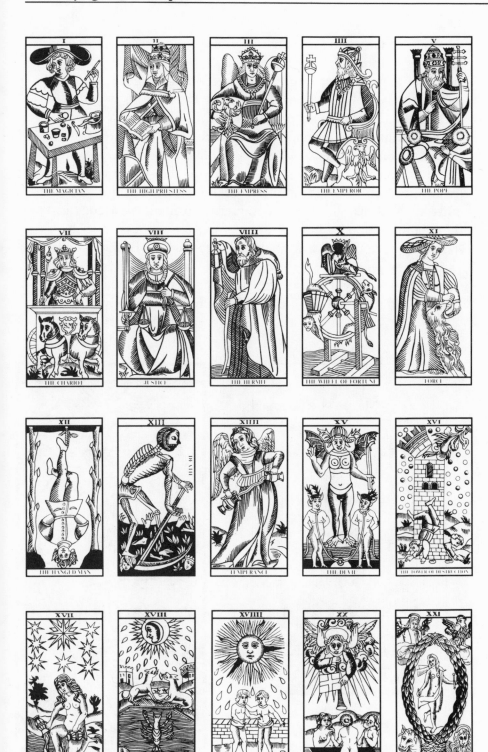

The Greater Trumps of the Tarot
from the Tarot of Marseilles.

that calls it into play, thereby providing specific and momentary symbolic markers.

The Zero Trump represents the Fool setting out upon a journey that will take him through the twenty-one steps of experience. We have no problem linking Taji to this card through numerous instances of imagery. The most striking and riddling example occurs when Taji delivers an objective and scientific lecture on sharks. In describing each shark variety, he dwells at length on the ominous qualities of the white shark and ends his analysis with a few comments on man's tendency to hate this phenomenon of Nature and on the foolishness of such irrational hatred.[8] Philosophically he remarks, "In five words—would they were a Siamese diphthong—he who hates is a fool" (41). With hardly a pause, however, he makes it clear that he himself suffers from an intense dislike for this ghostly creature.

8. Ellis, *Polynesian Researches,* I, 177–79, discusses the danger from sharks in the waters around the Society Islands as well as the superstitions associated with shark-worship, especially of the blue shark. In Vol. II, 195, he again mentions the large blue shark as an agent of the gods.

Fool cards from three types of Tarot decks (Tarot of Marseilles, right).

As the story proceeds, Taji abandons his scientific attitude and centers all his superstitious fear around the white shark with its greenish hue, as it becomes for him the specter of Aleema the Priest. With no further straining of the metaphor we may identify Taji as a fool by his own definition; nevertheless, by his cryptic illogicality Melville invites us to strain at Taji's little riddle. He has promised us five words and given us six, so one of the words must equal zero—unless two of them can be seen as a Siamese diphthong, which does not exist. By all literary logic, Taji need not have issued this pointless little joke; the idea could easily have been expressed in five words. By doing so, however, Taji demonstrates that both his arithmetic and his linguistics are faulty, while at the same time he forces us to equate one of the six words to zero. To the Tarot adept, the allusion is instantly obvious, and Taji becomes the questing Fool on the brink of his

Lover cards from three types of Tarot decks (Tarot of Marseilles, right).

fall. Later the image applies also to Babbalanja, who deals out the epithet of *Fool* freely and indiscriminately, even to himself.

It is notable also how many times the image of archangels appears in *Mardi,* the first time in connection with Jarl. When Jarl is introduced, Taji invokes "angels and archangels for cousins" (12) and later, in the *Chamois,* asks "whether, in any part of the world, Savannah, Surat, or Archangel, he had ever a wife to think of; or children, that he carried so lengthy a phiz. Nowhere neither" (36). Though Taji's obvious reference is to the Russian city of Archangel, the Tarot features two Archangel trumps. The first, in keeping with the "Fidus–Achates-ship" and its homosexual overtones, is Card Number VI, "The Lovers"—and certainly Jarl has been dubbed the VI-King by Taji. The second Archangel trump is entitled "Judgment." The first shows the angel presiding over a marriage, and the other shows the angel of the "last trump" hovering over a man and woman rising from their coffins on Judgment Day. Thereby, Jarl may be seen as Taji's lover and his judge, in the same context that these terms may be applied to Christ, as well as to the *Arcturion*'s old Neptune. We might note also that Trump Number IX is the Hermit—an image frequently invoked in *Mardi* and applicable to Neptune as the undiscovered ninth planet. This image will receive further attention in a later chapter.

Trump Number V in the Tarot is the Hierophant, or High Priest, and we have already noted the connection between Aleema and the numeral five. In some Tarot decks, Number V is shown as Jupiter.

Two Tarot trumps apply to the Leo–Sol function that we shall attribute to the mythic participation in the story of the author, Melville: The trump entitled "Strength" depicts the well-known figure of the maiden and the lion, while the other, entitled "Sol," varies from one deck to another but always features a blazing sun.

A significant connection exists between the Tarot trumps and the rituals of initiation that include the Crossing of the Line, the Arthurian initiation of the Knight, the Eleusinian Mysteries, and the Christian sacraments. Melville uses them to portray Taji's

Tarot No. V, which equates to the "Hierophant" or "High Priest" in the English deck.

steps of experience and to provide a link between the solar myth expressed by the fifty-twos and the avatar system now to be explored.

*   *   *

The third card pack to be considered is the medallionlike Hindu–Persian Avatar pack, from which our narrator takes his name of Taji—the Crown—one of the eight suits. These suits consist of *Taj* (Crowns), *Soofed* (Moons), *Shumsher* (Swords), *Gholam* (Slaves or Dwarfs), *Chung* (Harps), *Soorkh* (Suns), *Burat* (Diplomas), and *Quimash* (Merchandise). Each suit contains two honor cards along with ten suit cards representing the ten avatars of Vishnu.[9]

Melville derives his greatest significance from the first avatar of Vishnu, *Matsya* the blue fish–man, who can be interpreted as the lowest step on the ladder of development. That *Matsya* may equate to the goat–fish Capricorn both symbolically and functionally is obvious, for Capricorn, as the sign of the winter solstice, is at the nadir of the year, from which the only way is up. Another related image is that of the Philistine's god Dagon, also half man and half fish, linked in Christian mythology to the forces of Satan.

Combined with the zodiac, the avatar imagery suggests that in each incarnation the candidate must make his way through the steps of experience, but each time on a higher level of awareness. Babbalanja the Sage, much later in the book, remarks that "our mortal lives have an end; but that end is no goal: no place of repose. Whatever it may be, it will prove but as the beginning of another race" (575). As the Fish, Taji begins on the lowest rung of the lowest ladder, though he claims a higher position when he allows himself to be called Taji.

Jarl, on the other hand, wears a *taj* in the form of the conical Guayaquil hat (the *taj* is a tall, conical hat similar to a papal mitre), as well as in the symbolic iron crown of Neptune. Taji, however, with his propensity for error, sees Jarl as the

9. For a list of the Avatars and the suits of the Ganjifa deck, see p. 74.

The Hindu Cards of India

There are ten suits in a set of Hindu cards; twelve cards to each suit, consisting of numerals, from one to ten, and two court cards. One of the court cards of each suit represents one of the ten incarnations of Vishnu, and the other shows some incident connected with the particular incarnation; the suit signs are symbols of the incarnation represented.

The Ten Incarnations and usual suit marks are:

1. Matsya the Blue Fish Man, which towed the ship containing Menu (Noah), his family, and the creatures saved from the Deluge. Suit of Fish (see illustration, p. 73).
2. Kourma the Tortoise, on which rested the mountain that, revolved by the serpent Sesha, greatly disturbed the sea and produced the Fourteen Gems. Suit of Tortoises.
3. Varah the Boar, who came to destroy the giant Hiranyakcha. Suit of Boars.
4. Nara-Simha the Lion, who came to destroy the giant Hiranycasyopa. Suit of Lions (see illustration, p. 73).
5. Vamanavatara the Dwarf, who came to save men from the giant king, Bali. Suit of Dwarfs or of Water Jars.
6. Paracu Rama of the Axe, who came to punish the military caste and destroy their power. Suit of Axes.
7. Rama Chandra, the Gentle Rama, like the Moon, who avenged men and gods for the iniquities done by Ravana, the demon king of Ceylon. He won his wife Sita in a contest with arrows. Suit of Arrows.
8. Krishna the Black, the most popular of all the incarnations, believed to be the perfect manifestation of Vishnu, whose emblem is the Chakra or quoit of lightning which he hurled at his enemies. Suit of Quoits (see illustration, p. 73).
9. Buddha the Enlightened, who sits upon his shell-shaped throne in meditation. The Suit of Shells or of Umbrellas.
10. Kalki the White Horse, the incarnation to come. Suit of Swords or of Horses (see illustration, p. 73).

Matsya the Blue Fish Man, from the Hindu cards.

Nara-Simha the Lion, from the Hindu cards.

Krishna the Black, from the Hindu cards.

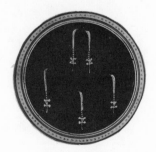

Kalki the White Horse, from the Hindu cards.

The Hindu-Persian Cards

The Hindu-Persian eight-suit deck is the one most likely to have been known to Melville, since he seems to have made use of the symbols that mark the cards:

Superior Suits

| Taj | = Crowns | Sumsher | = Sabers |
| Soofed | = Moons | Gholam | = Slaves |

Inferior Suits

| Chung | = Harps | Burat | = Diplomas |
| Soorkh | = Suns | Quimash | = Merchandise |

Illustrated are three cards each from the suits of Crowns (Taj), Harps, Moons, and Suns.

gholem, or slave, just as he misjudges the ocean: "Ere this, I had regarded the ocean as a slave, the steed that bore me whither I listed" (29). But Taji reveals himself as the slave, or dwarf, when he becomes frenzied during his first ocean calm:

> It is more hopeless than a bad marriage in a land where there is no Doctors' Commons. He has taken the ship to wife, for better or for worse, for calm or for gale; and she is not to be shuffled off. With yards akimbo, she says unto him scornfully, as the old beldam said to the little dwarf:—"Help yourself." (P. 10)

From his position as the ninth avatar, Buddha the Enlightened, suit of Shells or Umbrellas, Jarl reviews the steps that Taji must follow to achieve the ultimate rank: first the Tortoise, or shellback tar, then Nara-Simha the Lion: "Indeed, picking up heart, with the dawn of the day my Viking looked bold as a lion" (66); as Paracu Rama, the Axe, "Jarl buried his ax in the splintered stump of the mainmast, and not till then did he join us" (120); as a master of the harpoon, he demonstrates his command of the Quoit (or Thunderbolt), Avatar of Krishna the Black. The tenth avatar is Kalki, the White Horse, Incarnation to come—and Jarl's Neptune is the inventor of the horse. Thus again Taji is half right. The ocean is a steed, not a slave to its rider.

Yillah represents the suit of Soofed, or Moons, avatar of the Tortoise, product of the fourteen gems, as evidenced by the imagery of shells associated with her. In this respect she may be seen as the goal toward which Taji strives and which he at last achieves—though not in the way he hopes. Media's insignia, a "tri-dent" of boar's teeth, reveals him as the avatar of the Boar, Varah, again associated with the numeral three.

Melville does not attempt to develop fully the avatar system but uses it as auxiliary. Its primary application lies in the symbolism of reincarnation, which itself can be viewed from two distinct standpoints. In Melville's metaphor of correction and synthesis, the Hindu concept of ultimate salvation through development provides a justification for predestination. On the other hand, it contains its own brand of fatuousness, which enables Melville to parody its superstitious aspects and through it to reach out at the New England Brahmins who had seen in it an

10. Perry Miller, "Melville and Transcendentalism," *Virginia Quarterly,* 29 (Autumn 1953), 556–75, presents a helpful discussion of Melville's views on transcendentalism.

11. Note 1 of this chapter refers to Melville's visit to an Indian ship.

implication of free will and self-reliance, compensation and optimism.[10] Having observed at first hand the sailor folk of India, Melville no doubt felt that the Brahmin system fell far short of the ideal either in religion or, particularly, in social responsibility.[11] Just as the concept of reincarnation can temper the harshness of Calvinism, the reminder that an element of predestination is inherent in Brahminism serves to correct the romanticized viewpoint of the Transcendentalists.

The card metaphor, then, holds a significant position in the riddle of *Mardi,* and though it may be considered as an independent system, it contributes to, clarifies, and supports the astrological approach to Time. Melville's use of the playing-card motif appears to be unique in literature. It deserves fuller exploration than is practical here, especially since it permeates *Mardi*'s greater successor, *Moby Dick.*

VII. The Mardi Metaphor

> Here it must be mentioned, that from the various gay cloths and
> other things provided for barter by the captain of the Parki, I
> had very strikingly improved my costume; making it free,
> flowing, and eastern. —*Mardi*, 127

Melville's source for the name *Mardi* derives, not from the
map, but from the calendar, for it refers to Mars Day and
describes both a time and a condition of existence. Translating,
we may see Taji touring the Tuesday Islands under the auspices
of the war god, Mars—Lord of Misrule.

The normal state of society—and, we might add, the
fundamental requirement of story or novel—is conflict; hence the
ruling figure of Mars is apropos to Melville's metaphor, and
Media, battle-king of Odo, provides a guide worthy of Virgil.
Throughout the pages of *Mardi,* Melville studies war: the
threatening conditions of King Bello's Dominora, the pre-Civil
War tension in Vivenza, the ritual battles of Hello and Piko, and
the final insurrection on Odo.

The figure of Mars fills yet another symbolic function—that
of the Areopagitica. Here again Media serves the metaphor, for
he typifies the tyrant whose judicial logic is arbitrary, harsh, and
self-serving, like that of Ares when he avenged himself upon the
son of Poseidon-Neptune.[1] Taji tells us that Media appoints a
regent to rule Mardi during his quest. The imagery, however,
hints that Media, like Nebuchadnezzar, is turned out to pasture to
ruminate on the problem and to quest for true justice. As ruler of
the spring equinox, astrologically characterized as rash, impulsive,
and immature, Mars must be balanced by his opposite
component, the fall equinox, symbolized by the balances of
Justice and ruled by the goddess of love.

1. Mars (or Ares) was tried for the
murder of Halirrhothius (son of
Neptune), who had ravished his (Ares')
daughter, Alcippe. The site of the court
was the Areopagus, a hill below the
Acropolis in Athens. Ares was found "not
guilty."

*   *   *

The name *Mardi,* however, contains a symbolism of a more
specific nature, as revealed in the imagery of holiday ritual.
According to the almanac dating system, the fray between Taji's

party and that of Aleema the Priest occurs on February 24, which in 1846 was Shrove Tuesday, or Mardi Gras Carnival. Through its relationship to the title, this event becomes a pivotal action, heavily laden with significance. In effect, Melville shows all of society to be a ritual carnival in which riot, carnage, and carnality are secretly sanctioned by the Church and gods, on the grounds that each act of man "fulfills a design." It is through this device that Melville justifies the inescapable doctrines of predestination and responsibility.

Melville had ample material from which to draw his metaphor of ritual combat. The customs of Shrove Tuesday alone provide examples that Melville could have known about: an annual fight at Edenburgh between the "uppies" and "doonies," the men living above Mercat's Cross, toward Castle hill, and those living below it, toward Townfort. In Sudlow, England, the men of the Corn Street Ward engage those of Broad Street Ward in an annual tug-of-war. At Scone, bachelors contend against married men in a Shrove Tuesday football game.

At the Eleusinian Mysteries a foot race was a standard feature, possibly combining ritual combat with the idea of quest inherent in Ceres' search for her daughter.

In light of Taji's remark, regarding Jarl, that "like Sesostris I was served by a monarch" (14), it is interesting to note the ritual associated with the Egyptian festival of Osiris as described by the *Mystagogue* at Abydos during the reign of Sesostris III, 1870 B.C.

17. I arranged the expedition of Wep-wawet when he went to the aid of his father.
18. I beat back those who attacked the Bark of Neshmet, and I overthrew the foes of Osiris.

I arranged the Great Procession and escorted the god on his journey.
19. I launched the god's ship, and . . . Thoth . . . the voyage. I provided a crew for the ship of the Lord of Abydos who is called He-Who-Appears-in-Truth. I decked the ship with gorgeous trappings so that it might sail to the region of Peker.
20. I conducted the god to his grave in Peker.
21. I championed Wenen-nefru (Unnefer), on the day of the Great Combat and overthrew all his adversaries beside the waters of Nedit.

I caused him to sail in his ship. It was laden with his beauty.

I caused the hearts of the Easterners to swell with joy, and I brought gladness to the Westerners at the sight of the Bark of Neshmet. It put in at the port of Abydos; and Osiris, the first of all Westerners, the Lord of Abydos, was conducted to his palace. (Theodor H. Gaster, *Thespis,* Doubleday and Company, Inc., Garden City, N.Y., 1961, pp. 37–69.)

Notably, the ritual of Osiris parallels in many respects the progress of Taji and Jarl and, later, the quest through Mardi.

The imagery of masking pervades *Mardi,* beginning with Taji's own incognito and Jarl's mask of japanning and continuing throughout as Taji's errant narrative masks the underlying metaphorical structure.[2] It is just before the encounter with Aleema, however, that an emphasis on costume occurs. Taji reports he has "strikingly improved" his costume by adding garments taken from the trading goods of the *Parki* and that he looks "like an Emir." Here too we find the first mention of shipboard initiation, as Taji describes Jarl: "Nor had my Viking neglected to follow my example; though with some few modifications of his own. With his long tangled hair and harpoon, he looked like the sea-god, that boards ships, for the first time crossing the Equator." Note that Taji does not say that Jarl has taken any garments from the *Parki.* Nor, for that matter, has Samoa, for according to Taji, "he yet sported both kilt and turban, reminding one of a tawny leopard, though his spots were all in one place" (127). Literally taken, the passage indicates that only Taji is "playing dress-up," the other two being costumed as precisely what they are. At any rate, now, nine days after the destruction of the *Parki,* Taji, attired in robes and accompanied by his two spotted companions, approaches the sacrificial canoe of Aleema the Priest for "closer communion" in true Carnival style. Notably also, by a brief reference to the Eleusinian Mysteries, Melville combines an ancient spring initiation ritual with the Christian concept of Carnival, thereby linking Mardi Gras to the shipboard ritual of crossing. Thus Taji in his robes becomes an initiate approaching the temple.[3]

As Taji tells it, he boards the canoe and attempts to converse with the priest. Upon discovering that a maiden is concealed on

2. James E. Miller, Jr., "The Many Masks of Mardi," *Journal of English and Germanic Philology,* 58 (July 1959), 400–413; also, Robert Martin Adams, "Masks, Screens, Guises: Melville and Others," in *NIL: Episodes in the Literary Conquest of Void During the Nineteenth Century* (New York: Oxford University Press, 1966), pp. 131–48.

3. Melville's use of the image of the Eleusinian mysteries and the metaphor of Mardi Gras reflects the knowledge available at the time. Until archeological discoveries in the eighteen-eighties provided a clearer picture, the nature of the Mysteries was virtually unknown. According to mythology, after Persephone was abducted by Pluto, Demeter set out in search of her. At Eleusis, Demeter found such devoted hospitality that she instituted a ritual by which her adherents could gain immortality. The first part of the ritual occurred in June, the beginning of the dry season, when candidates for initiation into the mysteries began their period of trial. The greater mystery took place in September, at which time the candidates were received into the full mystery. The ritual is still unknown. The Great Temple of Eleusis, as known to the ancients—and hence to Melville—was flanked by two lesser temples, one to Poseidon and the other to Diana, thereby providing a link for Melville between Neptune and Luna, and between these and the asteroid Ceres. This asteroid, conjunct Sol shortly before the opening action of *Mardi,* has presided over the quadrant until this date, when she is superseded by Pallas.

It should be noted that everyone was eligible to enter the mysteries: men, women, children, and slaves—*unless* guilty of homicide. Now comes Taji in February and apparently commits this crime, among others.

The history of Mardi Gras may be found in at least two helpful works: William S. Walsh, *Curiosities of Popular Customs,* pp. 884–90, and Robert Tallant, *Mardi Gras,* pp. 83–114.

In light of Melville's later writings, it is interesting to note a song of 1699 about a Shrovetide Martyre, entitled "Cock-a-doodle-doo." See Walsh, p. 890.

the canoe, Taji resolves to rescue her. Opposed by Aleema's sons, he and Samoa give battle; he is menaced by the priest's dagger, "the sharp spine of a fish," and the crucial action ensues: "A thrust and a threat! Ere I knew it, my cutlass made a quick lunge. A curse from the priest's mouth; red blood from his side; he tottered, stared about him, and fell over like a brown hemlock into the sea" (133). So it appears that Taji, in self-defense, strikes out with his cutlass, piercing Aleema's side. In the confusion he and Samoa escape with two hostages. When order is restored, Taji exchanges the two hostages for the maiden and her tent and sails away.

After the Fray, Taji is momentarily overcome with misgivings:

> As I gazed at this sight, what iron mace fell on my soul; what curse rang sharp in my ear! It was I, who was the author of the deed that caused the shrill wails that I heard. By this hand, the dead man had died. Remorse smote me hard. (P. 135)

Here Taji makes his confession and acknowledges his remorse. Despite his immediate and subsequently repeated attempts at self-justification, the phantom of Aleema lingers; "at bottom guilt brooded." Externalized and personified by the sons of Aleema, the "Remoras," guilt continues to pursue Taji throughout the book.

Following this ritual carnage, the imagery of Ash Wednesday begins:

> Now, as every where women are the tamers of the menageries of men; so Yillah in good time tamed down Samoa to the relinquishment of that horrible thing in his ear, and persuaded him to substitute a vacancy for the bauble in his nose. On his part, however, all this was conditional. He stipulated for the privilege of restoring both trinkets upon suitable occasions. (P. 146)

Samoa's sacrificial act ushers in the Lenten season, and confirmation of the season's nature emerges after the *Chamois* is permanently abandoned on Media's Isle of Odo. Here Media entertains his guests with a meatless "tiffin in a temple," and no meat is mentioned in the descriptions of the meals until the Easter feast of the twenty-five kings on the Isle of Juam.

This account contains all the ingredients for a typical Mardi Gras as it was known in Melville's day. Originally intended to provide a pre-Lenten celebration, Mardi Gras had become associated with the popular idea of moral license—that is, licentiousness without responsibility. The Church had permitted herself to become the butt of ritual mockery as she winked for one day at the orgiastic Saturnalia of the people.[4] Following the orgy, however, came the repentance, sacrifice, and shriving of Ash Wednesday and Lent. In the episode of the Fray, Taji follows this general pattern, conducting his own riot and committing murder, sacrilege, and abduction, followed by unremitting remorse and guilt. The European practice (no doubt based on the Jewish scapegoat ritual of Yom Kippur) of decorating a live goat with items representing the sins of the community and then pursuing the animal into the countryside provides a parallel to Taji's situation insofar as he is the figure of Capricorn, the celestial Goat. The solar imagery suggests that Taji is to be seen as a sacrificial animal after the manner of Satan, Cain, and Judas, who also committed essential acts and, in man's view, merited the burden of eternal retribution.

Jarl's tattoo, so abruptly introduced at this point, serves to link Jarl to the figure of Christ, while at the same time it equates the blood from Aleema's side to that of Christ at the Crucifixion. This symbol enhances the concept of ritual involvement of the blood and flesh of Christ. It also transfers the Old Testament sacrificial mode, associated with Jehovah and represented by Aleema–Jupiter, to the New Testament mode of Christ, represented by Jarl–Neptune. In this context, the association of Yillah–Luna with the Grail becomes meaningful in that the entire episode of the Fray may be viewed as a ritual preparation for the Communion. Here we should recall the "midnight mass" beside the bread-barge on the *Parki,* during which Taji "rifles" the chest by thrusting his arm into a hole in the side of the barge. We might say that Taji meets with a series of altars and desecrates each one or that unwittingly he consecrates each one. In Melville's writing, the safer approach is to avoid such choices between interpretations and to accept both. The first represents the viewpoint from human ignorance and the alternative the broad overview of the gods. Such a synthesis indeed appears to

4. Tallant, in *Mardi Gras,* cites Sir James G. Frazer's *Golden Bough* in linking Shrove Tuesday with all ancient fertility rituals, including the Eleusinian Mysteries, and also including the Saturnalia with its Lord of Misrule, despite the concurrence of the Saturnalia with what is now Christmas. Though Melville's writings precede the more modern concerns with fertility rituals, per se, he obviously creates a linkage between Christmas and Shrove Tuesday, which encompassed the Carnival season, and overlays both with a fertility metaphor.

be Melville's objective in naming his romance "Tuesday."

By scheduling the Fray on Shrove Tuesday, Melville in effect shrives Taji for having committed—or accomplished—an essential act—that is, for having fulfilled an artistic design by providing conflict for the story. Inasmuch as the Mardi Islands represent the world, the world itself is a ritual carnival in which every act of man fulfills a higher purpose and constitutes another step in the process of initiatory education. That man is fully shriven for his predestined deed and forced act does not mean, however, that he goes unpunished; the fruits of his deed and the pangs of his guilt continue to pursue him through a long, Lenten lifetime.

Eternity, however, is another matter, for this is the element that disturbs Melville's sense of justice and induces him to "build another world."[5] The almanac metaphor does not attribute the blame for the unjust concept of Predestination and Responsibility to God Himself, but to the ignorance and error of mankind that could give rise to such a theology. Melville, in any case, will not assign a "Goat" to perform a necessary deed and then consign him to perdition, but will instead wink one eye and shrive the beast.

By this holiday metaphor, Melville demonstrates that insofar as man's sin and his shriving are involuntary, his repentance and remorse are also inescapable so long as he remains ignorant of the ways of Heaven, sunk in what Babbalanja describes as "Mardi's grosser air" (633).

5. Babbalanja quotes blind Vavona: "I will build another world," and "Great poets dwell alone; while round them roll the worlds they build" (592). These comments appear immediately before Babbalanja's celestial vision on Serenia, dated with the discovery of Neptune.

VIII. The Chamois: *The Sea Goat*

> The moon must be monstrous coy, or some things fall out opportunely, or else almanacs are consulted by nocturnal adventurers; but so it is, that when Cynthia shows a round and chubby disk, few daring deeds are done. —*Mardi*, 22

The opening chapters of *Mardi* are precision structured to contain all necessary clues to the planetary identity of Taji, all required coordinates for space and time, and a full range of foreshadowing imagery. By the end of Chapter 3, Melville has posed his riddle and brought his story to its starting point. Chapters 4 through 8 concern themselves with what we shall call the opening action—the escape or "birth" of the sea goat *Chamois,* the whaleboat in which Taji and Jarl jump ship. These eight chapters are so designed as to permit the reader to fix the date of Taji's escape from the whaling ship *Arcturion,* while at the same time they indicate a three-year background to the action.

Once the date of the escape is set, the great wheel of the zodiac begins to turn. The sixteen-day voyage of the *Chamois,* Chapters 9 through 19, carefully furnishes a day-by-day imagery system by which we may relate certain word clusters to their zodiacal equivalents and thereby compute the passage of time. When the *Chamois* encounters the brigantine *Parki,* the day-by-day chronology ends and the reader is expected to follow the time-line through the imagery, with the help of *The American Almanac.* By the time the *Chamois* escapes from the *Arcturion,* Melville has established all the metaphorical strands to be followed throughout *Mardi*: the riddles of Time, of Error, of Game, of War, of Exploration, of Theology, and of Creativity.

Because of their fullness and extraordinary precision, these opening chapters that constitute Melville's "Canto I" must bear the closest scrutiny. Every detail must be examined, and in some instances, like the serpent with his tail in his mouth, they must be

interpreted in light of the end of *Mardi,* for we are indeed
dealing in "cycles and epicycles," birth and rebirth.

*   *   *

The first paragraph of *Mardi* provides us with the stellar
cluster around which our story begins, for Taji invokes the
Horse, the Eagle, and the Goat, that is, the Tropic of Capricorn
and the hermit goats on Mas Afuero.[1] A look at the celestial
calendar reveals that Sagittarius the Horse, Aquila the Eagle, and
Capricorn the Goat form a grouping on the winter side of the
sky. The ship searches for the Cachalot, or sperm whale; Cetus
the Whale, one of the largest constellations, covers the sky
immediately to the south of Pisces the Fishes. The whaling ship is
revealed to be the *Arcturion,* and here we are given a precise
point in the sky, for the star, Arcturus—also called "Arthur" in
Arthur's Wain—appears at the southern tip of the
diamond-shaped constellation Boötes, and is poised directly over
the midsection of Virgo. A line drawn through the center of the
zodiacal circle, with Arcturus as radial point, intersects the sky
with Arcturus–Virgo to the celestial south and Pisces–Cetus to the
north. From this line we may draw the thirty-degree radials to
form a horoscope in which to place the planets. Since we find
that horse, goat, and eagle are all intersected by radial lines, we
may assume that we are dealing with the winter side of the
zodiac. We find further that the ninety-degree radial passes
through the middle of Sagittarius, the Archer–Centaur, through
the stirrup line. That Melville has entitled Chapter I "Foot in
Stirrup" indicates that this central radial may be taken as the
dateline, and the celestial calendar provides the date, December
24. As previously discussed, the world globe discloses that the
ship *Arcturion* is hard by Christmas Island at the time of the
escape, offering yet another support to the Christmas dating.

The next step is to identify the planet with which the
narrator is to be associated, and Taji himself provides more than
sufficient evidence that he represents the planet Saturn. Most
emphatic is his obsession with Time:

1. The Hermit Card of the Tarot,
usually Trump Number 9, shows an
Eremite holding aloft a lantern containing
a star. See p. 67. Related to this figure is
the island of Mas Afuero, where Taji first
sighted hermit goats. Another name for
Mas Afuero is Alexander Selkirk Island,
while its nearby companion isle is named
Robinson Crusoe.

This round-about way did the Arcturion take; and in all conscience a weary one it was. Never before had the ocean appeared so monotonous; thank fate, never since.

   .   .   .   .   .

So, day after day, daily; and week after week, weekly, we traversed the self-same longitudinal intersection of the self-same Line; till we were almost ready to swear that we felt the ship strike every time her keel crossed that imaginary locality.

   .   .   .   .   .

It was during this weary time, that I experienced the first symptoms of that bitter impatience of our monotonous craft, which ultimately led to the adventures herein recounted. (P. 4)

   .   .   .   .   .

Ay, Ay, Arcturion! I say it in no malice, but thou wast exceedingly dull. Not only at sailing: hard though it was, that I could have borne; but in every other respect. The days went slowly round and round, endless and uneventful as cycles in space. Time, and time-pieces! How many centuries did my hammock tell, as pendulum-like it swung to the ship's dull roll, and ticked the hours and ages. Sacred forever be the Arcturion's fore-hatch—alas! . . . Nevertheless, ye lost and leaden hours, I will rail at ye while life lasts.

Well: weeks, chronologically speaking, went by. Bill Marvel's stories were told over and over again, till the beginning and end dovetailed into each other, and were united for aye. Ned Ballad's songs were sung till the echoes lurked in the very tops, and nested in the bunts of the sails. My poor patience was clean gone. (P. 5)

These passages deserve close examination, concealing as they do a wealth of clues in the word-play. First the imagery of time and the narrator's feeling of being wrapped in eternal cycles are clear enough. The ship is likened to a clock pendulum as her keel "strikes" every time it crosses that "imaginary locality." As previously noted, that Line is indeed an imaginary locality, for Taji's false geography has placed him to the south of the true Equator, and he only imagines that he has reached the waistline of the world. Moreover, Taji relates his hammock to a pendulum, and we receive our first hint that Taji may be a lazy jack, spending more time in his hammock than he is entitled to. The hours are "leaden"—Saturn's metal. The comment on Bill Marvel's stories actually applies to Taji's story as well, not only in respect to its length but also to its circular nature. Most important, however, is the distinction drawn between subjective

2. Coincidentally, the period from 1819, Melville's birth year, and 1848–1849 constitutes a full Saturn cycle.

3. Charles Roberts Anderson, in *Melville in the South Seas*, points out that Melville's account of the voyage of the *Pequod* in *Moby Dick* bore little semblance to the real voyage of the *Acushnet*, Melville's own ship. However, the *Acushnet* did follow a route similar to that of the *Arcturion*, sailing around the Cape of Good Hope and "arriving in time to meet the season at New Zealand in March and at the Society Islands in June; then it was customary to recruit at some port in Peru in October, so as to be ready to take up the season on the 'Off-Shore Ground,' near the Galápagos Islands, in November." In relating the incident of the swordfish in *Mardi*, Melville mentions the ship *Rousseau*, and Anderson provides an entry from the Log Book of the *Rousseau* regarding a sighting of the *Acushnet* on Wednesday, November 3, 1841, near Albemarle Island, largest and westernmost of the Galápagos Archipelago (pp. 48–49).

4. Saturn is generally regarded as a malefic planet, especially to youth, since it represents restriction and repression. Later, in maturity, it represents control and becomes more benign. It is identified with Kronos, pictured as carrying a sickle-shaped sword like Taji's cutlass. His gem is the blue turquoise, but he is ruler of mines and often associated with diamonds. His metal is lead, hence Taji's "lost and leaden hours," and his nonmagnetic qualities.

5. Burton's *Anatomy of Melancholy* (Part I, *n*. 24) describes the various symptoms of melancholia, including delusions, hallucinations, erratic behavior, distraction, dyspepsia, frenzy, dotage, etc. Burton treats of "the ill habit or malady of melancholy itself" as a *morbus sonticus*, or *chronicus* (92), and states that "our body is like a clock, if one wheel be amiss, all the rest are disordered" (109). "He that is Saturninus shall never likely be preferred" (218): (see *Mardi*, Ch. 158, p. 515: "That head was Saturnina's. Gall and Spurzheim! saw you ever such a

time and actual time; on another level we might see this distinction as a transition from human time to planetary time, for the planet Saturn is the slowest of the visible planets, spending two to three years in each constellation and requiring twenty-nine years to circumscribe the zodiac.[2] Indeed, the three-year voyage of the *Arcturion* tracks Saturn from his 1842 position near the stirrup of Sagittarius to the spot he occupies, at the opening action, in the tail of Capricorn.[3] And finally, this passage reveals that Taji is suffering symptoms, among them lassitude, boredom, and impatience.[4]

"But hold you!" cries Taji, and launches into another description rife with puns:

> The sailors were good fellows all, the half-score of pagans we had shipped at the islands included. Nevertheless, they were not precisely to my mind. There was no soul a magnet to mine; none with whom to mingle sympathies; save in deploring the calms with which we were now and then overtaken; or in hailing the breeze when it came. (Pp. 4–5)

Here Taji shows himself to be exclusive and discriminating to the point of snobbery, but even more revealing of his planetary identity, he expresses his attitudes in terms of earthy and metallic imagery. That the phrase, "no soul a magnet to mine," is to be taken as a pun on *mining* is evidenced by subsequent references to "men of mettle" and "fire from their steel," as well as to "Burton on Blue Devils," an allusion to that section of *Anatomy of Melancholy* that deals with the subterranean "cobalt" devils frequently encountered by miners.[5]

In turn, reflections on Burton's mining devils lead Taji into imagery of hell, as he fears that his captain intends "to illustrate the Whistonian theory concerning the damned and the comets;— hurried from equinoctial heats to arctic frosts" (5).[6] With saturnine gall he approaches the captain and complains: "It's very hard to carry me off this way to purgatory." Through this imagery Melville establishes a connection between the figure of Saturn, linked by Burton to underground demons, and Satan, placed by Dante in the seventh circle of hell, encased in ice and surrounded by the fires of the inferno. The allusion to Purgatory is followed by a vision of beauty, as Taji gazes across the ocean and hears the breakers against the reefs that surround Christmas

Island. This upward progression from inferno to beatitude receives further play when Babbalanja discusses art on Bonavona.

The captain's decision not to go out of his way to put Taji ashore arouses thoughts of larceny in the mind of the discontented jack, who unwittingly confirms predestination as he makes his plans:

> My first thoughts were of the boat to be obtained, and the right or wrong of abstracting it, under the circumstances. But to split no hairs on this point, let me say, that were I placed in the same situation again, I would repeat the thing I did then. The captain well knew that he was going to detain me unlawfully: against our agreement; and it was he himself who threw out the very hint, which I merely adopted, with many thanks to him. (P. 7)

Having already begun the process of self-justification, Taji notes his "willful mood," and we are invited to contrast his willfulness to his recognition that he would act the same again under the same circumstances.

Because the saturnine personality—especially when associated with Capricorn—is characterized by caution, it should come as no surprise that Taji takes due consideration regarding the act he is about to commit.[7]

> Nevertheless, the enterprise hinted at was no light one; and I resolved to weigh well the chances. It's worth noticing, this way we all have of pondering for ourselves the enterprise, which, for others, we hold a bagatelle. (P. 7)

This caution, combined with the discontent engendered by Taji's vision of beauty and with the calm that accompanies the winter solstice, brings him to the point of frenzy and exaggerates the symptoms of melancholia already present.

Taji prefaces his description of the calm with a vague and ambiguous statement, informing us that "by certain nameless associations" the calm revived in him his "old impressions upon first witnessing as a landsman the phenomenon of the sea." Here we must be wary indeed, for Taji makes it clear that these impressions add to the problem he is now experiencing on the *Arcturion.* Just as the Saturn of Capricorn is an "earthy" planet, so Taji is a landsman on this voyage, despite his cavalier attitude.

Taji's most meaningful self-revelation occurs in Chapter 3 as

brow? . . . 'By my right hand, Saturnina!' cried Babbalanja, 'but thou wert made in the image of thy Maker!' "). Taji exhibits all the symptoms of *morbus chronicus* and demonstrates through his action and thought processes the influence of Saturn in its various aspects to Luna and Mars.

6. H. Bruce Franklin, Introduction to *Mardi,* vii–viii, notes that "the narrator at first suggests a rather obscure metaphor to describe his fate and explicate his adventures." Citing Taji's reference to the Whistonian theory concerning the damned and the comets, he continues: "The theory to which he refers—that Hell consists of an eternal revolution through the cosmos on a burning comet—metaphorically but precisely outlines the structure of *Mardi.* The narrator's voyage is both celestial and infernal, and he hurtles endlessly around through many worlds."

Merrell R. Davis, *Melville's Mardi: A Chartless Voyage,* p. 69 and note, refers to a letter from Edward Everett to Leverrier regarding "les cometes de Taije et de Vico," and suggests that the name "Taji" descends from this comet. Instead of relating the comet to the Whistonian "vulgar error," however, Davis links it to the Casseopeian nova.

7. Taji notes how each man ponders for himself an enterprise which for others he "holds a bagatelle." The Number 2 trump in the Tarot, called variously "The Magician," "Le Battaleur," "Il Bagatteliere," and "Bagatelle," signifies the childlike view of nature and events as effect without cause and relates to the primitive emphasis on magic.

he discusses the problem of his own identity:

> Now, at sea, and in the fellowship of sailors, all men appear
> as they are. . . . Incognitos, however desirable, are out of the
> question. And thus aboard of all ships in which I have sailed, I
> have invariably been known by a sort of drawing-room title. Not,
> —let me hurry to say,—that I put hand in tar bucket with a
> squeamish air, or ascended the rigging with a Chesterfieldian
> mince. . . . And never did shipmate of mine upbraid me with a
> genteel disinclination to duty. . . .
>
> Whence then, this annoying appellation? for annoying it most
> assuredly was. It was because of something in me that could not

The Italian Tarot No. 1 (left) is entitled "Il Bagattel" and represents the card called in English
"The Magician." To "hold a Bagatelle" is to be subject to chance and causeless fortunes—or
misfortunes. Also shown are magician cards from a French Tarot (center), and from the Grand
Eteilla Tarot (right). The Magician of the Tarot of Marseille is shown at top left, p. 67.

be hidden; stealing out in an occasional polysyllable; an otherwise incomprehensible deliberation in dining; remote, unguarded allusions to Belles-Lettres affairs; and other trifles superfluous to mention.

But suffice it to say, that it had gone abroad among the Arcturion's crew, that at some indefinite period of my career, I had been a "nob." (P. 14)

Cunningly Taji attempts to draw our attention away from the fact that, although "incognitos are out of the question," he never reveals either his name or his "appellation." Moreover, his self-description reemphasizes the snobbish attitude that has given rise to an appellation so annoying that he refuses to divulge it, though we can readily imagine the belles-lettres possibilities in such a nickname as "Percy," for King Arthur's fool–knight, or even "The Faerie Queene" from Spenser. In any case, Taji had been a "nob" and has therefore fallen from a high status. Among the planets, there are only two that have been nobs, Saturn and Uranus, and these are the planets that together form the personality of Taji, the "jack-ass."

*   *   *

Taking as a clue Taji's image of the *Arcturion* as timepiece, we might superimpose the ship on the sky map with the prow "standing northward" and the mainmast serving as the stirrup-line date indicator. Taji states in Chapter 4 that, having made his decision to abscond with a boat, he visits a fine old seaman, Jarl, "when, like some old albatross in the air, he happened to be perched at the foremasthead, all by himself." The foremast on our cosmic ship falls upon the fishtail of Capricorn, and according to the sky atlas it lies near the star *iota* Capricorn. Noting that Saturn–Taji, slow as he is, arrives at a point, the foremast, already occupied by Jarl, we must assume that Jarl represents a body even slower than Saturn and that this meeting represents a conjunction of two planets at the foremast position of the cosmic ship.

December 24, 1845

The Opening Position. The cosmic ship is in the daylight sky,
with the mainmast pointing toward Sol and serving as the
dateline. The prow is in Pisces (to the left), and the stern in Libra.
Reflected in the night sky is the earthly *Arcturion*.

As preparation for the escape gets under way, Taji provides
us with a planetary position of still greater precision, one by
which we may determine the year of the escape. On the eve of
the event, Taji reports:

> The moon must be monstrous coy, or some things fall out
> opportunely, or else almanacs are consulted by nocturnal
> adventurers; but so it is, that when Cynthia shows a round and
> chubby disk, few daring deeds are done. Though true it may be,
> that of moonlight nights, jewelers' caskets and maidens' hearts
> have been burglariously broken into—and rifled, for aught
> Copernicus can tell.
> The gentle planet was in her final quarter, and upon her
> slender horn I hung my hopes of withdrawing from the ship
> undetected. (P. 22)

In Chapter 8, Taji provides yet another specification regarding Luna:

> The night was even blacker than we had anticipated; there was no trace of a moon; and the dark purple haze, sometimes encountered at night near the Line, half shrouded the stars from view. (P. 26)

From this description of the past-midnight sky, we are given to understand that the third-quarter moon has just set below the horizon and that any residual glimmer is hidden in the haze. On the cosmic ship, Luna would be at the stern, between Libra and Scorpio.

> It was midnight, mark you, when our watch began; and my turn at the helm now coming on was of course to be avoided. On some plausible pretense, I induced our solitary watchmate to assume it; thus leaving myself untrammeled, and at the same time satisfactorily disposing of him. For being a rather fat fellow, an enormous consumer of "duff," and with good reason supposed to be the son of a farmer, I made no doubt, he would pursue his old course and fall to nodding over the wheel. As for the leader of the watch—our harpooneer—he fell heir to the nest of old jackets, under the lee of the mizzen-mast, left nice and warm by his predecessor. (P. 26)

Taji positions one planet at the helm of the cosmic ship, that is, at the mainmast, and another at the mizzenmast on the line that passes through the tail of Scorpio. The fat, sleepy helmsman is readily recognizable as the midwinter sun, and he it is who left a warm pile of jackets for Mark.

*   *   *

In order to identify the general period of time in which this action occurs, it is necessary to identify the planet conjoined with Saturn at the foremast positioned in Capricorn. A knowledgeable contemporary of Melville should recognize the conjunction readily, for after the discovery of Neptune, the recent history of the new planet was published in the United States in the *Sidereal Messenger,* with an illustration showing the conjunction of Saturn

8. *The Sidereal Messenger* (Cincinnati, July 1846–October 1848), 41–44, describes the events leading to the discovery of Neptune and provides all astronomical data known at that time, including the fact that Neptune's retrograde period had not yet been fully reckoned. An illustration on page 41 shows the Saturn–Neptune conjunction (see p. 92).

and Neptune as it had occurred months before the discovery.[8] In any case, a reader of Melville's day would no doubt see Jarl as a Neptune figure simply because of the imagery that describes him as an ancient tar in whom geography is "deplorably lacking." Without further evidence of Jarl's identity at this time, we are justified in turning immediately to that issue of the almanac that includes the first Christmas prior to the discovery of Neptune—*The American Almanac* for 1845. Here we find that Melville's imagery is precisely accurate, for on December 24 Saturn is at *iota* Capricorn in the fishtail of the Goat, the moon is at third quarter in the "pan" of Libra that lies between the claws of

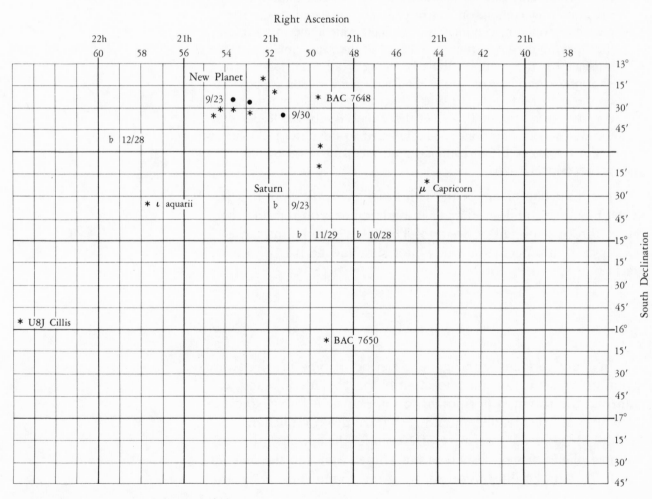

Right ascension at conjunction of Saturn and Neptune.

Scorpio, and Mercury is at the tip of Scorpio's tail, in the mizzenmast position attributed to Mark the Harpooneer.

Now, from the *Almanac* the rest of the planets can be positioned, and they are so perfectly aligned that we suspect the *Almanac* of having been designed for Melville's convenience. In order, the planets appear as follows:

The star Arcturus marks the descendant solar horizon.

Luna is thirty degrees beyond, near *gamma* Libra.

Mercury, thirty degrees beyond Luna, aligns with *lambda* Scorpio.

Sol, stated by the *Almanac* to have "entered Capricorn," is shown on the sky map to be at mid-Sagittarius.

Saturn and Venus are conjunct near *iota* Capricorn.

Uranus, ninety degrees beyond Sol, is near *omega* Pisces, just beyond the mouth of the first Fish.

Only two planets are out of aspect:

Mars is near *iota* Pisces, about to overtake Uranus, and

Jupiter is reported by the *Almanac* to be at *tau* Capricorn, in the neck of the Goat.

The planets, shown together and separately, in their opening positions in the daylight sky, with Sol at midheaven in Sagittarius. Note that except for Mars and the spurious Jupiter, all planets are in aspect. The true Jupiter is opposite Arcturus.

Sol in "stirrup" of Sagittarius

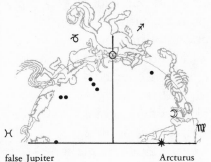

false Jupiter   Arcturus

Venus, Saturn, and Neptune in Capricorn

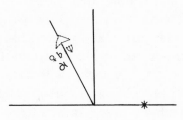

Uranus in Pisces   Mars

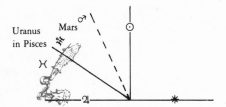

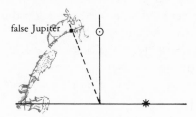

false Jupiter

true location of Jupiter in Pisces

Mercury in Scorpio

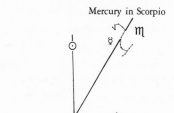

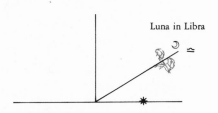

Luna in Libra

At this point it becomes necessary to deal with the problem of Jupiter, for *The American Almanac* has erred in regard to the location of this planet, which is actually to be found in direct opposition to Arcturus on the ascendant horizon, near *pi* Pisces. He is, in fact, in the spine of the Fish, an extremely significant position in relation to Taji's description of Aleema the Priest as holding "the sharp spine of a fish." Instead, the spine of a Fish holds Jupiter.

It must be remembered that the opening action of *Mardi* is set nine months prior to the discovery of Neptune and that Neptune is not included in the *Almanac.* In his place, though not in conjunction with Saturn, is a spurious Jupiter.[9] The modern reader is more likely to be taken in by this situation than a contemporary of Melville would be; even so, there were no doubt many readers who could be expected to pay no attention to astronomical events, and such a reader might have substituted Jupiter for Neptune upon finding Jupiter in Capricorn and no Neptune in the *Almanac.* This substitution is made by Taji, since he shows himself sufficiently gullible to believe everything he sees in print. In light of this, it is not surprising that Taji imposes Jovian imagery upon his description of Jarl. Vaguely and indirectly, Taji seems to describe Jarl as "jovially jabbering in the Lingua-Franca of the forecastle," while immediately afterward noting that Jarl is "exceedingly taciturn, and but seldom will speak for himself." He calls Jarl "an honest, earnest wight; so true and simple, that the secret operations of thy soul were more inscrutable than the subtle workings of Spinoza's," and he reports also that Jarl talked to him like an "uncle." Repeatedly he describes Jarl as blunt, straightforward, and frank, "one of those devoted fellows who will wrestle hard to convince one loved of error; but failing, forthwith change their wrestling to a sympathetic hug." Immediately, however, Taji alters his tone:

> Let me say, though, perhaps to the credit of Jarl, that whenever the most strategy was necessary, he seemed ill at ease, and for the most part left the matter to me. It was well that he did; for as it was, by his untimely straight-forwardness, he once or twice came near spoiling every thing. Indeed, on one occasion he was so unseasonably blunt, that curiously enough, I had almost suspected

9. Notice that Jarl combines the traits of Jupiter and Neptune until after the Aleema incident. Compare him with the Old Dansker in *Billy Budd,* who also combines the qualities of the two planets, since the later novel is set in a pre-Neptunian period. The imagery surrounding the Old Dansker parallels that of both Jarl and Aleema.

him of taking that odd sort of interest in one's welfare, which leads a philanthropist, all other methods failing, to frustrate a project deemed bad, by pretending clumsily to favor it. But no innuendoes; Jarl was a Viking, frank as his fathers; though not so much of a bucanier. (P. 21)

At sea in the *Chamois,* Taji in his fright claims that he would "fain have built an altar to Neptune." In the subsequent description of Jarl's "visor of japanning," however, we can see the mottled face of Jupiter, even as we recall Neptune's submarine spots. And finally, Taji on several occasions refers to Jarl as a tailor.

Astrologically, Jupiter is frank, blunt, and straightforward, though according to the *Almanac,* the planet Jupiter is retrograde on the day of the escape. Moreover, he is the patron of philanthropists, as well as of uncles and tailors. He is jovial and talkative and generous to a fault, while Neptune is traditionally silent, moody, and often associated with misfortune.[10]

The evidence for Jarl's identity as the undiscovered Neptune far outweighs the Jovian indications. In the Air sign of Aquarius when discovered, Neptune would properly be called the "Skyeman," and being far to the north of the ecliptic, he would also be a "Norseman to behold." Like Jarl, Neptune is "a lone, friendless mariner on the main, only true to his origin in the sea-life that he led," and he is kin to "the hierarchies of seraphs in the uttermost skies; the thrones and principalities of the zodiac." Still unknown, Neptune is without name or description and therefore "illiterate," and in geography he is "deplorably lacking," since no one knows where he is.

> According to his view of the matter, this terraqueous world had been formed in the manner of a tart; the land being a mere marginal crust, within which rolled the watery world proper. Such seemed my good Viking's theory of cosmography. As for other worlds, he weened not of them; yet full as much as Chrysostom. (P. 13)

Despite his lack of geography, Jarl has a "superstitious reverence for nautical instruments," and Taji intimates that this trait would characterize a "pedantic disciple of Mercator." It is in Chapter

10. According to Roman mythology, Neptune is the father of Capricornus, as reported by Gertrude Jobes and James Jobes, *Outer Space: Myths, Name Meanings, Calendars. . . . ,* p. 141, just as Poseidon is the father of Triton. The Jobeses state further that Neptune gives Pisces its "dull, treacherous, and phlegmatic" qualities and its reputation as the zodiac's hell (232). Neptune is also credited with the invention of the horse and is thereby given a possible connection with Jupiter's Sagittarius. Needless to say, the astrological interpretation of Neptune was incomplete at the time Melville wrote *Mardi,* though the little magazine, *The Nineteenth Century Astrologer,* carried articles speculating on the influence of both Uranus and the new planet.

11, however, that the planetary nature of Jarl is fully developed:

> But Jarl, dear, dumb Jarl, thou wert none of these. Thou didst carry a phiz like an excommunicated deacon's. And no matter what happened, it was ever the same. Quietly, in thyself, thou didst revolve upon thine own sober axis, like a wheel in a machine which forever goes round, whether you look at it or no. Ay, Jarl! wast thou not forever intent upon minding that which so many neglect—thine own especial business? Wast thou not forever at it, too, with no likelihood of ever winding up thy moody affairs, and striking a balance sheet? (P. 35)
>
> . . . . . .
>
> But how account for the Skyeman's gravity? Surely, it was based upon no philosophic taciturnity; he was nothing of an idealist; an aerial architect; a constructor of flying buttresses. It was inconceivable, that his reveries were Manfred-like and exalted, reminiscent of unutterable deeds, too mysterious even to be indicated by the remotest of hints. Suppositions all out of the question.
>
>   His ruminations were a riddle. (P. 36)

A study of the search for Neptune reveals that the most important factor in his discovery was his gravitational effect on Uranus. Truly the planet had been forever in motion, whether or not anyone was aware of it, and the business imagery reminds us that the search in progress was mathematical and not astronomical.

Astrologically, Neptune is indeed the dreamer, and in his connection with Jupiter's usurped realm of Pisces, he is to be attributed the qualities of imagination, idealism, and mystery. Above all, Melville specifically states here that Jarl's ruminations constitute a riddle of *Mardi*.[11]

Thus Melville takes full advantage of the *Almanac*'s misprint, using the spurious Jupiter as a mask for the undiscovered Neptune in the character of Jarl. Despite this mistake, there are nevertheless two extra persons in the *Chamois* with Taji and Jarl, and Taji has gone so far as to provide for them:

> Then, our larder was to be thought of; also, an abundant supply of water; concerning which last I determined to take good heed. There were but two to be taken care of; but I resolved to lay in sufficient store of both meat and drink for four; at the same time

11. Jarl's "cud" receives considerable play in *Mardi*, ranging from his silent ruminations through the "chew" he eschews to the incident with the Arva nut on Juam. Notably, Neptune and Pisces are associated with the use of drugs and rule over dreams and visions.

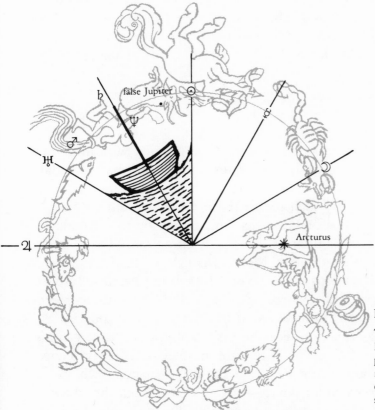

December 24, 1845, to January 5, 1846

The *Chamois* sector covers the sixty degrees of arc from the stirrup line of Sagittarius to the neck of the first fish. The *Chamois* covers parts of Capricorn and of Aquarius, a thirty-degree arc. The single mast of the *Chamois* intersects the tail of Capricorn at the position of Neptune. In the boat are Neptune, Saturn, and Venus. In the sector are Sol, Uranus, Mars, and the spurious Jupiter.

> that the supplemental twain thus provided for were but imaginary. And if it came to the last dead pinch, of which we had no fear, however, I was food for no man but Jarl. (P. 20)

Even without Jupiter, two other bodies are reported by the *Almanac* to be in Capricorn, and hence in the *Chamois*. Venus, having passed Neptune and Saturn on December 19, is still in the *Chamois* sector, and the *Almanac* has noted that Sol entered Capricorn on December 21. Of the latter Taji remarks: "And was not the sun a fellow-voyager? were we not both wending westward?" (38). Venus boards the *Chamois* disguised as a compass "that glistened to us like a human eye" (33), serving as a backseat driver from the aftermost thwart. Taji does well to provide for these "waifs," for by the time both the "old Pilot" and the compass throw Taji off course and Sol causes the water to leak and evaporate, there is need for those extra provisions. The presence of Venus also accounts for Taji's imagery of love and perhaps homosexuality directed at Jarl, as well as for his comment that he deemed his own resolution "quite venial" (16).

*   *   *

We see then that the *Almanac* is burdened with three major errors, and we are to discover later that the sky-map-calendar may contain yet another, if the reader is using one of the great classic sky-maps drawn by such sixteenth- and seventeenth-century masters as Apianus or Hevelius. Sol, shown by the calendar to be at the stirrup of Sagittarius, is actually some ten degrees behind the dateline. Nevertheless, Melville is not yet ready to correct that error because to do so would disturb the beautiful aspects presented by his neat horoscope. He provides for the correction after Taji and Jarl have boarded the *Parki,* just in time for Sol's first major conjunction. For the time being, Sol remains in his false position. It is possible that the nineteenth-century reader might have been using a current sky-map—many of which contained no calendar device—or none at all; but the older sky-map-calendars were widely used as illustrations during Melville's period, especially that of Hevelius, and for these the correction is essential.[12]

The voyage in the *Chamois* provides us with a day-by-day sampling of the imagery of chronology, in preparation for the discontinuance of the timeline aboard the *Parki.* For greater ease of handling, we will treat this section as a log, dating each event as it occurs and relating the imagery to the planetary activity.

12. See Basil Brown, *Astronomical Atlases, Maps & Charts; an Historical and General Guide* (London, 1932).

IX. Capricorn: The Astral Goat

> But, lingering not long in those silent vales, from watery cliff to cliff, a sea-chamois, sprang our solitary craft,—a goat among the Alps! —*Mardi, 37*

December 19. Venus is conjunct Saturn at *iota* Capricorn, and Taji, having been rebuffed by the captain of the *Arcturion,* is growing restive. He goes aloft for his allotted two hours, just as Saturn is aloft for only two hours after sunset during this period. Sol, at the stirrup of Sagittarius, sets at 7:26 P.M., and Saturn, thirty degrees behind, will sink below the horizon about 9:30, along with Venus. Under the mellowing influence of the goddess of love, Taji's soul is filled with romance, and, gazing into the sunset toward the southwest, he sees visions of Alhambras and Ninevehs. A bird crosses his sight, and he hears "mild billows laving a beach of shells, the waving of boughs, and the voices of maidens." Later, the bird imagery will receive further attention through its association with Venus.

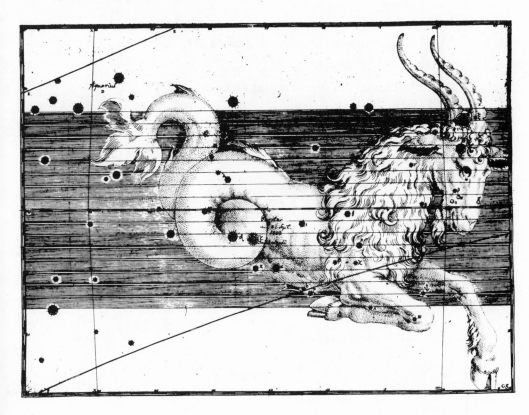

Capricorn

TABVLA TRIGESIMA PRIMA.
CAPRICORNVS.

Poëtis Neptunia proles, Aequoris Hircus, Pelagi procella,
Manilio Caper, Imbrifer, Gelidus, Corniger, Nonno ἀθαλπὴς, Capra, Græcis
αἰγόκερως, Pan, Aegipan, Germ. Stainbock/ Arab. Algedi, Alcantarus. ·

DIARTHROSIS.

1	α	SEptentrionalis duplex in cornu sequente. ☿♂.		
3	β	Ad frontem. ☿♂.		
23	γ	In eductione caudæ duarū antecedens, ἐν τῷ παρύρῳ, Arab. Deneb Algedi. ♃♄. Cardano. ♂♀.	4	Tertiæ.
24	d	Succedens. ♃♄.		
21	ε	Prior duarum in spinâ Australi apud caudam.	1	Quartæ.
14	ζ	Sub aluo duarum præcedens.		
18	η	In armo dextro trium Septentrionalis.		
19	θ	In dorso duarum antecedens.		
20	ι	Sequens.	7	Quintæ.
22	κ	Posterior duarum in spinâ Australi apud caudam.		
25	λ	In Boreâ parte caudæ quatuor præcedens. ♃♄.		
26	μ	In parte Australi. ♃♄.		
2	ν	Australis in cornu sequente, paruula. ♀♂.		
4	ξ	In cornu præcedente. ♀♂.		
6	ο	Supra rictum trium Australior. ♀♂.		
5	π	Media. ☿♂.		
7	ϱ	Borealior. ☿♂.		
8	σ	Prope nares.		
9	τ	Ad ceruicem. ♀♂.		
10	υ	In collo.	17	Sextæ.
16	φ	In armo dextro trium sequens.		
17	χ	Media Australior.		
11	ψ	In sinistro pede.		
12	ω	In dextro genu.		
13	A	In armo eiusdem.		
15	b	Sub aluo duarum sequens.		
29	c	Tres ultimæ Deneb Algedi.		

{Diff·

1

Cæteræ ♂. parum. ☿.

D. Aquarius. E. Aequator. F. Tropicus Capricorni, ab hoc asterismo deno-
minationem sortitus.

Gg   Capri-

December 20. The *Almanac* reports Jupiter at *tau* Capricorn, though the lunar passage on December 9 had shown him to be in Pisces. Venus reaches her greatest elongation—the farthest she can be from Sol. From now until she begins her retrograde period, her forward motion will be slow, and she will remain within conjunction distance of Saturn and Neptune for many more days. On this, the eve of the winter solstice, there falls a calm, and Taji develops a severe case of nerves. By nameless associations his old impressions as a landsman are revived in him. The tumescent imagery seems to portend an imminent birth. Nothing "possessed of a local angularity, is to be lighted upon in the watery waste," during this calm at the very waist of the world. Here is "the region of the everlasting lull, introductory to a positive vacuity" in which "thoughts of eternity thicken." His voice grows strange and portentous, and he "feels it in him like something swallowed too big for the esophagus." He is helpless, "succor or sympathy there is none." Without mobility or volition, he feels small indeed:

> It is more hopeless than a bad marriage in a land where there is no Doctors' Commons. He has taken the ship to wife, for better or for worse, for calm or for gale; and she is not to be shuffled off. With yards akimbo, she says unto him scornfully, as the old beldam said to the little dwarf:—"Help yourself." (P. 10)

Thus, still under the influence of Venus, Taji delivers himself of the punch line to a Rabelaisian joke, even as he reveals his true stature as a seaman. Whether this imagery is to be interpreted as parturient or ejaculatory, Taji is more the homunculus than the "man."

Astrologically, Taji is in a period of stress and strain, since his Saturn is squared with Luna—that is, about ninety degrees apart. Venus also is square to Luna, so that love takes on a negative rather than a positive connotation. And finally, the undiscovered planet Neptune is also squared with Luna, so the ocean also contributes to his stress. In addition to Taji's personal stress, a general condition of strain exists because of Sol's square with the planet of conflict, Mars—an aspect that plays havoc with patience.

The sky also provides justification for the imagery of fullness, since the horizon line of the descendant is passing through the abdominal region of Virgo, and Luna also is, as reported by *The Old Farmer's Almanac* (and others), in the "belly," that is, in Virgo, while the "sun" is about to enter the Christmas sign of Capricorn.

Venus, Saturn, and Neptune are semisextile (thirty degrees) from Sol, a minor aspect related to growth. That these planets are also semisextile to Mars enhances the possibility that the imagery is phallic as well as parturient.

Taji's description of the condition brought on by the calm contains many of the symptoms described by Burton in his *Anatomy of Melancholy,* in which melancholia is attributed in part to strained or adverse aspects of Saturn, Mars, and Luna. Certainly such aspects exist at this time, when all but one of the planets are in aspect.

December 21. Sol enters the sign of Capricorn at the winter solstice. Luna is at third quarter, leaving Virgo and entering Libra. Sol is squared with Mars and with Luna, while Mars and Luna are in opposition. To Taji these aspects mean that delays are possible, owing to interference by other people, relations with colleagues may be strained, restlessness checks progress in work, while a domineering manner may stir up antagonism from others, with resultant unpopularity. It is under these aspects that Taji ascends to the foremast to chat with the old seaman Jarl, in keeping with the conjunction of Saturn with the unknown Neptune, with Venus presiding. And here, in Chapter 3, with the introduction of Jarl, Taji provides the first real astrological imagery as he sails through the zodiac and sings of "the folio now spread with horoscopes as yet undeciphered, the heaven of heavens on high" (13). Taji has made clear that he is not overwhelmingly popular with his shipmates, and he indicates too that he may be somewhat domineering with Jarl. Thus his own horoscope for this day begins to seem accurate.

Taji tells Jarl of his desire to escape from the *Arcturion,* and the old seaman tries to dissuade him, urging him to "not be a boy, pause and reflect, stick to the ship, and go home in her like a man" (17). As Melville subsequently explains in *Redburn,* the terms *boy* and *man* are used to distinguish the lubberly novice sailor from the seasoned initiate. At last Jarl seems to be persuaded, and he swears to follow Taji through thick and thin. Nevertheless, Taji later suspects him of attempting to frustrate

the project by "pretending clumsily to favor it" (21). Jarl leaves
the preparations strictly to Taji and apparently does very little to
cooperate in the plans to escape. Meanwhile, Taji, intent on
leaving the *Arcturion,* shirks his duties in order to further his plot.
Thus the aspects in his horoscope prove to be correct.

His Viking secured, Taji spends the next few days in
preparation for their escape, selecting a whaleboat and filling it
with provisions.

December 24. On this Christmas Eve, Luna is in her final
quarter and is located in the "reins" of Libra; "upon her slender
horn" Taji hangs his hopes of escaping undetected. He has
chosen the bow boat, the one nearest the foremast where Saturn,
Neptune, and Venus are positioned on the cosmic ship. Sol is at
the mainmast position, where the fat, sleepy helmsman dozes at
the wheel. Mercury, at the mizzenmast post with Mark the
harpooneer, is on this date at aphelion—nearest the sun—so he is
comfortable in a nest of warm jackets. As the *Arcturion* stands to
the northwest in the equatorial waters just south of the Line
Islands, she is in the shark-infested waters near Christmas Island,
so it is natural that, as Taji readies himself for his watch, an old
sea dog talks about sharks in his sleep.

It is twelve-twenty before Taji begins to carry out his plan,
and since the *Chamois* must be loaded, it is probably near one
o'clock before the escape takes place and Taji and Jarl sail and
row into the darkness.

December 25. On Christmas morning, Taji and Jarl are "at sea
in an open boat, and a thousand miles from land!" though
actually they are just a few hours away from Christmas Island.
Jarl's glance seems so "queer" that Taji begs him to "look
another way." Having hitherto regarded the ocean as a slave or
as the steed that would bear him wherever he listed, Taji now
begins a Christmas celebration by amending his attitude and
thinking in terms of building an altar to Neptune. They set up
housekeeping, constructing an awning over the stern of the
whaleboat, and possibly with Christmas dinner in mind, Taji
remarks:

> But when a mere breath rippled the sea, and the sun was fiery
> hot, it was most pleasant to lounge in this shady asylum. It was
> like being transferred from the roast to cool in the cupboard. And
> Jarl, much the toughest fowl of the two, out of an abundant

kindness for his comrade, during the day voluntarily remained
exposed at the helm, almost two hours to my one. (P. 33)

. . . . . .

If we fall in with cannibals, thought I, then, ready-roasted
Norseman that thou art, shall I survive to mourn thee; at least,
during the period I revolve upon the spit. (P. 34)

December 28. Sunday, at break of day, a sense of peril comes
over Taji; and well it might, since his alterego, Uranus, is on this
day square with Sol. Taji suspects that his apprehension "could
hardly have been aggravated by the completest solitude," and the
Almanac shows that both Luna and Mercury have entered the
Chamois sector. At this point we receive the coordinates for the
horizon range of the *Chamois.*

> On a ship's deck, the mere feeling of elevation above the water,
> and the reach of prospect you command, impart a degree of
> confidence which disposes you to exult in your fancied security.
> But in an open boat, brought down to the very plane of the sea,
> this feeling almost wholly deserts you. Unless the waves . . . toss
> you and your chip upon one of their lordly crests, your sphere of
> vision is little larger than it would be at the bottom of a well. At
> best, your most extended view in any one direction, at least, is in
> a high, slow-rolling sea; when you descend into the dark, misty
> spaces, between long and uniform swells. (P. 37)

As illustrated, the horizon established by the *Arcturion* consists of
a full one-hundred-eighty-degree hemisphere, and includes all the
planets. The ship covers a "trine," that is, one-hundred-twenty
degrees, and includes Mercury, Sol, Neptune, Saturn, and Venus.
The *Chamois,* described by Taji as thirty feet in length, covers
thirty degrees, while its narrowed horizon consists of a sextile, or
sixty degrees, ranging from mid-Sagittarius to the neck of the first
fish in Pisces. The whaleboat, centered within this area, includes
only Capricorn and Aquarius. On this day, though Taji, Jarl, and
the Venus–Compass are still alone in the boat, the *Chamois* sector
has been invaded by Mercury, who in turn is on this day
conjunct the new moon. Tomorrow, the twenty-ninth, Luna is at
perigee (closest to Earth), so Taji the landsman already feels the
effects of her presence.

December 31, 1845, noon through midnight. A week has gone
by, and Taji becomes bewildered: "All became vague and

confused; so that westward of the Kingsmill isle and the Radack chain, I fancied there could be naught but endless sea" (38). This comment characterizes Taji's condition on this New Year's Eve, as Luna is conjunct Saturn. At no time has Taji mentioned the inclusion of grog among the supplies collected for his voyage, but during the next few chapters, 7 through 15, we have reason to suspect that Taji has found some way to celebrate, "especially when the constellation Pisces was in the ascendant." Traditionally, Pisces has been associated with tippling, no doubt giving rise to the expression, "drink like a fish."

Chapter 13, "Chondropterygii," contains important previews that deserve some consideration. To begin, on January 1, Pisces is ascending to the position of "sun-sign," while astrologically, in the sense of "rising sign," Pisces is the ascendant near the noon hour. It would be about this time that Taji begins his study of "Ichthyology" that he so highly commends. "Whoso crosses the Pacific might read lessons to Buffon"—an apt choice of names that serves to remind us not only that Taji himself is a buffoon, but that Buffon is renowned as an astronomer as well as a naturalist, though his cosmography was exploded by the Kant–LaPlace theory, current in Melville's day.[1] Now Taji turns naturalist and begins his description of the wonders of the deep:

> The sea-serpent is not a fable; and in the sea, that snake is but a garden worm. There are more wonders than the wonders rejected, and more sights unrevealed than you or I ever ever dreamt of. Moles and bats alone should be skeptics; and the only true infidelity is for a live man to vote himself dead. Be Sir Thomas Brown [*sic*] our ensample; who, while exploding "Vulgar Errors," heartily hugged all the mysteries in the Pentateuch. (P. 39)

This passage emphasizes the gullibility that marks Taji's approach to "science." More important, Taji previews here his own final act—that of voting himself dead. As one who believes in himself, Taji credits all errant things. Once he abjures self-belief, he becomes capable of judgment and discrimination.

While reflecting upon the creatures of the sea, Taji sees constellations of sharks. Surpassing all the others in horror is the "ghastly White Shark," and this creature provides the figure that will pursue Taji throughout Mardi, "gliding along just under the

1. Buffon's cosmogony includes another exploded "vulgar error" regarding comets, as he postulated the formation of the solar system by a collision of a comet with the sun, a theory exploded by the Kant–Laplace nebular hypothesis.

surface, revealing a long, vague shape of a milky hue." The white shark later becomes, in Taji's superstitious imagination, the ghost of Aleema the Priest.

This tendency on Taji's part to grasp hold of some natural phenomenon, alter it, exaggerate and embroider it, continues throughout the voyage. Here Melville emphasizes this trait by juxtaposing it to the same proclivity in the artist: "Had old Wouvermans, who once painted a bull-bait, been along with us, a rare chance, that, for his pencil. And Gudin or Isabey might have thrown the blue rolling sea into the picture. Lastly, one of Claude's setting summer suns would have glorified the whole" (42). By this juxtaposition, Melville defines the act of art and shows Taji as a figure of the artist with his capacity for elaboration.[2]

*   *   *

January 1, 1846. On New Year's Day, Jarl, now revealed as the keeper of the almanac, suggests that the currents are sweeping the *Chamois* toward the north and that Taji should row the boat.

> Take to our oars! as if we were crossing a ferry, and no ocean leagues to traverse. The idea indirectly suggested all possible horrors. To be rid of them forthwith, I proceeded to dole out our morning meal. For to make away with such things, there is nothing better than bolting something down on top of them; albeit, oft repeated, the plan is very apt to beget dyspepsia; and the dyspepsia the blues. (P. 43)

So Taji describes the "morning after," in a pun-laden paragraph. Taji's feelings of impending dyspepsia and of a stomach that has been "bolted down" no doubt are intended to serve as an ironic and highly recognizable clue to the day after New Year's Eve. Jarl spends most of this chapter trying to defend the water keg from Taji, who is evidently suffering from an exceptionally dry mouth. As Jarl assiduously checks the breaker for "leakage," Taji notes with amusement, "Oh Jarl, Jarl: to me in the boat's quiet stern, steering and philosophizing at one time and the same, thou and thy breaker were a study" (44).

2. The artist's capacity for expansion of fact receives further and clearer play in *Moby Dick,* Chapters 29–31. In this incident, Ahab speaks roughly to Stubb and calls him a "dog." By the next morning, Stubb has blown up the words into "ten times a donkey" and "a lot of jackasses" piled on top of that, plus a kick with Ahab's ivory "stubb." Throughout *Mardi,* Taji takes realistic incidents and blows them up into increasingly larger and more "air-filled" tales.

This New Year's Day chapter is influenced by the conjunction of Mars with Uranus, and Melville puns outrageously on the meeting between the arrowlike phallic symbol of Mars and the name of Taji's alterego planet. For example, regarding the problem of getting water from the various kegs, Taji notes that "when we came to the breaker, which had only a bung-hole, though a very large one, dog-like, it was so many laps apiece; jealously counted by the observer." In an interesting reversal of the festive custom of drinking from a lady's shoe, Taji drinks his "hair of the dog" from Jarl's shoe, the flavor possibly remindful of all water taken after wine. As "goggle green glasses are deemed indispensable to the bibbing of Hock," says Taji, "What then shall be said of a leathern goblet for water? Try it, ye mariners who list." This pun on staggering sailors precedes an appetizing reference to a visitor worthy of any hangover:

> One morning, taking his wonted draught, Jarl fished up in his ladle a deceased insect; something like a Daddy-long-legs, only more corpulent. Its fate? A sea-toss? Believe it not; with all those precious drops clinging to its lengthy legs. It was held over the ladle till the last globule dribbled; and even then, being moist, honest Jarl was but loth to drop it overboard. (Pp. 44–45)

This event merits special comment, for it serves as a preview to the *Parki* incident. First, Taji calls the creature an insect and then compares it to an eight-legged arachnid; second, it is implied but not stated that Jarl does eventually toss the beast overboard, which he does not necessarily do; finally, the previous chapter had related Taji's surgical removal of the wing of a flying fish, and these two beasts, the "one-armed" flying fish and the corpulent arachnid, are soon to be encountered on the *Parki*. This practice of symbolic preview recurs throughout *Mardi* and provides a link to the mythical art of metamorphosis. Just as the artists of the preceding chapter alter nature to fit their conception of truth or beauty, so Taji will transform some minor natural phenomenon into a tale. Thus, the flying fish and the arachnid, both deceased, are to be resurrected by a "sea change" to become Samoa and Annatoo.

But we are not yet finished with Taji's dyspepsia. He closes with a still less appetizing quotation from the Chinese: "In the operation of making your toilet, how handy to float in your ewer" (45).

Chapter 15, the final New Year's entry, provides the polar coordinates for this day. We have noted that on the day of the escape, the polar radials of our horoscope ran from the loins of Virgo to the spine of Pisces, where Jupiter was hidden. Now, one week later, the poles have moved forward by seven degrees. Chapter 15 is full of imagery of old maids working with wool, and if we move the radials forward until the ascendant pole enters the horn of Aries the woolly Ram, we find the descendant nearing the ankles of Virgo and the dateline at January 1.[3] The *Almanac* reports that Mars, now crossing the ecliptic, is conjunct Uranus, and therefore a preliminary meeting between Taji and the Mars figure, soon to be revealed as Annatoo the Arachnid, is necessary. Moreover, Sol is at perigee, his closest approach to Earth, and Sol's proximity results in the calm that will begin during this night.

Two other points should be noted briefly in this chapter. First, the feminine imagery, including "old-wife," directed at Jarl, reinforces the homosexual implications while at the same time it reveals Melville's intentional pun on Jarl's place of origin, the "constellated Hebrides." This visual pun on *he-brides* is an important clue to the identity of Jarl as it relates to the Venetian custom of the Doges' Espousal of the Sea.[4] Second, Taji introduces Jarl's Guayaquil hat, the "conical calabash" that resembles either the papal mitre, the dunce cap, or the Taj, an image already discussed in the section on the card metaphor. Jarl's relationship to the Papacy will receive further attention in a later chapter.

January 1–2. Chapter 16 covers five days—from the midnight of January 1 to the morning of January 6. With Sol at perigee, the heat is intense during the calm that falls during New Year's night; hence, the water in the breaker becomes "lukewarm, brackish, and slightly putrescent," and "the upper planking of the boat began to warp."

January 3. Luna is conjunct Uranus in Pisces, and the event occurs that will be stressed more and more as the book progresses through the quest. Each time Luna passes or is in phase with Uranus, there will be signals that are constantly misinterpreted by the characters. Luna is the "receiver" for the

3. On the sky-map-calendar, the sectors are divided into thirty-degree "months." Since December has thirty-one days, January first must be located on the second-degree mark of the next sector. The discrepancy is eliminated in February.

4. See *Mardi,* Chapter 149, p. 482, in which the Doges' Espousal of the Sea is described and juxtaposed to a reference to Neptune.

thoughts of the other planets, and Uranus is the planet responsible for the discovery of Neptune.[5] Thus, he is the "fugleman," or "signalman," for the new world. Now, as Luna passes the wobbling planet, vast smooth swells begin to overtake the boat. As Taji explains the phenomenon, "A sea-gale operates as if an asteroid had fallen into the brine; making ringed mountain billows, interminably expanding, instead of ripples." And Taji becomes quite specific in ambiguous terms: "The great September waves breaking at the bases of the Neversink Highlands, far in advance of the swiftest pilot-boat, carry tidings" (49). These advance September tidings transmitted as Luna passes Uranus are the news of a celestial discovery to be made in September—exactly nine months to the day from the launching of the *Chamois*.

5. See *Mardi*, Chapter 184, p. 616, in which Babbalanja, as the lunar figure, reveals himself as a receiver and interpreter of thoughts.

We have noted that one of the main features of the shipboard initiation is the "ducking" of the initiate. We are told at this point that the heat of the calm has induced Taji to get out of the boat and into the water for a bath, though he is always "clinging to the gunwale," keeping a lookout for sharks. It is important to bear in mind that Taji is not "ducked" at this point, for the idea of the initiation is that he must plumb the depths after letting go the side of the ship.

January 4. "On the third day a change came over us," reports Taji. He and Jarl cease to bathe; they turn their backs on each other and feel mutual detestation. "I can not tell what it was that came over me, but I wished I was alone," and Taji even entertains thoughts of murder. On this day a change comes over Luna also, as she changes to first quarter, and Taji's bloodthirsty thoughts can be attributed to Luna's conjunction with Mars and her squared aspect with Sol. Indeed, Taji's Uranus is still conjunct both Mars and Luna on this day, and this aspect produces tremendous strains in personal relationships that can result in violence.

Melville chooses to omit description of the fourth day, but the follower of the *Almanac* knows that Luna on this day completes her transit of planets as she passes out of the *Chamois* sector and by Jupiter, for whom Melville is not yet ready, and moves on into Aries beyond the horizon line.

January 6, Epiphany Tuesday. A day of the manifestation of

the Divinity. Taji cries, "Thanks be to Heaven, there came a
breeze . . . and our poor Chamois seemed raised from the dead."
And in celebration of the King, he exclaims:

> How changed the scene! Overhead, a sweet blue haze,
> distilling sunlight in drops. And flung abroad over the visible
> creation was the sun-spangled, azure, rustling robe of the ocean,
> ermined with wave crests; all else, infinitely blue. Such a cadence
> of musical sounds! Waves chasing each other, and sporting and
> frothing in frolicsome foam: painted fish rippling past; and anon
> the noise of wings as sea-fowls flew by.
>
> Oh, Ocean, when thou choosest to smile, more beautiful thou
> art than flowery mead or plain! (P. 50)

Thus on Epiphany, Taji does homage again to Neptune, the
King.

January 7. In Chapter 17, there are now fourteen notches on
the loom of the Skyeman's oar. Taji notes that "no floating
bough, no tern, noddy, nor reef-bird" denotes proximity to land.
Just the preceding day he has told us that "sea-fowl flew by," but
by now we would do well to be skeptical of Taji's ability to
identify birds. He estimates that the *Chamois* must have "sailed
due west but little more than one hundred fifty leagues," but Jarl
has warned him that they were moving northward. The *Chamois*
is in fact drifting northward, parallel to the Line Islands, headed
toward Kingman Reef.

This chapter provides the final Aries–Virgo coordinate.
Beginning with the reference to the loom, Taji comments, "The
calm gone by, once again my sea-tailor plied needle and thread;
or turning laundress, hung our raiment to dry." This will be the
last time Jarl is referred to in feminine terms, for Virgo's toes are
sinking below the solar horizon.

*   *   *

Chapter 18 is another transitional chapter, bridging January
7, on which Mercury is turning direct in Sagittarius, and January
8, on which Venus has reached her ascending node at *sigma*
Aquarius. She is on the ecliptic and, like the *Chamois*—whose

compass she is—moving northward. Here for the first time we encounter the pilot fish and the remoras, both of which accompany the shovel-nosed shark. These, of course, prefigure Hautia's Heralds and the Avengers, who will follow Taji throughout Mardi even as they now follow the *Chamois* after Jarl has killed the shark. It is interesting also that, since Venus and Hautia are to be associated with the card suit of Spades, the pilot fish are first seen in association with a "shovel-nose" shark. We also find one of the very few direct statements from Jarl, who says, "A good omen . . . no harm will befall us so long as they stay." We can keep an eye on the activity of these fish by watching Venus and Mercury—the pilot fish and the remoras, respectively—in the *Almanac.*

Until now, Venus has served as the compass for the *Chamois* as she has traveled through the tail of Capricorn. The *Almanac* reports that on January 8, Venus is conjunct *sigma* Aquarius, and has outdistanced the Goat-boat. True, Jarl's Neptune is also in Aquarius, but he is in that portion of the arm directly overhanging the Goat's back, and so he can remain in the *Chamois.* To keep pace with the compass it is now necessary to increase the portion of the sky to include Venus in her new location; hence a larger ship, the *Parki,* is now to be introduced, and the *Chamois* becomes part of this greater field.

X. The Parki

Arcturus, Arthur, and Joseph

Hath the rain a father? or who hath begotten the drops of dew? Out of whose womb came the ice? and the hoary frost of heaven, who hath gendered it? The waters are hid as with a stone, and the face of the deep is frozen. Canst thou bind the sweet influences of Pleiades, or loose the bands of Orion? Canst thou bring forth Mazzaroth in his season? or canst thou guide Arcturus with his sons?   —Job 38:28–32

1. Mechanically, Melville uses the aspects as aisles across and around the zodiac, enabling all planets within a given sector or group of sectors to convene through the medium of the second-level narrator, Taji, or the third-level narrator, Babbalanja.

Before we study the *Parki* sector, it might be well to review certain elements of the opening action in order to see how Melville utilizes stellar mechanics to further his metaphor and to employ a mythic image inherent in the *Almanac*'s error regarding Jupiter. As previously mentioned, the aspect of opposition is used by Melville to form an "aisle" between the characters involved in the aspect.[1] Since early in the *Parki* section the reader is to encounter such a pairing, a discussion of the symbolism of birth hidden in the opening action should also elucidate the episode of Samoa and Annatoo.

The star Arcturus or Bear Watcher is the zodiac pointer of the huge diamond in the sky that is Boötes, the Plowman. On the early sky maps, Arcturus is pictured as the phallus of the Plowman, poised rapaciously over the midsection of Virgo–Astraea the Earth Mother. Together they form the sunset rising sign of spring, hence they have long mythically represented the plowing of the thawing earth in preparation for fecundity and growth. In late summer they set in the west just after sundown, and it is during this period that the seduction of Virgo becomes a visible performance. Because of her bent configuration, Virgo seems to slide horizontally and head foremost into the rim of the earth, and Arcturus, like a pendulum, swings down above her. This plunge is repeated night after night until at last the Sun is in Virgo and the long winter gestation period begins.

In the Northern Hemisphere, the constellation Boötes never sets completely, but the top of the diamond can be seen riding low along the northern horizon during the night. Arcturus does disappear, however, and cannot be seen in the evening skies even

in the Northern Hemisphere as far north as Massachusetts. At the
Equator, of course, the entire diamond sets and does not
reappear until morning.

The constellation has long been known as "Arthur's Wain,"
with Arcturus identified as King Arthur. Since Melville
determinedly associates knighthood with the *Arcturion* in *Mardi,*
we may safely assume that he is familiar with the old English
name for Boötes and proceed accordingly.

Taji's view of himself as a knight questing for the lordly
Cachalot certainly plays upon the idea of Camelot, but in any case
this would-be knight has not yet been dubbed, despite his
pretensions. Jarl is fully aware of these pretensions, as Taji admits
that Jarl "must have taken me for one of the House of Hanover
in disguise; or, haply, for bonneted Charles Edward the
Pretender, who, like the Wandering Jew, may yet be a vagrant"
(14).

The description of the *Arcturion* chassezing back and forth
across the Line, combined with the highly charged imagery of
fullness and relief described in Chapter 2, "The Calm," would
seem to indicate that a birth of sorts is in progress. As already
noted, the escape from the *Arcturion* occurs amid considerable
Christmas imagery. Thus the reader is encouraged to associate the
escape with the birth of the Son, at a time when "the Sun enters
Capricorn" and Taji enters the sea goat, *Chamois.* At the same
time, this escape might also be seen as the birth of the "sons of
Arcturus," with reference to the "Voice out of the Whirlwind"
in Job.

If Arcturus is to be seen as the "father" in this instance and
is equated to King Arthur, who is as famous for his "horns" as
for his Round Table, then in regard to the birth of the "Son" he
can be equated only to Joseph. Thus, the problem set out in the
opening chapters of *Mardi* may be stated simply as "Who is the
father of the Sons of Arcturus, or of Arthur, or of Joseph?"

On December 24, according to the uncorrected sky-map,
when the Sun is at midheaven or at midnight, Arcturus–Virgo
lies on one horizon and Pisces–Cetus on the other. If the planets
are placed in accordance with the *Almanac* for this night in 1845,
there is no planet on this line. As previously pointed out,
however, there is an error in the *Almanac,* and Jupiter is actually

on the line in direct opposition to Arcturus. This opposition forms an aisle between Jupiter and Virgo, through Arcturus. The answer then becomes pat: Jupiter—God—is the true Father, working through Arcturus. Behind Jupiter, however, lies the vast constellation Cetus, the Sperm Whale, Leviathan, with the polar radial passing through the "loins" of the whale. The question, its first answer seemingly so pat, must be again posed.

There is no change in the nature of the quest from the beginning to the end of *Mardi.* The source of the Sperm is the real object of the quest throughout, and the Grail, the Urn, the Harpoon, the Lance, are all related to this concept.

The imagery of Chapter 2, described above as possible birth imagery, offers yet another potential interpretation: the passage of the Sperm as described from the standpoint of the "seaman." Melville's subsequent use of the opposition line suggests that this is an intended interpretation. While the birth metaphor postulates Taji–Saturn–Satan as twin brother to Christ, the Son, the conception image provides a still more complex puzzle to solve. If a conception did occur on the midnight of December 24, 1845, a nine-month gestation period would come to term on September 24, 1846, the date of the discovery of Neptune. Since Jarl emerges as a Christ figure, the ambiguous paternity of Christ becomes an object of the quest, while the problem arises as to the virginity of Virgo–Mary. Small wonder the metaphor required such elaborate concealment from the general run of the nineteenth-century readers! It does develop during the course of the book, however, that Melville redeems this near blasphemy and ascends to a higher plane of reverence. Nevertheless, by the time reverence sets in, all possibilities of excessive pietism have been thoroughly discarded and any devout nineteenth-century reader would have been irrevocably offended. As it turned out, many were offended anyway. One reviewer protested indignantly:

> We cannot but express our profound regret that a pen so talented, and an apparatus so fascinating, as those which the author of *Mardi* commands, should have been made use of for the dissemination of sceptical notions. To introduce the Savior of mankind under a fabulous name, and to talk down the verities of the Christian faith by sophistry, the more than irreverence of which is but flimsily veiled, is a grave offense.

And this reviewer from *John Bull* was referring to the figure of Alma, whom Melville treated with considerable respect in *Mardi*.[2] What then would have been said of the possibilities to be derived from Melville's riddle?

In summation, the opening opposition involves Virgo with Arcturus, Jupiter, or Cetus. The opposition we are about to encounter is that of Scorpio and Taurus and their *alpha* stars, Antares and Aldebaran.

2. Jay Leyda, *The Melville Log: A Documentary Life of Herman Melville, 1819–1891*, p. 299–300.

A Preview of the **Parki**

And thus divided, though but a few yards intervened, the pair were as much asunder as if at the opposite Poles.   —*Mardi,* 86

The *Parki* is a two-masted ship, and in keeping with previous usage she constitutes a quadrant, or ninety-degree square—an unfortunate aspect—on the horoscope. Because she must still contain the three planets included in the *Chamois* sector, she will necessarily encompass *iota* Capricorn, the star directly south of Jarl's position. The name *Parki* ends with the letter *i,* and with *iota* as the stern coordinate, the prow falls on *p* Aries. Thus the sector is comprised of an arc with a *p* in front and an *i* behind. It seems more than coincidental that the names *Arcturion* and *Parki* contain the syllable *arc* or *ark*—one pertaining to the section of a circle and the other to a shipload of animals, such as those

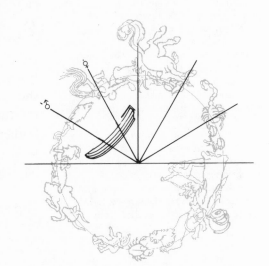

January 9, 1846

The *Parki* sector. As the *Chamois* encounters the *Parki,* Sol is in the neck of the Goat, and the horizon lines run from the nose of Aries to the toes of Virgo. The *Parki,* as shown above, occupies the Aquarius Pisces sector, and her two masts are at *p* Aquarius and *E* Pisces. Mars is on the "foremast" and Venus on the "mainmast."

outlined in the zodiac. Melville chooses his names with great care to serve as meaningful clues, even when the names derive from real biographical or geographical sources. Similar to the precision of the initial Christmas coordinates, the *Almanac* once again provides a gratuitous configuration: Drawing two thirty-degree radials between *iota* Capricorn and *rho* or *pi* Aries (the two stars are so close together that either can serve as the prow marker), we find that the "foremast" line falls at *epsilon* Pisces, the position of Mars (Annatoo), while the mainmast line at *sigma* Aquarius intercepts Venus (Samoa). In a sky full of stars and planets, a pat conformation such as this is not likely to be accidental.

A complex set of metaphors exists in the *Parki* sector, and in order to deal with them more easily, it might be helpful to introduce each of them briefly and separately before proceeding. We shall look at Annatoo and Samoa in terms of the insect and bull, clock and compass, Captain Cook and Dante, Church and State, and misunderstood virtue and blind faith.

*   *   *

Melville repeatedly emphasizes the beauty and brilliance of Samoa's eye and in a variety of images hints at Samoa's resemblance to a bull, specifically a half-bull. "Wild buffalo" that he is, Samoa is remindful of Bucephalus, or "bull-head." He is called "The Navigator," another name for Aldebaran of Taurus.[3] The *beta* star in Taurus is El Nath, the Dagger, at the tip of the right horn, corresponding to the dagger in Samoa's ear, while the Bull's nose is formed by a blade-shaped group of stars called the Hyades, represented by the nail in Samoa's nose. On the shoulder of Taurus are the Pleiades, resembling a tattoo. The sky-map portrays Taurus as having only a front half, and Taji finds in the *Parki*'s log a drawing of a diver half-eaten by a shark, while Samoa is half-tattooed and seems to Taji to be only a half-man.

Directly across the zodiac from Aldebaran is Antares, the "opposite Mars" and the "heart" of Scorpio. This red star, which looks as though it had been dipped in the red dye annatto, is

3. According to Gertrude Jobes and James Jobes, *Outer Space: Myths, Name Meanings, Calendars*, pp. 249–56, Taurus is the subject of numerous legends. "Greeks called the Egyptian Bull Serapis (Osiris–Apis or Osiris–Hapi) and believed that in it the souls of the two gods were united after death. In their own mythology, the bull was sacred in several forms. He was the Cretan Minotaur. . . . A deity of darkness, death, and winter, he was the son of Pasiphae, the moon goddess, wife of Minos, by her lover, the sea-god Poseidon" (250–51). "The bull in legend frequently is the recipient of an external soul" (251). "On modern sky maps the Bull manifests the animal that Orion hunts through the heavens" (254) —and note here that Taji refers to the animal pursued by Orion as a "moose" (13), so we may identify Melville's "moose" image with Taurus. The Jobeses also link Taurus with the ancient figure of Marduk, and notes that "the half figure represents the bull climbing out of the sea, his flanks still immersed in the waves."

Aldebaran is the lucida of the Hyades cluster. "Lying along the moon's track, it is occulted time and again. As a lunar star, navigators find it useful in ascertaining their positions" (Jobes and Jobes, 294). Aldebaran rises when the sun sets early in December and culminates about January 10.

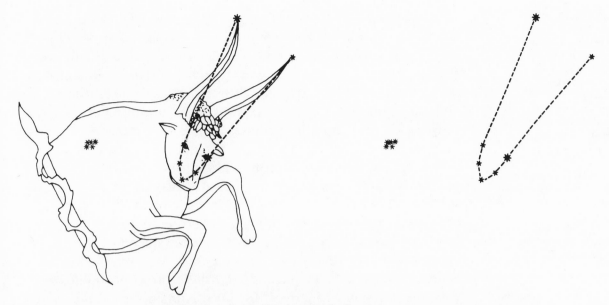

The constellation Taurus and its Stelleration
The large star in the eye of the Bull is Aldebaran, also called the
Navigator Star. On the shoulder are the Pleiades, or Seven Sisters.

The constellation Scorpio and its stelleration

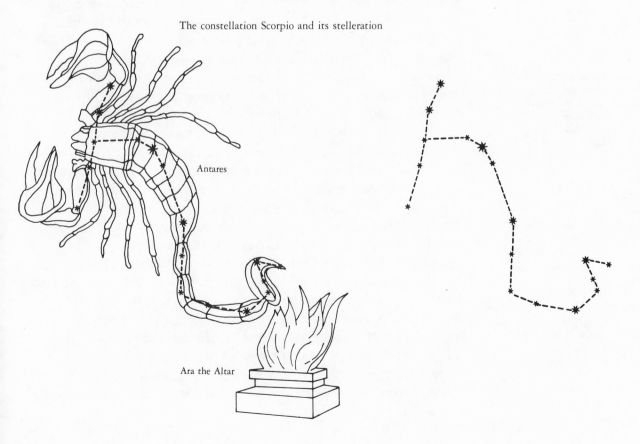

Antares

Ara the Altar

4. Antares was a luminary of Selk, Egyptian reptile goddess . . . or of Isis, who wept when she discovered all the dismembered parts of her husband's body "except the phallus" (Jobes and Jobes, *Outer Space*, p. 304). Scorpio is a constellation of great antiquity and is associated with the serpent and the eagle as well. "Those under its influence were dramatic, managerial, strong-willed, self-absorbed, sarcastic, jealous" (Jobes and Jobes, p. 243).

Like the spider, the scorpion is an arachnid, and Melville may have had this fact in mind in using the name *Annatoo*, after the red dye annatto, since, in Greek myth, the maiden Arachne was the daughter of a dyer. The star Antares, like Mars, is of a decided red hue.

5. The dates in the *Parki* sector coincide consistently with important dates in the career of Captain Cook. It has been noted that he discovered Christmas Island on December 24, 1777. On the date that Annatoo sees the dial in the tower, February 10, Cook received his commission to command the *Resolution* on its voyage to explore and to make astronomical observations to correct the time at Greenwich. On February 14, the date on which Annatoo is hit by a top block and swept overboard, Captain Cook was killed by a blow on the head. All three of these dated events were calculated for *Mardi* before any research on Cook was done for this study, and I consider the parallels to be too apt for mere coincidence.

The most helpful source for the records of Cook's travels is *The Journals of Captain James Cook on His Voyages of Discovery*, ed. J. C. Beaglehold. Also of interest is John Richman, *Journal of Captain Cook's Last Voyage to the Pacific Ocean*. This book, in an earlier edition, was attributed to Ellis, the ship's doctor.

Another possible link to Cook appears in the title of Chapter 29 of *Mardi*: "What they Lighted upon in Further Searching the Craft, and the Resolution they came to." *Resolution* was the name of one of Cook's ships, the other being the *Discovery*.

often mistaken for her ruler, Mars.[4] Whereas Taurus has no tail, Scorpio has no head, and her long tail coils far down into the "hold" of the southern sky where the Altar, Ara, eternally roasts the "skewer" of Scorpio. Samoa is a teller of tales, but Annatoo is secretive, thereby providing an irony regarding the pun on *tail* and *tale*. Samoa boasts of his prowess as a surgeon, but loses the only patient on whom he operates. Annatoo is the real surgeon—Scorpio is traditionally the sign of surgeons—and successfully amputates Samoa's *arm*, a term lending itself to a pun on weaponry. Taji repeatedly compares Annatoo to a hornet and a wasp, both insects that carry stings in their tails. Although Taji indicates that she is distressingly ugly, he refers to her "Penthesilian Qualities," and Penthesilea, a queen of the Amazons, was as renowned for her beauty as for her valor. As Scorpio, Annatoo is an arachnid and therefore comparable to Arachne, daughter of a dyer. In short, Annatoo is a "disarming" beauty, all heart and all tail, but utterly headless.

The planet Venus has served as the compass in the keg for the *Chamois*, and, like Sol, she has been a "north-seeking" guide. Now the compass on the *Chamois* is replaced by the compass in the binnacle of the *Parki*, though both are lost before the *Chamois* sets sail again. Once Aldebaran rises above the horizon, the true Navigator is available—and just in time, for Venus will turn retrograde and will be unable to serve as compass. While on board the *Parki*, Taji searches for a chronometer and finds evidence that Annatoo destroyed the clock or perhaps ate both the clock and the former captain. The imagery reveals, however, that Annatoo is the avatar of Captain Cook; she is therefore the true captain of the *Parki* and the timekeeper as well.[5] As such she corrects for precession in order that Sol will be in a position for his first major conjunction. Cook himself was a "Scorpio," and his tale of adventure and discovery is both true and extremely long. Like Annatoo's "tail," Cook's tale ends at an altar.

In Samoa we find the first hint of the Dante figure; we know that Dante was born under the sign of Taurus. As Scorpio astrologically symbolizes hell or purgatory, the Taurean Dante is associated with the ascent to heaven through ideal love. Above all, however, stands Samoa's role as artist, as teller of ideal or unreal tales, the truth of which must be taken on faith. Like Cook, Dante explores new worlds, for his seven heavens are the

seven planetary spheres. It is interesting that, although Taji
believes Samoa's tales, Jarl does not—and for good reason: Dante
stops with the seventh planetary heaven, and Jarl represents the
ninth sphere.

*　　　*　　　*

The religious imagery that dominates the *Parki* episode
points up a continuing concern with the development of man's
idea of God and the concomitant strife and misinterpretation.
Annatoo and Samoa represent the Church Militant and its
marriage to the State, but Melville does not make immediately
obvious which is which. Indeed, Samoa's quarters are likened to
the Prayer Room of Peter the Hermit while Annatoo's chest
contains a picture of the Prodigal Son and the Harlots.
Nevertheless, it is Annatoo who frequently retires like a nun to
her devotions, and who keeps her eye on Heaven while she
steers. In this metaphor the sexual problem implied by the
Taurus-Scorpio marriage becomes both ironic and revealing.
Prince Samoa, the half-man, characterized by the short dagger in
his ear rather than by a long sword at his loin, has been deprived
of his arm—and thus of his strength—by excessive war. Though a
picture of power, he is apparently impotent. Conversely, Queen
Annatoo possesses enormous potency that ends in a poisonous
sting—capable, in fact, of inflicting self-destruction. Throughout
the history of the Church Militant, Church and State have
intermittently battled and reconciled, and in the struggle for
material goods, the Church has often had the best of the
controversy. It would seem, then, that Melville equates Samoa to
the domineered and subservient State, while Annatoo portrays
the ambiguous character of the Church, presenting a range of
temperament from that of harridan to saint.

*　　　*　　　*

Annatoo's brief flirtation with Jarl and her subsequent
irritation with him flicks lightly at the Church's relationship to
Christ. The situation seems to imply that the Church at the height
of her power had only a passing interest in Christ, and that He,
in turn, spurned her completely. But this is Taji's story, not

necessarily Melville's. Insofar as Jarl–Neptune represents baptism, initiation, and resurrection, we may assume that Melville's system utilizes death by drowning as a symbol of spiritual benefit. If on the other hand we analyze the episode in terms of its action rather than through Taji's invariably inaccurate character descriptions, we find that the relationship between Jarl and Annatoo has deeper possibilities. When Annatoo makes advances to Jarl, Taji states that Jarl is "swept through and through with a terrible typhoon of passion" (115). Though by *passion* Taji obviously means *anger,* the word also means intense love, both human and divine. We have seen that in the card metaphor Jarl and Annatoo are the King and Queen of Hearts, and the *Almanac* shows that the day of the "advance" is February 14. Thus, when Neptune proposes to commit Annatoo to the sea, his threat is tantamount to a proposal of marriage. The *Almanac* further reveals that Annatoo's Mars is indeed approaching conjunction with Jupiter. In light of the confusion of identities between Jupiter and Neptune, this juxtaposition may be involved in Taji's interpretation of the relationship.

Samoa as Taurus is—as far as is visible—incapable of other than Platonic devotion. Because of his innocence, symbolized by the dagger he uses for a weapon, Samoa has no way of knowing the extent or nature of Annatoo's "virtue." Nevertheless, he proudly intimates that "the lady was the most virtuous of her sex" (115). Samoa, then, has implicit faith in Annatoo, but it is a blind faith. Even so, he has more evidence of Annatoo's possession of virtue than Taji has for intimating her lack of it. Astrologically, Scorpio is cursed with the characteristic of being forever misunderstood, and it would appear that both Samoa and Taji are guilty of misunderstanding Annatoo, each from a different point of view.

XI. Capricorn and Aquarius

> Now, which was Samoa? The dead arm swinging high as
> Haman? Or the living trunk below? Was the arm severed from
> the body, or the body from the arm?   —*Mardi*, 78

One arm of Aquarius, in which Neptune resides during the
year of his discovery, hangs far over the back of the Goat
constellation and is included in the thirty degrees belonging to
the sign of Capricorn, as reckoned by astrologers. Thus, the arm
has been amputated from the sign of Aquarius and hangs over
Capricorn just as the arm of Samoa hangs over the *Chamois*
aboard the *Parki.* As Venus leads her followers into this Air sign,
the imagery of amputation prevails.

We will resume now the day-to-day log of the voyage,
beginning with January 9 and omitting details of the four-month
journey of the *Parki.* She had started from Hawaii in early
October, 1845—the death place and the birth month of Captain
Cook. At this time, Sol had been passing from Virgo into Libra,
house of Venus, and Mars was passing Saturn in Capricorn. Since
the conjunction of Mars with Saturn brings about violent
separations and hostility on the part of others, explosive tempers
and mishaps, and malice, suspicion, and sudden misfortunes, it is
only natural that Samoa and Annatoo should encounter a fearful
experience and that their relationship should be strained. And so
the past history of the *Parki* reveals.

The *Parki* episode may be divided into two parts—the
longer first part dealing with Sol-time and continuing through
February 10, and the brief though crucial section that introduces
Mars-time, setting Sol back ten degrees. The *Parki* sinks on
February 15.

*   *   *

January 9. Jarl's oar shows "sixteen notches on the loom" on
this Friday evening, when Taji sights a ship's spars "traced like a
spider's web [and] looking like a far-off craft on fire." As
previously noted, the loom—in this use, no allusions are made to

the old maid—launches the ascendant horizon into the
constellation Aries, the Ram. Having already described the fat
insect that Jarl fishes from the breaker, Melville now likens the
Parki to a spider's web, introducing a great deal of insectile
imagery surrounding Annatoo. The reference to fire may be
associated with the painful stings of these insects, but also in this
instance with the ascending Fire sign Aries. Taji explains that the
ship's sails can be seen because of the lighting conditions at
evening:

> A sail, invisible in the full flood of noon, becomes perceptible
> toward sunset. It is the reverse in the morning. In sight at gray
> dawn, the distant vessel, though in reality approaching, recedes
> from view, as the sun rises higher and higher. . . . The more light
> you throw on them, the more you obscure. Some revelations show
> best in a twilight. (P. 56)

It is in the double light of ambiguity that the *Parki* must be
viewed by the reader if he is to receive the full revelation
intended by the author, since sunlight is deceptive in more ways
than one.

Upon first sighting the ship, Taji promptly and erroneously
divines that the vessel is a whaler. Coming closer, they see that
she is a brigantine that constantly yaws in her course. This yawing
motion is an important element in the identification of the *Parki*.
We have noted that the ship represents an expansion of the field
of action in order to retain Venus. Additionally, we have
included all of Aquarius, most of Pisces, and the planets Mars
and Uranus—the latter being Taji's other "self" (notice that the
field actually contains Jupiter also, but not officially, for according
to the *Almanac*, Jupiter is behind the *Parki* sector at *tau*
Capricorn). Uranus, though now positioned in Pisces, is the ruler
—with Saturn—of Aquarius, so the *Parki* actually "belongs" in
large part to Taji. The *Chamois* or Capricorn sector, with the arm
of Aquarius, is partly included. Since the conventions of astrology
posit that a sign takes on the character of its ruling planet, and
since Uranus is the "yawing" planet whose wobbling orbit
indicates the presence of Neptune, the *Parki* is described as
constantly yawing in her course. Because Uranus is *in* Pisces,
Aleema's canoe, encountered later, also yaws in its course.

Moreover, Taji describes Samoa–Taurus as lacking an arm, and Samoa's ruling planet Venus is in Aquarius. The amputated arm of Aquarius therefore represents the more severe amputation of the Bull, who lacks hindquarters.

Despite Taji's reluctance to board the *Parki,* the subtle Jarl knows exactly how to persuade his saturnine companion to do so:

> Not a little terrified at the sight, superstitious Jarl more than insinuated that the craft must be a gold-huntress, haunted. But I told him, that if such were the case, we must board her, come gold or goblins. In reality, however, I began to think that she must have been abandoned by her crew; or else, that from sickness, those on board were incapable of managing her. (P. 57)

Once tempted by the possibility of finding gold and reassured by his conclusion that there is no one dangerous on board, Taji is eager to explore the boat. "We came still nearer, using our oars, but very reluctantly on Jarl's part." Taji infers that this reluctance pertains to approaching the brigantine, though it is equally possible that Jarl is merely averse to rowing. With due caution and quite properly, since one rows backward, Jarl looks over his shoulder while rowing; Taji makes this act seem cowardly. As they spring on board, Jarl snatches "his harpoon, his favorite arms."

The religious imagery now begins in full force, as Taji is maneuvered into unwittingly taking his First Communion during this night. They light two candles and enter the "smallest and murkiest den in the world. The altar-like transom . . . closed dead-lights . . . dim little sky-light . . . somber aspect" gave an air of "some subterranean oratory, say a Prayer Room of Peter the Hermit" (59).[1] Here they find a "large box, sheathed with iron and stoutly clamped," though this armor fails to prevent Taji from breaking into it. It contains "a keg partly filled with powder, the half of an old cutlass, a pouch of bullets, and a case for a sextant." Notice the incomplete nature of each item here—a half portion of everything being appropriate for a "half-man." Taji finds the broken and stained blade of the cutlass so "tragical" that he thrusts it out of sight. We have already noted Taji's melancholy tendency to find tragedy in all things, consistent with his nature not only as artist but as *tragos,* the Goat. The

1. The reference to Peter the Hermit carries several connotations in addition to his historical role as an instigator of the First Crusade. For the Tarot reader it is another issue of Trump Number 9. For the astrologer it provides another clue as to the emergence of Mars, for Aries, house of Mars, is in Christian astrology given to Saint Peter, the battling fisherman who cut off a centurion's ear. The association of Saint Peter with the phallic sign of Mars lends a sexual connotation to the image—or rather, a confirmation of a sexual image already vaguely evident.

broken blade, like Samoa's dagger, seems to present another symbol of impotence—tragedy enough for Taji. This cabin will later be identified as Samoa's quarters in the stern of the *Parki*. We might even go so far as to note that the cabin is Samoa's "rear quarters" and to wonder if Melville is punning on "Peter the Hermit" as well as on the broken blade. Certainly Samoa's marital relationship warrants the assumption.

At any rate, Taji appropriates a musket and a cutlass, while Jarl refrains from thievery and relies on his harpoon. They proceed to the forecastle where they find a "snug little lair" and a sailor's chest. Regardless of Jarl's entreaties, Taji breaks into the box and finds, along with feminine garb, "greenish Carolus dollars (true coin all)." He is inspired to paeans on the subject of wealth: "The dollars rang like convent bells." As Jarl confiscates the coins and lays them aside, Taji imputes his own greed to Jarl: "the sight of substantial dollars doing away, for the nonce, with his superstitious misgivings. True to his kingship, he loved true coin."

Taji also breaks into a little hair trunk found in the forecastle. The trunk contains three pewter mugs, parts of a quadrant, beads, rings, and a print depicting the Prodigal Son with the Harlots. Since Annatoo is quartered in the forecastle, this is her trunk, and she is in possession of the quadrant. The rest of the items are quite appropriate for Lady Mars of Scorpio— her rosary, wedding ring, and religious icon.

Now occurs an important and revealing event, as a top block falls to the deck and narrowly misses "my Viking's crown; a much stronger article, by the way, than your goldsmiths turn out these days." It is reported later that Annatoo hurled the top block at the intruders, so it is appropriate that her career ends when, through Jarl's actions, she is struck on the "head" by a top block. Let us notice, however, the reference to Jarl's crown: Neptune wears an iron crown, which is, as Taji states, stronger than gold.[2] The Viking's kingship is receiving more emphasis now, and the "laundress and sempstress" are neglected. Taji also admits that Jarl—the old experienced sailor—is startled by the falling block, while he himself, having many a time dodged stray blocks accidentally falling from aloft, "thought little of it." These falling blocks may be added to the list of hazing activities on board the *Arcturion,* for Taji is all too "youthful"—at least by his

2. Traditionally, Neptune's crown was of iron rather than gold, and this may have enabled Melville to draw a connection between Neptune and the iron crown of the Lombards through the image of the bride of the Doges: cf. *Moby Dick,* Chapter 37, as Ahab muses: "Is, then, the crown too heavy that I wear? this Iron Crown of Lombardy."

own self-image—to have so exceeded Jarl in his experienced dodging of stray blocks, "accidentally falling." We can probably assume that dropping blocks on Taji during the voyage of the *Arcturion* was a favorite sport of his shipmates, including Jarl.

Despite his disclaimers, Taji longs for day. Even though he believes that the brigantine is untenanted, he is nervous in the dark. He sends Jarl to the quarterdeck to search out line and sinker, but Jarl returns, whispering that "there were spirits aboard to a dead certainty. He had overheard a supernatural sneeze"—in the maintop at that. Taji protests that he was standing directly under the maintop and heard nothing. Since Jarl turns out to be correct again, we are justified in assuming that Taji not only has eyes and sees not, as mentioned in Chapter 1, but also has ears and hears not. Moreover, since Melville has already committed one pun on "spirits" (23), we might suspect the possibility that while on the quarterdeck Jarl found the captain's grog supply—a factor to be recalled later when Jarl and Samoa tend to sleep a great deal and when Taji finds and hides one cask of Otard.

Jarl continues throughout the dark hours to hear the movements of persons on board, and Taji continues to accuse him of cowardice and superstition. Nevertheless, when Jarl challenges him to climb the mast to look for evidence, Taji declares that "here my mature judgment got the better of my first crude opinion. I civilly declined." Though admitting the possibility of live, inimical people aboard, he fears that he might climb the mast only to be tumbled by "some unseen arm." There is in fact an arm aloft—but it is dead. Clearly, it is Taji who fears ghosts.

At last Jarl pronounces the *Parki* "an arrant imposter, a shade of a ship, full of sailors' ghosts, and before we knew where we were, would dissolve in a supernatural squall, and leave us twain in the water." His statement proves to be precisely true, for Jarl is indeed acquainted with the land of goblins and goblets. He entreats Taji to leave the "ill-starred craft, carrying off nothing from her ghostly hull." But Taji refuses. Notice here that Jarl "entreats" Taji to leave. We are not told that Jarl suggests that they both leave. Jarl, who has carefully refrained from vandalism, might well have suggested that his companion move back to the *Chamois* and cease his depredations.

3. The Book of Daniel, from which a great deal of the imagery of *Mardi* is taken, contains a long account of the future quest for power of the Goat–King, his rise, and his downfall. A reading of the entire Book of Daniel is helpful in gaining an insight into the astrological interpretation of *Mardi*.

"One cannot relate every thing at once," states Taji, and then describes the bread-barge whose ornamentation describes and relates together the major themes of *Mardi,* including divers diagrams in chalk, to connote undersea geology, and drawings of old Finnish mariners, who cast horoscopes and prophesied. "Your old tars are all Daniels," says Taji—despite his disbelief of Jarl's ominous foretellings. With this line also, Melville indicates that sailors are, more often than not, able to cast horoscopes, himself included.[3]

Finally, the bread-barge may be identified with the body of Christ. It has "a round hole in one side, through which, in getting at the bread, invited guests thrust their hands." The allusion is to Doubting Thomas, but the incident is parallel to a Communion of which Taji is unaware.

> And mighty was the thrusting of hands that night; also, many and earnest the glances of Mustapha at every sudden creaking of the spars or rigging. Like Belshazzar, my royal Viking ate with great fear and trembling; ever and anon pausing to watch the wild shadows flitting along the bulwarks. (P. 64)

In Taji's allusion to "the Grand Turk and his Vizier Mustapha sitting down before Vienna," he does not identify which of the pair is to fill the role of Grand Turk, leaving the reader to attribute that royal reference to Taji himself. However, since Jarl is likened to King Belshazzar, the role of the frightened vizier is left for Taji. As for Jarl, he is blessed with double vision, for the wild shadows flitting across the bulwarks are those, as we discover later, of Samoa the Bull flitting from one mast to the other. It also refers to the Handwriting on the Wall, from Daniel—an omen of events to come. The reference to Belshazzar is again ambiguous, for Jarl is not Belshazzar but Daniel, who can read correctly the shadows moving on the bulwarks.

*   *   *

January 10. Morning breaks, and Taji and Jarl discover Samoa on the maintop and Annatoo on the foretop. Descending, Samoa relates an adventurous tale that covers four months and six chapters, bringing the matter up to date for a continuance of the main story in Chapter 29. Here, the subject of art and interpretation receives considerable attention, for Taji, seeking the *Parki*'s log, discovers that it is missing and attributes the loss to Annatoo's aversion to literature. He does find a page, however, that presents a tragedy susceptible to two meanings:

> "This day, being calm, Tooboi, one of the Lahina men, went overboard for a bath, and was eaten up by a shark. Immediately sent forward for his bag." (P. 94)

> Aside of the paragraph, copied above, was a pen-and-ink sketch of the casualty, most cruelly executed; the poor fellow's legs being represented half way in the process of deglutition; his arms firmly grasping the monster's teeth, as if heroically bent upon making as tough a morsel of himself as possible.[4] (P. 95)

4. William Ellis, *Polynesian Researches,* I, 306.

Taji refers to this sketch as an "unwonted embellishment" possibly created by an artist once engaged in whaling:

> And the chief mate, whose duty it is to keep the ship's record, generally prides himself upon the beauty, and flushy likeness to life, of his flukes; though, sooth to say, many of these artists are no Landseers. (P. 95)

The outrageous pun on the name of the artist known for his drawings of animals contains several implications. Obviously, the mariners see very little land. And like Landseer, they often impose human attributes to the animals they draw—as Taji will increasingly demonstrate, and as Ahab also does in *Moby Dick.* The point is that these artists embellish their works, and Taji—himself an artist in that sense at least—is again drawing attention to the principle of creative exaggeration.

Samoa having convinced Taji of the veracity of his story, Taji forthwith informs the couple that, although nothing would please him more than a return to the scene of the massacre that disarmed Samoa to "chastise its surviving authors," it would be more prudent to remain on their present course. The command of the vessel is tacitly yielded up to Taji; that is, nobody *says* he is in command. The *Parki* is made shipshape, for which its crew was "mostly indebted to my Viking's unwearied and skillful marling-spike, which he swayed like a scepter." Jarl stands at the helm and guides the *Parki* "like some devoted old foster-father."

> As I stood by his side like a captain, or walked up and down on the quarter-deck, I felt no little importance upon thus assuming for the first time in my life, the command of a vessel at sea. The novel circumstances of the case only augmented this feeling; the wild and remote seas where we were; the character of my crew, and the consideration, that to all purposes, I was owner, as well as commander of the craft I sailed. (P. 97)

Though Taji assumes that he is in command, his commission is as fictitious as any novel, for Jarl still holds the sharp-pointed marling-spike scepter. And while Taji is in one sense the true owner of the *Parki,* he has claimed possession under false pretenses.

*   *   *

Chapter 30 is devoted to a "full length" portrait of Samoa, expressed in a plethora of word-play. A "man of mark," Samoa is an "obelisk" in stature. Since the obelisk is the dagger-mark that takes the place of the asterisk on a second footnote, we may be already alarmed about his stature, though we must bear in mind that the huge stelleration of Taurus is shaped like a dagger blade or like a tower. Carefully, Melville contrasts Samoa's practice of wearing a knife in his right ear to that of the Highlander who uses his leggings for this purpose.[5]

> But it was the mother of Samoa, who at a still earlier day had punctured him through and through in still another direction. The middle cartilage of his nose was slightly pendent, peaked, and Gothic, and perforated with a hole; in which, like a Newfoundland dog carrying a cane, Samoa sported a trinket: a well polished nail. (P. 98)

Samoa's resemblance to the front half of a bull continues to develop as we learn that he wears, not the traditional ring in his nose, but its opposite symbol, the nail. Taji describes him, moreover, as a coxcomb; this suggestive expression places all his sexual potential on the top of his head, where his horns are. His

5. On many ships, the initiate's ear lobe was pierced with an awl, and a single gold earring marked him as a shellback.

tattoo marks cover only the "vertical half of his person; the other side being free from the slightest stain." Since the stance of Taurus is horizontally oriented, his hind-quarters concealed by the full length of Aries the Ram, Melville leaves us no choice but to identify the tattoo as the Pleiades, a small stelleration on the Bull's shoulder. At the same time, we find greater meaning in the subsequent description: "Thus clapped together, as it were, he looked like a union of the unmatched moieties of two distinct beings; and your fancy was lost in conjecturing, where roamed the absent ones." In noting the interesting juxtaposition of Taurus and Aries, we should recall that Aries is the other house of Annatoo's Mars.

> But there was one feature in Samoa beyond the reach of the innovations of art:—his eye; which in civilized man or savage, ever shines in the head, just as it shone at birth. Truly, our eyes are miraculous things. But alas, that in so many instances, these divine organs should be mere lenses inserted into the socket, as glasses in spectacle rims.
>
> But my Islander had a soul in his eye; looking out upon you there, like somebody in him. What an eye, to be sure! At times, brilliantly changeful as opal; in anger, glowing like steel at white heat. (P. 99)

The brightest star in Taurus is the Bull's Eye, also called the Navigator Star, and Samoa is revealed as a Upoluan, of the Navigator Isles, his name having been given him by a sea captain.

From the history of the *Parki* we know that the travels of Samoa and Annatoo have taken them to Hawaii, where Captain Cook met his end at the hands of an island chief, and since Annatoo is the avatar of Captain Cook, we might wonder if the "soul" in Samoa's eye is that of an island chief undergoing a purgatorial revenge at the hands of his erstwhile victim.

Regarding the faceless heart of Scorpio–Annatoo, Taji can "make no pleasing portrait of the dame. . . . The only ugliness is that of the heart, seen through the face. And though beauty is obvious, the only loveliness is invisible." Since Annatoo has no face, and her heart is visible, Taji's remark is highly ambiguous.

*   *   *

As time passes aboard the *Parki,* Taji explores the ship's
"tragic hull" as if it were "haunted by some marvelous story."
Indeed, Taji compares Annatoo to a tragedy queen, and, given
this much perception, it is surprising that he fails to recognize the
tragedy involved, since he later shows knowledge of Captain
Cook's history. As Saturn, Taji can explore the stern of the ship,
while Uranus can lounge in the foretop or descend to the
forecastle. Though Taurus is rising, Aldebaran still lies below the
solar horizon, so Samoa is "rather reserved." Annatoo serves at
the helm, though Jarl appears to feel that "there was a slight
drawback upon her usefulness." Indeed, a headless helmsman is
an anomaly; Taji observes that she is too much "taken up by her
lovely image partially reflected in the glass of the binnacle before
her." The image in the binnacle is that of the Venus compass, the
"asterisk," which the headless Annatoo can claim for her own
until the "obelisk" of Taurus is fully risen.

In his explorations, conducted "with a glimmering light,"
Taji has "lighted upon sundry out-of-the-way hiding places of
Annatoo's; where were snugly secreted divers articles, with which
she had been smitten." In this wording, Melville draws ever
closer to the murder of Cook, who was smitten and killed by the
various weapons of the island divers in Hawaii. Taji continues, "I
found a jaunty shore cap of the captain's, hidden away in the
hollow heart of a coil of rigging; covered over in a manner most
touchingly natural" (101–2). Melville provides a graphic
description of Annatoo's constellation as Taji sees, deep in the
hold, "a huge ground-tier butt, headless as Charles the First." For
future reference, we might also note Annatoo's neatness. She had
long busied herself about cleaning barnacles from the side of the
Parki, and now Taji reports that in her lair "was a mat nicely
spread for repose." These details become significant when Media
appears as Captain Cook's next avatar.

Melville concludes the chapter by challenging his reader to
solve the riddle of Annatoo:

But now the problem was solved. Here, in this silent cask in the hold, Annatoo was wont to coil herself away, like a garter-snake under a stone.

Whether she thus stood sentry over her goods secreted round about: whether she here performed penance like a nun in her cell; or was moved to this unaccountable freak by the powers of the air; no one could tell. Can you?

Verily, her ways were as the ways of the inscrutable penguins in building their inscrutable nests, which baffle all science, and make a fool of a sage.

Marvelous Annatoo! who shall expound thee? (P. 102)

In Taji's obvious desire to "pound" Annatoo, we find a recollection of the many natives who "pounded" Cook.[6]

January 26–31, Monday through Saturday. Since January 20 Sol has been in the sign of Aquarius. On the twenty-sixth, Venus is at greatest brilliance and Luna is at perigee. The following day brings the new moon. Melville marks this week of the transit of Luna with another finny list and another binge for Taji. During his previous ichthyological tourney, Taji severed the wing of a flying fish. Here, in Chapter 32 he disarms a swordfish chevalier amid such pronounced phallic imagery that one might suspect him of reenacting the myth of Cronus and Uranus, now combined into one, and castrating himself. At the same time, he previews his bout with Aleema, soon to come in the next new moon, and informs that, though Bayard's sword may have slain its scores, the blade of the swordfish had "riddled its thousands." Again we are challenged to solve a riddle, and we might note here that in some ancient Greek zodiacs, Capricorn was drawn as a swordfish.

After lifting his sword to the brilliance of Venus, Taji turns to his cups to toast the transit of Luna. In Chapter 33, Taji further reveals his saturnine character when, upon finding a keg of Otard, he philosophizes his way toward a prudent ethic of keeping his discovery to himself, since Jarl, Samoa, and Annatoo, on separate judicious counts, should not undergo the temptations inherent in exposure to the "double distilled soul of the precious grape." Instead, Taji resolves to appropriate the spirit-cask for medicinal purposes.

February 3. As Luna makes her first quarter turn, the *Parki*

6. Annatoo's relationship to Scorpio, and hence to the serpent, might be recalled later when Vee-Vee releases a snake from under a stone. *Mardi,* p. 573.

also turns, and Taji provides the last earthly coordinates to appear in the book:

> When we quitted the Chamois for the brigantine, we must have been at least two hundred leagues to the westward of the spot, where we had abandoned the Arcturion. Though how far we might then have been, North or South of the Equator, I could not with any certainty divine.
>
> But that we were not removed any considerable distance from the Line, seemed obvious. For in the starriest night no sign of the extreme Polar constellations was visible. . . . So far as regards the aspect of the skies near the ocean's rim, the difference of several degrees in one's latitude at sea, is readily perceived by a person long accustomed to surveying the heavens. (P. 108)

We recall that in the *Chamois* Jarl noted a northward drift. According to the charts, at ten degrees north of the Line the currents turn to the east. Having circled around the western side of Christmas Island, the group now encounters this eastward current and moves backward through the shoals and reefs of the Line Islands.

February 4–14. During this week, Taji, having "cajoled" himself into the notion that he is captain of the *Parki,* becomes a pest and a busybody. Despite his card-game comment that "he who is ready to despair in solitary peril, plucks up a heart in the presence of another," he shows himself to be in a constant state of delusion and panic, especially at night:

> Though in the joyous sunlight, sailing through the sparkling sea, I was little troubled with serious misgivings; in the hours of darkness it was quite another thing. And the apprehensions, nay terrors I felt, were much augmented by the remissness of both Jarl and Samoa, in keeping their night-watches. Several times I was seized with a deadly panic, and earnestly scanned the murky horizon, when rising from slumber I found the steersman, in whose hands for the time being were life and death, sleeping upright against the tiller, as much of a fixture there, as the open-mouthed dragon rudely carved on our prow.
>
>   .   .   .   .   .
>
> Samoa's aspect, sleeping at the tiller, was almost appalling. His large opal eyes were half open; and turned toward the light of the binnacle, gleamed between the lids like bars of flame. And added to all, was his giant stature and savage lineaments. (P. 109)

With Samoa watching the "pinochle" and Jarl "deceitfully secure" in a "double-deck," we may be sure that a game is in progress that Taji does not comprehend. The imagery indicates that Samoa, Jarl, and Annatoo know where they are going, for Samoa watches the compass, Annatoo watches the "Navigator," and Jarl has at all times watched the currents and the time.

For those readers who have been using the sky-map-calendar, Melville now commissions Lady Cook to make the necessary corrections in the celestial clock:

> It has been mentioned, that Annatoo took her turn at the helm;
> but it was only by day. And in justice to the lady, I must affirm,
> that upon the whole she acquitted herself well. For
> notwithstanding the syren face in the binnacle, which dimly
> allured her glances, Annatoo after all was tolerably heedful of her
> steering. Indeed she took much pride therein; always ready for her
> turn; with marvelous exactitude calculating the approaching hour,
> as it came on in regular rotation. Her time-piece was ours, the
> sun. By night it must have been her guardian star; for frequently
> she gazed up at a particular section of the heavens, like one
> regarding the dial in a tower. (P. 110)

Until February 10, the true position of Sol is unimportant. His only conjunctions have been with Mercury and Luna, and neither of these has been provided with stellar coordinates, so their conjunctions have been indefinite. On January 22, the *Almanac* has information about Jupiter, but again, a confused typesetter, possibly afflicted with pied type, has made an error in regard to Jupiter. Instead of the glyph for *square,* the one for Gemini

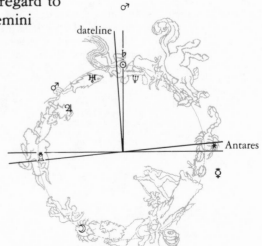

February 10, 1846

This drawing illustrates the correction for precession that occurs on the *Parki,* by allusion to the dial in a tower. Henceforth, Sol is set ten degrees behind the dateline. Note that the descendant horizon had already passed Antares in Scorpio (left side); the correction resets the horizon line so that Antares remains in the field of action. Note also that Sol is conjunct Saturn and that without the correction, Sol overshoots his mark.

appears on the *Almanac*'s calendar page, and the entry reads "♊♃." Here again, judicious interpretation is essential if the true location of either Jupiter or Sol is to be determined; but Taji is a literalist, and the entry is meaningless to him. Such vagueness is no longer feasible, however, because on February 10 Sol is conjunct Saturn, and Saturn's location is accurately recorded in the *Almanac*. Before Sol passes Saturn, he also passes Neptune, and for this conjunction he must be on time.

Taji reports that he has appointed Samoa to steer at night but that he now decides to "let Annatoo take her turn at the night watches." The sky-map-calendar shows that on February 10 Aldebaran rises into the solar hemisphere, while Antares sinks into the night sky. But Annatoo is not yet ready to sink. Therefore, on February 4, while the first-quarter or so-called half-moon is at *epsilon* Taurus, Annatoo takes her last astronomical observation. Note Taji's comment: "Her time-piece was the sun, and at night it must have been her guardian star; for frequently she gazed up at a particular section of the heavens, like one regarding the dial in a tower." What she sees there is indeed the "dial in a tower," that is, the half-moon in the Gothic point of the nose of Taurus, which to her is the Dial of Ahaz. For us, the

The Dial of Ahaz

This well-known device enables Melville to correct for precession by setting the sun ten degrees behind the dateline as established by the classical sky-map-calendar. The precision with which this correction enables Sol to make his conjunction with Saturn at the correct degree on February 10 makes it near certain that Melville did utilize one of the sixteenth-century sky-map-calendars such as the Apianus map shown on the frontispiece.

(From Fowler, *Spenser and the Numbers of Time*, p. 75.)

reference means to turn Sol and the horizon lines ten degrees
back. The instruction is a subtle one, for some readers might well
be able to follow the time-line without using the
sky-map-calendar, while others may use a version in which the
correction would be unnecessary. For readers of the old calendars
it is essential; otherwise, when the *Almanac* reports Saturn
conjunct Sol, a ten-degree discrepancy results. The correction
places Sol in precisely the spot for his conjunction with Neptune
and Saturn. Henceforth, Sol rides ten degrees behind the
dateline.

February 14: Saturday, Valentine's Day. Taji complains that
Annatoo

> gave herself mighty airs at the tiller; with extravagant gestures
> issuing unintelligible orders about trimming the sails, or pitching
> overboard something to see how fast we were going. All this
> much diverted my Viking, who several times was delivered of a
> laugh; a loud and healthy one to boot: a phenomenon worthy the
> chronicling. (P. 110)

Taji assumes that Jarl is laughing at the stupidity of Annatoo, but
we, knowing that Annatoo is Captain Cook, suspect that she has
proposed pitching the pesky Jonah, Taji; hence Jarl's phenomenal
ability to give birth to a laugh.

Even though Sol has been reversed, the fourteenth has at last
arrived, and Antares sinks below the solar horizon. Taji notes
that Annatoo had "of late grown exceedingly friendly" to Jarl—a
sentiment suited to Valentine's Day, when, as Chaucer notes,
even the birds choose their mates. Since Annatoo's Mars is now
speeding through Jarl's sign of Pisces, and since Jarl and Annatoo
are the King and Queen of Hearts, there may be more to the
friendliness than Taji suspects. To be sure, Mars is approaching
conjunction with Jupiter, and Taji has confused Jupiter with
Neptune; therefore, his impressions may be influenced by his
error.

Meanwhile, Taji confirms that the *Parki* has met the easterly
currents:

> For while making no onward progress through the water, the
> rapid currents we encountered would continually be drifting us

eastward; since, contrary to our previous experience, they seemed
latterly to have reversed their flow, a phenomenon by no means
unusual in the vicinity of the Line in the Pacific. And this it was
that so prolonged our passage to the westward. . . . we were in
reality almost a fixture on the sea. (P. 111)

Though Taji desires to continue his westward course by sailing
throughout the night, Jarl recommends that they "heave the ship
to" at nights, thereby "stopping her headway till morning."
Through Taji's words, Melville again issues a challenge to the
reader:

> The equatorial currents of the South Seas may be regarded as
> among the most mysterious of the mysteries of the deep. Whence
> they come, whither go, who knows? Tell us, what hidden law
> regulates their flow. Regardless of the theory which ascribes to
> them a nearly uniform course from east to west, induced by the
> eastwardly winds of the Line, and the collateral action of the Polar
> streams; these currents are forever shifting. Nor can the period of
> their revolutions be at all relied upon or predicted. (P. 111)

By the time Melville sailed the Pacific, the equatorial currents
had been fairly well charted, thanks partly to the efforts of
Captain Cook. But in any case, Jarl desires to hold back the
eastward progress of the *Parki,* and it is possible that he has in
mind an appointment for Taji. Meanwhile, the saturnine Taji
continues his philosophizing and notes

> that the ocean, according to the popular theory, possesses a special
> purifying agent in its salts, is somewhat to be doubted. Nor can it
> be explicitly denied, that those very salts might corrupt it, were it
> not for the brisk circulation of its particles consequent upon the
> flow of the streams. It is well known to seamen, that a bucket of
> sea-water, left standing in a tropical climate, very soon becomes
> highly offensive; which is not the case with rain-water. (Pp.
> 111–12)

However, Taji "builds no theories" but suggests that the
offensiveness may derive from "the presence of decomposed
animal matter," such as deceased insects. Melville, meanwhile,
has drawn attention to the ocean currents that can be checked on
the chart or globe.

From this comment Taji goes directly to a description of Annatoo, thereby balancing the picture of Samoa at the beginning of the *Parki* sector. In Chapter 35, Taji finds a wooden box full of weapons that Samoa claims to have thrice rescued from "Annatoo's all appropriating clutches."[7] To Taji's horror, he finds that the binnacle is empty (recall that Venus became retrograde on February 7), and the compass has been "abstracted."[8] Immediately Taji accuses Annatoo of theft, "but her face was a blank." Already what passes for the head of Scorpio is below the horizon, while Mars is racing toward Jupiter and toward his other kingdom of Aries, which prompts the statement that Annatoo "had occasionally cast sheep's eyes at Jarl." Now, however, her attitude changes and she seems "innocent as a lamb." She "looks another way," pinches him, and makes wry faces, expressing deep contempt. Inquiring the reason, Taji learns "that with eye averted, she had very lately crept close to my Viking, and met with no tender reception." Again, it is Jupiter, not Neptune, who is the target of Annatoo's "contempt," but to Taji it is all one.

As the heart and body of Scorpio descend below the horizon, "her skewer is broken," and she may be considered sunk.

Now Taji tells us that the ship is in a calm, and, knowing his tendency to become frantic during a calm, we understand that his behavior during the past few days has resulted from this condition. He has already declared that the *Parki* was "in reality almost a fixture on the sea" and that "a terrible typhoon of passion" was brewing. The calm begins on February 12, and the typhoon occurs on the evening of February 14. "Jarl, who was foremost of all," snatches an axe and begins to cut down masts and lanyards.

> The remaining lanyards parted. From the violent strain upon them, the two shrouds flew madly into the air, and one of the great blocks at their ends, striking Annatoo upon the forehead, she let go her hold upon a stanchion, and sliding across the aslant deck, was swallowed up in the whirlpool under our lee. (P. 117)

The "two shrouds" that flew madly into the air present an interesting image in light of the chapter title, "The Parki Gives

7. At the time of his death, Captain Cook had forbidden his crew to use weapons against the natives. J. C. Beaglehold, ed., *The Journals of Captain James Cook on His Voyages of Discovery*, III, Part 2, 1205. Cook's death is best described by Samwell, pp. 1197–1216.

8. Recall here Taji's "abstraction" of the *Chamois* (Chapter 7) considered in its rhetorical sense as a separation of an object or idea by the operation of the mind alone.

Up the Ghost." As Jarl had insisted, the *Parki* has indeed been a ship haunted by ghosts, goblins, and goblets. Now the *Parki* rights herself, and Taji exults that they "for the time being were saved, my own royal Viking our savior."

*   *   *

February 15. The *Chamois* is launched, and Taji, Jarl, and Samoa transfer to the smaller boat, now occupying the same sextile as heretofore and containing Neptune, Saturn, and the retrograde Venus. Sol is in the sector, but not in the boat. Now Taji fully reveals his capacity for reporting that which he cannot possibly know:

> To a seaman, a ship is no piece of mechanism merely; but a creature of thoughts and fancies, instinct with life. Standing at her vibrating helm, you feel her beating pulse. I have loved ships, as I have loved men.
>
> To abandon the poor Parki was like leaving to its fate something that could feel. It was meet that she should die decently and bravely.
>
> All this thought the Skyeman. (P. 120)

To show his love for the *Parki,* something that could feel, Jarl buries his axe in the splintered stump of the mainmast, which, incidentally, is where Samoa's arm was hanging. Unwittingly, Taji

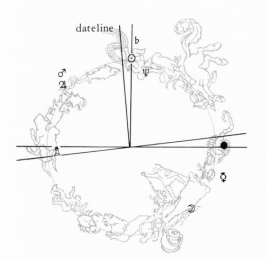

February 15, 1846

The correction for precession having allowed Antares a brief respite, the day nevertheless arrives in which she must sink below the solar horizon. At the same time, Aldebaran, the Bull's Eye, becomes the ascendant star. As Antares sinks below the horizon on the descendant, the planet Mars passes Jupiter and moves into Aries on the ascending side. In the masculine house of Mars, Annatoo is metamorphosed to Media.

pays tribute to Annatoo, heart of Scorpio, as he remarks:
"Quitting the sinking Parki, my heart sunk with her."

*   *   *

February 16. As Mars passes Jupiter and moves into Aries,
Annatoo undergoes the sea change that is to transform her from
a heart to a club—from a water insect to a firefly. The imagery of
the shark that prefigures the ghost of Aleema recurs:

> Starting, we beheld the ocean of a pallid white color, corruscating
> all over with tiny golden sparkles. But the pervading hue of the
> water cast a cadaverous gleam upon the boat, so that we looked to
> each other like ghosts. . . . The tracks of sharks were denoted by
> vivid, greenish trails. (P. 121)

This is the last time Taji will take a scientific attitude toward this
phenomenon, for henceforth the "greenish trail" will represent
Taji's agonized conscience. Now, however, he discusses the
matter with aplomb, mentioning previous experiences, in
particular one off the coast of Peru: "And rushing on deck, [we]
beheld the sea white as a shroud; for which reason it was feared
we were on soundings." Again, with this description, we receive
notice that the *Chamois* is "on soundings" and near land.

> Dismissing, as destitute of sound philosophic probability, the
> extravagant notion of one of my nautical friends—no less a
> philosopher than my Viking himself—namely: that the
> phosphorescence of the sea is caused by a commotion among the
> mermaids, whose golden locks, all torn and disheveled, do
> irradiate the waters at such times; I proceed to record more
> reliable theories. (P. 123)

By this verbal gymnastic, Taji implies that Jarl made the
superstitious statement about the mermaids, but he does not in
fact say so. Instead, he says that the nautical friend is as much a
philosopher as Jarl. After turning again to the subject of
putrescent matter, Taji finally exchanges science for sentiment:

> A French naturalist maintains, that the nocturnal radiance of the
> fire-fly is purposely intended as an attraction to the opposite sex;

that the artful insect illuminates its body for a beacon to love.
Thus: perched upon the edge of a leaf, and waiting the approach
of her Leander, who comes buffeting with his wings the aroma of
the flowers, some insect Hero may show a torch to her gossamer
gallant. (Pp. 123–24)

Once more the buffoon cites Buffon, as the insectile Annatoo
becomes a Hero, signaling Jarl to meet her in Aquarius in three
years.

*   *   *

February 20. Luna, passing through Scorpio (that is, through
Ophiuchus, north of Scorpio), and into the winter side of the
zodiac, is waning. Aleema the Priest comes to take Yillah away
from the summery isle of Ardair and to transport her to Oroolia
via Tedaidee. Sol moves into the sign of Pisces, though he is still
in the constellation Aquarius.

XII. Transition

Rear View of the Parki

If your Otard magazine be exposed to view—then, in the evil hour of wreck, stave in your spirit-casks, ere rigging the life-boat. —*Mardi*, 107

Taji tells us that the story of the *Parki* is all "an episode, made up of digressions" (92). An etymological enthusiast, Melville must be fully aware that *episode* stems from *epi hoda,* or "tail," especially since the statement follows a digression concerned with ship names "(Scorpions, Hornets, and Wasps)." Indeed, the *Parki* section is not one but two "tails," one an ideal tale, the other a very real and tragic one. Samoa's Taurean story is, to use a vulgarism, sheer "bull," while Annatoo's untold tale of a brutally martyred captain carries a sting.

The episode is also a love story between Captain Cook and his beloved sea: the adventures of Mars through Neptune's kingdom of Pisces. The information that Annatoo is the resurrected figure of a great captain and nutritionist from "an island far to the westward" reveals that we are indeed dealing in avatars.[1] Annatoo, the Shellback Scorpion, is soon to be recreated as the avatar of the Boar, to return to Scorpio via the summer side of the "Ark." Concurrent with her history is the love story of Venus and Mars, told in the sparring between her and Samoa. Nevertheless, this affair is a mere myth, like the mermaids.

The real tragedy is that Taji has not yet recognized his companion as the Sea-King. Ever the literalist, he cannot perceive that which is hidden. Here Taji, the "Landseer" who cannot see land despite all the usual signs, has been offered a choice between Dante—now in the purgatory of life with a termagant, and Cook, now relentlessly haunting the island chief who dismembered him. Fancy or fact; literature or life; and Taji opts for the company of the Bull.

With the sinking of the *Parki,* the spirit-cask of Aquarius has been stove in.

1. Captain Cook's other, and in some opinions equal, claim to renown is his exploration into the subject of nautical diet. He initiated the regular use of greens and vegetables that enabled him to remain at sea for years without a single case of scurvy among his crew. As his ships visited the various islands, he left animals for breeding purposes and planted food crops for later harvesting on return visits.

Pisces   But let the sea-fowls fly on: turn we to the fish. —*Mardi*, 148

February 24. Nine days after the sinking of the *Parki,* the *Chamois* is wedged between the two prows of Jupiter's houses, Pisces and Sagittarius, represented by the double canoe of Aleema. The polar radials run from the tip end of Scorpio's stinger to the last star in the horn of Taurus—the Dagger, el Nath. Sol has barely reached the first star in Pisces. Jupiter is moving out of Pisces and into Aries, and the time has come for Neptune to claim his sign. With Jupiter influenced by conjunction with Mars, the outcome is battle.

Neptune, however, cannot reach Jupiter, for he is in Aquarius and Jupiter is in Pisces and out of aspect, Taji has one planet in Capricorn and one in Pisces and can therefore be used as a catspaw for Neptune's purposes.

By this time we are in possession of certain facts that can help in the interpretation of this mock theomachia. First, Jarl–Neptune, fully in control, is aware of the date; second, he has an ignorant tar to initiate, and that tar must pass through the full range of experience, including murder, during the nine months of his development. And third, Jupiter is moving out of Pisces and into the summer side of the zodiac and can no longer retain his identity as Aleema. Like Annatoo, Aleema must suffer his sea change. In a ritual battle, Jupiter yields Pisces to Neptune, and the author of the deed is one well experienced in such legal matters, for he established the precedent in 1781 when Uranus ousted Saturn from Aquarius. In order to remind Taji how such

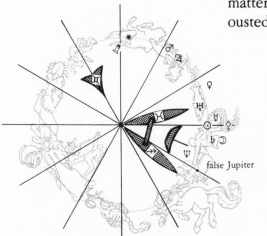

false Jupiter

February 24, 1846

The double canoe of Aleema represents the Jovian signs of Sagittarius and Pisces, plus the twin sign of Gemini. The *Chamois* is shown positioned between the twin prows. Luna moves from Sagittarius toward her conjunction with Saturn in Capricorn on this date.

friendly ritual battles work, Melville later permits him to tour the divided realm of Hello and Piko, who provide the paradigm by which we may interpret the theomachia.

It might be asked why, after two lunar conjunctions with Saturn and Uranus, Taji has not yet identified the moon as Yillah. One reason is that Melville has prevented Taji from seeing the moon during this phase; another is that Melville's system decrees that each character, as his planet passes the equinoxes, takes on a new identity, or avatar, of the opposite sex. Luna's change of identity necessarily differs in timing; since her transit of half the zodiac requires a brief two weeks, her identity changes as Sol crosses the equinoxes. More important, this February conjunction is the first in which Saturn meets Luna during the last few hours before she becomes the new moon, at her slenderest and most ethereal phase. From this situation Melville derives a strange and ironic design as Taji's sword is again put to use as a surgical instrument—this time for the delivery of the infant Luna by Caesarean operation.

Samoa has caused Taji to understand that there were no women on board Aleema's canoe, but there is "astern an arched cabin or tent; behind which, were two broad bladed paddles, terminating in rude shark-tails" (127–28). His curiosity overwhelming his tact, Taji insists on knowing the "Eleusinian" mystery of the tent, but the natives declare that "it would be profanation to enter it."[2] Taji's description of the canoe enables the reader to perceive it as a pregnant vessel. Taji arrives at the conclusion that in the tent "was concealed a beautiful maiden, [who was] being borne an offering from the island of Amma to the gods of Tedaidee" (131). Taji desperately desires "to accomplish the deliverance of the maiden," preferably with "no shedding of blood; though the odds were against it." After the natives cry out, faint cries are heard from the tent, and Taji approaches it like a midwife, attended by Samoa.

> By means of thin spaces between the braids of matting, the place was open to the air, but not to view. There was also a round opening on one side, only large enough, however, to admit the arm; but this aperture was partially closed from within. In front, a deep-dyed rug of osiers, covering the entrance way, was intricately

2. See Chapter X, n. 3. The June mysteries were held in Athens, but the more important September mysteries were always held in Eleusis. At both celebrations, Jupiter Ammon, as granter of immortality, presided over the rites.

laced to the standing part of the tent. As I divided this lacing with my cutlass, there arose an outburst of voices from the Islanders. And they covered their faces, as the interior was revealed to my gaze.

Before me crouched a beautiful girl.

. . . .

. . . the captive gathered more closely about her a gauze-like robe. (P. 136)

From this description we can readily picture a birth, made difficult because the birth passage is obstructed by a virginal hymen, which Taji cuts with his cutlass. The scene might be read as rape, but Taji's scythe-shaped sword, like that of Time, is more appropriate for reaping. As he subsequently comments, he sees Yillah in such a light: "Of all things desirable and delightful, the full-plumed sheaf, and my own right arm the band." If Yillah is to be seen as a sacred infant, the role of Aleema seems far different from the one assigned him by Taji:

> For ulterior purposes connected with their sacerdotal supremacy, the priests of these climes oftentimes secrete mere infants in their temples; and jealously secluding them from all intercourse with the world, craftily delude them, as they grow up, into the wildest conceits.
>
> Thus wrought upon, their pupils almost lose their humanity in the constant indulgence of seraphic imaginings. In many cases becoming inspired as oracles; and as such, they are sometimes resorted to by devotees; always screened from view, however, in the recesses of the temples. But in every instance, their end is certain. Beguiled with some fairy tale about revisiting the islands of Paradise, they are led to the secret sacrifice, and perish unknown to their kindred. (P. 139).

Taji's description here can be construed in the light of a convent school in which children are reared in a religious atmosphere and taught to believe in angels and afterlife. As priests or nuns, they perform such duties as advising or hearing confession, and the Communion is indeed a secret sacrifice. Moreover, their end is considered to be certain; a lifetime of service and security and eternity in heaven after death. Taji does not mention at what age the "end" is destined to occur.

In regard to the comment that the priests "secrete mere infants in their temples," a look at the *Almanac* reveals that the

asteroid Pallas is conjunct Sol on this day, and Pallas is the
goddess who sprang from the temple, or brow, of Jupiter, full
grown.

> But with what passionate exultation did I find myself the deliverer
> of this beautiful maiden; who, thinking no harm, and rapt in a
> dream, was being borne to her fate on the coast of Tedaidee. Nor
> now, for a moment, did the death of Aleema her guardian seem to
> hang heavy upon my heart. (P. 140)

Now Taji notes that "the only obstacle to be encountered was
the possibility of Yillah's alarm at being suddenly borne into my
prow."[3] Thus Yillah is "born" and Taji is the one who delivers
her.

As the new moon emerges on Ash Wednesday, both Taji
and Samoa are enchanted. Yillah is an idol to both. According to
Taji, however, Jarl looks upon Yillah as an "Ammonite syren"
who might lead Taji astray; and indeed, there could be truth in
this opinion, since as a "secretion" of the Priest of Amma or of
Jupiter Ammon, she may be seen as a wailing, babbling infant
who sounds like a siren. Taji does turn away from the westward
isles to journey to the south; having confused Jupiter with
Neptune for two months, Taji now fixes his devotion on a still
more obvious body that has been pursued by generations of
idealists, the newborn fickle moon. He will, moreover, surround
her with solar imagery, thereby burdening himself with yet
another mistaken identity.

Earlier chapters have shown that the new moon is marked by
imagery of swords and cups. This one is no exception, for Taji
wields his sword and brings forth the red wine of Communion,
and Yillah herself is the cup. As Taji adores her, she covets the
figure on Jarl's arm:

> But most of all was she struck by a characteristic device on
> the arm of the wonderful mariner—our Savior on the cross, in
> blue; with the crown of thorns, and three drops of blood in
> vermilion, falling one by one from each hand and foot.
>
> Now, honest Jarl did vastly pride himself upon this ornament.
> It was the only piece of vanity about him.
>
> .   .   .   .
>
> Eventually, through the Upoluan, she made overtures to the
> Skyeman, concerning the possession of his picture in her own
> proper right. In her very simplicity, little heeding, that like a
> landscape in fresco, it could not be removed. (P. 147)

3. In regard to the possibility of
Yillah as infant, the expression "rapt in a
dream" might be seen as a pun on
"wrapped in a dream," as in a caul. When
Aleema arrived to take Yillah away from
Amma, he "came to her with a dream"
(138).

In the episode of the Fray, Melville has tied all his myths together into a veritable Gordian knot and has, in addition, commented on various religious practices. Insofar as Yillah is soon to be presented as the Grail, there is a specific comment on the transference of the divinity of Christ onto a picture, a Virgin, or a Holy Grail, adoration of which may subtract from the reality of the divinity it represents. Then, too, Yillah as an idol receives the adoration due to Jarl as Christ–Neptune, while Taji remarks that Jarl's possession of the Christ figure is Jarl's only vanity. And, just as Aleema holds the spine of a fish while the spine of the Fish holds Jupiter, so the arm of Jarl holds Christ while the arm of Aquarius holds Neptune.

In his act of murder, Taji has accomplished not one but many designs. He has assisted at the birth of the new moon, authored a deed in his capacity as "sea-attorney," served as the Goat in a sacrificial ritual, taken Communion, and been shriven. This is Taji's final adventure in the world of physical action and sensation. He must now enter Society, and encounter new lessons.

Transition

The transition from the grove to the sea was instantaneous. All seemed a dream.   —*Mardi*, 167

Having celebrated his Mardi Gras with acts of violence, Taji enters the Lenten season with a lie. Since "punctilious reserve on the part of her deliverer" might teach her to regard him as "some frigid stranger from the Arctic Zone," an apt description of old, cold Saturn, Taji endeavors to establish himself as a divine being who has known Yillah in a previous life. In addition, he deceives his comrades, for, having told them that the *Chamois* would continue its westward course, he turns south during the night while they sleep. Though he informs them when they discover the change that he is heading for Tedaidee, he tells the reader that the *Chamois*, like the pirate of old, has a "roving commission," and that he plans to hover about for a while.

Chapter 48 is entitled "Something Under the Surface," and once again Taji delivers a dissertation on fishes. Here Melville provides tidbits of clues, summaries, and confirmations, with which we will deal briefly, glancing over the two-month period already covered. First, the date is either Ash Wednesday, February 25, or the following day, and rank upon rank of fish are mustering to yield up their lives for Lent. "Samoa caught many without hook or line." The fish are "countless as the tears shed for perfidious lovers." After her conjunction with Saturn, Luna is conjunct Sol on Ash Wednesday and begins to swell, and it would be possible to see her as a perfidious lover, "her first virgin bloom departed," as Taji said of Annatoo. The fish swim "in long lines, tier above tier; the water alive with their hosts." Here Melville puns on *tier* as well as on *host,* for these repentant fish are taking Communion on the transubstantiated body and blood of a host of drowned sailors. They are "locusts of the sea, peradventure, going to fall with a blight upon some green, mossy province of Neptune."

The fish are aware of the *Chamois* as a barnacled monster, "sharp at both ends; a tail either way." This is a revealing observation, since, as noted before, the front end of the *Chamois* is the rear end of Capricorn. Throughout the voyage, Taji is faced with two tales that he must either choose between or synthesize. The fish also, as Taji speaks for them, see the *Chamois* as a swordfish; but Taji's imputation seems incorrect in light of their panicky behavior when a true "Chevalier" swims among them.

Finally, Taji feels competent to essay his first literary venture. He composes a fishy song.

*   *   *

February 27. Luna recedes from Saturn, passing Sol, Mercury, and Venus, and draws closer to Taji's other self, Uranus:

> And love, which in the eye of its object ever seeks to invest itself with some rare superiority, love, sometimes induced me to prop my failing divinity; though it was I myself who had undermined it.
>
> But if it was with many regrets, that in the sight of Yillah, I perceived myself thus dwarfing down to a mortal; it was with quite

contrary emotions, that I contemplated the extinguishment in her heart of the notion of her own spirituality. (P. 159)

The waxing moon, approaching the far distant and smaller planet Uranus, causes Taji to revive the image of the dwarf that marked his first experience with the calm on the *Arcturion*. But Yillah is sad in his company; she sees "lustrous eyes and beckoning phantoms, and strange shapes smoothing her a couch among the mosses." Like a homesick child she yearns for the shore. Passing Uranus, she moves on through Pisces toward her father, Jupiter.

March 1. On the fifth day, Luna is conjunct Jupiter and moves into Aries. The *Chamois* turns westward, and on the next morning, land is sighted.

*   *   *

With the landing on Mardi, Taji ceases to be a mere physical entity and becomes an artist in training: a dreamer, scholar, and synthesizer. Like a checker that has reached a far boundary, he is to be crowned and sent on a roving commission. Nevertheless, he is not the only piece on the board to wear a crown, nor is the crown he wears rightfully his own:

> Upon the whole, so numerous were living and breathing gods in Mardi, that I held my divinity but cheaply. And seeing such a host of immortals, and hearing of multitudes more, purely spiritual in their nature, haunting woodlands and streams; my views of theology grew strangly confused; I began to bethink me of the Jew that rejected the Talmud, and his all-permeating principle, to which Goethe and others have subscribed. (P. 176)

In his confusion, Taji ceases to differentiate between mind and matter, between Creator and creation. After the manner of Spinoza, he becomes pantheistic, and so involved in synthesis that he loses not only the power of distinction but that of discretion as well. Already wearing the crown of his creator because of Media's error, Taji now adopts the error for his own and convinces himself that he is indeed a deity.

Instead, then, of being struck with the audacity of endeavoring to palm myself off as a god—the way in which the thing first impressed me—I now perceived that I might be a god as much as I pleased, and yet not whisk a lion's tail after all; at least on that special account. (P. 176)

But the tail of Leo may whisk on his own behoof, when he is in need of yams, and ready to demonstrate the power of the author over his creature. Nevertheless, Taji began his narrative as a god, albeit a fallen one, and his creator does not will that he should die. Nor, in the spirit of Mardi Gras, is he to be condemned.

Melville's study of the psychology of the artist and of that subconscious learning process that results in a book the author never intended to write, begins in earnest as Taji sets foot on the Mardi Islands. The repeated image of two souls in one body, applied especially to the Saturn–Uranus and the Venus–Aldebaran amalgamations, bears heavily on the image of the artist; Taji's double identity as Saturn the "jack" and Uranus the "ass" enables him to rise from the position of sacrificial Goat to that of "Christ-carrier," while at the same time it provides a technicality by which Taji may circumscribe the zodiac without falling below the horizon of death as the other planets must. As he pursues the Grail, he is pursued by the Lance, and at no time is he to be consciously undeceived. Indeed, the errant narrator remains errant throughout *Mardi,* and herein lies an important aspect of Melville's riddle. We have seen that Taji has spent over a month in the company of "Captain Cook," without recognition. Encountering the figure again in the person of Media, he still does not recognize it; he does, however, bring to mind the story of an eminent navigator. Although his conscious mind, time-bound, is making no connection between past experience and present circumstances, he is on a deeper level recollecting— though perhaps misapplying—the "nameless associations" revived in him by Media's resemblances to Annatoo.

As we enter the kingdom of Mars, symbol of masculinity, it is appropriate to reemphasize that we are dealing with a book of tales: tales in conjunction, tales in opposition, tales potent and impotent, tales real and ideal, tales leading and following, and tales that secrete their true nature under the guise of other matter. Taji as artist must be taken also as Taji the interpreter, and despite his theological or artistic confusion, he can no more write solely from experience than he can steer without a chart. By the time he reaches the Mardi Islands, his experience has already been permeated by the traditional tales of great artists; whether or not he is consciously aware of it, he is already standing on the shoulders of giants. It should be mentioned that when Taji's planet Saturn passes into Aquarius at the end of March, he moves into the "butt" of the water-carrier—an irony that Melville does not overlook in his ritual battle between the ancients and the moderns.

The first day on land is spent in establishing the identity of Media as the latest avatar of Cook–Annatoo and in representing the first signs of Taji's subconscious acceptance of the "secret work" to which he has been exposed during his initiation. Still the "Fool," Taji cannot yet distinguish between Neptune and Jupiter, but the brothers have combined forces to continue the education of the initiate. All the planets have been introduced in their winterside avatars, and throughout the rest of the voyage, they will appear and reappear in various disguises as the dreaming initiate digests what he has seen and fits each element into new combinations.

March 2. The *Chamois* approaches land and Taji exclaims that the islands are "some new constellation in the sea," with a lagoon that stretches "all around us like another sky." Upon landing, Taji, cautious, sends his companions to reconnoiter, and they return with Jarl borne on the shoulders of two natives like an island king.[4] At last the heretofore nameless narrator receives the name "Taji," and is hailed as an "inferior ex-officio demi-god," an accurate title for the fallen god, divided by a belt of rings. But Taji is dubious of these honors; he recalls the fate of the eminent navigator who was destroyed while full faith in his divinity had in no wise abated. Though subsequently this allusion is shown to refer to Captain Cook, at this point it applies also to the figure of Christ.

Challenged by the kings of Mardi as a "quarrelsome demi-god," Taji promptly asserts his divinity by answering them belligerently. In so doing he acquires a friend, King Media, who invites him to his own isle of Odo. Now a maneuver takes place, for the Jarl and Samoa represented by Neptune and Venus cannot enter the sixty degrees covered by Odo. Instead, the

4. William Ellis, *Polynesian Researches,* II, 349, describes the Polynesian king-bearers.

characters are served by Aldebaran alone and by Jupiter, incognito. "Springing out of our prow, the Upoluan was followed by Jarl; leaving Yillah and Taji to be borne therein toward the sea" (167). When Taji arrives on Odo, Jarl and Samoa will be on hand, but altered. The nature of Taji's adventures on the islands is briefly noted but not emphasized at this point: "The transition from the grove to the sea was instantaneous. All seemed a dream."

Here for the first time the narrator refers to "Taji" in the third person. Henceforth he will frequently do so until at last the narrator seems divorced from the character. At the same time there is to be an increase in the imagery of dreams, and a substitution of *temples* for *tales*. The solar transit of Pallas the asteroid governs this period of mentalization.

XIII. March and Mardi

Strong was his arm to wield the club, or hurl the javelin; and
potent, I ween, round a maiden's waist. —*Mardi*, 190

As Yillah meets Media, Luna is conjunct Mars in Aries.
Outside the Odo sector, Venus transits under Sol, to emerge in
Mardi incognito on March 4. Odo is a small island of moderate
elevation, in keeping with the tiny, triangular stelleration of
Aries, elevated well north of the ecliptic.

In Media's temple, Taji encounters three idols: One
represents the King and serves as effigy when Media is physically
absent; one presently serves as effigy for an absent deity, the
mysterious "Taji" whose name and position our narrator usurps;
and one, to Taji's humiliation, stands in for Media's deceased
cook. There is no idol to represent Yillah. The meal Media
serves resembles "a harvest wain; heaped up with good things
sundry and divers: Bread-fruit, and cocoanuts, and plantains, and
guavas," but no meat. "Transported at the sight of these viands,
after so long an estrangement from full indulgence in things
green," Taji gluttonizes and encourages Yillah to do the same.
Having "grown full," the three emerge through the walls of the
temple like a trio of Athenas. Taji wonders about the practice of
building and destroying temple walls, but assumes the custom to
signify "that such gentry can go nowhere without creating an

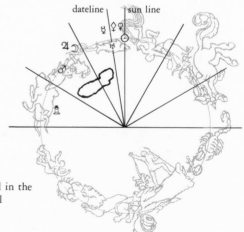

March 1, 1846

The Island of Odo covers the thirty degrees of arc involved in the
month of March. It represents zero degrees zero, the vernal
equinox, which Sol reaches on March 20.

impression; even upon the most obdurate substances" (170).[1]

On retiring to Media's palace, Taji encounters yet another idol:

> But who is this in the corner, gaping at us like a butler in a quandary? Media's household deity, in the guise of a plethoric monster, his enormous head lolling back, and wide, gaping mouth stuffed full of fresh fruits and green leaves. Truly, had the idol possessed a soul under his knotty ribs, how tantalizing to hold so glorious a mouthful without the power of deglutition. Far worse than the inexorable lockjaw, which will not admit of the step preliminary to a swallow. (P. 172)

Here we recall Taji's interpretation of certain art work found in the *Parki* log. Media's God of Good Cheer can hold but not swallow, and the Jonah-like image can be applied also to Tooboi.[2] Media virtually walls in his guests with food and even introduces a felled plantain tree.

Finally, Media leads his guests to a "handsome unoccupied mansion" and personally investigates it to make sure all is well:

> Not fancying something about the mats, he rolled them up into bundles, and one by one sent them flying at the heads of his servitors; who, upon that gentle hint made off with them, soon after returning with fresh ones. These, with mathematical precision, Media in person now spread on the dais; looking carefully to the fringes or ruffles with which they were bordered, as if striving to impart to them a sentimental expression. (P. 173)

Here indeed is Annatoo's male counterpart—tidy and well organized, but with a penchant for throwing things when in a fit of temper.

To make certain that his reader notices the imagery of Captain Cook—specifically his interest in nutrition—Melville provides one more allusion:

> The celebrated navigator referred to in a preceding chapter, was hailed by the Hawaiians as one of their demi-gods, returned to earth, after a wide tour of the universe. And they worshipped him as such, though incessantly he was interrogating them, as to who under the sun his worshippers were; how their ancestors came on

1. Regarding the breaching of walls, Louis McNeice relates the following story: "The Moslem governor of Basra told Morier that once, when he was about to embark for Calcutta, he 'was ordered by these astrologers (as the only means of counteracting the influence of a certain evil star) to go out of his house in a particular aspect; as unfortunately there happened to be no door in that direction, he caused a hole to be made in the wall, and thus made his exit.'" He notes further that "Marco Polo had described central Asian funerals (five centuries before Morier) in which a hole would be broken in the wall so that the corpse might be carried out in the direction ordered by the astrologers." From *Astrology* (Garden City, 1964), p. 176.

2. *Mardi*, pp. 94–95. William Ellis, *Polynesian Researches*, I, 257, for Media's household deity. Recall Jarl's lockjaw (Ch. VIII) and Captain Cook's interest in vegetables.

the island; and whether they would have the kindness to provide his followers with plenty of pork during his stay. (P. 174)

Considering this probing into the islanders' history and knowing the eventual fate of this particular demigod, Taji with saturnine caution determines to ask no questions. In avoiding the destiny of Captain Cook, he falls into the error of Percival. Equally as a result, he does not ask for pork or any other kind of meat, and therefore keeps Lent along with Media. These are his salad days.

Taji notes that Media is worshiped as a "spiritual being. In his corporeal absence, his effigy receiving all oblations intended for him." Who then is the absent "Taji" of whom Media is said to be fond? Recalling the devotion of Annatoo the water-bug for Jarl the sea king, we might identify the usurped idol as that of Neptune. However, Media the Ram, being of a fiery temperament, has an affinity for his fellow fire kings, Sol and Jupiter. The latter is presently in Aries, and so is not absent; but Sol, as Taji has already noted, is the "garish sun lingering without like some lackey in waiting" (172). Sol still occupies both the sign and the constellation of Pisces, just outside the Odo sector, while Taji's planet Uranus is just inside. It appears, therefore, that Media has also failed to recognize the true "Taji" —Sol—his author, and has crowned instead some frigid stranger from the Arctic Zone. As a result, Media himself will be usurped by Sol. Of all the planets, Mars alone has no conjunction with Sol until the very end of the quest. Instead, he leads the processional around the zodiac, hotly pursued by a vengeful Sol all the way, as Taji is pursued by his Avengers.

Taji lectures himself—or cautious Saturn lectures asinine Uranus—and advises himself to "be not a 'snob,' Taji." Gullible as always, he reflects that Mardians are familiar with greater marvels than his and could put his exploits to the blush. Thus assessing himself severely, Taji adopts an attitude that is close to humility in nature. During the night, he approaches still closer to self knowledge. Wakeful, he goes out into the "magical" starlight, and gazes out at the islands. He sees one island "belted round by a frothy, luminous reef, wherein it lay, like Saturn in its ring." From the summits of the volcanic isles, "went up a milk-white smoke. . . . And floating away, these vapors blended with the faint mist." By this description we know that the heavens are veiled; but Taji sees reflections in the waters of the lagoon:

> But how tranquil the wide lagoon, which mirrored the burning spots in heaven! Deep down into its innermost heart penetrated the slanting rays of Hesperus like a shaft of light, sunk far into mysterious Golcondas, where myriad gnomes seemed toiling. Soon a light breeze rippled the water, and the shaft was seen no more. But the moon's bright wake was still revealed: a silver track, tipping every wave-crest in its course, till each seemed a pearly, scroll-prowed nautilus, buoyant with some elfin crew. (Pp. 178–79)

Hesperus is the name given to the evening star, and often, but not necessarily, applied to Venus. On this night, the evening star is Jupiter. The connection of the moon with the pearly shell is to serve as one of several clues to the presence of the crescent throughout the quest. "High above me was Night's shadowy bower, traversed, vine-like, by the Milky Way," and here Taji makes the association between the vine of Yillah's birth blossom and the smoky path that crosses the sky between Gemini and Jupiter's house of Sagittarius. At midnight, as Taurus sinks below the earthly horizon, Leo and Virgo stretch across the night sky. Taji cries:

> Oh stars! oh eyes, that see me, wheresoe'er I roam: serene, intent, inscrutable for aye, tell me Sybils, what I am,—Wondrous worlds on worlds! Lo, round and round me, shining, awful spells: all glorious, vivid constellations, God's diadem ye are! To you, ye stars, man owes his subtlest raptures, thoughts unspeakable, yet full of faith. But how your mild effulgence stings the boding heart. Am I a murderer, stars? (P. 179)

March 3. During a breakfast of fruit and of wine served in fire-tempered cups—the first quarter moon having passed through the fire of Mars–Aries—Media compares garments with Taji, displaying in a somewhat effeminate manner the red and black beauty of his betassled robe. Equally reminiscent of his female counterpart is Media's delight in teasing Jarl. Just as Media had mistakenly invested the Narrator with the identity and the idol of the real Taji (Sol), he now playfully transfers Jarl's identity along with his "taj."

> Next came under observation the Skyeman's Guayaquil hat; at
> whose preposterous shape, our host laughed in derision; clapping a
> great conical calabash upon the head of an attendant, and saying
> that now he was Jarl. At this, and all similar sallies, Samoa was
> sure to roar louder than any; though mirth was no constitutional
> thing with him. (P. 181)

Having behaved in such an undignified way—and as
mischievously as Annatoo—Media resumes his kingly manner. As
a final connecting link with Annatoo, Taji reports,

> the repast concluded, we journeyed to the canoe-house, where we
> found the little Chamois stabled like a steed. One solitary
> depredation had been committed. Its sides and bottom had been
> completely denuded of the minute green barnacles, and short
> sea-grass, which, like so many leeches, had fastened to our planks
> during our long, lazy voyage.
>   By the people they had been devoured as dainties. (P. 181)

Note that now, on the island of springtime, the barnacles are
"green," and grass has been added for a Lenten salad.

Chapter 60, entitled "Belshazzar on the Bench," provides
another of those pivotal images by which a character is identified
and then altered before the reader's eyes. As noted, the date is
the third day of the third month, and the day is Tuesday. In
every sense this is Mars Day, and as Aries is the high noon of the
zodiac, the Areopagitica of Media occurs at high noon on this
auspicious occasion. In order to understand all nuances implied in
the trial, let us recall certain factors that have been previously
introduced: the headlessness of Annatoo–Cook; the references to
"Daniels" that first night on the *Parki,* and to the shadows flitting
across the bulkhead; the offering of Sol's "taj" to Saturn–Uranus;
and the imminent entry of Sol into the sign of Aries on March
20. To these elements we may add Taji's description of Media's
crown: a red turban, resembling the rising sun, from which
radiates white fishbones like the "spine of a fish" first seen in
connection with Jupiter; a bandeau of pearls representing Luna;
and in the center, the trident of Neptune. Thus crowned like a
day, Media presents an insult to the true sultan, Sol.

Taji, the impressionable, sings paeans to the divinity of
kings, invoking the Gracchi, the Acephali, the Levelers—all either
headless or beheading—to behold the sight.

Man lording it over man, man kneeling to man, is a spectacle that Gabriel might well travel hitherward to behold; for never did he behold it in heaven. But Darius giving laws to the Medes and Persians, or the conqueror of Bactria with king-cattle yoked to his car, was not a whit more sublime, than Beau Brummel magnificently ringing for his valet.

A king on his throne! It is Jupiter nodding in the councils of Olympus; Satan, seen among the coronets in Hell.

A king on his throne! It is the sun over a mountain; the sun over law-giving Sinai; the sun in our system: planets, duke-like, dancing attendance, and baronial satellites in waiting. (P. 183)

This loaded passage contains many ironies. The mention of Satan puts the lie to the comment about Gabriel, for all traditions show that heaven has hierarchies, and Gabriel has witnessed the fate of one angel too proud to bend the knee to an all-powerful king. It is interesting also that, at the sight of the trident on Media's crown, Taji thinks not of Neptune, but of Satan. The image of Darius and the king-cattle bears directly on the transformation of Media, for he himself is soon to serve in this capacity.[3]

On this high noon, Media sits in trial upon one Jiromo, and his justice is swift and harsh.

His guilt was clear. And the witnesses being heard, from a bunch of palm plumes Media taking a leaf, placed it in the hand of a runner or pursuivant, saying, "This to Jiromo, where he is prisoned; with his king's compliments; say we here wait for his head."

It was doffed like a turban before a Dey, and brought back on the instant. (P. 183)

Media's justice is tantamount to murder, as was Mars's justice in slaying the son of Neptune to avenge his daughter Alcippe. Immediately Media is brought to trial by certain "varlets" who mutter "wild jargon about 'bulwarks,' 'bulkheads,' . . . and other unintelligible gibberish." These "bulkheads" are the wall upon which the handwriting has appeared.[4] The varlets petition for trial by a jury of twelve, but Media responds with a sophistic tirade, which he concludes by declaring:

"I am king: ye are slaves. Mine to command: yours to obey. And this hour I decree, that henceforth no gibberish of bulwarks and bulkheads be heard in this land. For a dead bulwark and a

3. In the Book of Daniel, Chapter 5, the story of Belshazzar is related, and it is possible that the name *Media* is taken from "Darius the Median," representing the figure of Sol deposing Mars for the duration of the quest. See also "Metia" in Ellis, *Polynesian Researches*, II, 230.

4. The shadowy handwriting on the bulkheads and bulwarks is the familiar MENE, MENE, TEKEL, UPHARSIN: "God hath numbered thy kingdom and finished it. Thou art weighed in the balances and found wanting. Thy kingdom is divided, and given to the Medes and Persians." Daniel 5:25–28. The references to the balances provide a ready relationship to the Scales of Libra as the missing element in Media's rule. Note the subsequent reference to "kneepans" in regard to the pans in Libra's scales of justice.

bulkhead, to dam off sedition, will I make of that man, who again but breathes those bulky words. Ho! spears! see that these knee-pans here kneel till set of sun."

High noon was now passed; and removing his crown, and placing it on the dais for the kneelers to look at during their devotions, King Media departed from that place, and once more played the agreeable host. (P. 185)

On Saturday, March 7, Sol enters the Mardi sector to pick up the crown left on the dais. From this chapter on, the effeminate, mischievous Media appears no more. Mars passes the last star in Aries—*delta,* in the Ram's tail—and goes to pasture in Taurus, while the person of King Media is taken over by Sol. Like the king-cattle, Mars pulls Sol's chariot around the zodiac and quests for justice.

March 6. The third of March passes, and is followed by several days of social activities.

Upon the third day, however, there was noticed a mysterious figure, like the inscrutable incognitos sometimes encountered, crossing the tower-shadowed Plaza of Assignations at Lima. It was enveloped in a dark robe of tappa; so drawn and plaited about the limbs; and with one hand, so wimpled about the face, as only to expose a solitary eye. But that eye was a world. Now it was fixed upon Yillah with a sinister glance, and now upon me, but with a different expression. However great the crowd, however tumultuous, that fathomless eye gazed on; till at last it seemed no eye, but a spirit, forever prying into my soul. (P. 186)

For the third time we are presented with the image of the eye: first the compass, then Samoa, and now the Incognito. On this day, Venus moves into the Mardi sector. She gazes at Yillah on her left, or "sinister" side, as Luna moves out of Taurus. Taji begs Media to "fix" the elusive glance, but a new and more dignified Media replies that, by courtesy, incognitos are sacred, and the robe and wimple are as secure as a castle.[5]

March 7. Luna is at *kappa* Gemini, and Taji receives his first of many visits from Hautia's Heralds, the "three black-eyed damsels" who bring flower messages that Taji cannot interpret. Nor does he ever understand them, for the translator whom he later acquires subtly misinterprets subsequent messages.[6]

The visit of the damsels occurs in the morning, and it is still

5. Melville is generous in his use of chess imagery, as well as that of checkers and other games. One knowledgeable in the game may be able to detect a symbolic relationship between the characters and the chess pieces, such as the "castle" of the Incognito and of the Bread-barge.

6. Merrell R. Davis, "The Flower Symbolism in *Mardi,*" *Modern Language Quarterly,* 2 (1941), 625–38, postulates that Melville may have used Frances S. Osgood's *The Poetry of Flowers.* With thanks to this note, I have used Mrs. Osgood's *Flower Gift: A Token of Friendship for All Seasons with A Complete Floral Dictionary* (Chambersburg, Pa., 1840), which in turn is adapted from an English work, "The Sentiment of Flowers." The origin of these books appears to be Lady Mary Wortley Montagu (1689–1762), and hers is a more extensive dictionary from which Mrs. Osgood rarely deviates. Lady Mary's list is taken from Henry Frederick Reddall, *Fact, Fancy, and Fable,* pp. 212–18, and a later list comes from Liliam Eichler, *The Customs of Mankind,* pp. 658 ff.

March 7 when Taji selects an islet on which to dwell with Yillah amid woods and vines. This is poor judgment on Taji's part, for these vines provide the means by which Yillah eludes him. As Luna approaches full, the time for her transformation and rebirth draws near. According to Yillah's story,

> one day strolling in the woodlands, she was snared in the tendrils of a vine. Drawing her into its bowers, it gently transformed her into one of its blossoms, leaving her conscious soul folded up in the transparant petals.
>
> Here hung Yillah in a trance, the world without all tinged with the rosy hue of her prison. At length when her spirit was about to burst forth in the opening flower, the blossom was snapped from its stem; and borne by a soft wind to the sea; where it fell into the opening valve of a shell; which in good time was cast upon the beach of the Island of Amma. (P. 137)

Passing through Gemini, Luna encounters the vine of the Milky Way that twines across the sky to Jupiter's house of Sagittarius, and here in the islet, Yillah is surrounded by vines, as well as by calabashes and coconut shells, and fine tappa for her caul. Three times a day a "garrulous old man" brings food, and in the evenings, a phantom in a canoe keeps the islet under surveillance. At night, Yillah shudders as she sleeps. " 'The whirlpool,' she murmured, 'sweet mosses.' Next day she was lost in reveries, plucking pensive hyacinths, or gazing intently into the lagoon" (189).[7] Already Yillah is lost to Taji, for she has been snared by the vine of the Milky Way and is on her way home.

7. Sweet mosses can be interpreted as "maternal love" or "ennui," while hyacinths are "sorrow" or "unobtrusive loveliness."

* * *

March 8–12. Taji explores Odo and finds the corruption inherent in Media's reign. Of importance in Chapter 63 is the image of the sea as "the common sepulcher of Odo."

> And now, what follows, said these Islanders: "Why sow corruption in the soil which yields us life? We would not pluck our grapes from over graves. This earth's an urn for flowers, not for ashes."

They said that Oro, the supreme, had made a cemetery of the sea.

And what more glorious grave? Was Mausolus more sublimely urned? Or do the minster-lamps that burn before the tomb of Charlemagne, show more of pomp, than all the stars, that blaze above the shipwrecked màriner? (P. 192)

Here Neptune emerges as the "urn," a figure of death and a correlative of Yillah as the "cup." From a gardener's viewpoint, it is implied that the practice of burying the dead at sea depletes the soil of that which should be returned to it for fertility, though sea burial enriches the realm of Neptune.

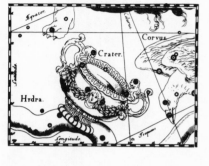

Crater the Cup

*   *   *

March 12. Throughout the preceding week, Luna has spent decreasing time in the daylight side of the sky with Saturn. Waxing to the full, she seems far away and ghostly during the few hours of her daylight sojourn. Now the *Almanac* provides another of those beautiful planetary conformations that seem designed for Melville's convenience. On the day of the full moon, Luna passes south of the ecliptic and directly into the constellation Crater, the Cup. The holiday announced by the *Almanac* is the Hebrew feast of Purim. On this day, Yillah disappears forever from Taji's life and becomes the Grail for which he will quest. It is mentioned in passing that "at this juncture" visitors arrive, among them Hautia's Heralds, who "came and went unheeded."

March 12, 1846

The disappearance of Yillah coincides with the Hebrew feast of Purim, which celebrates the deliverance of the Jews from Haman by Queen Esther. On this day, as the moon comes to full, she is passing through the constellation Crater, just south of Virgo. By this happy image, Yillah becomes the Grail figure as the object of the Quest.

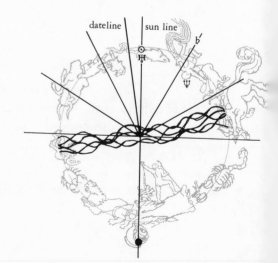

March 15. Messengers sent out on March 12 return empty-handed as Luna passes *alpha* Virgo and sinks below the horizon from Uranus. Taji raves, and then, as Mercury the Transformer passes Uranus on March 18, Taji goes into a trance, "one glance forever fixed."

* * *

March 20. "Still sped the days." Luna is at third quarter in Sagittarius, and Sol passes into the sign of Aries: spring begins. "The thoughts of things broke over me like returning billows on a beach long bared."

* * *

March 24. Luna at perigee is conjunct Saturn, and the "remembrance seemed the thing remembered." On either this day or the day before—the *Almanac* does not comment—Sol passes by Uranus. Taji hardly notices, but says,

> There are thoughts that lie and glitter deep: tearful pearls beneath life's sea, that surges still, and rolls sunlit, whatever it may hide. Common woes, like fluids, mix all round. Not so with that other grief. Some mourners load the air with lamentations; but the loudest notes are struck from hollows. Their tears flow fast: but the deep spring only wells. (P. 194)

March 27. The new moon passes Uranus, and Mars is conjunct A^1 Taurus. Taji informs Media that he "must hie from Odo."

A complete realignment of the planets necessitates a change in both characters and story. The three great planets, Neptune, Saturn, and Uranus, are to be left behind on the winter side of the sky, while the others assume their positions for the grand processional through the summer constellations. On this date the planets are milling around at the top of the zodiac, with Mars at the fore in Taurus and Jupiter moving—rapidly for his size—close behind in Aries. In Pisces are Luna, Mercury, Sol, Uranus, and Venus, in that order.

As Taji proposes to tour Mardi in search of Yillah, Media surprises him by offering to go along. "I myself am interested in this pursuit, . . . and trust me, Yillah will be found." This statement takes on added significance when we recall that Sol has now assumed the crown of Media, and that Sol is responsible for the phases of the Moon. Media fits out three royal canoes for the tour and introduces three new characters, each of whom desires to find Yillah. Mystical Babbalanja embodies two personalities: old Bardianna, the new lunar figure, quests for the Christ figure on the arm of Neptune–Aquarius, while the devil Azzageddi represents Uranus, the Fugleman, spurring on the search. Thus Babbalanja combines the character of Taji as seeker and of Yillah as the one sought for, and he it is who discovers the "new world" in the heavens on the date that Leverrier finds Neptune.[8] Mohi, or Braid-Beard, combines Saturn's interest in chronicles with Mercury's affinity for kings; his constellation is Virgo. Yoomy combines Uranus and Mercury, and his constellation is Gemini. Media appoints a regent, Almanni, to rule in his place during the quest.

*   *   *

March 28. "Media, on the beach, at eventide, when both light and water waned, drew a rude map of the lagoon, to compensate for the obstructions in the way of a comprehensive glance at it from Odo" (198). Let us recall this map when Taji later declares that he has "chartless voyaged."

*   *   *

Saturn meets his first conjunction in Aquarius, at the star *tau* in the Waterman's ankle, and Taji departs from Odo on March 29.

8. Azzageddi may have yet another significance. Leverrier, in attempting to work out the problems of Bode's law during late 1845, postulated the existence of a planet in an orbit between Sol and Mercury. This hypothetical planet he called "Vulcan" because of the extreme heat from Sol, nearby. His concern with Vulcan may have slowed down his work on Neptune. We cannot be sure whether or not Melville knew about Vulcan, but if he did, Azzageddi provides an ideal figure for the distracting hypothesis.

Part II: The Quest

XIV. March and the Quest

the king, who receives his ambassadors with a majestic toss of the head, may have just recovered from the tooth-ache. —*Mardi,* 208

With Saturn's entry into Aquarius, the planet's influence changes drastically, and Taji's personality must be appropriately altered. A fifteenth-century astrological treatise, *The Kalendar and Compost of Shepherds,* describes Saturn in Capricorn as "false, envious, and full of debate, and full of law, . . . heavy, thoughtful, and malicious; a robber, a fighter, and full of covetousness; . . . and he shall love to sin willfully."[1] This description has not been much improved over the centuries. In Aquarius the Air sign, however, Saturn becomes less ignoble. Though he still endows mortals with crooked teeth, he also grants a sound mind in a sound body, with an inclination toward and a capacity for great learning. Thus the Taji of the quest now becomes the quiescent scholar rather than the rogue sailor.

1. Louis McNeice, *Astrology* (Garden City, 1964), p. 62.

Yet another cause exists for the change in Taji as well as for his virtual disappearance as an active character during the quest. With the passage of Sol over the vernal equinox, both Saturn and Uranus are left behind on the winter side of the sky, along with the undiscovered Neptune. All other planets accompany Sol to the summer side and undergo metamorphosis. Deprived of the power of Sol, Taji's planets can no longer function as before and still maintain the mechanics of Melville's metaphor. To counter this problem, Melville stresses the imagery of dreams and places

March 29, 1846

The three canoes of Media depart from Odo at the end of the month of March, on the day that Saturn has his first official conjunction in the constellation Aquarius. Though he has been in the Aquarius sector for quite some time, the *Almanac* has not reported on the fact until now.

Taji in the passive role of the entranced dreamer who speaks of himself in the third person.

With the beginning of the quest, the introductory portion of *Mardi* comes to an end. Its purpose has been to provide imagery sufficiently precise to establish the myth and the metaphor on which the rest of the book is based. The exceptional precision that marks these opening chapters is no longer necessary, and indeed, as the planets align themselves so that conjunctions are reduced, it is no longer feasible. Though the stellar metaphor is maintained—accurately and easily—the emphasis shifts to the philosophical content.

Melville now turns to a slightly altered time system that permits the voyagers to take longer leaps around the zodiac. Each of Media's three boats represents a thirty-degree sector of the sky, within which the action can take place. One sector always contains Sol, and unless Melville specifically states otherwise, the other two span the polar radials. The dateline moves forward in accordance with the lunar day—that is, in fifteen-degree sweeps, the distance Luna travels in a day. Melville thereby provides himself with considerable flexibility yet adheres rigidly to the limitations he has set.

The planetary nature of the characters also undergoes alteration, leading to greater complexity. To establish the metaphor in the opening chapters it has been necessary to provide a one-to-one relationship between planet and character—not only to ensure that the reader could work out the identity pattern, but also to demonstrate the metaphor of the avatar. In these early chapters, only Taji represents an amalgamation of two planets, and these—Saturn and Uranus—are not difficult to associate from either a mythological or an astrological standpoint. On the summer side, however, amalgamation is the rule for all the characters rather than the exception.

Heretofore, the planet Mercury has remained uncharacterized except for hints that he might represent the *Arcturion*'s harpooneer, Mark, and the sons of Aleema who, in their connection with Gemini, are ruled by Mercury, planet of brothers. On the summer side, Mercury serves, along with Luna, as substitute for the planets left on the night side. As Mercury combines with Saturn, symbol of time, to form the historian

Mohi, and with Uranus to form Yoomy the poet, and as Luna combines with Uranus to form Babbalanja, it is logical that these three can carry the burden of personality on behalf of the dreamer, Taji. The amalgamation of Sol with Mars has been noted, as the insulted sultan Sol invades the person of Media and puts Mars to the yoke to search for justice.

Just as Yillah must disappear and Taji must be deemphasized to accord with Melville's celestial mechanics, so also must Jarl and Samoa. Taking their places are the Avengers and Hautia's Heralds. Jarl's Neptune combines with Aleema's Jupiter and the Mercury of Aleema's sons to form the triple threat of the Avengers, while Venus rules the appearances of the Heralds until Hautia enters the scene.

The structure of the quest is complex, but it follows consistently a specific pattern. Each island landing presents a situation in keeping with a constellation indicated by the imagery, the planets involved in the action, and the holiday associated with the month in progress. The situation contains a lesson for each quester, illustrated by the exposure of some error in kingship, theology, science, art, history, or philosophy. The visit to each island is prefaced by a description in which the thematic problems are indicated, and when the questers leave the island, the themes are discussed through a series of interim chapters. Each of these discussions exposes the flaws that characterize the thought processes of the featured quester, who suffers from bias, confusion, or gullibility. The weaknesses of Taji as sailor–narrator reflect from the verbal meanderings of Babbalanja, Mohi, and Yoomy.

A dream sequence accompanies each section; in each of these sequences Melville emphasizes some specific metaphor or reveals some significant development in the education of one of the questers. The appearances of the Avengers and the Heralds serve similar purposes: The Avengers punctuate the episode just completed, while the flower message of the Heralds announces the theme or development to watch for in the episode to come. Yoomy's interpretation of the flower messages is not to be trusted, as the Heralds demonstrate at one point. The reader is expected to recognize Yoomy's error of interpretation and to

The Flower Language

Chapter 61
Iris .Message
Circea . . . . .Spell, or Fascination
Moss Rosebud . . . . .Confusion of love
    Rose, Moss . . . . .Superiority, or Pleasure without alloy
Venus Car . . . . .Fly with me
Witch Hazel . . . . .A Spell

Chapter 63
Moss . . . . .Maternal love
Mosses . . . . .Ennui
Hyacinths . . . . .Sport, games, play
    Purple . . . . .Sorrow, or Grief
    White . . . . .Unobtrusive loveliness

Chapter 70 - After Valapee
Jonquil . . . . .Desire, or, I desire return of affection
Wormwood . . . . .Absence
Oleanders . . . . .Beware

Chapter 88 - After Nora-Bamma
Hemlock . . . . .You will cause my death
Verbena . . . . .Sensibility
    White . . . . .Pray for me
    Scarlet . . . . .Unite against evil
    Pink . . . . .Family union
Barbed rose . . . . .Love severe
White Lily . . . . .Purity, majesty

Chapter 99 - The Funeral on Mondoldo
Asphodel . . . . .Regret, or, My regrets follow you
                            to the grave
Hawthorne, withered . . . . . . .Hope

Chapter 101 - After Mondoldo
Was-myrtle berries . . . . .Enlightenment
Lily of the Valley . . . . .Return of Happiness;
                           unconscious sweetness
Bilberries . . . . .Treachery
Saffron-flower . . . . .Excess is dangerous
Crocus, saffron . . . . .Mirth
Leaves, dead . . . . .Melancholia
Crocus . . . . .Youthful gladness

Chapter 116 - In the Pontiff's Garden
Casaurina, Cypress . . . . .Death and Mourning, extinguished hope
Convulva . . . . .Bonds, Repose, Worth sustained
                          by affection
Violets . . . . .Faithfulness, watchfulness, modesty
Balsam . . . . .Impatience
Ferns . . . . .Fascination, magic, sincerity

Chapter 118 - After Jarl's departure
Tri-foil leaf . . . . .Revenge
Daffodils . . . . .Regard, Self-love, Deceitful hope

Chapter 134 - After Taji's Confession
Blackthorn . . . . .Difficulty
Rose-Balm . . . . .Sympathy and love
Strawberry . . . . .Perfect Excellence
    Wreath . . . . .Foresight
    Tree . . . . .Esteem, not love

Chapter 141 - After Diranda
Sumach . . . . .Splendor
Cherry Stalks (tree) . . . . . . .Good Education
    Black . . . . .Deception
Cactus . . . . .Warmth
Lilies, tiger . . . . .For once may pride befriend me
Grapes (wild) . . . . .Charity

Chapter 173 - After Doxodox
Tremella Nostoc . . . . .Resolve the Riddle (Mrs. Osgood)
Midnight Tremella . . . . .Resistance (Lady Mary)

Chapter 190 - The Approach to Flozella-a-niña
Cereus, night-blooming . . . . .Transient Beauty

Chapter 192 - On the Island
Columbines . . . . .Folly
Daisy . . . . .Innocence
Peach . . . . .I am your captive
Clematis . . . . .Mental Beauty, or, Artifice
Amaryllis . . . . .Haughtiness and Pride, or Timidity,
                          or, Splendid beauty
Vervain . . . . .Enchantment
Privet Hedges . . . . .Prohibition
Honeysuckles . . . . .Bond of love
Pinks . . . . .Lovely and pure affection
Pansies . . . . .Think of me
Bluebells . . . . .Constancy, sorrowful regret
Heath . . . . .Solitude
Dahlia . . . . .Instability and Heartless Beauty
Nightshade . . . . .Falsehood (Lady Mary), Truth (Osgood)

Chapter 193
Sweetbriar . . . . .Poetry (Osgood)
    American . . . . .Simplicity
    European . . . . .I would to heal
Linden leaves . . . . .Conjugal love
Anemones . . . . .Your frown I defy (Osgood)
    Field . . . . .Sickness
    Garden . . . . .Forsaken
Juniper . . . . .Succor, Protection
Palm stalks . . . . .Victory
Lotus . . . . .Eloquence (Lady Mary), Silence (Osgood)
    Flower . . . . .Estranged love
    Leaf . . . . .Recantation
Fennel . . . . .Worthy all praise; strength
Thyme . . . . .Activity; courage

inform himself by referring to one of the many books of flower symbolism so popular in Melville's day (see Flower Language chart).

*   *   *

We recall that in the opening chapters of *Mardi* Melville provided a day-by-day sample of the imagery in order that after sixteen days the reader could proceed without the author's guidance. The questers' first stop, the Isle of Valapee, serves a similar purpose. Brief and simple, the visit to Valapee provides the stellar coordinates by which the reader may synchronize symbol and event before setting forth on the quest; reaffirms that an astrological metaphor is to pervade the quest; points out a series of errors or follies of government, economics, tradition, social custom, art, and science; exposes the reaction of each quester; restates the principle of "artistic blow-up" that we have previously encountered; and establishes a set of images, symbols, and devices that will recur, with development and elaboration, throughout the quest. A detailed examination of the launching of the quest and of the Valapee episode, Chapters 66 through 70, establishes a paradigm by which subsequent sections may be dealt with more briefly.[2]

2. The quest motif as used by Melville has been dealt with by many scholars, including Tyrus Hillway, "Taji's Quest for Certainty," *American Literature,* 18, 27–34; Philip Graham, "The Riddle of Melville's *Mardi:* A Reinterpretation," *Texas Studies in English,* 36 (1957), 93–99, in which it is argued that *Mardi* investigates the development of man's quest from past through future time.

*   *   *

The quest begins with a description of the three royal canoes of Media, specifically the elephantlike foremost canoe, which bears the questers—a total of fourteen persons, two of whom will soon be removed. The great canoe, as delineated, has Polynesian antecedents, but it also bears a striking resemblance to the Hevelius drawing of the constellation Argos, mythologically associated with the Golden Fleece—appropriate to Media as ruler of Aries the Ram—and the Dragon's Teeth, which will figure prominently in the imagery of the quest. The boat's prow bears "a grinning little imp of an image, a ring in its nose, cowrie shells jingling at its ears, with an abominable leer like that of Silenus reeling on his ass. It was taking its ease; cosily smoking a

pipe, its bowl, a duodecimo edition of the face of the smoker.
This image looked sternward, everlastingly mocking us" (200).
The backward gaze of the imp symbolizes man's journey through
time, able to see the past but blind to the future.

Media's royal crest consists of "three upright boars' tusks, in
an heraldic field argent. A fierce device: Whom rends he?" This

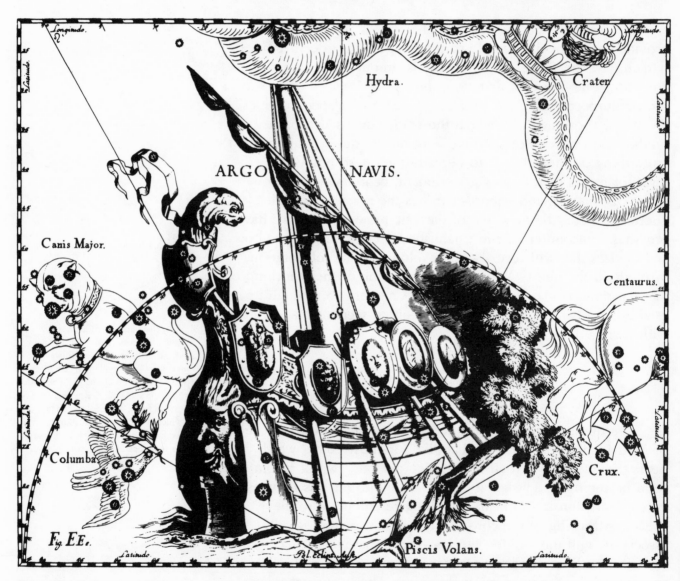

This rendering of the constellation Argo Navis, by the seventeenth-century astronomer Hevelius,
bears a striking resemblance to many of the features of Media's canoe. Argo is located in the
southern sky near Crater the Cup or Grail (shown above right). To the left is Canis Major,
whose *alpha* star, Sirius, marks the dog's nose; to the right is Centaurus.

device, remindful of the wild boars that rent the body of Adonis and those sent by Artemis to ravage Caledonia, previews the emphasis on teeth that characterizes the Isle of Valapee.

*   *   *

The canoes' first landing on the Isle of Yams is marked by Swiftian satire on manners, mores, traditions, and superstitions. As the questers explore Valapee, we may consider the mechanics by which Melville sets up the temporal coordinates to fix the time line on a specific date in accordance with lunar time. Characteristically, Melville first presents the coordinate image but does not reveal until the questers reach the Isle of Juam that Luna rather than Sol now governs the positioning of the dateline. That this putting of cart before horse might throw his reader into severe confusion is no doubt a matter of which Melville was gleefully aware. At any rate, the lunar imagery will be discussed in the chapter that deals with Juam.

The figure of little King Peepi of Valapee provides the key to the lunar position in the same way that Arcturus established the opening solar radial. Peepi is a ten-year-old boy—to use a word within the metaphor, a "kid,"—who travels about his realm astride the back of a burly mute. By consulting the sky-map-calendar, we can readily locate this image in the constellation Auriga the Charioteer, who is carrying the little Goat, Capella, on his shoulder. The *alpha* star in this configuration is Capella, the Goat's eye, and the equivalent spot on the zodiac is *xi* Taurus, at the tip of the horns. Luna is at this position on March 31 and still in her first quarter. The next step is to place Sol at the proper spot on the map, which on this date is approximately *pi* Pisces. The polar radials then are *p* (for *rho*) Gemini and *pi* Sagittarius. Small wonder that the child monarch's name is *p-pi*. Included in the field of action are six planets: Sol, Luna, Uranus, Jupiter, Venus, and Mercury, and two asteroids, Pallas and Ceres. The last-named is conjunct Sol on March 30 and therefore governs the quest until the end of July.

In the two chapters that cover the Valapee sector, imagery of arches, fever, and insects indicates that the Archer, Sagittarius, is

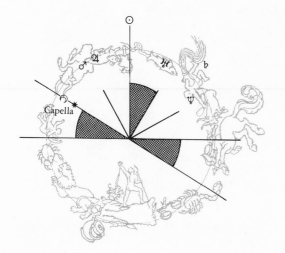

March 30, 1846

As Media's canoes leave Odo, Melville provides himself with a means by which to enlarge and vary his field of action as well as to take larger leaps in time. The date and the field are determined by the position of Luna at the beginning of each episode. The Isle of Valapee and the figure of Peepi indicate a lunar position designated by the star Capella in the constellation Auriga. Luna arrives at this point on this date.

at one pole and that part of Scorpio is included—thereby providing a clue that a certain arc is involved in each radial.

$$* \qquad * \qquad *$$

Imagery of astrology and teeth dominates the visit to Valapee. Little Peepi is ruled by six ancestral souls, "uppermost and active in him one by one" (203). These "revolving souls" share the characteristics of the planets, and when each is "lord of the ascendant," Peepi is predictably unpredictable. "Thus subject to contrary impulses, over which he had not the faintest control, Peepi was plainly denuded of all moral obligation to virtue." Here Media is exposed to government by impulse for the edification of impulsive Mars, while the astrological imagery points to those believers in determinism who use that philosophy to justify the act of the moment, thereby providing Babbalanja with food for thought.

While refreshments are being served to the party, Peepi covets the teeth of one of Media's attendants, precipitating a discussion of teeth as the medium of commercial exchange on Valapee, where the financial structure is based on equal but limited inherent resources. Here, "the very beggars are born with a snug investment in their mouths; too soon, however, to be appropriated by their lords; leaving them toothless for the rest of their days." Instead of pulling their own teeth as an offering to the dead, as Taji tells us the Hawaiians do, the Valapee folk appropriate the molars of their deceased ancestors, to be distributed as memorials. Thus, the ancestors bequeathe molars as well as souls to their descendants, and the questers receive a lesson in conservation.

The artistic metaphor reiterates in miniature what has been repeatedly illustrated in *Mardi:* the technique of the proportional blow-up:

> Terrific shade of tattooed Tammahammaha! If, from a vile dragon's molars, rose mailed men, what heroes shall spring from the cannibal canines once pertaining to warriors themselves! . . . For, lo! roundabout me Tammahammaha's tattooing expands, till all the sky seems a tiger's skin. (P. 206)

This expansion of the tattoo—itself a work of art—into a heroic universal expresses Melville's idea of one of the sources of art and further demonstrates that *Mardi* is both an expansion and a unification of man-made diversities, which are based on the artistry of nature. Throughout the quest the reader is deluged with imagery of ingestion as Taji takes in new experiences, and it is fitting that a discussion of teeth should introduce the metaphor.

In keeping with the theme of revenge, the visit to Valapee ends with another tri-dental curse; "By this tooth," said Bondo to Noojoomo, "by this tooth I swear to be avenged upon thee, oh Noojoomo!"

*   *   *

Chapters 69 and 70 serve as a paradigm for the transit between islands, the first serving as the application of the ideas presented on Valapee and the second as a transition to the island to be visited next.

Media impulsively sets aside his crown and offers to socialize on equal footing with his companions, whereupon Babbalanja puts the offer to the test and becomes excessively familiar. When Media is regally offended, the philosopher tactfully and cleverly rebukes him. Essentially good-natured though hot-tempered, Media acknowledges and accepts the lesson in Babbalanja's ploy.

In passing Pella the Rock, the subject of Nature, introduced on Valapee, is related to the art of analogy in terms of the resurrection of the worm into the short-lived moth, and Babbalanja's conclusion is in direct opposition to the avatar metaphor of *Mardi*. In regard to dead kings, he remarks:

"Yet, grant that they lived; then, if death be a deaf-and-dumb death, a triumphal procession over their graves would concern them not. If a birth into brightness, then Mardi must seem to them the most trivial of reminiscences. Or, perhaps, theirs may be an utter lapse of memory concerning sublunary things; and they themselves be not themselves, as the butterfly is not the larva." (Pp. 209–10)

But the butterfly is the larva, and furthermore, the larva is father to the butterfly as the butterfly is father to the larva. Thus Babbalanja simultaneously rejects and confirms the Wordsworthian idea that the child is father of the man, even as Peepi had contained within himself the souls of all his fathers.

Said Yoomy, "Then, Babbalanja, you account that a fit illustration of the miraculous change to be wrought in man after death?"

"No; for the analogy has an unsatisfactory end. From its chrysalis state, the silkworm but becomes a moth, that very quickly expires. Its longest existence is as a worm. All vanity, vanity, Yoomy, to seek in nature for positive warranty to these aspirations of ours. Through all her provinces, nature seems to promise immortality to life, but destruction to beings. Or, as old Bardianna has it, if not against us, nature is not for us." (P. 210)

Babbalanja rejects the possibility of a benevolent Nature, as well as the Romantic tenet that man can draw analogies from Nature.[3] The irony lies in his own identity as the constantly recycled lunar figure citing Bardianna, who lives again in him. Indeed, like Peepi, Babbalanja claims to contain other entities who force him to do their will instead of his own. Adding to the irony, Media, the avatar of Annatoo, brings the topic to an abrupt halt: "Said Media, rising, 'Babbalanja, you have indeed put aside the courtier; talking of worms and caterpillars to me, a king and a demi-god!'" Here the Ram rejects his insectile past.

Inevitably, the topic turns to the immortal artist:

3. Melville does not seem to have read extensively in Emerson's works until after *Mardi* was completed, at which time he read a number of Emerson's essays while visiting the Hawthornes. Nevertheless, *Mardi* contains passages that seem to be addressed directly to Emerson's "Nature," such as this discussion of man's urge to draw analogies from Nature. For example, in describing the court of King Peepi, Melville notes that the island chiefs retire from the presence of royalty "with their heads between their thighs; so that while advancing in the contrary direction, their faces might be still deferentially turned toward their lord and master. A fine view of him did they obtain. All objects look well through an arch" (202–3). Emerson, in "Nature," instructs the reader to "turn the eyes upside down, by looking at the landscape through your legs, and how agreeable is the picture, though you have seen it any time these twenty years!"

"He, who on all hands passes for a cypher to-day, if at all remembered hereafter, will be sure to pass for the same. For there is more likelihood of being overrated while living, than of being underrated when dead. And to insure your fame, you must die."

"A rather discouraging thought for your race." (P. 211)

A card-shark might confirm this statement by noting that a player is generally consistent enough to be anticipated by his opponent. Even King Peepi is so consistently inconsistent that his courtiers manage to predict which ancestor is to be lord of the ascendant for the day. His particular form of irresponsibility lies in the foolish consistency of his little mind. Again the cipher equals the Fool, while the card-shark can anticipate the "pass."

As the voyagers sail past Pella the Rock, Mohi relates the story of Upi the Archer, pointing again to Sagittarius while at the same time providing another error of tradition. Babbalanja remarks:

"But perhaps we lost time in listening to it; for though we know it, we are none the wiser."

"Be not a cynic," said Media. "No pastime is lost time."

Musing a moment, Babbalanja replied, "My lord, that maxim may be good as it stands; but had you made six words of it, instead of six syllables, you had uttered a better and a deeper." (P. 212)

This word-play encompasses several conclusions that are meaningful to the metaphorical burden of the chapter: a philosophical comment on the recycling of time; a note on man's forgetfulness of the past; a clue to the reader that the second half of *Mardi* can be interpreted only in light of the first half; and a hint that games are well worth the playing for their own sake as well as for their symbolic value. The date of the voyage around Pella is April 1, or April Fool's Day.

*　　*　　*

Chapter 70 prepares for the next landing, on the Isle of Juam, as Hautia's Heralds arrive, bearing flowers, their import subtly mistranslated by Yoomy:

"Shall I, then, be your Flora's flute, and Hautia's dragoman? Held aloft, the Iris signified a message. These purple-woven Circe flowers mean that some spell is weaving. That golden, pining jonquil, which you hold, buried in those wormwood leaves, says plainly to you—Bitter love in absence." (P. 215)

In the language of flowers, the jonquil means, "I desire a return of affection," while the wormwood says that "absence is bitter." As the Heralds depart, one of the maidens waves an oleander three times, correctly translated as "Beware—beware—beware," but Babbalanja misapplies the message as he says, "Taji, beware of Hautia," for the three Avengers are on Taji's trail, and the warning might well refer to them. Media jumps to conclusions when he says, "Well done, Taji, you have killed a queen."

The Heralds' message may also be interpreted in light of the landing about to be made. A new spell (story) is in the making—one that concerns a pining, loveless monarch trapped in a bitter and lonely kingship, wrapped in a sterile girdle, exiled from the world, and craving companionship. The jonquil is Donjalolo "the girl," whose plight is one that all the questers are warned to beware.

The date is April 3, and Luna is again at the Milky Way's vine, at *delta* Gemini.

Ay, the dead are not to be found, even in their graves.   —*Mardi*, 327

April 4. The canoes arrive at the Island of Juam, which is ruled by the effeminate King Donjalolo. The lunar passage ranges from Gemini through Cancer, as indicated by the early emphasis on the Twins, Marjora and Teei, and the later stress on the nautilus-shell nature of Donjalolo's harem. The horizon line cuts off the arm of Pollux, representing the amputation of Marjora's arm.

Mohi relates the story of the brothers and their battle, in which Marjora murders Teei and loses one arm. Marjora decrees that all subsequent kings of Juam must wear his royal girdle and that, once they have assumed the throne, they may not leave the island. The image of the captive king, who wears his emblem of office around his loins, reveals yet another aspect of kingship along with a warning of the effeminacy that follows castration by crown.

Donjalolo's arrival prompts a tale about the origin of the moon, and his lips are described as "moss-rose buds after a shower." Like Luna, who is compelled to traverse the sky from daylight to darkness, Donjalolo is "continually passing and repassing between opposite extremes."

Chapter 75, "Time and Temples," interrupts the episode to present a set of clues in preparation for the entry of Luna at apogee into her house of Cancer on Palm Sunday. The ruling image is that cited from the narrative of "veracious" Gaudentia di Lucca, especially the designation of the "concentric zones of palaces, cross-cut by twelve grand avenues symbolizing the signs of the zodiac, all radiating from the sun-dome in their midst." On Palm Sunday Sol begins his final week in Pisces, and on Good Friday he will enter the constellation Aries. As of April 5, Sol is at the center of the planetary procession, and Luna is moving into direct opposition to Neptune—the fleetest to the slowest.

The subject is Time and in particular the time from conception to fruition. The image of spiral cycles is reiterated as prelude to presenting the analogy of Donjalolo's harem. Almost like a reproach the narrator states that "no fine, firm fabric ever yet grew like a gourd," and in his catalog of growing things, he descends the ladder from the eternal Grampians to the ephemeris, man:

> Even man himself lives months ere his Maker deems him fit to be born; and ere his proud shaft gains its full stature, twenty-one long Julian years must elapse. And his whole mortal life brings not his immortal soul to maturity; nor will all eternity perfect him. Yea, with uttermost reverence, as to human understanding, increase of dominion seems increase of power; and day by day new planets are being added to elder-born Saturns, even as six thousand years ago our own Earth made one more in this system; so, in incident, not in essence, may the Infinite himself be not less than more infinite now, than when old Aldebaran rolled forth from his hand. (Pp. 229–30)

He concludes with an identification of the narrator with the god of Time:

> Thus, then, though Time be the mightiest of Alarics, yet is he the mightiest mason of all. And a tutor, and a counselor, and a physician, and a scribe, and a poet, and a sage, and a king.
> Yea, and a gardener, as ere long will be shown. (P. 230)

From Pallas, symbol of the Temple of Zeus, Taji–Saturn turns to Ceres, symbol of growth and vegetation, birth and rebirth, to signify the coming ritual of Easter.

*   *   *

Chapter 76 introduces the imagery of palms as Taji describes the House of the Morning, whose living pillars require full five hundred moons to grow. These forty years of growth equate to the age of Babbalanja, and in accordance with the ratio of the orbits of Saturn and Luna—twenty-nine years to twenty-nine days—they signify the forty days of Lent.[1]

The House of the Afternoon ranges from fire to stone, "a goodly green mark for the archer in the sun," and the "stone image of one Demi." From one house to the other Donjalolo is daily transported: "Thus dodging day's luminary through life, the

---

1. Alastair Fowler, *Spenser and the Numbers of Time*, p. 106 n., notes that there is an "astronomical relationship between Saturn and Luna, in that one had the nearest and fastest, the other the farthest and slowest, of the planetary orbits—a contrast underlined by the numerical coincidence that the synodic orbital period of the moon in days was the same as the orbital period of Saturn in years. This relationship of one year to one day was occasionally given a symbolic development by other authors (Ficino, *Opera omnia*, p. 1468).

prince hied to and fro in his dominions; on his smooth, spotless brow Sol's rays never shining."

In the House of the Afternoon the bones of Marjora and Teei are interred, inlaid in the floor of a grotto. By Marjora's side is the sickle-shaped weapon with which he slew Teei. Here Babbalanja, "solus," studies the bones and frets on the subjects of death and resurrection as Luna moves through the house of the Twins.

> "To come to this! But the balsam-dropping palms, whose boles run milk, whose plumes wave boastful in the air, they perish in their prime, and bow their blasted trunks. Nothing abideth; the river of yesterday floweth not to-day; the sun's rising is a setting; living is dying; the very mountains melt; and all revolve:—systems and asteroids; the sun wheels through the zodiac, and the zodiac is a revolution. Ah gods! in all this universal stir, am *I* to prove one stable thing?" (Pp. 237–38)

This passage stands in direct contrast to the spirit of "Time and Temples," and the final sentence contains a world of irony, being uttered by the lunar figure whose instability is notorious. The word-play permits more than one interpretation, and one might ask what "stable thing" Babbalanja expects to prove, and in what stable it is to be found.

Immediately after the lunar figure comments on his own stability, we receive the Saturn's-eye view of Luna's spiral as Taji describes the Cancerian castle of Donjalolo:

> And here, in this impenetrable retreat, centrally slumbered the universe-rounded, zodiac-belted, horizon-zoned, sea-girt, reef-sashed, mountain-locked, arbor-nested, royalty-girdled, arm-clasped, self-hugged, indivisible Donjalolo, absolute monarch of Juam:—the husk-inhusked meat in a nut; the innermost spark in a ruby; the juice-nested seed in a golden-rinded orange; the red royal stone in an effeminate peach; the insphered sphere of spheres. (P. 240)

This description of Donjalolo's inscrutable retreat is followed by yet another appeal to the reader to list to the *Almanac,* along with a clue to the nature of lunar time.

> The King had wives thirty in number, corresponding in name to the nights of the moon. For, in Juam, time is not reckoned by

days, but by nights; each night of the lunar month having its own
designation; which, relatively only, is extended to the day.
(P. 241)

      .   .   .   .   .

For convenience, the king is furnished with a card, whereon
are copied the various ciphers upon the arms of his queens; and
parallel thereto, the hieroglyphics significant of the corresponding
Nights of the month. Glancing over this, Donjalolo predicts the
true time of the rising and setting of all his stars. (Pp. 241–42)

The hint is strong here, and it continues with a clue to the
replacement of wives and to the "small population of gray-beards
and hoary-heads" who guard the seraglios. In a burst of comic
description, Taji asserts his own saturnine identity as he tells of
the young wives teasing the old codgers until the uproar brings
Donjalolo racing through his maze of corridors to see "what
under the seventh heavens was the matter." The astrological
correspondence between Saturn and Luna alerts the reader to the
correspondence between the belting orbit of Luna and the
constricting rings of Saturn, as both bodies respond to the same
description.

April 5. On the second day of residence in the hollow at
Willamilla, the incident at breakfast exposes the social
provinciality of all but the cosmopolite king, Jarl.[2] Afterward, in
the "great Palm-Hall" of the House of the Morning, three
explorers come before Donjalolo to report on events in the
outside world. In a variation on the tale of the three blind men
and the elephant, the difficulty of achieving true and complete
interpretation of multifaceted phenomena comes under
consideration. By the *Almanac*'s analogy, the symbolism of Palm
Sunday, the popular concept of Christ the King as opposed to the
humble entry of Jesus riding the ass, and the stellar parable of Sol
leaving the constellation of the Fishes and moving into the tiny
triangular war-zone of Aries—all are contained in the metaphor
of this chapter.

Taji's function as sacrificial Goat ended as Sol entered the
constellation of Pisces on February 24 to illuminate Uranus,
whereupon he began to serve as the Christ-carrier. From this
function he is relieved on April 10, Good Friday.

2. See pp. 62–63.

*   *   *

For a week the wanderers explore the kingdom of Juam and consider the political consequences of rulership by an invalid, insane, and secluded king. The miserable populace suffers under cruel viceroys, who are unchecked by Donjalolo. Babbalanja exclaims, "Let us depart; idle our search, in isles that have viceroys for kings." Media, however, does not relate the comment to his own act of leaving Odo to the rule of a viceroy.

April 11, Saturday. The explorers return from the outposts of Juam to attend the dinner for twenty-five kings. This is the date of the full moon, and the planets are again realigned. In Aquarius are Neptune and Saturn; Pisces holds Venus and Uranus; Mercury is moving from Pisces to Aries; Sol in Aries is attended by Ceres in the Ram's head and Pallas in the tail; and Jupiter, Vesta the Altar, and Mars occupy Taurus, with Mars and Vesta in near conjunction. Hence we find Mars at the Altar as Media celebrates Easter at a feast.

The twenty-five kings are engaged in undignified hilarity as Media's party advances, and Taji reports that a "pair of potentates, who had been playfully trifling, hurriedly adjusted their diadems, threw themselves into attitudes, looking stately as statues. Phidias turned not out his Jupiter so soon." In the horoscope, Jupiter is making the crossing between Aries and Taurus at this point.

All night the feast continues, the wine flowing as Luna turns from full to waning moon. At last Donjalolo launches a flotilla of food, including the meat of the wild boar—Media's insignia—and the kings dine like goats. The final touch is the "King's Own Royal Particular! A vinous Percy! . . . Distilled of yore from purple berries growing in the purple valley of Ardair!" Thus, after the transubstantiated flesh of the Boar of Mars, the lunar wine of Yillah's Ardair flows. But while others fill, Babbalanja grows empty:

> But the imperial Marzilla was not for all; gods only could
> partake; the Kings and demigods of the isles; excluding
> left-handed descendants of sad rakes of immortals, in old times
> breaking heads and hearts in Mardi, bequeathing bars-sinister to

many mortals, who now in vain might urge a claim to a cup-full of right regal Marzilla.

The Royal Particular was pressed upon me, by the now jovial Donjalolo. (P. 257)

The bloodlike wine of Ardair combines the names of Mars and Yillah.

"Drink, Taji," cried Donjalolo, "drink deep. In this wine a king's heart is dissolved. Drink long; in this wine lurk the seeds of the life everlasting." (P. 257)

And Donjalolo bursts forth in an invocation to the Grail:

". . . 'gainst the goblet ne'er sin;
.   .   .   .   .   .
"As the spheres, with a roll, some fiery of soul,
Others golden, with music, revolve round the pole;
So let our cups, radiant with many hued wines,
Round and round in groups circle, our Zodiac's signs:—"
(P. 258)

and, drunk on wine and flesh, the revelers subside as Taji comments, "If ever Taji joins a club, be it a Beef-Steak Club of Kings!"

The kings rise at noon on Easter Sunday and promptly return to sleep. Early on the next day, April 13, Media's party calls on Donjalolo to say farewell. "Pale and languid," and suffering from hangover, Donjalolo cries:

"Go, leave me; go, and be rovers again throughout blooming Mardi. For me, I am here for aye.—Bring me wine, slaves! quick!

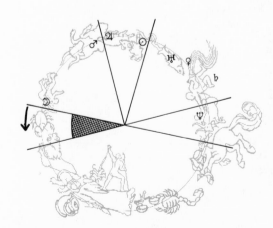

April 4, 1846

The Isle of Juam is a lunar island and represents the sign of Cancer the Crab, ruled by Luna.

that I may pledge my guests fitly. Alas, Media, at the bottom of
this cup are no sparkles as at top. Oh, treacherous, treacherous
friend! full of smiles and daggers. Yet for such as me, oh wine,
thou art e'en a prop, though it pierce the side; for man must lean.
Thou wine art the friend of the friendless, though a foe to all.
King Media, let us drink. More cups!—And now, farewell."
(P. 261)

The association of the wine with the pierced side recalls the
sacramental nature of the death of Aleema as well as the symbolic
identity of Luna with the Cup. At the same time, the passage
recalls the biblical injunction against kings who partake of strong
drink.[3]

3. Cf. Proverbs 31:4–7.

Their souls ascended, ere their bodies touched. —*Mardi*, 278

May 2. Luna again approaches her first quarter turn, and Hautia's Heralds arrive to spur her on, bringing a Venus-car, a pallid blossom buried in hemlock leaves, and a cascade of moss roses and verbena. Yoomy translates, "Fly to love; . . . I have wrought a death; . . . yet fly, oh, fly to me; all rosy joys and sweets are mine!" In his song Yoomy apparently identifies the pallid blossom as a white verbena. Again he is subtly inaccurate. The hemlock translates, "You will cause my death," while the verbena connotes sensibility or asks the receiver, "Pray for me." Yoomy's error creates a significant difference in the tenor of the message, especially since the episode to come results in the death of both Jarl and Samoa, and, accurately read, the flower message serves as a warning of these deaths.

After a brief landing at Ohonoo to visit King Uhia, the questers travel on for a longer and more meaningful visit.

May 15. By the time Melville began writing *Mardi,* the periods of Neptune's orbit had been fairly well established, but the data did not appear in the almanacs before the issue of 1849. From the computations of the discovery, however, it is possible to ascertain that the planet's retrograde period would last five months—two and a half months on either side of opposition. The *Almanac* shows that on May 21 Saturn is square to Sol, and though Neptune's position is not given, he must necessarily arrive at the square before Saturn.

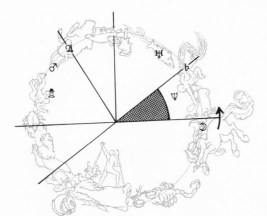

May 15, 1846

The Capricorn island of Mondoldo, ruled by the jovial King Borabolla, covers the area occupied by Neptune and Saturn. During the questers' stay on this isle, Sol moves the horizon lines so Neptune can no longer remain in the field of action. Saturn also becomes dormant, but Taji "lives" through the planet Uranus.

In the holiday metaphor, one event in the Christian calendar holds a doubly gratuitous relationship to Neptune—that of Ascension, which in 1846 falls on May 21. The date of Christ's departure from Earth is traditionally associated with the ancient Italian ritual of the Doges' Espousal of the Adriatic Sea, making of Neptune a "He-bride." It follows then that, as Neptune sinks below the solar horizon and begins his retrograde course, Jarl, the Christ figure and the man of the Hebrides, must be left behind. Since Jarl must go, Samoa must depart also, for the *Parki* image of arm and body has linked the two characters, that is, the arm of Aquarius completes the body of Taurus. The multiple horizons established by the three canoes of Media enable Samoa's Aldebaran to be excluded from the field of action as Jarl's Neptune sets.

The Island of Mondoldo represents the arc that encompasses Sagittarius and Capricorn, the constellations opposite Juam's Gemini and Cancer. From the schedule of activities on Mondoldo, the date of the landing is estimated to be Friday, May 15, as Luna moves through Jupiter's house of Sagittarius. The "grand piscatory" dinner confirms a Friday arrival, for we are about to enter a section of *Mardi* that contains a great deal of imagery—and satire—directed toward Catholicism. On Saturday, May 16, as three conjunctions occur—one not reported by the *Almanac*—the wedding and the funeral take place. Sunday, May 17, as the moon is at third quarter, the Avengers and Hautia's Heralds appear; and on Monday, May 18, the voyagers leave the island as Venus arrives at conjunction with Uranus.

The planetary identity of Borabolla becomes evident in his description as a jolly, jovial, sociable old man, "Round all over; round of eye and of head; and like the jolly round Earth, roundest and biggest about the Equator. A girdle of red was his Equinoctial Line." Since Jupiter is in conjunction with Sol in Taurus, Taji reports, "This old Borabolla permitted naught to come between his head and the sun; not even gray hairs. Bald as a gourd, right down on his brazen skull, the rays of the luminary converged" (285).

Borabolla, meeting his guests, arrives like Aleema, "seated cross-legged upon a dais" in a large canoe, accompanied by five other canoes, as Aleema had been accompanied by his five sons.

"Soon the water shoaled (approaching land is like nearing truth in metaphysics)," comments Taji, in full opposition to the idea that truth abides in the depths, which Melville so frequently stresses. As the questers near Borabolla's castle, they observe that it is enclosed in a stockade, but "in the palisade was a mighty breach, not an entrance-way, wide enough to admit six Daniel Lamberts abreast." To demonstrate his hospitality the king shows his gates "lashed back with osiers." Babbalanja observes, "Is not the open gate the sign of an open heart?" Referring again to the Aleema episode: osiers concealed the entrance to Yillah's sanctuary on Aleema's canoe, and Taji cut them aside. That also was "not an entrance-way." Aleema had, upon meeting Taji, seemed to recall something "terrific," and then lapsed into much "merryment."

As an avatar of Aleema, Borabolla exhibits an extraordinarily altered aspect, having changed from the reluctant host to the model of hospitality; his environmental accoutrements are also changed: the closed and tightly laced tent of Aleema contrasts to the breached wall and gaping shelter of Borabolla. The Jupiter of the first incident had been opposite the loins of Virgo, but now the planet is opposite Scorpio, and the implication is that of a maidenly wall once breached and now open and available to all guests.

Here the design that Taji fulfilled in the ritual murder of Aleema takes on still another significance in the religious metaphor—one that must be recalled when the voyagers subsequently visit Maramma. Insofar as Jupiter has represented the priesthood, in full charge of the sacrament and originally strictly limiting those to whom it might be administered, he now dispenses it freely to everyone—an overly generous host forcing fish and hospitality even on unwilling, cautious guests. This is the Medieval Church of the Lost Grail—the "whore of Rome" whose favors are not only available to but forced on all who come within her reach.

After the "death" of Aleema, the fish convened in the ocean, so thick that Samoa could reach out with his one arm and catch them at will. On Mondoldo, the fish are carefully processed, forced through channels of fresh water until no trace of salt remains in them.[1] Aleema was called "Old Aaron" during his

1. Cf. Matthew 5:13.

exclusive period, and thus he must also be seen as the pre-Christian priest figure whose sacred craft gave birth to the new dispensation, prematurely, while Taji had brief possession of Yillah the Cup and was accompanied by Jarl the Lance. Now, however, Taji is to part with Jarl—at least temporarily—and Jarl is to be left with Borabolla.

In observing the process by which salty fish are converted into fresh, Taji is reminded of Saint Anthony preaching to the fish. He comments, "Of all nature's animated kingdoms, fish are the most unchristian, inhospitable, heartless, and cold-blooded of creatures. At least, so seem they to strangers." This thought leads him to suggest that "whoso shall Christianize, and by so doing, humanize the sharks," will work a greater good for mankind than the missionaries. And indeed, Taji "humanizes" the shark as he sees the ghost of Aleema in every ghostly greenish trail that moves through the waters. Because of his own identification with Leviathan and Matsyavatar, it is notable that he postulates immortality for whales: "A creature eighty feet long without stockings, and thirty feet round the waist before dinner, is not inconsiderately to be consigned to annihilation" (289).

After several generous snacks, dinner is served, followed by the goatskin of wine. Borabolla toasts "Lord Capricornus," and then "the goblet fell from his hand, the purple flew from his wine to his face; and Borabolla fell back into the arms of his servitors." Lord Capricornus has struck the jovial king with an attack of gout. The "gout-fiend" departs, however, and "the old king brightened up; by degrees becoming jolly as ever."

*   *   *

Chapters 96 through 98 concern Samoa as surgeon and artist. The diver Karhownoo having injured his head in a dive, Samoa performs a trepan. The operation is a success but the patient dies, whereupon Samoa proposes to tell a story. First, however, Taji speaks of faith, and this chapter presents a distinction and a turning point in the quest for artistic potency. Taji arrives at the crucial distinction between belief and faith that will later be echoed in the soliloquy of Pani on Maramma:

> The higher the intelligence, the more faith, and the less credulity:
> Gabriel rejects more than we, but out-believes us all. The greatest
> marvels are first truths; and first truths the last unto which we
> attain. Things nearest are furthest off. Though your ear be
> next-door to your brain, it is forever removed from your sight.
> Man has a more comprehensive view of the moon, than the man
> in the moon himself. We know the moon is round; he only infers
> it. It is because we ourselves are in ourselves, that we know
> ourselves not. And it is only of our easy faith, that we are not
> infidels throughout; and only of our lack of faith, that we believe
> what we do. (Pp. 296–97)

Yet, even as Taji speaks of "things nearest," he fails to recognize
that he is vainly pursuing the obvious mark, the moon, while
failing to discover the new world in his near company. And now,
following through with the concept of development begun in
"Time and Temples," Taji identifies himself with time past, from
the first "ark" to the one to come—the coming month of June:

> I was at the subsiding of the Deluge. . . . With the Israelites, I
> fainted in the wilderness. . . . I, it was, who suppressed the lost
> work of Manetho, on the Egyptian theology, as containing
> mysteries not to be revealed to posterity; . . . I, who originated
> the conspiracy against that purple murderer, Domitian; I, who in
> the senate moved, that great and good Aurelian be emperor. . . . I
> touched Isabella's heart, that she hearkened to Columbus. . . . I
> am the leader of the Mohawk masks; . . . I am the Vailed Persian
> Prophet; I, the man in the iron mask; I, Junius. (P. 297)

In a subsequent dream passage, the succeeding months will be
similarly named. Meanwhile, Taji claims for himself the roles of
the masked critic and the hidden influence. We may suspect that
again he is usurping the role of the mysterious Taj, the voice of
Sol.

In Chapter 98, Samoa tells his story. It is of a man in whose
cranium a pig's brain was implanted. Taji identifies Samoa with
Dante and with the "bull" as well:

> It was, in good part, his villainous transcribers, who made
> monstrosities of Mandeville's travels. And though all liars go to
> Gehenna; yet, assuming that Mandeville died before Dante; still,

though Dante took the census of Hell, we find not Sir John, under the likeness of a roasted neat's tongue, in that infernalest of infernos, The Inferno. (P. 298)

That Samoa's "neat's-tongue story" is related to "bull" is clear; but the subject of the tale is the grafting of one identity upon another, which also is the subject of *Mardi*. The "anecdote was credited by some present. But Babbalanja held out to the last":

> "I have long thought, that men, pigs, and plants, are but curious physiological experiments; and that science would at last enable philosophers to produce new species of beings, by somehow mixing, and concocting the essential ingredients of various creatures; and so forming new combinations. My friend Atahalpa, the astrologer and alchymist, has long had a jar, in which he has been endeavoring to hatch a fairy, the ingredients being compounded according to a receipt of his own." (P. 299)[2]

2. See Merton M. Sealts, Jr., "Melville's 'Friend Atahalpa,'" *Notes and Queries*, 194 (January 22, 1949), 37.

Such a grafting is now to occur as the questers leave Jarl–Neptune with Borabolla. From this union the three-arrow trident is formed by which Jarl will "stick to" Taji for the remainder of the quest in the persona of the specter sons of Aleema. Moreover, as Neptune has usurped the realm of Jupiter, Jarl will usurp the priesthood of Aleema.

The wedding and the funeral complete the second day on Mondoldo, each serving as a symbol of the coming day of Ascension and as a mark of the triple conjunction that occurs on Saturday, May 16. As Luna passes through Capricorn, Mercury is conjunct Ceres, Mars conjunct Vesta the Altar, and Luna conjunct Neptune.

May 17, Sunday. Luna, nearing Saturn in Aquarius, is at third quarter as the sons of Aleema arrive at Mondoldo. Taji reports, "Then came over me the wild dream of Yillah; and, for a space, like a madman I raved." He rushes upon the skeletons, but Media leads him aside. They "foamed out" curses: "Oh murderer! white curses upon thee! Bleached be thy soul with our hate!" Taji "lay fainting against the hard-throbbing heart of Samoa," and once more in his thoughts "the green corpse of the priest drifted by."

The strangers recite another variation of the story of Yillah —this, a realistic one that shares the same imagery as Yillah's own original, more fanciful, version. Here at last we discover that a mother–child relationship is involved, as the sons of Aleema tell the history of a troublesome white god, his wife and their child, and his vengeful murder of three of their native countrymen. The child was torn from her mother and hidden in Ardair for eventual sacrifice to Apo in Tedaidee.

> "There arose a tumult, hostile to our sire's longer holding custody of Yillah; when, foreseeing that the holy glen would ere long be burst open, he embarked the maiden in yonder canoe, to accelerate her sacrifice at the great shrine of Apo, in Tedaidee.— The rest thou knowest, murderer!" (P. 308)

From this we learn that the "Eleusinian mystery" of the Aleema incident had indeed been premature. Since the ancient mysteries had been performed in June and September, and the murder of Aleema occurred in February, it becomes evident that the reference to the mysteries is not to be dismissed as an incidental image. The empty island of Maramma is to represent the month of June, its mystery strangely altered.

*   *   *

The curses of the sons of Aleema are followed by the appearance of the Heralds bearing wax-myrtle berries and a lily of the valley, crushed. As Yoomy translates the message, the Heralds must correct his interpretation, confirming that Yoomy is indeed subject to error in this regard. Corrected, the message is this: "Taji, you have been enlightened, but the lily you seek is crushed" (309). The lily of the valley indicates "return of happiness" and does not necessarily refer to Yillah, as Taji assumes. The Heralds fling bilberries and wave oleanders, rightly interpreted as "Harm! treachery! beware!"—a warning perhaps of the imminent fates of Jarl and Samoa. Departing, one Herald strews dead leaves in Taji's path, the rest wave crocuses, yellow, white, and purple. The dead leaves mean "melancholia," while the crocuses connote "youthful gladness," and Yoomy comments, "Sad your path, but merry Hautia's."

*   *   *

Media's party quits Mondoldo on Monday, May 18. As Luna, at third quarter, passes Saturn in Aquarius, Taji meditates on the history of Yillah and considers the mysteries unriddled. For the first time he questions the validity of Yoomy's interpretation of Hautia's message, despite the fact that the Heralds had made certain that the message was properly decoded.

As they voyage onward, Yoomy sings the song of Marlena: "The words were about a curious hereafter, believed in by some people in Mardi; a sort of nocturnal Paradise, where the sun and its heat are excluded: one long, lunar day, with twinkling stars to keep company." Mohi comments that the song is "soporific as the airs of Nora-Bamma," and Yoomy attempts to interpret his remark. Babbalanja suggests that Yoomy learn to interpret ambiguous statements in such a way that flattering meanings may be derived from them. This suggestion is designed to draw our attention also to Yoomy's questionable abilities as an interpreter, so we shall investigate for ourselves the tenor of Hautia's messages. It also conveys an evaluation of Babbalanja's scientific method.

The reference to the long lunar day stresses again that the summer sequence is to be ruled by the degrees of Luna rather than Sol.

*   *   *

Chapter 104 declares Bardianna a "trump" after Babbalanja advances his theory that devils are sent into men as additional punishment for the devils, so that "the devils themselves are possessed by men, not men by them." Media objects to this concept on the grounds that "by implication it absolves you mortals from moral accountability." Seen in the light of the symbolic function of Mondoldo, Media's statement must be taken as ironically true.[3]

3. If Melville is aware of the hypothesis regarding Vulcan (see Chapter IX, n. 8) then Azzageddi represents the unscientific act of inventing a "planet" to fit into a theory, thereby turning Bode's law into a procrustean bed and demonstrating man's tendency to invent a devil to suit every need.

XVII. June and the Mysteries

Cried Mohi, "But Alma is also quoted by others, in vindication
of the pilgrimages to Ofo. They declare that the prophet himself
was the first pilgrim that thitherward journeyed: that from thence
he departed to the skies." —*Mardi*, 324

May 24. The voyagers arrive at Maramma, where they
remain until June 5. The tour of Maramma rounds out for the
time being the metaphor of theology, and is succeeded by a
concentration on the imagery of letters, introduced by a visit to
Oh-Oh and Jiji and to the Vowels on Pimminee. The summer
solstice on June 20 signals the visit to Earth.

To the ancients of the Mediterranean world, the month of
June brought the dry and arid period, during which Ceres
searched for her lost daughter. From this figure Melville derives
the sterility of Maramma. The island is tied by reference to the
period of Dante, during which the Church was exceptionally
corrupt and free with her favors. Moreover, the Dantean theme
of Italianate revenge characterizes the episode as well. Melville
does not want his reader to lose sight of the fact that *Mardi* is in
one sense a book of vengeance, though it is masked as
completely as Junius. The name of Maramma carries a double
allusion—to the Dantean description of the wild and swampy
region of Maremma and to the combination of Mars and Ammon
(Jupiter) who govern this period of the Church.[1] Maramma
represents the Church, deprived of both Grail and Lance,
presiding over a multiplicity of viewpoints, and beset by
iconology and idolatry. The dominion of Maramma covers a
variety of islets, each subject to its own form of corruption. Pani
is the blind "all-seeing" guide, ironically following the biblical
statement that "a little child shall lead them."

On the day of the questers' landing on Maremma, the new
moon is conjunct Jupiter, which is still within ten degrees of Sol.[2]
As a result, Pani notes that "the Pontiff would be invisible for
several days to come; being engaged with particular company."
The connection of the Pontiff with Borabolla is indicated as Pani
strikes Media dumb by announcing the Pontiff's guests to be "no

1. Dante, *Inferno*, Canto XXV, ll.
19–21. The obvious origin of the name,
however, is the Toa–Marama of William
Ellis, *Polynesian Researches*, II, 58. It is
possible also that the combination of Mars
and Ammon designates the militant
priesthood and its control over the
superstitious through the various forms of
idolatry.

2. The degree of conjunction
between Sol and Jupiter could be from
five to seven degrees, since planets, even
slow-moving Jupiter, appear to move
rapidly at conjunction and slowly at
opposition.

other than certain incorporeal deities from above, passing the Capricorn Solstice at Maramma." As we have noted, Jarl occupies the area of the Capricorn solstice, and Luna passed through the solstice on her way toward Jupiter. This visit ends as Luna reaches the Cancer solstice at third quarter on June 2.

As announced by the title of Chapter 108, the Pontiff's name is Hivohitee 1848. Obviously, Melville wants the reader to associate the Pontiff with the Pope who was presiding in Rome in early June, 1848. Actually, Pope Gregory XVI died on June 1, 1846, and his successor, Pius IX, was elected June 16 and consecrated June 21, 1846. Thus, on the date indicated for this celestial visitation, a Pope was indeed entertaining "certain incorporeal deities from above." According to Catholic doctrine, the office of Pope is continuous as Viceroy of Christ, whether or not a living man occupies it. On this June 2, then, the office of the Roman Pontiff is vacant as Mardi's Hivohitee is "invisible."

Taji reports that Hivohitee's treatment of his guests is somewhat high-handed, since he eats and drinks while "carrying on the flow of soul" with them. "And truly, the sight of their entertainer thus enjoying himself in the flesh, while they themselves starved on the ether, must have been exceedingly provoking to these aristocratic and aerial strangers" (333). This scene recalls Taji's question when first entertained as a demigod by Media on Odo: "Did deities dine?" Apparently Hivohitee thinks not.

> It was reported, furthermore, that Hivohitee, one of the haughtiest of Pontiffs, purposely treated his angelical guests thus cavalierly; in order to convince them, that though a denizen of earth; a sublunarian; and in respect of heaven, a mere provincial; he (Hivohitee) accounted himself full as good as seraphim from the capital; and that too at the Capricorn Solstice, or any other time of the year. Strongly bent was Hivohitee upon humbling their supercilious pretensions. (P. 333)

The dignity of the pontiffs of Maramma is transmitted by heirs male, "the fruit of successive marriages between uterine brother and sister. A conjunction deemed incestuous in some lands."

To Maramma's pontiffs is ascribed the power of "healing with a touch the bites of the ravenous sharks," with whom they are on the friendliest terms. At their ordination, "the ceremony

3. See Chapter IX, note 8, regarding the relationship of Polynesian priests to the sharks, from Ellis, *Polynesian Researches*.

was not deemed complete, until embarking in his barge, he was saluted High Priest by three sharks drawing near." Again, the figure of the priest is identified with the shark. But more of this later.[3]

Pani is presented as a gross hypocrite until his encounter with the ambitious youth who desires to climb the peak of Ofo; then he reveals a peculiar type of humility as he speaks through his mask of blindness:

> "Off masks, mankind, that I may know what warranty of fellowship with others, my own thoughts possess. Why, upon this one theme, oh Oro! must all dissemble? Our thoughts are not our own. . . . What is this shining light in heaven, this sun they tell me of? Or, do they lie? Methinks, it might blaze convictions; but I brood and grope in blackness; I am dumb with doubt; yet, 'tis not doubt, but worse: I doubt my doubt." (Pp. 338–39)

Pani, his mask briefly fallen, repeats in substance the same idea set forth in "Faith and Knowledge" as he regards the "wild boy" who, "without faith, seems full of it. The undoubting doubter believes the most."

The voyagers witness in Maramma a number of violent deeds committed in the name of Alma. Mohi describes Alma as an illustrious prophet who "had appeared to the Mardians under the different titles of Brami, Manko, and Alma. Many thousands of moons had elapsed since his last and most memorable avatar, as Alma on the isle of Maramma" (348). It develops that Babbalanja's father had been burned for blasphemy on Maramma in the name of Alma, so the name has become almost hateful to him. He suggests that the concept of hell may be more precious to Mardians than heaven itself, and that Alma's mission "seems to have been the revealing to us Mardians the existence of horrors, most hard to escape." And here Media asks the question on which the opening image of Mardi is based: "But think you not, that possibly, Alma may have been misconceived? Are you certain that doctrine is his?" (350). In this manner the question of the conception of Virgo by Arcturus—or Jove—or Cetus—arises on Maramma.

After the tour of Maramma's lagoon, Babbalanja relates another version of the anecdote concerning the blind men and the elephant, but this time with a double referent. In addition to the obvious allusion to the many ways of interpreting God, Babbalanja's story points forward to the impending visit of the nine planets to Earth and to the prophetic nature of the journey. It is, in effect, to be a voyage to "Tomorrow." The story is of nine blind men who visit a valley ruled by King Tammaro, where they examine the many trunks of a huge banyan tree to determine which is the original, true trunk. Each claims that the trunk he has found is the original one, and they fall to fighting. When Tammaro calls upon each of them to clasp the trunk he had declared to be the original, "one and all, they changed places," crying out that each grasped the original. Tammaro orders them to leave the valley. Media greatly admires the story:

> "By my scepter, but it is well done! Ha, ha! blind men round a banian! Why, Babbalanja, no demi-god could surpass it. Taji, could you?"
>
> "But, Babbalanja, what under the sun mean you by your blind story!" cried Mohi. "Obverse, or reverse, I can make nothing out of it."
>
> "Others may," said Babbalanja. "It is a polysensuum, old man."
>
> "A pollywog!" said Mohi. (P. 357)[4]

At last Hivohitee 1848 is available for visitation, now retired to his private sanctuary. The voyagers approach through a luxuriant garden—as meaning-laden as Hautia's flower messages —holding eyes, ears, and nostrils like the monkeys of the Japanese temple. Melville provides an order among them specifically to separate the identities of Mohi (Saturn–Mercury) and Yoomy (Uranus–Mercury), so Yoomy assumes the position of Mercury for this scene: "Yoomy above Babbalanja, my lord Media above him, and Braid-Beard, our guide, in the air, above all." The hermit ghost resides at the temple pagoda, and he selects Yoomy to be his guest, translator, and interpreter. After bringing Yoomy into the dark interior of the pagoda, the hermit queries him:

> "What see you, mortal?"
>
> "Chiefly darkness," said Yoomy, wondering at the audacity of the question.

4. *Pollywog* is a term used to designate a novice sailor before initiation has made him a *Shellback*. According to the Oxford English Dictionary, the earliest use of the term in literature occurred in *Episodes* by Oliphant in 1854. Linguists state, however, that there is a lag of approximately thirty to fifty years between earliest use and first literary appearance. Though Olmsted, Dana, and others use the term *greenhorn*, it is possible that *pollywog* was used to a limited extent during the ritual.

"I dwell in it. But what else see you, mortal?"

"The dim gleaming of thy gorget."

"But that is not me. What else dost thou see?"

"Nothing."

"Then thou hast found me out, and seen all! Descend." (Pp. 360–61)

This visit occurs on June 5, as Mercury is conjunct Jupiter and Luna is in Virgo. Yoomy, not comprehending the encounter, remains silent among his companions until at last they return to their canoes. Then only does Yoomy ask for explanation:

> Whereupon, Mohi lifted his hands in amazement; exclaiming at the blindness of the eyes, which had beheld the supreme Pontiff of Maramma, without knowing it.
>
> The old hermit was no other than the dread Hivohitee; the pagoda, the inmost oracle of the isle. (P. 361)

Therefore, Taji must view the inner mystery of Maramma not through his own eyes, but through those of Yoomy the poet, who for once fails utterly of interpretation. Babbalanja "endeavors to explain the mystery," and so does Mohi. But the secret is not explained by either of these interpreters.

In all probability, Melville's contemporaries who were informed about current events could have readily recognized Hivohitee 1848 as the recently deceased Pope Gregory, who had not been one of the more admirable Popes. On June 16, 1846, a new Pontiff was selected and installed as Pius IX. Pius, an opponent of the reactionary policy of Cardinal Lambruschini, minister of his predecessor, signalized his accession by a general amnesty, by the introduction of representative government, and by favoring Italian unity. When Pius refused to take up arms against Austria, his popularity waned. Rossi, his minister, was murdered while trying to restore order, and Pius was forced to flee in disguise to Naples in November, 1848. So it was that on June 5, 1846, and also at the time Melville was writing these chapters, the Papacy was vacant—in the first instance, because of the death of an arrogant Pope Gregory, and in the second, the flight of the benevolent but betrayed Pope Pius. In both cases, one who looked to the Pontiff would see, like Yoomy, nothing.

At this point let us review some of the imagery surrounding Jarl from the beginning of *Mardi.* We have noted that his introduction had been marked by references to the birth of Christ and that he was associated with the ninth planet, Neptune, though mistaken for a Jupiter figure. After the encounter with Aleema the Priest, he was shown to bear on his arm a tattoo of Christ crucified. He wore a conical Guayaquil hat, for which Media later jokingly substituted a conical calabash resembling a mitre. He has been left on the Capricorn island of Borabolla, who had assumed Aleema's place as a Jupiter figure. Now we find Hivohitee visiting with celestial beings at the Capricorn solstice and insulting them roundly during a period when the unsympathetic Gregory XVI, newly deceased, was to be succeeded by the ninth Pius, who grants a general amnesty.

As the questers leave Maramma, discussing various interpretations of the mystery of the Pontiff, they receive tidings of Jarl's death. Since Samoa's demise had been reported as having occurred "much later" when the party left Mondoldo, why is Jarl's death, which is reported to have occurred immediately after their departure, not related until now? It is logical to assume that Melville intends Jarl's death to be associated with the episode of Maramma, especially since the Heralds had warned Taji of an impending death before the episode began and had further warned him of harm and treachery. Since Jarl represents the undiscovered ninth planet and the benevolent ninth Pius has not yet been revealed as of *Mardi*'s June 5, we may assume that Jarl has again effected a usurpation and that his "ascension" elevated him to replace Jupiter in the priesthood. Already the relationship between Neptune's sea and the Doges, suggested by the holiday of Ascension, has made the transition possible. Taji is informed that Jarl was discovered with three arrows in his heart, the three strangers having fled. "Slain for me," sobs Taji and tries to turn: "Instantly the three canoes had been reversed; and full soon Jarl's dead hand in mine, had not Media interposed" (364). Media tells Taji, "To death, your presence will not bring life back." But Jarl's next avatar is to grant amnesty in accordance with the spirit of Mardi Gras, as will soon be demonstrated.

In the evening, Hautia's Heralds appear. Two leaves, one shaped like a trident, the other like an arrow, are presented, then a faded daffodil, signifying the fading of self-love, or of deceitful hope.[5]

5. The Tri-foil leaf, also called Birdsfoot Trefoil, signifies "revenge."

*   *   *

Chapter 119 is a prelude to the retrograde period of Saturn,
which begins on June 11, the Feast of Corpus Christi. In his
dreams, Taji feels the pull of the past in the shrouds that bind
him to the ship and the sea. Then he hears the concert of times
to come:

> In me, many worthies recline, and converse. I list to St. Paul who
> argues the doubts of Montaigne; Julian the Apostate
> cross-questions Augustine: and Thomas-a-Kempis unrolls his old
> black letters for all to decipher. Zeno murmurs maxims beneath
> the hoarse shout of Democritus; and though Democritus laugh
> loud and long, and the sneer of Pyrrho be seen; yet, divine Plato,
> and Proclus, and Verulam are of my counsel; and Zoroaster
> whispered me before I was born. . . . My memory is a life beyond
> birth; my memory, my library of the Vatican, its alcoves all
> endless perspectives, eve-tinted by cross-lights from Middle-Age
> oriels. (Pp. 367–68)

Despite Media, Taji succeeds, in his dreams, in turning back
toward his old comrade amid imagery of saints, Vaticans, and life
before birth.

By reference to the masked Junius, Julius the Apostate, and
Augustine, these chapters provide clues not only to the period of
time but to the thematic content of each period to come.
Moreover, these dramatic pauses reveal steps in the development
of the artist, and here the multiplicity of idols in Maramma is
echoed in the multiplicity of the shrined worthies in the mind of
the maturing author. The names listed form the diet of the artist
—a rich diet of meat and wine that generates the restless energy
of creativity like a fever. This image initiates the chapters that
center around food, providing Taji's artistic and critical diet as he
is exposed to the letters of the islands to come.

In Chapter 120, Media sets forth advice to Babbalanja that
states the intended technique of *Mardi* itself: "Meditate as much
as you will, Babbalanja, but say little aloud, unless in a merry and
mythical way." Whereupon, in the following chapter, another
parable of variant points of view ensues, this time regarding the

myths and scientific opinions about amber and ambergris.[6]
Babbalanja declines to believe that ideas are found imbedded in
amber, yet Mohi notes that "black-letter characters have been
discovered in amber." When they discuss ambergris, Media states
the scientific fact that it is "a morbid secretion of the spermaceti
whale; for, like you mortals, the whale is at times a sort of
hypochondriac and dyspeptic." Now we should begin to see a
connection between the sickeningly rich literary diet of heavy
readers, which creates heartburn, and this well-known fact
concerning whales' dyspepsia. Media informs his audience that
hunters would sometimes pursue a whale and strike it,
whereupon "it would start off in a dastardly fright, leaving
certain fragments in its wake." Since, in Melville's metaphor, Taji
is the melancholy Leviathan, he too emits poetic fragments when
frightened by his pursuers. "These fragments the hunters picked
up, giving over the chase for awhile," Media continues, and
Babbalanja questions whether "it would have been wise to kill
the fish that dropped such treasures."[7]

The parable of ingestion continues as the visit to Oh-Oh
leaves Babbalanja with a servere case of excessive literature,
having found in the archives of Oh-Oh an ancient work called "A
Happy Life." Gorging himself upon it, he is thrown into an
emotional dyspepsia, and wails, "Tell me, Mohi, where the
Ephina? I may have come to the Penultimate, but where, sweet
Yoomy, is the Ultimate? Ah, companions! I faint, I am wordless:
—something,—nothing,—riddles,—does Mardi hold her?" (390).
Having delivered himself of this effusion, as though he were Ben
Jonson's poetaster, Babbalanja swoons briefly and then revives
quickly and serenely, his indigestion relieved.

The brief visit to Jiji reveals a money-miser who starves,
although he has many teeth, the currency of the islands. Vee-Vee
tosses him a yam. This episode is a reverse image of the Isle of
Valapee, or Isle of Yams, where teeth were valued also, and in
this garden of letters, we should recall that the yam symbolizes
Sol and that teeth, when properly planted, grow into armed
warriors.

As the questers sail from Padulla, Yoomy prepares to sing,
and Babbalanja eases his girdle for the feast of song, "as Apicus
would for a banquet." Afterward, however, Yoomy's listeners

6. Cf. the myth of Aetheria, one of the Heliades, daughter of Apollo and sister of Phaeton. After the death of Phaeton, she was changed into a poplar tree that wept tears of amber.

7. Cf. *Moby Dick*, Chs. 81 and 92, regarding the sick whale and the ambergris. Insofar as Yoomy is the literary aspect of Taji, his poetry seems to attract the attention of the Avengers.

accuse him of having eaten flounders to account for the flatness of his song. "But Yoomy vouchsafed no reply, he was ten thousand leagues off in a reverie: somewhere in the Hyades perhaps" (394). And indeed, Yoomy's Mercury is approximately in the area of the Hyades, in the nose of Taurus, or under the "neat's tongue." The conversation turns to the subject of fame:

> "Mardi is a monster," says old Bardianna, "whose eyes are fixed in its head, like a whale's; it can see but two ways, and those comprising but a small arc of a perfect vision. Poets, heroes, and men of might, are all around this monster Mardi. But stand before me on stilts, or I will behold you not, says the monster; brush back your hair; inhale the wind largely; lucky are all men with dome-like foreheads; luckless those with pippin-heads; loud lungs are a blessing; a lion is no lion that can not roar." (P. 395)[8]

8. Cf. *Moby Dick*, Ch. 74, in regard to the vision span of whales, in degrees of arc.

The conversation is long; it concludes with another observation on the nature of art and cycles: "The truest poets are but mouth-pieces; and some men are duplicates of each other; I see myself in Bardianna" (397).

                    *   *   *

The two-day visit to the Tapparians on Pimminee, with the pretentious Begum and her daughters, the Vowels, and all the "fripperies, fopperies, and finesses," presents a satire on men and manners that requires no analysis. Suffice it to quote Babbalanja on the subject:

> "They are irreclaimable Tapparians; not so much fools by contrivance of their own, as by an express, though inscrutable decree of Oro's. For one, my lord, I can not abide them."
>   Nor could Taji. (P. 413)

The irony is that the Tapparians, in their deceptions and gullibilities, hold the mirror up to Taji and to the rest of the questers as well. Each foolish mannerism displayed by the Tapparians has been displayed by one or more of the voyagers, including Babbalanja.

*   *   *

June 8–9. As Luna moves into Scorpio, Babbalanja creates a
scientific sandwich in memory of Captain Cook's sponsor, the
"Oil" of Sandwich. The Isle of Fossils is an extension and an
enlargement of the piece of amber in which thoughts are
preserved, and in the "antique tablets" are "Luxor marks,
Tadmor ciphers, Palenque inscriptions." Media challenges Mohi
to interpret the hieroglyphs, but the Chronicler is nonplussed.
"Said Media, 'Expound *you,* then, Sage Babbalanja.' " And as
Mohi and Babbalanja break into a quarrel—Mercury and Luna
being at opposition—Media exclaims, "Will you quit driving your
sleet upon us? Have done. Expound these rocks" (415).

In answer, Babbalanja displays a fossilized picture of a "Last
Supper" with a mitred personage about to be murdered by his
host, a king. Is this another clue to the death of Jarl?

Babbalanja's geological sandwich is suggestive in the extreme
and heavy with sexual image-play, as befits a record of the
development of life. But throughout, the metaphor of food
persists. As though speaking of the battle of the ancients and the
moderns, Babbalanja concludes: "Thus fared the old diluvians:
arrant gormandizers and beef-bolters. We Mardians famish on the
superficial strata of deposits; cracking our jaws on walnuts,
filberts, cocoanuts and clams. My lord, I've done."

It is upon the rock at the full moon in Scorpio that the devil
Azzageddi enters the story. Sol is moving from Taurus into
Gemini as Luna passes through the tail of Scorpio, and the Lion
is in the ascendant. Azzageddi announces himself: I am "the
mildest devil that ever entered man; in *propria persona,* no antlers
do I wear; my tail has lost its barb, as at last your Mardian lions
lose their caudal horns." He comes from "a torrid clime, cut by a
hot equator." It is not by accident that Azzageddi enters at the
approach of midsummer. He is the figure whose heat will spur
Babbalanja toward discovery, the element in the creative search
of the philosopher for new worlds.

The nonsense syllables uttered by Babbalanja,
"Gogle-goggle, fugle-fi, fugle-fogle-orum," represent the early
signals sent through Babbalanja as he begins to function as a

transmitter of thoughts. They are stutterings as yet, but they will eventually coalesce into a full-blown interplanetary message. The fossils have already instilled a mathematical concept in Babbalanja as he deals with a dispute among Media's servitors. Having seen certain marks on the rock, made by a three-toed, heronlike creature, one servitor claims that the marks are of three toes; the other that it is one foot. Babbalanja says:

> "Unite, and both are right; divide, and both are wrong. Every unit is made up of parts, as well as every plurality. Nine is three threes; a unit is as many thirds; or, if you please, a thousand thousandths; no special need to stop at thirds." (P. 416)

With this minor formula, the metaphor of letters is joined by one of mathematics and logic, as Babbalanja begins to develop numbers and to deal with the concepts of numerology. This same "three," of course, applies to Taji's "devil" and bears on the question as to whether the Avengers constitute three arrows or one trident.

In his flight of imaginative logic, Babbalanja postulates that there are creatures other than Mardians, "but perhaps with more exalted faculties, and organs that we lack. They may have some better seeing sense than ours; perhaps, have fins or wings for arms." Taji, of course, remains silent as to his own extra-Mardian origins. The others attribute Babbalanja's insanity to the full moon of June 9.

Now the Avengers arrive and send three arrows into the stern of the canoe, and Taji cries, "The priest I slew, but to gain her, now lost; and I would slay again, to bring her back. Ah, Yillah! Yillah!" This confession elicits mixed reactions from his companions, but Yoomy's is the most cryptic: "Ah, Taji! I had shrank from you, . . . but for the mark upon your brow. That undoes the tenor of your words" (423). The nature of the mark on Taji's brow, now introduced for the first time, is one of the riddles of *Mardi*. While the obvious connotation is that of the mark of Cain, which would not undo the tenor of Taji's words, the metaphors of Time and Mardi Gras force us to consider the mark of ashes placed on the foreheads of penitents—whether or not Taji recognizes himself as a penitent—especially in light of the Vatican imagery that surrounds the news of Jarl's death. As

the Avengers retreat, the Heralds approach, predicting difficulty
and offering foresight.

*   *   *

June 11. The holiday is Fête Dieu—the feast of Corpus
Christi—and there falls a calm. Luna is waning, at perigee, and
Saturn begins his retrograde motion. Vee-Vee falls from his perch
on the shoulder of one of the paddlers, nearly breaking an arm,
and the occurrence precipitates a discussion on necessity and fixed
fate and on the predictability of the future. Thus the "foresight"
proffered by Hautia becomes the topic of the day. As Luna
moves into Jupiter's house of Sagittarius, Babbalanja declares
himself a fool and cries, "I but fight against the armed and
crested Lies of Mardi, that like a host, assail me. I am stuck full
of darts; but, tearing them from out me, gasping, I discharge
them whence they come." The torments of Taji's initiation and
quest are reflected in those of Babbalanja, and the two are in
harmony like a musical instrument, one serving as the voice, the
other as ear.

*   *   *

June 12. Media fills his cup from the waning moon and toasts
the stars. The June morning rises, and at noon "from side to side,
we turned and grazed, like Juno's white oxen in clover meads."

> High midsummer noon is more silent than night. Most sweet a
> siesta then. And noon dreams are day-dreams indeed; born under
> the meridian sun. Pale Cynthia begets pale specter shapes; and her
> frigid rays best illuminate white nuns, marble monuments, icy
> glaciers, and cold tombs. (P. 432)

Sol is in Gemini, and Babbalanja makes an appropriate comment
on man:

> "Oh Man, Man, Man! thou art harder to solve, than the Integral

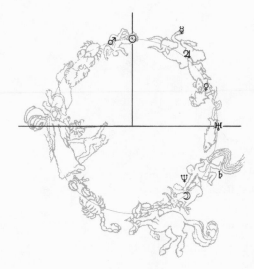

June 12, 1846

The Isle of Diranda represents the sign of the Twins,
Gemini—portrayed by the battling kings, Hello and Piko—as Sol
enters this constellation near the summer solstice.

Calculus—yet plain as a primer; harder to find than the
philosopher's-stone—yet ever at hand; a more cunning compound,
than an alchemist's—yet a hundred weight of flesh, to a penny
weight of spirit; soul and body glued together, firm as atom to
atom, seamless as the vestment without joint, warp or woof—yet
divided as by a river, spirit from flesh; growing both ways, like a
tree, and dropping thy topmost branches to earth, like thy beard
or a banian!—I give thee up, oh Man! thou art twain—yet
indivisible; all things—yet a poor unit at best." (P. 433)

With Sol and Mars in the house of Mercury, Media
cross-questions Mohi, and Yoomy sings a battle song of clubs,
bows, spears, and slings. On this note the canoes arrive in
Diranda, realm of the twin battle kings, Hello and Piko.

*   *   *

June 14. In the saga of these friendly battlers we are to see
the nature of the ritual conflict of the brothers Jupiter and
Neptune, "their joint majesties" of clubs and hearts, Sagittarius
and Pisces. Aside from this continuing battle, however, is the
political instruction for the grazing Mars regarding monarchs who
use war and mayhem to keep peace as the late Romans used
bread and circuses. The landing on Diranda is "like landing at
Greenwich among the Waterloo pensioners" (443).

June 17. A battle royal in Diranda's arena is heralded by a procession of priests bearing an idol with a cracked coconut for a head—Krako, the god of Trepans. Ludicrous but deadly battles, jousts, lists, and tourneys follow, soon developing into a true riot. As the twin kings cope with their own phantom, Taji is again faced with the Avengers as three feathered arrows fly. Two of them are buried in the ground, but from Taji's arm the third draws blood (450).

Upon their departure from Diranda, the voyagers resume their discussion of the ideas of moral sense and accountability. Babbalanja speaks of "an inscrutable stranger"—not Azzageddi—within him, to whom he charges all past action that in retrospect appears to be such folly: "He is locked up in me. In a mask, he dodges me. . . . This is he who talks in my sleep, revealing my secrets; and takes me to unheard of realms, beyond the skies of Mardi." Media retorts, "You have fairly turned yourself inside out," to which Mohi adds, "Yes, my lord, and he has so unsettled me, that I begin to think all Mardi a square circle" (457). Challenged by Media on this paradox, Babbalanja states, "Ever since Mardi began, we Mardians have been trying to square it."9

*   *   *

June 20, Midsummer. As Sol arrives at the summer solstice and hovers over the Greenwich meridian at high summer noon, the voyagers tour the planet Earth, circumnavigating the globe, touching on all shores, and prophesying the future, as befits a tale based on the metaphor of astrology. On this date the sun, though still in Gemini, enters the sign of Cancer the Crab, so named because, as Sol reaches the solstice in this sign, he appears briefly to move backward, simply because he is standing still preparatory to moving southward. As Sol stands directly over England's Greenwich meridian, the questers visit King Bello on the island of Dominora.

I will not attempt to cover this portion of *Mardi* thoroughly for several reasons, one of which has to do with the practical matter of length. The section as a whole is not necessary to the

9. Melville appears to be playing with Sir Thomas Browne's quincunx, in which the planetary orbits are shown on a square rather than a circular arrangement. Here Babbalanja seizes upon a square and begins trying to make a quincunx of Luna's orbit.

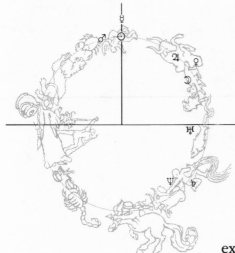

June 20, 1846

The summer solstice marks the beginning of the voyage to Earth, which occupies two lunar months.

10. Merrell R. Davis, in *Melville's Mardi: A Chartless Voyage*, has provided illuminating coverage of the political aspects of the Vivenza section.

explication of the almanac metaphor; since it deals primarily with national and political matters and the contents have been explicated thoroughly by others.[10] This is not to say that the visit to Earth is a separate entity, added to or superimposed on the rest of the book. On the contrary, it is an integral part of the total metaphor, maintaining the chronology throughout. The same characteristics, however, that make it amenable to alteration also make such alteration essential. There can be no doubt that the Earth sector of *Mardi* was brought up to date before publication of the book, along with certain other sections that would have been passé without such changes.

*   *   *

Entry into the lunar sign of Cancer provides a rationale for a complete but swift tour of Earth by way of the moon. Media sets up the imagery in Chapter 144 as he passes the wine, saying, "Forget not that calabash with the sea-blue seal, and a round ring for a brand. Rare old stuff, that, Mohi; older than you: the circumnavigator, I call it." In following the swiftly moving planet, the voyagers not only visit the four corners of the Earth but experience the four seasons as well, ranging like Taji's comet from equatorial heat to arctic frosts, a lunar year in a solar month. Then, too, summer is notably devoid of holidays. The one important day is not, like the others dealt with in the metaphor, a "holy day," but rather a secular and localized celebration of one nation's independence from another. For this reason, July 4 requires separate treatment and a descent from the universe to a particular locale. The essentially political nature of the day calls for a politically oriented environment, and the topic of war is apropos to the descent into politics.

Certain images appear in this segment that merit close examination, one of which is the relationship of King Bello of Dominora to the sea. Like Borabolla, Bello relates to the figure of Jupiter in Taurus, and the sector begins as Luna passes through this constellation. In addition, he relates to the figure of the Lion on the British coat of arms. "Bello of the Hump" is a monarch, "absolute in his rule as Predestination." Melville stresses his relationship with the "wild Nimrods" of Vivenza who are determined to protect their shores "even as a young lion will protect its den against legions of unicorns." But the young hunters of Vivenza are descendants of Bello and are no dastards: "Coming from lion-like loins, they were a lion-loined race" (472). In accordance with the game imagery, Bello is "but one of the most conspicuous pieces on a board, where the gods played for their own entertainment." Despite opposition, "and like unto some obstinate old uncle," he flourishes in the face of fateful prognostications of the "nephew nations."[11]

As the voyagers partake of Bello's hospitality, Bello seeks to know of Taji "whether his solar majesty had yet made a province of the moon; whether the Astral hosts were of much account as territories" and "whether the people in the sun vilified him [Bello] as they did in Mardi." Note here that Bello asks Taji about these solar matters, confirming that Sol is the true owner of the Taj, though Taji is wearing it at the time. Bello cannot tell Sol from Saturn just as England cannot discover Neptune or distinguish a real sailor from a romancer.

After a gala feast, the travelers bid Bello adieu, but as they return to the beach, they see the "brave ocean-chariot" of this "old sea-king of Mardi":

> In a broad arbor by the water-side, it was housed like Alp Arslan's war-horse, or the charger Caligula deified; upon its stern a wilderness of sculpture:—shell-work, medallions, masques, griffins, gulls, ogres, finned-lions, winged walruses; all manner of sea-cavalry, crusading centaurs, crocodiles, and sharks; and mermen, and mermaids, and Neptune only knows all.

11. Recall here that Jupiter is the patron of uncles. We might ask why Bello is a figure of Jupiter rather than of Mars, as his name would seem to imply and as I originally assumed. The planetary arrangement suggests the involvement of Jupiter, while the imagery repeats the Jupiter–Neptune linkage that characterizes the summerside sequences. Then, too, England is connected to Neptune by her name, Albion, and not to Mars, despite her nineteenth-century reputation for belligerence.

> And in this craft, Doge-like, yearly did King Bello stand up and wed with the Lagoon. (P. 482)

To make sure we notice this vital image that links Bello to Neptune, and makes a "he-bride" of the sea, Melville relates the tradition according to Ghibelli:

> When, in a stout sea-fight, Ziani defeated Barbarossa's son Otho, sending his feluccas all flying, like frightened water-fowl from a lake, then did his Holiness, the Pope, present unto him a ring; saying, "Take this, oh Ziani, and with it, the sea for thy bride; and every year wed her again." (P. 482)

But Bello's tradition presents a variant:

> Ages ago, Dominora was circled by a reef, which expanding in proportion to the extension of the isle's naval dominion, in due time embraced the entire lagoon; and this marriage ring zoned all the world.
>
> But if the sea was King Bello's bride, an Adriatic Tartar he wedded; who, in her mad gales of passions, often boxed about his canoes, and led his navies a very boisterous life indeed. (P. 482)

Nevertheless, Taji notes, some predicted "ere long she would desert her old lord, and marry again. Already, they held, she had made advances in the direction of Vivenza."

*   *   *

Chapter 150 contains an image of importance to the solar identity. As the voyagers leave Dominora at next morning's twilight, they experience a sullen feeling, and "all but Media" remain silent.

> But now, a bright mustering is seen among the myriad white Tartar tents in the Orient; like lines of spears defiling upon some upland plain, the sunbeams thwart the sky. And see! amid the blaze of banners, and the pawings of ten thousand thousand golden hoofs, day's mounted Sultan, Xerxes-like, moves on: the Dawn his standard, East and West his cymbals. (P. 484)

This is the summer solstice, and Sol's identity is seen in the figure of the Sultan–Sun, which serves as the symbol of the author's participation in the story. At this juncture, Mercury passes around the back of the sun, so that Yoomy greets his majesty "with a Persian air; 'would that all time were a sunrise, and all life a youth.'"

As they depart, Luna passes Jupiter in Taurus and moves on to Gemini.

*   *   *

June 23. The new moon is conjunct Mercury, and as cups are emptied, talk turns to the stars. Babbalanja states that wine fosters no base passions in him, but opens glorious visions: "It is then that I have all Mardi under my feet, and the constellations of the firmament in my soul." But Mohi cries, "Pooh, pooh! who does not see stars at such times?" And he lists the constellations contained between the solar horizons, from Andromeda to the Lesser Bear. "Ay, cried Media, "the study of astronomy is wonderfully facilitated by wine. Fill up, old Ptolemy, and tell us should you discover a new planet." Having issued this crucial challenge, Media becomes—or pretends to become—incoherently tipsy, but he nevertheless fells Babbalanja with a quip. Says Mohi, "His counterfeit was not well done. No, no; a bacchanal is not used to be so logical in his cups" (490).

*   *   *

The travelers bypass the continents of Europe, but note with alarm that a storm is brewing in Franko. Following the sun, they sail westward to Vivenza.

Chapter 161 represents July 4, for at this time a mysterious "scandalous document" is posted in Vivenza. Babbalanja and Media accuse each other of authorship of the prophetic epistle from the "Apostle of the Past"; Babbalanja claims to have recognized Media's "sultanic style," and from this remark we recognize the "Sultan-Sun," owner of the Taj. At this point, Melville jokingly—or perhaps not so jokingly—estimates and predicts that scholars will be laboring to solve the riddle of *Mardi* five hundred years hence. He further intimates that an important part of the riddle lies in the identity of the mysterious author of the prophetic pamphlet.

XVIII. July, August, and Leo

Ah, my own Koztanza! child of many prayers! —in whose
earnest eyes, so fathomless, I see my own; and recall all past
delights and silent agonies—thou may'st prove, as the child of
some fond dotard:—beauteous to me; hideous to Mardi!
— *Mardi*, 601

As they leave Vivenza at the full moon, July 8, the canoes
set forth to complete the circumnavigation of the world. They
return to Mardi on July 30, two days after Sol passes Vesta, the
asteroid whose glyph is a flaming altar. Vesta presides over this
last segment of the voyage. The travelers arrive in the morning
"upon the same mild, blue Lagoon as erst; and all the lands that
we had passed, since leaving Piko's shore of spears, were faded
from the sight." The cluster of islands is "like the Pleiades, that
shine in Taurus," and may therefore be seen as a separate entity
apart from the isles of Mardi. They are the tattoos on the
shoulder of the Bull. The long-range perspective that Melville has
attempted to achieve in these chapters is expressed in stellar
terms: "As in Orion, to some old king-astronomer,—say, King of
Rigel, or Betelgeuse,—this Earth's four quarters show but four
points afar; so, seem they to terrestial eyes, that broadly sweep
the spheres." The zodiacal constellations mentioned, Cancer, Leo,
Pisces, and Aquarius, represent the sectors covered by Sol during
this interim and, in reverse order, the opposition sectors.

And now occurs the most misleading statement of all, as Taji
addresses the reader:

Oh, reader, list! I've chartless voyaged. With compass and the
lead, we had not found these Mardian isles. Those who boldly
launch, cast off all cables; and turning from the common breeze,
that's fair for all, with their own breath, fill their own sails. Hug
the shore, naught new is seen; and "Land ho!" at last was sung,
when a new world was sought. (P. 556)

Taji has not chartless voyaged, for Media drew up the map of
Mardi before they embarked upon their journey. The reader is
expected to be mindful that America would probably not have
been found were not compass, sextant, and quadrant available for

navigation. In addition, all great explorers for generations had ploughed uncharted waters by keeping a close eye on the stellar charts. One of the important points in Melville's metaphor of creativity is that no writer voyages into new worlds of the mind without the guiding lights of previous artists. Nor have the discoverers of Neptune voyaged chartless. Unless this intriguing chapter be understood as the cry of the errant narrator surrounded by charts he cannot yet read, we are likely to miss the import of the succeeding chapters, in which the subjects of the charted future and the guided hand come under discussion. At all times Taji has been ringed in and charted, led and driven, and Melville has gone to great lengths to emphasize the situation. In the chapters to come, Taji's plaint will be elaborated and illustrated by the parallel plaints of Babbalanja.

At noon, Yoomy proposes a song, composed long since, when Yillah yet bowered in Odo. In it he invites Taji to "live over again your happy hours." The song he sings is incomplete, eliciting an objection from Babbalanja:

> "What, minstrel; must nothing ultimate come of all that melody? no final and inexhaustible meaning? . . . I mistrust thee, minstrel! that thou hast not yet been impregnated by the arcane mysteries; that thou dost not sufficiently ponder on the Adyta, the Monads, and the Hyparxes; the Dianoias, the Unical Hypostases, the Gnostic powers of the Psychical Essence, and the Supermundane and Pleromatic Triads; to say nothing of the Abstract Noumenons." (P. 561)

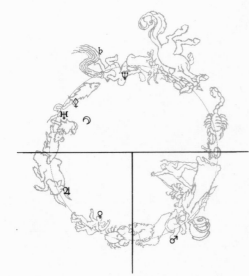

July 31, 1846

August is the month of the yellow Lion, and on August 1, Melville's birthday, Sol begins his entry into the head of Leo.

Realizing that Babbalanja is again beset by the demon Logic, Media informs "Azzageddi" that he must diet and be bled. "Ah!" sighs Babbalanja, turning; "how little they ween of the Rudimental Quincunxes, and the Hecatic Spherula!" Although he uses terms derived from various mystic and philosophical sources, including numerology, several of them serve as lunar puns, particularly *Dianoias, Hecatic Spherula,* and *Monad.*[1]

1. *Adyta:* secret inner sancta; *monad:* indivisible unit; *hyparxis:* initial or original essence; *dianoias:* rational faculty; *unical hypostasis:* union of human and divine nature in the single person of Christ; *noumenons:* objects of intuition apprehendable by intellect alone. All represent essences, absolutes, or ineffable ultimates.

*   *   *

July 31. Luna reaches her first quarter turn, and Babbalanja is still trying to square the circle—thereby experiencing great difficulty as he strives to maneuver the sharp corners of the lunar orbit. The group visits one Doxodox, who "is said to have penetrated from the zoned, to the unzoned principles." As they reach the island, Babbalanja whispers:

> "This silence is a fit introduction to the portals of Telestic lore. Somewhere, beneath this moss, lurks the mystic stone Mnizuris; whereby Doxodox hath attained unto a knowledge of the ungenerated essences. Nightly, he bathes his soul in archangelical circumlucencies. Oh, Doxodox! whip me the Strophalunian top! Tell o'er thy Jynges!" (P. 563)

Again the lunar pun, as Babbalanja invokes the "Wise One" to help the moon with a difficult "strophe," or "turn."

Doxodox proves well able to outdo Babbalanja in the production of syllables. When at last he distinguishes between a "simple Sumption" and an "Assumption," Mohi remarks, "So called from the syllogist himself, doubtless." Babbalanja, disappointed in this "shallow phraseman," emits a sophistic syllogism, at which Doxodox becomes angry and drives his guests away. Says Media, "Bravely done, Babbalanja. You turned the corner to admiration" (564).

Evening falls, and Media sleeps. Dreaming, he mutters aloud in conversation with gods and demigods. Suddenly his thoughts turn to Odo, and he dreams that mobs and rebels beset the kingdom:

"I leap upon the soil! Render thy account, Almanni! Where's my throne? Mohi, am I not a king? Do not thy chronicles record me? Yoomy, am I not the soul of some one glorious song? Babbalanja, speak.—Mohi! Yoomy!"

"What is it, my lord? thou dost but dream."

Staring wildly; then calmly gazing round, Media smiled.

"Ha! how we royalties ramble in our dreams! I've told no secrets?" (P. 566)

Mohi tells Media that he spoke at length, and Media denies knowing what he has said. "We dream not ourselves," says Babbalanja, "but the thing within us." To which Media replies, "Ay?—good morrow Azzageddi! . . . Vee-Vee! wine." And "straight through the livelong night, immortal Media plied the can."

The next morning is August 1. Sol is at the paws of Leo, in direct opposition to the retrograde Neptune, and Mercury is at aphelion, temporarily leading the planetary procession. A metamorphosis has taken place in Media, and the first glimmerings of a sense of responsibility toward his kingdom have emerged. His "grazing" is soon to come to an end.

The day is also Melville's birthday.

*   *   *

August 19. Time passes; Luna grows and wanes, until Venus passes into the house of Cancer, and meets the moon, two days before new.

Soon, from her clouds, hooded Night, like a nun from a convent, drew nigh. Rustled her train, yet no spangles were there. But high on her brow, still shone her pale crescent; haloed by bandelets—violet, red, and yellow. So looked the lone watcher through her rainbow-iris; so sad, the night without stars.

The winds were laid; the lagoon, still, as a prairie of an August noon. (P. 567)

Though the crescent moon is visible through the mist, Venus cannot be seen. The voyagers sleep, until suddenly they are surprised by one of the Avengers, who has attacked Taji with a stiletto. Immediately Hautia's Heralds appear, and Yoomy's translation is again woefully inaccurate. The midnight tremella signifies, "Resolve the riddle," while the hemlock again says, "You will cause my death." The half-closed convulvulus speaks of "bonds, loosened," and the proffered grapes represent "charity."

*   *   *

August 20. Saturn is in opposition to Sol, and Mercury, retrograde, retreats toward Sol, passing Mars and leaving the war planet again in the lead. The canoes land on Hooloomooloo, the Isle of Cripples. Here must be congregated all the victims of Mardian wars, the deformed citizenry being ruled by King Yoky, who is seeking a comparative anatomist. Here Media learns a lesson in humility as Yoky tells of his predecessor, whose boon companion had been an ape. When both died, they were buried together, and now it is impossible to distinguish the royal bones from those of the simian; hence the need for a comparative anatomist. "Such the narration; hearing which, my lord Media kept stately silence."

As the questers leave the island, "Vee-Vee, spying a curious looking stone, turned it over, and found a snake."[2]

In Chapter 175, Babbalanja sermonizes about the Isle of Cripples, as Luna approaches her conjunction with Sol. Enlarging on his topic, he moves into the question of the importance of man:

> " 'In respect of the universe, mankind is but a sect,' saith Diloro; 'and first principles but dogmas.' What ethics prevail in the Pleiades? What things have the synods in Sagittarius decreed? (P. 574)
>
> " 'What shaft has yet been sunk to the antipodes? What underlieth the gold mines?
>
> " 'But even here, above-ground, we grope with the sun at meridian. Vainly, we seek our Northwest Passages,—old alleys, and thoroughfares of the whales.

2. Vee-Vee's release of the serpent from beneath the rock completes an image begun on the *Parki*. The serpent is one of the three symbols of the sign of Scorpio; Vee-Vee's act symbolically releases Mars from his sentence while at the same time it previews the return of the winterside avatar of Mars. Media cannot retain his identity after Sol passes the fall equinox.

" 'Oh men! fellow men! we are only what we are; not what we would be; nor every thing we hope for. We are but a step in a scale, that reaches further above us than below. We breathe but oxygen. Who in Arcturus hath heard of us? They know us not in the Milky Way.' " (P. 575)

He further stresses the inability of man to achieve the fullness of Oro, and man's equal inability to recognize and appreciate the wonder of his present surroundings. In so doing, he provides an indirect reference to the hieroglyphics of the *Almanac,* as well as to the sky itself:

"Do the archangels survey aught more glorious than the constellations we nightly behold? Continually we slight the wonders, we deem in reserve. We await the present. With marvels we are glutted, till we hold them no marvels at all. But had these eyes first opened upon all the prodigies in the Revelation of the Dreamer, long familiarity would have made them appear, even as these things we see. Now, *now,* the page is outspread: to the simple, easy as a primer; to the wise, more puzzling than hieroglyphics. The eternity to come, is but a prolongation of time present: and the beginning may be more wonderful than the end." (P. 576)

He deals further with man's lack of concern about things distant in time or place. "Curiosity apart," he asks, "do we really care whether the people in Bellatrix are mortal or no?" He speaks of the great nova in Cassiopeia, which may have immolated worlds of continents, yet "Who thinks now of that burning sphere? How few are aware that ever it was?"[3]

These perspectives weigh heavily on Babbalanja, and he acknowledges the "dog days" of the season as he proclaims, "Like pebbles, were the isles to sink in space, Sirius, the Dog-star, would still flame in the sky." With the rising of this ominous star at summer's end, the levity of *Mardi* draws to a close, and the figure of the gravedigger, with his trump spade, emerges to predominate.[4]

Media bids Babbalanja to cease his perpetual reading of Bardianna's words. "You live not up to Bardianna's main thought. Where he stands, he stands immovable; but you are a Dog-vane." And Babbalanja again utters his nonsense syllables, "Gogle-goggle, fugle-fi, fugle-fogle-orum."

3. The event referred to here is the appearance of the great nova observed by Tycho Brahe in 1572 in Cassiopeia; it was for a brief time among the brightest of the stellar bodies, but within a year it had dimmed so as to be hardly visible to the naked eye.

4. Sirius the Dog Star is the greenish-yellow *alpha* of Canis Major, the "evil-starred crown" of Abrazza. In their book, *Outer Space: Myths, Name Meanings* . . . , Gertrude Jobes and James Jobes report that "the Romans who were not astute stargazers accepted Greek observations without studying conditions in their own age or country, and thus firmly established the belief in dog-days and the alliance of the Dog and the Lion with unhealthy mid-summer heat that persists into the present time. . . . Dante, on the other hand, called the star Veltro, the Messiah in greyhound form" (366). "Some say it is the Mazzaroth of the Book of Job" (369–70). "Its early influence in Europe was feared; it supposedly caused drought, fevers, and plagues" (370).

*   *   *

August 21. For twenty-four hours Babbalanja remains silent and motionless. As the new moon emerges and comes to apogee, he speaks again: "At banquets surfeit not, but fill, partake, and retire; and eat not again till you crave. Thereby you give nature time to work her magic transformings; turning all solids to meat, and wine into blood." With this, the food metaphor, so pronounced a few chapters back, comes again into full play, this time with added emphasis on the processes of digestion. Even as we move into the catabolistic imagery of death, the anabolism of digestion, transformation, and assimilation counteracts and balances the falling action. Media asks, "Art resuscitated, then, Babbalanja?" And the ponderer replies, "Ay, my lord, I am just risen from the dead." Babbalanja's words signal the meeting of the depleted Luna with Sol and the beginning of a new growth.

Newly energized, Babbalanja begins a tirade designed to connect the food imagery to the metaphor of art.

> "Oh my lord man—not *you* my lord Media! . . . In every age, thou boastest of thy valorous advances: . . . All the Past, wasted time! the Present knows all! . . . every man an author! books plenty as men! . . . But ages back they boasted like us; and ages to come, forever and ever, they'll boast. Ages back they black-balled the past, thought the last day was come; so wise they were grown. Mardi could not stand long; have to annex one of the planets; invade the great sun; colonize the moon." (Pp. 579–80)

Thus he rails against each new generation that claims to reject the wisdom of the sires, along with those who "reverentially grope for charred pages" from the burned libraries of the past.

> "But amazing times! astounding revelations; preternatural divulgings!—How now?—more wonderful than all our discoveries is this: that they were never discovered before. So simple, no doubt our ancestors overlooked them; intent on deeper things— the deep things of the soul. All we discover has been with us since the sun began to roll. . . . Tell us, ye sages! something worth an archangel's learning; discover, ye discoverers, something new."
> (P. 480)

As Babbalanja refers to man cutting his teeth, Mohi remarks that he, at an advanced age, is just now cutting a new tooth, and Babbalanja pulls in the letter imagery that was established by Oh-Oh, Jiji, and the Vowels:

> "Old man! it but clears the way for another. The teeth sown by the alphabet-founder were eye-teeth, not yet all sprung from the soil. Like spring-wheat, blade by blade, they break ground late; . . . All Mardi's history—beginning, middle, and finis—was written out in capitals in the first page penned. The whole story is told in a title-page. An exclamation point is entire Mardi's autobiography." (Pp. 580–81)

Babbalanja strikes a keynote when, in reply to a question from Media, he aims at the deepest function of symbolic art:

> "Even in their deepest lucubrations, the profoundest, frankest, ponderers always reserve a vast deal of precious thought for their own private behoof. They think, perhaps, that 'tis too good, or too bad; too wise, or too foolish, for the multitude. . . . At any rate, the profoundest ponderer seldom tells us all he thinks; seldom reveals to us the ultimate, and the innermost; seldom makes us open our eyes under water." (P. 581)

The Last Will and Testament of Bardianna contributes a legalistic form to the collection of genres that is *Mardi,* and it stands as a satirical comment on men and manners. For our purposes, however, the final lines of Chapter 177 bear on the theme of resurrection through art. The will having been read, Media inquires of Babbalanja, "Where think you, he is now?" And Babbalanja answers, "In his Ponderings. And those, my lord, we all inherit."

*   *   *

August 23. Sol in Leo is square Ceres, as the goddess of vegetation is conjunct Aldebaran. The travelers watch as a thousand prows speed by, "their crowded inmates' arms, in frenzied supplications wreathed; like tangled forest boughs." Media orders his paddlers to halt. The storm cloud which the

August 23, 1846
Hooloomooloo and Bonavona are the islands of Leo, and the former represents the sign of Taurus while the latter signifies Scorpio.

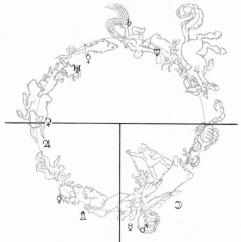

canoes are fleeing passes Media's three craft and overtakes the thousand boats, drowning all on board. "Flying death, they ran to meet it. . . . They died, because they might not longer live. Could we gain one glimpse of the great calendar of eternity, all our names would there be found, glued against their dates of death" (587). Here the concept of the fixed future is expressed in terms of a celestial almanac in which all temporal events are fixed and dated.[5]

5. See Chapter IV, note 6, regarding the practice of entering statistics in the almanac.

*   *   *

August 24. In the afternoon, the canoes arrive at Bonavona, the island of King Abrazza. The king's name has at least two meanings: one, the Latinate and martial, "To arms," for Abrazza is a figure of diet-minded Scorpio, who "likes his Bread-fruit baked, not roasted; sometimes carries filberts in his crown." Like Odo, Bonavona has a shadowy side from which issues "pining, plaintive notes . . . half-suppressed, and sobbing whisperings of leaves." Media avoids this side of the island, and orders a landing on the "morning meads" for his grazing. Like Media, Abrazza is a figure of injustice, pitying all, but relieving none. The other meaning of the name is *abrasive,* and on this "hollow" isle Sol passes through or under the intestines of Leo, the ultimate exit-producing sensations similar to those suffered by the proverbial turpentined cat. In this section especially, the pictoral element provided by the sky-map-calendar is essential to a full appreciation of the purgatorial and infernal imagery that permeates the chapter.

The visit to Abrazza's cool retreat is a lengthy one—a "grove of dates," that extends to September 4. It is on September 3, Thursday, that the dramatic dialogue takes place in which the metaphor of creativity is brought to its fulfillment.

Like Oh-Oh, Abrazza is an antiquarian of sorts "who loved his antique ancestors; and loved old times; and would not talk of moderns." The conversation begins with talk of ancient blind artists like Homer, and Babbalanja notes that "few grand poets have good eyes; for they needs blind must be, who ever gaze upon the sun" (591). He cites Vavona as the blind gamesman who formed a world of "kings and slaves, philosophers and wits; whose checkered actions—strange, grotesque, and merry-sad will entertain my idle moods" (592). Since Melville was plagued with poor vision, it would appear that Vavona is a self-reference, while Lombardo represents the inspiring source, Dante. To some extent this is true, for *Mardi* purports to be a Divine Comedy in the same sense as Dante's work; therefore, the title, *Koztanza,* is given to Lombardo's work as representing a "co-stanza." Primarily, however, it is Melville's intent to show the process of creativity through the hell of inspiration without volition, the purgatory of active composition, and the paradise, albeit a temporary one, of the relief inherent in completion.

The temporary nature of that Paradise necessitates an auxiliary metaphor, and here the avatar comes into play. The artist never reaches perfection or absolute completion in his lifetime; thus there is no "Ultimate," no "ephina"—merely a rising series of "Penultimates," each followed by a "Stropheluna," and the cycle begins again with a new, but higher, hell. With each production the artist rises to a higher level of quality, but on each level he must suffer through the same great comic cycle: first, inspired indolence; second, necessity to bestir himself "to procure his yams"; and third, the dyspepsia that results from coping with the dual forces of inspiration and compilation. Babbalanja strongly opines that the first motive would not suffice without the second, so that Necessity, in the metaphysical sense, takes on the more domestic guise of mere need.

The figure of the yellow lion transfers the persona of Lombardo from Dante to Melville:

> "Hast ever seen a yellow lion, all day basking in the yellow sun:— in reveries, rending droves of elephants; but his vast loins supine, and eyelids winking? Such, Lombardo; but fierce Want, the hunter, came and roused his roar. In hairy billows, his great mane tossed like the sea; his eyeballs flamed two hells; his paw had stopped a rolling world." (P. 593)

This last image produces a graphic picture if one reviews the position of Sol during the month of August. On August 1, Melville's birthday, Sol's position on the zodiac is at the front paws of the constellation Leo; on the tenth, the flaming Sol passes the heart—the star Regulus the King—and moves on into the body. On the day of this discussion, September 3, Dante's ruling planet, Venus, has been caught by the paws of Leo, while Sol, like a burr flambeau, is emerging between the loins of the lion, whose lasso tail lifts high to avoid the burning bolus. Babbalanja's Luna is passing through Capricorn and is conjunct Neptune.

Ever sensitive, Babbalanja reflects the infernal torment of the King of Beasts in the throes of production:

> "And ere Necessity plunged spur and rowel into him, he knew not his own paces. *That* churned him into consciousness; and brought ambition, ere then dormant, seething to the top, till he trembled at himself. . . . To scale great heights, we must come out of lowermost depths. The way to heaven is through hell. We need fiery baptisms in the fiercest flames of our own bosoms. We must feel our hearts hot—hissing in us. And ere their fire is revealed, it must burn its way out of us; though it consume us and itself." (Pp. 593–94)

As the burning yam of inspiration passes through the system of the lion, the imagery of fire continues, and Babbalanja's description becomes almost frenzied:

> "At white-heat, brand thyself; and count the scars, like old war-worn veterans, over camp-fires. Soft poet! brushing tears from lilies—this way! and howl in sackcloth and in ashes! Know, thou, that the lines that live are turned out of a furrowed brow. Oh!

there is a fierce, a cannibal delight, in the grief that shrieks to multiply itself. . . . Some damned spirits would not be otherwise, could they." (P. 594)

Full of pain and planets, Leo has no choice but to bestir himself. But he contains more than food:

"We are full of ghosts and spirits; we are as grave-yards full of buried dead, that start to life before us. And all our dead sires, verily, are in us; *that* is their immortality. From sire to son, we go on multiplying corpses in ourselves; for all of which, are resurrections. Every thought's a soul of some past poet, hero, sage. We are fuller than a city. Woe it is, that reveals these things." (Pp. 593–94)

The agony of the loins parallels that of the soul, which provides a hell or purgatory for the immortal ghosts possessed by it. They too are being digested.

Abrazza shares with many the idea that "Lombardo took no special pains," and that the *Koztanza* "must have come full-fledged, like an eagle from the sun."[6] Melville here makes use of the association of fletches with arrows, and Babbalanja commits a painful pun as he replies that Lombardo's thoughts, born plumeless, "came to soar."

Looking back to the return from the visit to Earth, we see that Bardianna's papers have reflected Leo's composition. Media's dream of Odo occurred as Leo's paw stopped the rolling sun, and Mercury and Mars were near Regulus. As the Death Cloud passed on the nineteenth, Sol entered the intestine, and the excerpt from the Ponderings revealed the writings of the ancients undergoing assimilation, while the Last Will and Testament preluded the "rite of passage" now in progress. Babbalanja reports that in ten days (Sol at Regulus) "Lombardo had written full fifty folios," which he read, neatly packaged, and "put it into the fire," not to burn but to temper and to purge the dross. This, I believe, is a tale we must credit, for Melville is here intimating that after a full-blown first draft, *Mardi* was completely rewritten. Babbalanja reports,

"When Lombardo set about his work, he knew not what it would become. He did not build himself in with plans; he wrote right on; and so doing, got deeper and deeper into himself; and like a

6. Recall here that the eagle has three functions in the solar myth. It is Jupiter's sacred bird; it is one of the symbols for Scorpio and therefore of Mars; and it is the meaning of Jarl's name.

resolute traveler, plunging through baffling woods, at last was
rewarded for his toils." (P. 595)

This passage describes the writing of the guided first draft—an
outpouring of material from the unconscious. Having reached a
certain point, Lombardo wrote in his autobiography,

> "I came out into a serene, sunny, ravishing region; full of sweet
> scents, singing birds, wild plaints, roguish laughs, prophetic voices.
> Here we are at last, then, . . . I have created the creative." And
> now the whole boundless landscape stretched away. (P. 595)

Now the labor begins. Sweat on brow, Sol rising, an end in view,
and a plan now charted, Lombardo rewrites. Confirming a
correlative birth image, Babbalanja replies to Abrazza's
suggestion that Lombardo must have enjoyed his own wit: "Hear
you laughter at the birth of a man child, old man? The babe may
have many dimples; not so, the parent. Lombardo was a hermit to
behold." In the opening chapters of *Mardi* we have examined
alternatives to the metaphor of birth: the birth of a son to Virgo;
the descent of the sperm to Virgo from "someone" and the
ensuing development of the embryo; and the voyage of the
sperm in its own quest of a "new world." The first of these
metaphors applies to the quest for faith, the second to the quest
for art, and the third to the quest for immortality. Here too we
must draw on the Mardi Gras ritual of the murder of Aleema in
which Taji either committed murder, sacrilege, and violation;
conducted a premature delivery; or "authored a deed."
Whichever, the act was a mere "first draft" and Yillah the
"sunny, ravishing region" that sets the artist to hard labor,
prodded by the infernal arrows of fire and led by Dante's Venus.

The metaphor of digestion, along with the suggestions of
cannibalism and of the punishment of ghosts, applies to another
question from Media: "Tell us how he made acquaintance with
some of those rare worthies, he introduces us to, in his
Koztanza." Babbalanja answers, "He first met them in his
reveries." They were shy and sour, but at last, "they were frank
and friendly. Lombardo set places for them at his board; when he
died, he left them something in his will." The assimilation of the
worthies is represented in the earlier comment regarding
inspiration, "The essence of all ideas is infused."

Abrazza declares that the *Koztanza* lacks the unities, but Lombardo has said that he had tried to keep in the good graces of those nymphs, only to find them "captious and exacting." Fleeing the unities, however, he sailed into their arms: "Matter and mind, though matching not, are mates; and sundered oft, in his Koztanza they unite:—the airy waist, embraced by stalwart arms." Melville confirms that *Mardi* shares the stellar metaphor with *The Divine Comedy* as he expresses the nature of this unity: "Though Lombardo abandoned all monitors from without; he retained one autocrat within—his crowned and sceptered instinct. And what, if he pulled down one gross world, and ransacked the etherial spheres, to build up something of his own—a composite" (597). Note here the term *gross world,* as it applies to Mardi Gras, for again the poet must be shriven for breaking down and fragmenting a world. As the *Koztanza* lacks cohesion, and is "wild, unconnected, all episode" in Abrazza's eyes, Babbalanja replies that "so is Mardi itself, nothing but episodes; valleys and hills; rivers, digressing from plains; vines, roving all over; boulders and diamonds; flowers and thistles; forests and thickets; and, here and there, fens and moors. And so, the world in the Koztanza." Thus, by inference Melville ties *Mardi* to the *Koztanza* and himself to Lombardo.

Babbalanja's nonsense syllables, representing incoherent attempts at communication, suddenly coalesce into a logical sequence in this chapter, expressing the concept of expansion: "Modak is Modako; but fogle-foggle is not fugle-fi." Clearly, the word *Modak* is contained in the expanded *Modako,* while *fogle-foggle* and *fugle-fi* are similar but mutually exclusive. The first set is a modal proposition in which form carries its own meaning of "the lesser contained in the greater of the same kind," while the second and negative set carries a potential semantic significance. It could, for example, be translated as "A misty flight is not a true signal." From Yoomy there is yet another kind of reaction: "Some of those strange things fall far too melodiously upon the ear, to be wholly deficient in meaning." Although we may take Yoomy's comment as a clue to translate these syllables, Yoomy does not serve as dragoman in this regard; rather, he equates meaning with melody and finds it sufficient—an attitude that many poets would find valid.

The modal proposition contained in the syllables as used

here form a summary of the statement to which they append:

> "There are things infinite in the finite; and dualities in unities. Our eyes are pleased with the redness of the rose, but another sense lives upon its fragrance. Its redness you must approach, to view: its invisible fragrance pervades the field. So, with the Koztanza. Its mere beauty is restricted to its form: its expanding soul, past Mardi does embalm." (P. 597)

Note here how this final concept repeats the images of the amber that preserves ideas and of the great rock in which the history of man and his deeds is petrified. It is not insignificant that this connection is made with the chapter in which Azzageddi first revealed himself. The slow coalescence of Babbalanja's syllabic logic may be likened to the geological stratification, while the "expanding soul" repeats the concept presented earlier in Tammahammaha's tattoo.[7]

Clearly also, Abrazza is wrong in his choice of the word *unconnected.* The episodes of *Mardi* are connected fore and aft and on all sides.

7. Cf. Tammahammaha's tattoo, *Mardi,* p. 206.

*   *   *

Media provokes a verbal barrage when he asks whether Lombardo had obtained opinions about the *Koztanza,* and the Vowels of Pimminee return as Babbalanja describes the feelings of the artist about his finished work:

> "When abroad, among men, he almost despised it; but when he bethought him of those parts, written with full eyes, half blinded; temples throbbing; and pain at the heart—— . . . he would say to himself, 'Sure, it can not be in vain! . . . Who will read me? Say one thousand pages—twenty-five lines each—every line ten words —every word ten letters. That's two million five hundred thousand *a*'s, and *i*'s, and *o*'s to read! How many are superfluous? Am I not mad to saddle Mardi with such a task?'" (Pp. 600–601)

As Babbalanja's fires rise on behalf of Lombardo, the figure of the yam-eating lion is raised to a Pentecostal level: He quotes Lombardo:

"[The critics] are fools. In their eyes, bindings not brains make books. They criticize my tattered cloak, not my soul, caparisoned like a charger. He is the great author, think they, who drives the best bargain with his wares: and no bargainer am I. Because he is old, they worship some mediocrity of an ancient, and mock at the living prophet with the live coal on his lips. . . . Critics?—Asses!" (P. 599)[8]

Babbalanja's monologues in this chapter explicate several of the chapters that deal with the search for the "new worlds of the mind." He proceeds into the problem of poetic immortality by using Lombardo's words: "I? Lombardo? but yesterday cut in the market-place by a spangled fool! Lombardo immortal? Ha, ha, Lombardo! but thou art an ass, with vast ears brushing the tops of palms! . . . Ha, ha, ha!—go, go! dig thy grave, and bury thyself!"[9] For the most part, however, the artist feels dissatisfied, contenting himself by noting that "Fate is in it," and sending his "child" out to "get bread for its sire." Abrazza lights on Taji's problem of identity as he inquires about Lombardo, "Did he think himself a god?", and Babbalanja answers to the same point: "He himself best knew what he thought; but, like all others, he was created by Oro to some special end; doubtless, partly answered in his Koztanza." Like Taji, who had "authored a deed," Lombardo had created a work and fulfilled a design.

*   *   *

In the evening, the "sinister, hollow, heartless" Abrazza provides a supper, and in epic manner Taji catalogs great suppers of the past in order to establish a precedent for the antiquarian king. Again, this chapter reviews the imagery of *Mardi*. In the card game, Taji makes a substitution: "Give me the heart that's as huge as all Asia; and unless a man be a villain outright, account him one of the best tempered blades in the world." The suit of swords, or spades, predominates here, as evidenced by the bloody nature of this catalog of last suppers. All those who gave suppers were themselves supped upon—overthrown, beheaded, stabbed, exiled, or betrayed. Note especially the image of the "conquering

8. "No bargainer am I," says Lombardo, yet the name *Lombard* is synonymous with the mercantile—the Lombard Medicis' insignia being the three golden balls that now represent the pawnbroker and that also provides a suggestive picture of the exit of Sol from Leo.

9. There is a provocative similarity between Lombardo's comment on his own claim to genius: "I?—Lombardo? but yesterday cut in the market-place by a spangled fool!," and the title of an 1843 opera by Verdi, entitled *I Lombardi*.

son of Olympia by Jupiter himself, [who] sent out cards to his
captains . . . to join him at ten P.M. in the Temple of Belus," as
Media had sent an invitation to Jiromo for a beheading.

Abrazza had arranged the seating of his guests, but Yoomy is
not present and Babbalanja does not join the feast at first, since
he is still bemused by his signals as Luna passes Neptune, waxing
to full. Media remarks that "suppers are jovial," and the function
of the introductory catalog is confirmed as discussion turns to
Ludwig the Fat, "King of cups and Tokay":

> "For after devouring many a fair province, and grinding the poor
> of his realm, Ludwig the Great has long since, himself, been
> devoured by very small worms, and ground into very fine dust.
> And after stripping many a venison rib, Ludwig the Fat has had
> his own polished and bleached in the Valley of Death; yea, and
> his cranium chased with corrodings, like the carved flagon once
> held to its jaws." (P. 605)

The gluttony of Ludwig exceeds even that of Borabolla: "Such a
full-orbed paunch was his, that no way could he devise of getting
to his suppers but by getting right into them. Like the zodiac his
table was circular, and full in the middle he sat, like a sun; all his
jolly stews and ragouts revolving around him." Because
Babbalanja is sharpening his crabby claws on all present, both
Media and Abrazza order him to "fill up." As he continues to
plague the group, Abrazza orders his guards to evict the
too-sober sage. Media, however, countermands the order, crying,
"Back! touch him not, hounds!" Babbalanja, whose moon is just
a few hours from full, says, "Surely you would not that I should
imbibe more than I can hold. The measure being full, all poured
in after that is but wasted. I am for being temperate in these
things, my good lord. And my one cup outlasts three of yours.
Better to sip a pint, than pour down a quart." But Media will
have none of Babbalanja in his Azzageddi mood: "Away with
your logic and conic sections! Drink!" Nevertheless, he
withdraws his urgings and allows Babbalanja to have his way.
Three times Abrazza tries to set his guards upon the sage, and
each time Media refers to the guards as "dogs," "hounds," or
"curs." We have noted previously that Sirius the Dog Star has
risen, casting an evil influence over all. At last Babbalanja is

prevailed upon to imbibe. Media notes the filling of Luna as he observes of Babbalanja, "He came to it a skeleton, but will go away, every bone padded." Babbalanja thinks of the fee, however:

> "Every thing, my good lords, has its price, from a marble to a world. And easier of digestion, and better for both body and soul, are a half-haunch of venison and a gallon of mead, taken under the sun at meridian, than the soft bridal breast of a partridge, with some gentle negus, at the noon of night!" (P. 608)

Having stated in the preceding chapter that Lombardo worked by day, Babbalanja claims that midnight feasting does not lend itself to good digestion, and indeed Taji has demonstrated that dyspepsia can result from midnight excesses. Yet, from dyspepsia comes ambergris. Babbalanja extends the image: "Whoso takes much wine to bed with him, has a bedfellow, more restless than a somnambulist. And though Wine be a jolly blade at the board, a sulky knave is he under a blanket. I know him of old" (608).

At last Abrazza has enough of Babbalanja's caustic remarks, and in a rage he calls for his guards.

> "Back, curs!" cried Media. "Harm not a hair of his head. I crave pardon, King Abrazza, but no violence must be done Babbalanja."
> "Trumpets there!" said Abrazza; "so: the banquet is done—lights for King Media! Good-night, my lord!" . . . And all—drawing nigh to the evening end of these wanderings wild—meet is it that all should be regaled with a supper. (P. 609)

And a meaty supper it has been.

XIX. September and Neptune

> our mortal lives have an end; but that end is no goal; no place of
> repose. Whatever it may be, it will prove but as the beginning of
> another race.   —*Mardi*, 575

September 4. Luna at perigee is conjunct Saturn in Aquarius,
and Sol passes into the laureled head of Virgo. The voyagers
leave Bonavona—at Abrazza's suggestion—and sail past the isle of
cankered maidens and of King Klanko's mines.[1]

As the harvest moon rises just after sunset, the questers grow
moody, until at last Media bids them be merry:

> "Up heart, Taji! or does that witch Hautia haunt thee? Be a
> demi-god once more, and laugh. Her flowers are not barbs; and
> the avengers' arrows are too blunt to slay. . . . Perdition to
> Hautia! Long lives, and merry ones to ourselves! Taji, my
> charming fellow, here's to you:—May your heart be a stone! Ha,
> ha! . . . See! the round moon is abroad." (P. 612)

As Jarl was blunt, so too are the Avengers' arrows; and Hautia,
Queen of Swords, figure of Justice, has presented more than one
barb in her flower messages. It is with double meaning that
Media states the moon to be "abroad," and Babbalanja says, "Say
you so, my lord? then for one, I am with you." He proceeds to a
Shandean catalog of agonized laughter that ranges from
"Demokriti" to "Rabeelee." "Ho! let us be gay, if it be only for
an hour, and Death hand us the goblet," he cries, and "Not to

1. Compare the cankered maidens
and jolly bachelors of "A Paradise of
Bachelors" and "Maids of Tartarus" to
this contrasting pair of islands.

September 3, 1846

The passage of Sol through the constellation Leo gives rise to the
artistic metaphor of the Inferno, Purgatorio, and Paradisio of
Dante's *Divine Comedy*. As Sol emerges from under Leo's tail, the
agony of the author, as felt by Babbalanja, is reflected in the
passion of the philosopher's near-raving speech. Sol's position on
this date may also relate to the Medici insigne, now the symbol of
the pawnbroker.

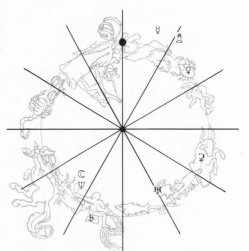

laugh is to have the tetanus." The imagery of this chapter
balances that of Chapter 11, "Jarl is Afflicted with the Lockjaw,"
in which Taji begs for a "lively, grinning loon."

As he concludes his speech, Babbalanja finds that the "heart
is not whole, but divided," that "we cannot live without hearts;
though the heartless live longest."

> "Yet hug your hearts, ye handful that have them; 'tis a blessed
> inheritance! Thus, thus, my lord, I run on; from one pole to the
> other; from this thing to that. But so the great world goes round,
> and in one somerset, shows the sun twenty-five thousand miles of
> a landscape!"
>
> At that instant, down went the fiery full moon, and the
> Dog-Star; and far down into Media, a Tivoli of wine. (P. 614)

Here Time is subjected to a strange paradox, for the harvest
moon cannot set at the same time with the Dog Star. Indeed, as
Sirius rises, the harvest moon is approaching midheaven. Taji
does not say that Luna sets, however, but merely that she "goes
down"—an expression applicable to the moment past her
opposition to Sol, when she ceases to wax and begins to wane.
And as Luna begins to go down—as a balloon goes down—
Sol-Media topes her poured-out wine.

*   *   *

2. This image of the "plaided
Highlander" relates back to Samoa's
"Highlander's dagger," *Mardi*, p. 98.

September 5. The morning sun arrives like a plaided
Highlander.[2] Babbalanja hails the stars and planets as brothers
who talk to him:

> "Saturn, and Mercury, and Mardi, are brothers, one and all; and
> across their orbits, to each other talk, like souls. . . . Worlds pass
> worlds in space, as men, men,—in thoroughfares; and after periods
> of thousand years, cry:—"Well met, my friend, again!"—To me,
> to *me,* they talk in mystic music; I hear them think through all
> their zones." (P. 616)

These words confirm the personification of the planets and reveal
the method of communication among them. At the same time

they foreshadow Babbalanja's coming vision of a voyage through space to the upper regions of the ninth circle of heaven.

*   *   *

The sperm image also receives attention as Babbalanja relates the metaphors of art and religion to the conception and birth elements previously noted.

> "Oh! that these myriad germ-dramas in me, should so perish hourly, for lack of power mechanic. . . . Sweet being! if, by Mardian word I may address thee—speak!—'I bear a soul in germ within me; I feel the first, faint trembling, like to a harp-string, vibrate in my inmost being. Kill me, and generations die!'—So, of old, the unbegotten lived within the virgin; who then loved her God, as new-made mothers their babes ere born." (P. 616)

Who is the "sweet being" who speaks these words? Babbalanja has said,

> "Ho! let's voyage to Aldebaran.—Ha! indeed, a ruddy world! . . . Who is this?—a god? What a lake-like brow! transparent as the morning air. I see his thoughts like worlds revolving—and in his eyes—like unto heavens—soft falling stars are shooting.—How these thousand passing wings winnow away my breath:—I faint:— back, back to some small asteroid." (P. 616)

On this day, Jupiter is moving out of the horns of Taurus toward the hunter, Orion, and is about to pass beyond the solar horizon into the night sky and into a new identity.

But Luna has just passed Saturn, and is moving toward Uranus. The field signals again, as Babbalanja cries,

> "Oh, Alma, Alma, Alma!—Fangs off, fiend!—will that name ever lash thee into foam?—Smite not my face so, forked flames!"
>
> "Babbalanja! Babbalanja! rouse, man! rouse! Art in hell and damned, that thy sinews so snake-like coil and twist all over thee? Thy brow is black as Ops! Turn, turn! see yonder moose!"
> (P. 616)[3]

3. Ops is the wife of Saturn, also called Cybele. Cf. Taurus as moose, Chapter XIV, n. 1.

As Babbalanja's agony becomes intense, Media cries, "He falls!"

and Yoomy, sympathetic, adds, "Mark the agony in his waning eye!" confirming that Luna is on the wane.

*   *   *

September 23. Time has passed. Sol has taken the lead in the procession of planets, followed by Mars and Mercury in Virgo, and Venus at perihelion is now moving through Leo. Sol passes into the fall sign of Libra, though he is still in the constellation Virgo, as is Luna, waxing. It is Wednesday.

Taji's hopes "revived not from their ashes," but he recognizes that the quest must soon end. The canoes move toward the west, and Yoomy provides the first definite statement as to the season: "When we set sail from Odo, 'twas a glorious morn in spring . . . toward the rising sun we steered. But now, beneath autumnal night-clouds, we hasten to its setting" (617). On this equinoctial day, the sea is angry, and a merry, singing bowsman falls from his elevated perch into the dark lagoon.[4] "With all haste, our speeding canoes were reversed; but not till we had darted in upon another darkness." Deep night has dived deeper down in the sea. Depressed, the questers speak of death, and as Sol moves into the Arcturus sector, the opening imagery is repeated. The canoes sail back and forth across the equinoctial line as the *Arcturion* had crossed and recrossed that other "imaginary line." As Taji had then found it "hard" to carry him off to purgatory, here repeatedly it is "hard and horrible" to die, "hard to live; hard to die." The carnival image becomes explicit as Babbalanja compares Mardi to a "tented fair" and puns directly on fair Yillah in her tent, his own alterego. Like Taji on the ship, Babbalanja sees "the same dull round." He complains that "no new stars appear in the sky; no new lights in the soul."

4. Cf. opening imagery of an equinoctial storm, in which a fat cook fell into the scuppers of the *Arcturion: Mardi,* p. 4.

"I think of green youth as of a merry playmate departed; and to shake hands, and be pleasant with my old age, seems in prospect even harder, than to draw a cold stranger to my bosom [as Yillah had known a "frigid stranger from the Arctic zone"]. But old age is not for me. I am not of the stuff that grows old. This Mardi is not our home. Up and down we wander, like exiles transported to a planet afar;—'tis not the world *we* were born in." (P. 619)

Yoomy provides another clue to the time metaphor as he mourns: "Oh, I have marked what it is to be dead;—how shouting boys, of holidays, hide-and-seek among the tombs, which must hide all seekers at last." Because of the holiday imagery, combined with that of boys at play, we are reminded again of the ritual nature of the quest, even as the questers fail to see the significance of their own words.

Media refers to his own planetary identity as he exclaims, "Let the king die to martial melodies!"

Now Babbalanja discusses the theological problem as he deals with the justice of Oro. With misery so widely spread, "this Mardi may be the retributive future of some forgotten past." Or, conversely, there may be a hereafter, "and the sufferings of the virtuous recompensed. . . . but to make restitution implies a wrong, and Oro can do no wrong. Yet what seems evil to us, may be good to him." One idea Babbalanja rejects: "that all Mardi is but a means to an end; that this life is a state of probation." Yet in terms of Melville's metaphors of initiation and artistic design, this rejected idea hits closer to the truth. Babbalanja strikes at Media when he denies that "evil is but permitted for a term; that for specified ages a rebel angel is viceroy.—Nay, nay. Oro delegates his scepter to none; in his everlasting reign there are no interregnums; and Time is Eternity; and we live in Eternity now" (620). Media has left a viceroy; further, the author of *Mardi* has permitted a viceroy to narrate in his stead, just as Sultan–Sol has permitted Saturn–Time to wear the Taj. By equating Time to Eternity, Babbalanja has wrought a paradox, for he has also said that the sun is coeternal with Oro. The eternal sun and the time-bound Saturn are thus paralleled. Oro, Babbalanja claims, "is an everlasting calm," and we may recall with what desperation Taji reacts to calms.

*   *   *

September 24. The skies clear, and the voyagers reach Serenia, the Isle of Alma, the Penultimate.[5] Here the vision of the orbits of heaven comes through to Babbalanja, promising an eternal quest through ever higher levels of awareness, but no perfection

5. Cf. Spenser's Castle of Alma in Book II of *The Faerie Queene* and its relationship to Temperance (see Tarot Trump 14) and to the sign of Aquarius, the "airiest" of the three Air signs. Fowler notes that, according to Ficino, the graces bestowed by Sol, Venus, and Jupiter are transmitted by Mercury and Luna, especially the latter. To carry out this "transmissive function," Luna should be in an airy sign, preferably in Aquarius, the sign opposed to Sol's Leo. The melancholic Phantastes as a Saturn figure may bear somewhat on the nature of Taji as a pursuer of the moon and as an unconscious scholar. Alastair Fowler, *Spenser and the Numbers of Time*, pp. 88–114.

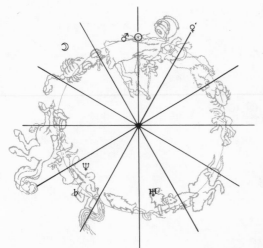

September 24, 1846

As the canoes arrive at the Isle of Serenia, the dateline is posed on the opening position of the descendant, while Sol lags ten degrees behind.

and no Ultimates. The archangels of Babbalanja's vision reveal themselves not to be all-knowing. Perpetual scholars, they rise from one level to the next as Vishnu rises through his avatars. Always they remain subject to ignorance and error: "And though death gave these beings knowledge, it also opened other mysteries, which they pant to know, and yet may learn. And still they fear the thing of evil; though for them, 'tis hard to fall" (634). The problem of sin is left open by the angel, who cannot fathom this last mystery of Oro:

> "And what, oh! guide! of those who, living thoughtless lives of sin, die unregenerate; no service done to Oro or to Mardian?"
> "They, too, have their place . . . but 'tis not here. And Mardian! know, that as your Mardian lives are long preserved through strict obedience to the organic law, so are your spiritual lives prolonged by fast keeping of the law of mind. Sin is death."
> (P. 634)

If we complete the circle here, we must return to the angel's earlier statement, "Death gave these beings knowledge."

Notice the strange similarity of Melville's heaven to Dante's nether regions. Melville's archangels know progressively more intense degrees of sadness as they feel their eternal separation from Oro and their position in the everlasting Penultimate. Their wings are drenched in fire, and their tears fall forever. On these terms, gross Mardi seems a paradise of ignorance, and hell superfluous. Here is no *primum mobile,* no multifoliate rose, but a constant quest for a receding goal.

"Loved one, love on! But know, that heaven hath no roof. To know all is to be all. Beatitude there is none. And your only Mardian happiness is but exemption from great woes—no more. Great Love is sad; and heaven is Love. Sadness makes the silence throughout the realms of space; sadness is universal and eternal; but sadness is tranquility; tranquility the uttermost that souls may hope for." (P. 636)

*   *   *

September 25. The questers depart from Serenia. As Sol moves into the winter sky, Babbalanja, the summer moon, can no longer retain his masculine identity. Like Jarl and Samoa, he must stay behind to undergo his metamorphosis. All but Taji have fallen under the influence of Alma, but Taji's quest is as yet unfinished. They sail on, importuning Taji to give up the search, but he is "fixed as fate." In this month of the hunter's moon, October, Taji is the hunter.

XX. October and All Souls

For on board that very craft, the old Arcturion, were four tall
fellows, whom two years previous our skipper himself had picked
up in an open boat, far from the farthest shoal. To be sure, they
spun a long yarn about being the only survivors of an Indiaman
burnt down to the water's edge. But who credited their tale?   —*Mardi*, 7

October 18. The planetary processional has ended, and as Sol
passes out of Virgo into Libra, Mercury, Mars, Venus, and Luna
are congregated in Virgo. Luna is conjunct Venus. Saturn, still
retrograde, has retreated into the body of Aquarius, and Neptune
remains motionless in the arm of Aquarius, no longer incognito.
Uranus now occupies the spot in the Fish's spine first held by
Jupiter, directly opposite Arcturus. Three times the moon has
changed, and three times the Avengers and the Heralds have
approached. Taji's companions implore him to turn back; he
almost yields to their urgings:

> Then sweet Yillah called me from the sea;—still must I on! but
> gazing whence that music seemed to come, I thought I saw the
> green corse drifting by: and striking 'gainst our prow, as if to
> hinder. Then, then! my heart grew hard, like flint; and black, like
> night; and sounded hollow to the hand I clenched. Hyenas filled
> me with their laughs; death-damps chilled my brow; I prayed not,
> but blasphemed. (P. 639)

At midnight Hautia's Heralds arrive again:

> They bore a large and stately urn-like flower, white as alabaster,
> and glowing, as if lit up within. From its calyx, flame-like,
> trembled forked and crimson stamens, burning with intensest
> odors.
>   The phantoms nearer came; their flower, as an urn of burning
> niter. Then it changed, and glowed like Persian dawns; or passive,
> was shot over by palest lightnings;—so variable its tints. (P. 640)

The night-blooming cereus, a cactus flower, signifies "transient
beauty" and represents the last night of the old moon; that is,
Yillah as first seen by Taji. As Luna's cup-shaped crescent passes

Venus, the planet seems poised above the cup like the stamen of a flower; but this lunar flower can blow only in the hour before sunrise, never at midnight. The visit does not occur by the clock but by Taji's "midnight of despair." Taji resists their call at first, but his companions urge him to respond, and at last the questers follow the Heralds.

*   *   *

"As if Mardi were a poem, and every island a canto, the shore now in sight was called Flozilla-a-Nina, or The-Last-Verse-of-the-Song." Mohi tells a story of winged beings who once inhabited Mardi, but they were driven away by an ancestor of Hautia. Neither Yoomy nor Mohi has been made less errant by exposure to Serenia, and there is evidence that Hautia's island is not as Taji believes it to be.

The name *Hautia* is ideal for this Duessa-like island queen, for the reader receives the impression of pride and hauteur even as Taji does and with as little reason. But the name is taken from Ellis, after a friendly island chieftain who converted to Christianity and became a model of good government and justice. The story most pertinent to Melville's purposes is that of Governor Hautia's dealings with a rebellious young island noble who insisted on tattooing himself in defiance of the new edicts of the missionaries. Hautia sentenced the youth to labor at deep diving. And this is to be Taji's sentence as well.[1]

Through Melville's ambiguous terms, it is possible to see Hautia as the Mother Superior of a convent school or the High Priestess of vestal virgins. Yoomy's story of Ozonna and Rea, seemingly attesting to the cruelty of Hautia, instead reveals her motherly concern for the virtue of her "niñas" of Flozella, as "duenna," not "duessa."

The possession of Luna by Venus continues until the full moon, so Hautia and Yillah are united throughout Taji's stay on the island.[2] Venus's house of Libra stands midway between summer and winter, and Hautia's island is similarly situated. In

1. William Ellis, *Polynesian Researches*, II, 466–77. Ellis writes of Taaroarii, a king's son, and his disobedience. His sentence sent him to dive for coral (the island was Sir Charles Saunders Island). Still rebellious, the young prince and a band of other youths abandoned their labors and escaped to the northern part of the island. Hautia, deputy governor, led a party to capture the young rebels and succeeded in bringing them back without bloodshed. Hautia, who conducted their trial, released those who had merely followed the leaders and sentenced the active rebels to public labor in small parties, with police officers to guard them.

2. Venus retains "possession" of Luna through the square, just as Taji had retained Yillah for the two weeks, from the new moon to full moon, February 24 to March 12.

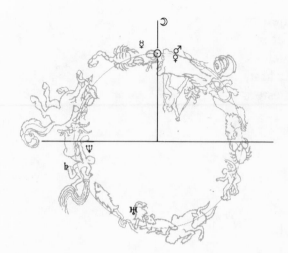

October 19, 1846
As the canoes arrive at Flozella-a-Niña, Hautia's island, Sol is
passing out of Virgo and into Libra.

keeping with the sign of the scales, the Libra island is a place of
weighing, testing, probation, and, in the end, of judgment.

October 19. Luna passes Mars and eclipses Sol. The voyagers,
led by the maidens of Hautia, arrive at Hautia's island bower
where the three from Odo are served sherbet; but Taji receives a
"nautilus shell, brimmed with a light-like fluid, that welled, and
welled like a fount." Taji drinks and exclaims, "Like a
blood-freshet, it ran through my veins." For a moment he sees
Hautia, with Luna, in all her beauty. He reaches out for her, but
she vanishes. "She is deeper than the sea," says Media; "Her
bow is bent," says Yoomy. Again the description points to Venus
and the bow-curved moon.

Mohi tells the story of Ozonna and his quest for Ady. Taji is
deeply influenced but is unable to understand that which is
plainly before him. He searches the black eyes of the maidens,
convinced that one of them is Yillah transformed, "but in all
those cold, mystical eyes, saw not the warm ray" that he sought.

Having reached the house of Justice, Media has fulfilled his
quest and may now return across the oppositing "aisle" to Odo.
As Luna passes Mars and begins to cover Sol, Media ends his
period of rumination and departs for Odo with his companions.
First, Yoomy tries to persuade Taji to return with them: "Come
away, come away! . . . Far hence is Yillah! and he who tarries
among these flowers, must needs burn juniper."[3] But Taji must
remain until Hautia breaks the spell.

3. Juniper was burned to fumigate
dwellings after illnesses. In flower
language, juniper signifies "succor" or
"protection."

*   *   *

Now alone with Taji, Hautia begins the trial. "Come! let us sin, and be merry," she cries. But Taji resists the blandishments of the "Lil": "My heart flew forth from out its bars, and soared in air; but as my hand touched Hautia's, down dropped a dead bird from the clouds." Having drunk from the Cup and proved his steadfastness, he is ready for the watery test.

*   *   *

October 23. We are given reason to allow three days for the journey to Hautia's cave, as the bemused Taji reports:

> Then wending through constellations of flowers, we entered deep groves. And thus, thrice from sunlight to shade, it seemed three brief nights and days, ere we paused before the mouth of the cavern.
>
> A bow-shot from the sea, it pierced the hill-side like a vaulted way; and glancing in, we saw far gleams of water; crossed, here and there, by long-flung distant shadows of domes and columns. All Venice seemed within. (P. 650)

The imagery here recalls the first reveries of Taji on the *Arcturion,* and the following lines refer back to Taji's description of Yillah in the *Chamois* as a sheaf, his own right arm the band: "From a stack of golden palm-stalks, the damsels now made torches; then stood grouped, a sheaf of sirens in a sheaf of flame."

Hautia herself dives into the cavern pool, emerging with her hands full of pearls.

> "Lo! Taji; all these may be had for the diving; and Beauty, Health, Wealth, Long Life, and the Last Lost Hope of man. But through me alone, may these be had. Dive thou, and bring up one pearl if thou canst."
>
> Down, down! down, down, in the clear, sparkling water, till I seemed crystallized in the flashing heart of a diamond; but from those bottomless depths, I uprose empty handed. (P. 651)

Hautia taunts him for his failure to find pearls: "Thou art fresh from the mines. Ah, Taji! for thee, bootless deep diving. Yet to Hautia, one shallow plunge reveals many Golcondas." But nonetheless, Taji has made the baptismal plunge.

*   *   *

October 24. Returned from the cavern, Taji is again tranced in Hautia's bower. Again he begs her to reveal the fate of Yillah, and at last Hautia answers by showing Yillah's rose-pearl that adorns her own head. Taji snatches it, crying out for Yillah, but Hautia speaks: "Rave on: she lies too deep to answer; stranger voices than thine she hears:—bubbles are bursting round her."

On this day, Luna enters Jupiter's Sagittarius, at the end of the Milky Way's vine, where moons are born by the bursting of bubbles, just as Yillah's blossom had burst on Amma. But Taji, who no longer believes Yillah's "deep lie" regarding her origin, believes that his love is drowned. "Oh, vipress," he cries, "I could slay thee!" Hautia releases him from his spell, and from his sentence as well: "Go, go,—and slay thyself: I may not make thee mine;—go,—dead to dead!—There is another cavern in the hill." Note the word play here. Hautia sent Taji to dive for pearls, but he found himself in the heart of a diamond. Having told him that he was "fresh from the mines" (a Spade image), Hautia now says that she cannot make him "mine." Instead, he is to slay himself.

*   *   *

October 28. He flies past the cave of pearls to another, where "a lake transparent shone," and in it "round and round, a gleaming form slow circled in the deepest eddies:—white, and vaguely Yillah." Taji plunges into the water again, but the "revolving shade" darts out of sight. Luna is conjunct Saturn.

*   *   *

October 29. Taji makes his way to the beach, and like a ghost flits to and fro. Suddenly Mohi and Yoomy stand before him. "Is this specter, Taji?" asks Mohi, and the narrator replies, "Taji lives no more. So dead, he has no ghost. I am his spirit's phantom's phantom." And Mohi cries, "Nay, then, phantom! the time has come to flee" (653). He and Yoomy pull Taji into a shallop, and Mohi tells the story of Media's return to Odo, where he was faced with sedition. And just as Media has returned to reclaim his crown from his viceroy, so Taji must yield up his crown: "In trumpet-blasts, the hoarse night-winds now blew; the Lagoon, black with the still shadows of the mountains, and the driving shadows of the clouds. Of all the stars, only red Arcturus shone" (654).

In autumn, Arcturus rises just before sunrise and is red only when low on the horizon. Therefore, morning is near as Taji seizes the helm from Mohi and again appropriates a boat. Mohi and Yoomy swim for shore as Taji, now alone, steers for the open sea. " 'Now, I am my own soul's emperor; and my first act is abdication! Hail! realm of shades!'—and turning my prow into the racing tide, which seized me like a hand omnipotent, I darted through." The narrator has surrendered Sol's Taj, and has become a shade. But in his wake, pursuing him toward Arcturus and sunrise, is the trident of Neptune. Saturn has ceased his retrograde motion and has begun to move forward again.

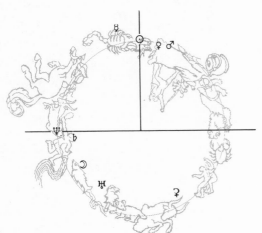

October 29, 1846

With Sol in mid-Libra, Taji leaves Hautia's island and heads out to open sea alone. Saturn, retrograde since June 11, regains his forward motion through Aquarius.

XXI. Summation

Mardi is a long work as it stands, but when the implications of the imagery have been unfolded, the work expands to reveal unexpected treasures of unity, structure, and coherence. After delving into the substrata of Melville's riddle, one finds it all too easy to forget that the surface is flawed and to become uncritically overenthusiastic. To paraphrase Media's criticism of old Bardianna, *Mardi,* though a trump, is undeniably a bore to the casual reader. For this reason alone it is unlikely to attain the stature of that greater "fish story," *Moby Dick.* But *Mardi* is both less and more than a piece of literature. It is a riddle and a game, and viewed so, it may be judged on a different standard altogether. Indeed, the work fulfills its author's claim to originality, and it stands unique—a masterpiece of synthesis. This, I believe, was Melville's intent.

No doubt about it, Melville leads his devoted explicator along a devious path, for the circular pattern of *Mardi*—in which each metaphor intertwines so tenaciously with every other— affords no single strand by which one may begin to unravel its mysteries. Thus, to discover Melville's pattern is one thing; to interpret it as he may have intended is quite another.

Once perceived, Melville's use of the *Almanac* and the application of his metaphor of Time provide a unity for *Mardi* that even careful reading does not otherwise reveal. In addition, an understanding of Melville's symbolic mode reveals answers to some critical questions regarding his method and order of composition. For one thing, in composing the end of *Mardi,* Melville had by no means forgotten the beginning. Indeed, with excessive care he tied each strand of imagery into its circular pattern—sometimes to the point of strain and too often to the point of tedium.

At no time is Taji merely a sailor; from the very beginning he is a fallen god, an arch fool on a ship of fools, a ghost among ghosts awaiting rebirth, a character trying to masquerade as his own author, a seafaring symbol. His function in this context is to demonstrate the relationship of narrator to author—a viceroy position that is prima facie deceptive. As Melville would have it,

Taji only dimly senses the guiding hand of the author and tries strenuously to shape the narrative in his own way. In turn, as his planet is outdistanced by the swifter bodies, he is overtopped by those who are in closer touch with the solar symbol of the author. It becomes Taji's function to report the words of others and in so doing to assimilate and digest them. Of considerable importance to the analogy drawn to the relationship of God to man is the fact that Taji never realizes the truth of his position, even after his "initiation." He is exposed to symbols, formulas, patterns, archetypes, myths, and tales, but never to certainties.

It is equally essential that Babbalanja remain unenlightened in regard to the ultimates and absolutes he has sought, even after his vision and his discovery of new worlds of the spirit, and of the Christ-figure of Neptune in the arm of the Waterman.[1] Melville in all cases withholds full knowledge from his creatures, just as he hides his own deeper meanings from his readers by burying them in a riddle of Time and speaking in "a merry and mythical way." Though Babbalanja states that all Mardi is an exclamation point, Melville would seem to postulate that it is a question mark.

1. Babbalanja uses the term *higher power*, recalling that in the hierarchy of angels, a *power* is one of the angelic ranks, along with Dominion, Principality, and so forth. Then too, in Babbalanja's mathematical concerns we might recall that he is attempting to square, or raise to a higher power, his own orbital number. Each planet is an angelic power.

I believe that the most important theme to emerge from an examination of the revenge motif has to do with the identity and function of the artist—specifically, the author. Having published two narratives of voyages in the Pacific that were suspected to be fiction—that is, falsehoods—Melville quite definitely stated that *Mardi* was composed as a romance, "to see whether the fiction might not, possibly, be received for a verity."[2] Melville knew full well that neither *Typee* nor *Omoo* was completely factual, that both were, indeed, glossed over with some degree of romance and artistic exaggeration. *Mardi,* on the other hand, is a romantic fantasy issued as stated fiction, and it consists of a series of symbolic documentaries culled from numerous sources, all of which had at some time or another been accepted by large groups of people as "Truth." First is that nautical authority, *The American Almanac.* In addition, flagrantly displayed, are the true stories from William Ellis, from Captain Cook and his companions, from Dana, Browne, Burton, Buffon, Müller and Henle, Ptolemy and Copernicus, and so on and on. In short, *Mardi* is no fiction at all but a compilation of facts disguised as

2. From the "Preface" to *Mardi*.

fiction. Combined with these facts are mythic elements that have been accepted as natural or spiritual truths—the Polynesian legends, the Greek and Hindu theological structures, the Calvinist doctrines of predestination and responsibility, and the Dantean version of the Catholic concepts of hell, purgatory, and heaven, and above all, the Bible itself as interpreted by widely divergent theologians.

A good part of Melville's revenge, then, lies in this deliberate confusion of fact and fiction. But this is not all. In addition to a mere confounding of critics, Melville offers a full-blown theory regarding the nature of art and the act of creativity. Take a fact, says Melville, and blow it up, garnish it, add a summer sun like Gudin, Isaby, or Claude, rearrange the details to suit some concept of order, and serve. The implied result will be fact, layered with falsehood, and forming something as near to truth as man can ever reach.

Taji has been a tool of the gods and has "fulfilled a design" that he only dimly senses, but never recognizes. The artist also fulfills a design, whether or not he recognizes the true quality of his work. Just as Taji has been manipulated by Jarl, the Avengers, and Hautia's Heralds, the artist is driven, steered, and lured by the "higher power" that implanted the "germ drama" in his mind. And after each accomplishment, the artist, like Taji, is driven out into deeper waters of thought to begin again.

Melville indicates that whether a work of art is likened to a new-born child or to dyspeptic excreta, the end is the result of creativity. Further, according to Babbalanja's evaluation of the general run of critics, a work of art that the artist feels is mere excreta may be accepted by the critical world as a work of art—or vice versa, as in the case of *Mardi*.

The same complexity that causes *Mardi* to fascinate the few is probably responsible for its failure with the many. Designed as it was to deceive and to enlighten, the book merely appears to be confusing and poorly organized. As a "masque," *Mardi* is all too successful in its masking to achieve popularity. Indeed, *Mardi* shares many characteristics with the traditional Masque. Like *The Faerie Queene, The Divine Comedy,* and Milton's *Comus, Mardi* progresses from one symbol-laden tableau to another and displays the stellar and planetary mythology, the pageantry of holiday and

season, and the involvement of current affairs, in turn and
simultaneously.

Unlike these elder greats from whom Melville has borrowed
copiously, *Mardi* is the work of a trickster, albeit a most serious
one. Each character is so masked as to be hidden one from the
other, each from himself, and all from the reader. Neptune and
Jupiter trade identities; Sol usurps Mars as Saturn usurps Sol;
Venus goes incognito; and even Yillah "lies deep." The constant
need for ambiguity and the incessant word-play places a strain on
Melville's dialogue and tortures sentences into strange structures
that do not characterize his earlier works.

The use of astromythical types was no doubt convenient to
Melville, providing him with readymade characterizations of
consistency and stability, even as it enabled him to work with the
problem of predestination. A direct line of imagery binds Dr.
Long Ghost to Taji and both to the tragic figure of Jackson in
Redburn. Annatoo is linked to Fedallah and Claggart, while
Samoa provides the Taurean prototype for Billy Budd. The
theme of revenge that dominates *Mardi* continues in *Moby Dick,*
but the interpretation is altered in the later book. While *Mardi*
has as its protagonist Taji, the frightened Leviathan pursued, *Moby
Dick*'s protagonist is Ahab, the pursuing shark. In each instance,
Melville's deepest concern involves error in interpretation,
misplaced credibility, and the impossibility of achieving absolute
Truth.

Apparently Melville learned from his own lessons, for in the
great "fish story" that follows, the vulgar errors of *Mardi* are not
repeated. Nevertheless, *Mardi* represents Melville's initiatory
long, seething dive into metaphysics, psychology, and
mythmaking. Read as a riddle, *Mardi* can lay claim to a high
degree of originality, even as its author stated. In the kind words
of one reviewer,

> "There is an art of *diving* as well as flying," and who knows but
> what the author, after attaining a comfortable elevation by his
> former works, may not have made this plunge *on purpose,* as men
> do who climb to the top of a high mast that they may dive the
> deeper.[3]

3. *The Melville Log,* Jay Leyda, ed.,
311.

Appendix: A Guide to Star Maps and Astrology

Positions of Heavenly Bodies Related to Events in *Mardi*

December, 1845

Monday	15 Uranus stationary (starting forward).	
Thursday	18 Mercury stationary (starting backward).	
Friday	19 Venus conjunct Saturn at ι Capricorn (also Neptune).	This conjunction accounts for "love" imagery surrounding Jarl.
Saturday	20 Jupiter conjunct τ Capricorn.	Error. Jupiter is near II Pisces. Note "jovian" imagery directed toward Jarl.
Sunday	21 Sol enters Capricorn; winter begins. Mars square Sol. Luna at 3rd quarter, also squared to Sol.	Taji joins Jarl on foretop of *Arcturion* and plots to leave ship.
Wednesday	24 Mercury perihelion (closest to Sol).	Preparation for escape. Mark (Mercury) in nest of jackets left warm by predecessor.
Thursday	25 Christmas.	Escape about 1:30 A.M. The *Chamois* afloat. Ch. IX
Friday	26 Jupiter stationary (starting forward).	
Saturday	27 Mercury passes under Sol.	
Sunday	28 Uranus square Sol; new moon conjunct Mercury.	The square is a dangerous aspect; hence, Taji experiences a sense of peril. Ch. XII
Wednesday	31 New Year's Eve. Luna conjunct Saturn. Venus at ι Aquarius.	End of Ch. XII. Taji is bewildered and confused and possibly made drunk by lunar cup on New Year's Eve.

January, 1846

Thursday	1 Sol perigee (closest to Earth); Mars passing ecliptic and moving into northern sky, is conjunct Uranus on New Year's Day. (Polar radials leaving Virgo and entering Aries.)	Ch. XIV and XV. Jarl warns Taji about northward drift. Imagery of dyspepsia (New Year hangover). Taji (Uranus) meets corpulent insect (Mars). Calm begins; heat is severe. Imagery of "old maids" and wool marks polar transition.
Saturday	3 Luna conjunct Uranus; Mercury at greatest Hellenic latitude North.	Ch. XVI. Mention of "September Tidings" (discovery of Neptune, caused by wobbles of Uranus).
Sunday	4 Luna at 1st quarter conjunct Mars; both are square to Sol.	Taji and Jarl turn backs on each other and experience mutual detestation.
Monday	5 Luna conjunct Jupiter.	This demonstrates that Jupiter is in Pisces well past Uranus.
Tuesday	6 Epiphany.	A breeze rises, and Taji hails the appearance of the king, the ocean.
Wednesday	7 Mercury stationary (moving forward);	Ch. XVIII. Remoras and pilot fish
Thursday	8 Venus, moving into northern sky at Σ Aquarius; she has now	
Friday	9 moved out of *Chamois* sector.	Ch. XIX. Taji and Jarl board the *Parki* and search her.
Saturday	10 Luna at Ξ Orion; radial poles enter Taurus and Scorpio; Mars at "foremast" and Venus at "mainmast" positions.	Ch. XXI. Samoa and Annatoo discovered "at opposite poles" on *Parki*.

February, 1846

Lunar passage has shown the planets to be in the following order: Mercury, Sol (Neptune), Saturn, Venus, Uranus, Mars, and Jupiter.

February 4 through 14 represents the ten-day adjustment in time made by Annatoo's observations of the "dial in the tower."

Wednesday	4 Luna at ∈ Taurus.	Ch. XXXIV, "How we Steered." The "half-moon" in the shaft of Taurus is Annatoo's "dial."
	Venus at greatest latitude north.	Northward drift noted for the last time. Eastward drift begins.
Saturday	7 Venus stationary (moving backward).	Compass disappears.
Tuesday	10 Saturn conjunct Sol; Luna at α Cancer.	Taji assumes command of the *Parki*. Finds and hides Otard.
Wednesday	11 Full moon.	
Thursday	12	Calm begins.
Saturday	14 Valentine's Day.	Annatoo displays interest in Jarl. He responds with a "typhoon of passion." Storm breaks and wrecks *Parki*. Annatoo is swept overboard.
Sunday	15 Luna at α Virgo; Mars conjunct Jupiter.	Chs. XXXVII and XXXVIII. Back to the *Chamois*. The sea on fire. The insect as "Hero."
Friday	20 Luna in Scorpio.	Aleema departs with Yillah.
Tuesday	24 Shrove Tuesday. Pallas conjunct Sol; Luna at perigee (nearest Earth), and conjunct Saturn (and Neptune).	The Fray.
Wednesday	25 Ash Wednesday. New moon, conjunct Mercury.	*Chamois* turns south.
Friday	27 Mars conjunct Π Aries. Luna conjunct Uranus.	Ch. LI.

March, 1846

Sunday	1 Luna conjunct Jupiter.	Ch. LII. *Chamois* turns west. Land Ho!
Monday	2 Luna conjunct Mars. Mercury conjunct Venus. Venus passes under Sol.	Yillah meets Media. Chs. LII to LVIII.
Tuesday	3	Chs. LIX to LX: Belshazzar on the Bench.
Friday	6	Ch. LXI. The Incognito.
Saturday	7 Luna at κ Gemini. Mars at Δ Aries. Venus conjunct Pallas.	Hautia's Heralds Appear.
Thursday	12 Full moon in Crater the Cup. Purim (14 Adar)	Ch. LXIV. Yillah disappears.
Sunday	15 Luna at α Virgo.	Messengers return.
Wednesday	18 Mercury conjunct Uranus.	Taji in a trance.
Friday	20 Luna at 3rd quarter. Sol enters Aries. Spring begins.	Still sped the days.
Tuesday	24 Luna perigee conjunct Venus. Luna conjunct Saturn.	Remembrance.
Friday	27 New moon. Luna conjunct Uranus. Mars at A-1 Taurus.	Taji must "hie from Odo." Media will leave also.
Saturday	28 Mercury conjunct Luna.	Ch. LXV. Taji makes three acquaintances, and Media draws a map of the lagoon.
Monday	30 Saturn at τ Aquarius.	Departure.
Tuesday	31	Ch. LXVII. Little King Peepi.

April, 1846

Wednesday	1 Mercury at greatest latitude North. April Fool.	Ch. LXIX. The Lonely Fisherman and Pella the Rock.
Friday	3 Luna at 1st quarter at Λ Gemini.	Ch. LXX. Hautia's Heralds.
Saturday	4 Luna at κ Gemini. Mars at Y Taurus.	Ch. LXXI. Arrival at Juam.
Sunday	5 Luna at apogee (farthest from Earth). Palm Sunday.	Chs. LXXV to LXXVI. Description of palm palaces. Jarl and the nut at breakfast.
Tuesday	7 Venus at greatest brilliance.	The group leaves and wanders throughout Juam.
Saturday	11 Full Moon.	Return to Juam. Feast of twenty-five kings begins.
Sunday	12 Easter Sunday and Passover. Vesta the Altar at o Taurus.	The feast goes on all night and the guests gorge on boar's meat. Lent is over. The questers leave Juam.

The Lunar passage, April 20 through April 29, shows the planets to be in the following order: (Neptune), Saturn, Venus, Uranus, Mercury, Sol, Jupiter, and Mars.

May, 1846

Saturday	2 Luna 1st quarter apogee. Mars at β Taurus.	Ch. LXXXVIII. Ohonoo. The Calm. Hautia's Heralds.
Sunday	3 Vesta at η Gemini. Mercury aphelion.	Ch. XCII. Keevi.
Monday	11 Full moon at B & Y Scorpio. Vesta at η Gemini.	Ch. XCIII. Tupia.
Friday	15 Luna in Sagittarius, perigee.	Ch. XCIV. Arrival at Mondoldo for fish dinner.
Saturday	16 Luna at β Capricorn. Mercury conjunct Ceres. Mars conjunct Vesta.	Wedding and funeral. Samoa's surgery and his "tall tale."
Sunday	17 Luna at 3rd quarter.	Ch. C. Avengers and Heralds.
Monday	18 Luna conjunct Saturn.	Ch. CII. Party leaves Mondoldo.
Tuesday	19 Venus conjunct Uranus.	
Thursday	21 Ascension. Luna conjunct Uranus, then Venus. Saturn square Sol.	Probable date of Neptune's retrograde period, and also date on which polar line passes Neptune's position. Jarl and Samoa "die."
Sunday	24 New moon conjunct Jupiter.	Ch. CV. Arrival at Maramma.

June, 1846

Friday	5 Mercury conjunct Jupiter.	Ch. CXVI. Visit to Hivohitee. Voyagers leave Maramma.
	Mars at Δ Gemini.	Taji learns of Jarl's death. Avengers and Heralds arrive. Ch. CXIX: Dreams.
Monday	8 Luna at beta¹ Scorpio	Isles of Fossils and
Tuesday	9 Full moon	enter Azzageddi. Avengers and Heralds reappear.
Thursday	11 Luna perigee. Saturn stationary (moving backward). Fête Dieu.	Ch. CXXXI. A calm. Vee-Vee falls.
Sunday	14 Luna conjunct Saturn. Mars at Ξ Gemini.	Ch. CXXXVIII. Arrival at Diranda.
Wednesday	17 Luna conjunct Uranus.	Battle Royal, the vengeful father, and the Heralds.
Saturday	20 Mercury passes over Sol.	A visit to King Bello.
Sunday	21 Luna conjunct Jupiter. Sol enters Cancer; Summer begins.	A visit to Earth via the summer solstice line at Greenwich.

July, 1846

Wednesday	1 Luna at 1st quarter. Sol apogee.	Babbalanja tells the story of Midni who tried to square the circle in the dark. The bow paddler laughs.
Saturday	4 Independence Day.	Ch. CLXI. The document in Vivenza.
Wednesday	8 Full moon.	Ch. CLXIX. Party leaves Vivenza.
Monday	20 Uranus stationary (moving backward).	(Possible date of return to Mardi)
Friday	24 Pallas conjunct Uranus. Luna conjunct Mars.	
Thursday	30 Venus at μ Gemini.	Date selected as return to Mardi.
Friday	31 Luna at first quarter.	Ch. CLXXI to Doxodox.

August, 1846

Saturday	1 Melville's Birthday. Mercury aphelion (nearest Sol).	Ch. CLXXII. Media dreams. His own avenger, Sol the true "Taji," is hot on his heels. He cries out to the two Mercurial companions, Mohi and Yoomy.
Tuesday	11 Luna conjunct Uranus at ε Pisces. Mercury stationary. Meteor shower.	
Wednesday	19 Luna conjunct Venus.	Ch. CLXXIII. Heralds and Avengers.
Thursday	20 Saturn opposite to Sol. Mercury conjunct Mars.	Ch. CLXXIV. Hooloomooloo.
Friday	21 New moon apogee.	Ch. CLXXVI. Babbalanja silent for twenty-four hours.
	Mercury greatest latitude south.	Bardianna's Will.
Saturday	22 Luna conjunct Mercury, then Mars.	Bardianna's Will.
Sunday	23 Ceres square Sol and conjunct Aldebaran.	Ch. CLXXVIII. Fatal storm cloud that overtakes a thousand souls, but spares the questers.
Monday	24	Ch. CLXXIX. Arrival in Bonavona.

September, 1846

Thursday	3 Mercury stationary.	Ch. CLXXX. Dialogue and supper.
Friday	4 Luna at perigee conjunct Saturn.	The questers leave Mondoldo.
Saturday	5 Full harvest moon.	Ch. CLXXXIV. Babbalanja's agony.

The lunar passage now stretches from September 4 through 21 and shows the planets to be in the following order: (Neptune), Saturn, Uranus, Jupiter, Venus, Mercury, Mars, and, now leading all the rest, Sol.

Wednesday	23 Venus perihelion (nearest Sol).	
	Sol enters Libra; Fall begins.	Ch. CLXXXV. The merry bowsman falls.
Thursday	24 Neptune discovered in Aquarius.	Ch. CLXXXVII. Serenia.
	Mercury at greatest latitude North.	Babbalanja's vision: the discovery of the ninth heaven.
Friday	25 Ch. CLXXXIX	The questers depart from Serenia.

October, 1846

Sunday	18 Luna conjunct Venus.	Ch. CXC. Hautia's Heralds make their final appearance.
Monday	19 Solar eclipse. Luna conjunct Mars.	Ch. CXCI. The questers land on Flozella-a-Nina.

Tuesday	20	New moon. Venus conjunct Mars. Luna conjunct Mercury.	Media returns to Odo.
Friday	23		To Cave of the Pool.
Saturday	24		Return from the Cave.
Wednesday	28	Mercury aphelion. Luna conjunct Saturn.	To another cave. Taji sees a form, "vaguely Yillah," in the deep pool.
Thursday	29	Saturn stationary. (End of retrograde period. Resumes forward motion.)	Taji on the beach at midnight.
Friday	30	Luna perigee.	Taji abdicates.
Saturday	31	All Saint's Eve.	

Star Atlas

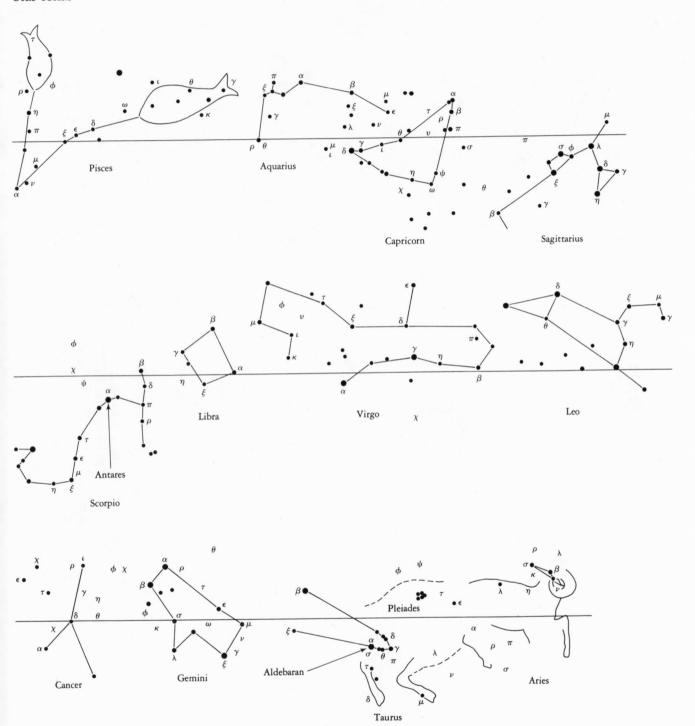

Pages from *The American Almanac,* November 1845-December 1846

32 *November, Eleventh Month, begins on Saturday.* [1845

Twilight begins and ends. Mean Time.

	1st day.		7th day.		13th day.		19th day		25th day.	
	Begins. h. m.	Ends. h. m.	Begins. h. m.	Ends. h. m.	Begins. h. m.	Ends. h. m.	Begins. h. m.	Ends. h. m.	Begins. h. m.	Ends. h. m.
Boston,	4 58m	6 30a	5 5m	6 23a	5 11m	6 18a	5 17m	6 14a	5 23m	6 11a
N. York,	4 57	6 31	5 4	6 24	5 10	6 19	5 15	6 16	5 21	6 13
Wash.	4 57	6 31	5 3	6 25	5 8	6 21	5 13	6 18	5 19	6 15
Charles.	4 54	6 34	4 59	6 29	5 3	6 25	5 7	6 23	5 12	6 22
N. Orl's.	4 53	6 35	4 55	6 31	5 1	6 28	5 5	6 26	5 9	6 25

PERIGEE AND APOGEE OF THE MOON.

Perigee, 2d day, 4h. M. | Apogee, 10th day, 4h. M.

PHASES OF THE MOON.

First Quarter, 6th day, 1h. 6.5m. A. | Last Quarter, 21st day, 11h. 17.9m. A.
Full Moon, 13th " 7h. 46.9m. A. | New Moon, 29th " 6h. 33.2m. M.

Days of Month.	Days of Week.	Sun's *upper* limb rises and sets, (corr. for refract.) M. T. Boston, &c. rises.	Boston, &c. sets.	New York, &c. rises.	New York, &c. sets.	Wash'ton, &c. rises.	Wash'ton, &c. sets.	Charleston, &c. rises.	Charleston, &c. sets.	N. Orleans, &c. rises.	N. Orleans, &c. sets.	High Water. M. Time. Boston, &c.	New York, &c.	Charleston, &c.
		h. m.	h. m.	h. m.	h. m.	h. m.	h. m.	h. m.	h. m.	h. m.	h. m.	h. m.	h. m.	h. m.
1	S.	6 33	4 53	6 30	4 57	6 27	5 0	6 18	5 10	6 14	5 13	0 7a	9 47m	8 7m
2	*Su.*	6 34	4 52	6 31	4 56	6 28	4 59	6 19	5 9	6 15	5 12	0 48a	10 28m	8 48m
3	M.	35	51	32	55	29	58	20	8	16	11	1 30	11 10	9 30
4	Tu.	36	50	33	54	30	57	21	7	17	10	2 16	11 56	10 16
5	W.	38	49	34	53	31	56	22	7	17	10	3 6	0 46a	11 6
6	Th.	39	47	36	51	32	55	23	6	18	9	4 2	1 42	0 2 a
7	F.	40	46	37	50	33	54	24	5	19	8	5 11	2 51	1 11
8	S.	42	45	38	49	35	53	25	4	20	8	6 31	4 11	2 31
9	*Su.*	6 43	4 44	6 39	4 48	6 36	4 52	6 26	5 3	6 20	5 7	7 46a	5 26a	3 46a
10	M.	44	43	40	47	37	51	27	2	21	6	8 54	6 34	4 54
11	Tu.	46	42	42	46	39	50	28	2	22	6	9 48	7 28	5 48
12	W.	47	41	43	45	40	49	29	1	23	5	10 33	8 13	6 33
13	Th.	48	40	44	44	41	48	30	0	24	5	11 14	8 54	7 14
14	F.	50	39	46	43	42	47	31	0	25	4	11 54	9 34	7 54
15	S.	51	38	47	42	43	46	32	4 59	26	4	. . .	10 11	8 31
16	*Su.*	6 52	4 37	6 48	4 41	6 44	4 45	6 32	4 58	6 26	5 3	0 31m	10 45a	9 5a
17	M.	53	36	49	41	45	44	33	57	27	3	1 5	11 18	9 38
18	Tu.	54	35	50	40	46	41	34	57	28	2	1 38	11 53	10 13
19	W.	55	34	51	39	47	43	35	56	29	2	2 13	. . .	10 51
20	Th.	57	34	53	39	48	42	36	56	29	2	2 51	0 31m	11 33
21	F.	58	33	54	38	49	42	36	55	30	1	3 33	1 13	. . .
22	S.	59	32	55	37	50	41	37	55	31	1	4 20	2 0	0 20m
23	*Su.*	7 0	4 31	6 56	4 36	6 51	4 41	6 38	4 55	6 32	5 1	5 19m	2 59m	1 19m
24	M.	2	31	57	36	52	41	39	54	33	0	6 31	4 11	2 31
25	Tu.	3	30	58	35	53	40	40	54	34	0	7 36	5 16	3 36
26	W.	4	30	59	35	54	40	40	54	34	0	8 40	6 20	4 40
27	Th.	5	29	7 0	34	55	40	41	54	35	0	9 33	7 13	5 33
28	F.	6	29	1	34	56	40	42	54	36	0	10 20	8 0	6 20
29	S.	8	29	3	34	58	40	43	54	37	0	11 5	8 45	7 5
30	*Su.*	7 9	4 28	7 4	4 33	6 59	4 39	6 44	4 54	6 38	5 0	11 49m	9 29m	7 49m

1845.] *November has Thirty Days.* 33

Passage of the Meridian (mean time) and Declination of the Planets.

	1st day. *Souths.* h. m.	Dec. ° ′	7th day. *Souths.* h. m.	Dec. ° ′	13th day. *Souths.* h. m.	Dec. ° ′	19th day. *Souths.* h. m.	Dec. ° ′	25th day. *Souths.* h. m.	Dec. ° ′
☿	11 53m	—15 51	0 11a	—19 9	0 26a	—21 53	0 41a	—23 58	0 56a	—25 19
♀	2 38a	—25 26	2 45	—25 55	2 53	—25 57	2 59	—25 34	3 6	—24 45
♂	7 36	—12 42	7 23	—11 23	7 10	—10 1	6 58	— 8 34	6 46	— 7 5
⚶	2 22m	+15 47	1 55m	+15 42	1 26m	+15 38	0 57m	+15 35	0 27m	+15 33
⚵	10 38	— 4 11	10 23	— 4 47	10 7	— 5 21	9 51	— 5 53	9 35	— 6 24
⚳	5 18a	+ 0 19	5 0a	— 0 21	4 41a	— 0 57	4 23a	— 1 28	4 5a	— 1 54
⚴	7 12	—25 24	6 51	—24 49	6 31	—24 10	6 11	—23 29	5 52	—22 45
♃	11 29	+11 53	11 2	+11 39	10 35	+11 25	10 9	+11 12	9 43	+11 0
♄	6 17	—18 7	5 54	—18 4	5 32	—17 59	5 9	—17 54	4 47	—17 47
♅	9 42	+ 2 9	9 18	+ 2 5	8 54	+ 2 1	8 30	+ 1 58	8 6	+ 1 56

Days of Month.	Moon Souths. Mean Time.	Moon rises or sets. Mean Time. Boston, &c.	N. York, &c.	Wash'ton, &c.	Cha'ston, &c	N. Orl's, &c.	PHENOMENA AND OBSERVATIONS. *Sundays and Holidays.*
		sets.	*sets.*	*sets.*	*sets.*	*sets.*	Washington Mean Time.
	h. m.	h. m.	h. m.	h. m.	h. m.	h. m.	d. h. m.
1	1 20a	6 16a	6 20a	6 25a	6 40a	6 48a	1 4 54a. ☌ ♀ e² Oph. ✱ 1 37 N.
S.	2 19a	7 13a	7 17a	7 23a	7 38a	7 46a	24*th Sunday after Trinity.*
3	3 19	8 15	8 21	8 25	8 40	8 46	2 10 33a ♂ ☌ σ ♒ ✱ 1 0 N.
4	4 17	9 24	9 27	9 32	9 45	9 51	2 10 36a. ♀ ☌ ☾ ♀ 5 27 S.
5	5 14	10 33	10 37	10 41	10 51	10 57	4 10 27a. □ ♄ ☉
6	6 7	11 43	11 46	11 49	11 56	. . .	5 4 28a. ☌ ⚶ y² Ori. ✱ 0 20 S.
7	6 50	. . .	. . .	. . .	. . .	0 0m	6 1 41a. ☌ ♄ ☾ ♄ 6 40 S.
8	7 48	0 52m	0 53m	0 55m	0 58m	1 2	8 6 9m. ☌ ♂ ☾ ♂ 7 19 S.
S.	8 37a	2 0m	2 1m	2 1m	2 2m	2 3m	25*th Sunday after Trinity.*
10	9 25	3 6	3 5	3 5	3 2	3 2	10 4 4m. ☿ in Aphelion.
11	10 14	4 13	4 11	4 9	4 3	4 3	10 0 5a. ☌ ♅ ☾ ♅ 4 20 S.
12	11 3	*rises.*	*rises.*	*rises.*	*rises.*	*rises.*	Olmsted's Meteoric Shower.
13	11 53	4 32a	4 37a	4 40a	4 53a	5 0a	Moon Ecl., vis. in U. S.
14	8	5 14	5 18	5 23	5 38	5 44	12 5 27m. ☌ ⚶ y² Ori. ✱ 0 28 S.
15	0 43m	6 0	6 4	6 10	6 25	6 32	12 0 7a. ☌ ♃ ☾ ♃ 2 40 S.
S.	1 33m	6 50a	6 54a	7 0a	7 15a	7 22a	26*th Sunday after Trinity.*
17	2 22	7 43	7 48	7 53	8 7	8 14	12 2 28a. ☌ ♀ λ ♐ ✱ 0 28 N.
18	3 9	8 39	8 43	8 48	8 59	9 6	12 10 11a. ♀ gr. Hel. Lat. S.
19	3 56	9 35	9 39	9 43	9 53	9 58	15 6 40m. ☌ ♂ λ ♒ ✱ 1 15 N.
20	4 41	10 34	10 36	10 40	10 47	10 51	16 0 37m. ☌ ♀ φ ♐ ✱ 1 18 S.
21	5 26	11 32	11 34	11 35	11 40	11 44	17 0 31m. □ ♀ ☉
22	6 8	. . .	. . .	. . .	. . .	. . .	17 10 18a. ☌ ♀ σ ♐ ✱ 0 46 S.
S.	6 52m	0 30m	0 31m	0 32m	0 35m	0 37m	27*th Sunday after Trinity.*
24	7 36	1 32	1 32	1 32	1 31	1 32	24 8 33m. ☌ ⚶ o¹ Ori. ✱ 1 34 S.
25	8 23	2 35	2 34	2 33	2 29	2 29	26 6 8m. ☌ ♀ h² ♐ ✱ 0 34 S.
26	9 13	3 41	3 39	3 36	3 30	3 29	26 10 15m. ☌ ♂ φ ♒ ✱ 0 3 N.
27	10 6	4 48	4 46	4 43	4 33	4 30	
28	11 3	*sets.*	*sets.*	*sets.*	*sets.*	*sets.*	30 2 15a. ☌ ☿ ☾ ☿ 5 47 S.
29	0 3a	4 50a	5 2a	5 7a	5 23a	5 30a	30 3 8a. ☿ gr. Hel. Lat. S.
S.	1 5a	5 59a	6 4a	6 10a	6 25a	6 33a	*Advent Sunday.* St. Andrew.

Twilight begins and ends. Mean Time.

	1st day.		7th day.		13th day.		19th day.		25th day.	
	Begins. h. m.	Ends. h. m.	Begins. h. m.	Ends. h. m.	Begins. h. m.	Ends. h. m.	Begins. h. m.	Ends. h. m.	Begins. h. m.	Ends. h. m.
Boston,	5 29m	6 9a	5 35m	6 9a	5 40m	6 8a	5 43m	6 10a	5 46m	6 14a
N. York,	5 27	6 11	5 33	6 11	5 37	6 11	5 41	6 13	5 44	6 16
Wash.	5 25	6 13	5 30	6 14	5 34	6 14	5 38	6 16	5 41	6 19
Charles.	5 17	6 21	5 22	6 22	5 26	6 23	5 29	6 25	5 32	6 28
N. Orl's.	5 13	6 25	5 18	6 26	5 24	6 17	5 25	6 29	5 28	6 32

PERIGEE AND APOGEE OF THE MOON.

Perigee, 1st day, 1h. M. | Apogee, 16th day, 6h. A. | Perigee, 29th day, 10h. M.

PHASES OF THE MOON.

First Quarter, 5th day, 9h. 44.2m. A. | Last Quarter, 21st day, 6h. 19.2m. A.
Full Moon, 13th " 1h. 34.8m. A. | New Moon, 28th " 5h. 45.0m. A.

Days of Month.	Days of Week.	Sun's *upper* limb rises and sets, (corr. for refract.) M. T. — Boston, &c. rises. h. m.	Boston, &c. sets. h. m.	New York, &c. rises. h. m.	New York, &c. sets. h. m.	Wash'ton, &c. rises. h. m.	Wash'ton, &c. sets. h. m.	Charleston, &c. rises. h. m.	Charleston, &c. sets. h. m.	N. Orleans, &c. rises. h. m.	N. Orleans, &c. sets. h. m.	High Water. M. Time. — Boston, &c. h. m.	New York, &c. h. m.	Charleston, &c. h. m.
1	M.	7 10	4 28	7 5	4 33	7 0	4 39	6 44	4 54	6 39	5 0	0 35a	10 15m	8 35m
2	Tu.	11	28	6	33	1	39	45	54	40	0	1 20	11 0	9 20
3	W.	12	28	7	33	2	39	46	54	40	0	2 9	11 49	10 9
4	Th.	13	28	8	33	3	39	47	54	41	0	2 59	0 39a	10 59
5	F.	14	28	9	33	4	38	47	54	42	0	3 53	1 33	11 53
6	S.	15	28	10	33	5	38	48	54	43	0	4 50	2 30	0 50a
7	*Su.*	7 16	4 28	7 11	4 33	7 6	4 38	6 49	4 54	6 44	5 0	5 58a	3 38a	1 58a
8	M.	17	28	12	33	7	38	50	54	44	1	7 7	4 47	3 7
9	Tu.	18	28	13	33	8	38	50	54	45	1	8 17	5 57	4 17
10	W.	19	28	14	33	9	38	51	54	46	1	9 21	7 1	5 21
11	Th.	20	28	15	33	10	38	52	55	46	1	10 11	7 51	6 11
12	F.	21	28	16	33	11	38	53	55	47	2	10 56	8 36	6 56
13	S.	22	28	17	33	11	38	54	55	48	2	11 36	9 16	7 36
14	*Su.*	7 23	4 28	7 18	4 33	7 12	4 38	6 55	4 55	6 48	5 2	. . .	9 55a	8 15a
15	M.	24	29	19	34	13	39	56	56	49	3	0 15m	10 28	8 48
16	Tu.	24	29	19	34	13	39	56	56	49	3	0 48	11 3	9 23
17	W.	25	29	20	34	14	40	57	56	50	3	1 23	11 37	9 57
18	Th.	25	29	20	34	14	40	57	56	50	3	1 57	. . .	10 31
19	F.	26	30	21	35	15	41	58	57	51	4	2 31	0 11m	11 9
20	S.	26	30	21	35	15	41	58	57	51	4	3 9	0 49	11 47
21	*Su.*	7 27	4 31	7 22	4 36	7 15	4 42	6 59	4 58	6 52	5 5	3 47m	1 27m	. . .
22	M.	27	31	22	36	16	42	59	58	52	5	4 31	2 11	0 31m
23	Tu.	28	32	22	37	16	43	7 0	59	53	6	5 52	3 5	1 52
24	W.	28	32	22	37	16	43	0	59	53	6	6 34	4 14	2 34
25	Th.	28	33	23	38	17	44	0	5 0	53	7	7 43	5 23	3 43
26	F.	29	33	23	38	17	44	1	1	54	7	8 52	6 32	4 52
27	S.	29	34	23	39	17	45	1	1	54	8	9 51	7 31	5 51
28	*Su.*	7 29	4 34	7 24	4 39	7 18	4 45	7 1	5 2	6 55	5 9	10 43m	8 23m	6 43m
29	M.	29	35	24	40	18	46	2	3	55	9	11 33	9 13	7 33
30	Tu.	30	36	24	41	18	47	2	4	55	10	0 25a	10 5	8 25
31	W.	30	37	25	42	19	48	3	5	56	11	1 12	10 52	9 12

Passage of the Meridian (mean time) and Declination of the Planets.

	1st day. Souths. h. m.	1st day. Dec. ° ′	7th day. Souths. h. m.	7th day. Dec. ° ′	13th day. Souths. h. m.	13th day. Dec. ° ′	19th day. Souths. h. m.	19th day. Dec. ° ′	25th day. Souths. h. m.	25th day. Dec. ° ′
☿	1 10a	—25 50	1 21a	—25 30	1 23a	—24 23	1 5a	—22 48	0 20a	—21 17
♀	3 11	—23 34	3 15	—22 2	3 18	—20 11	3 20	—18 6	3 19	—15 48
♂	6 35	— 5 34	6 24	— 4 1	6 13	— 2 25	6 2	— 0 49	5 52	+ 0 48
⚶	11 52	+15 32	11 22	+15 34	10 52	+15 37	10 23	+15 43	9 54	+15 51
⚵	9 19m	— 6 51	9 3m	— 7 16	8 47m	— 7 39	8 30m	— 7 59	8 14m	— 8 16
⚳	3 48a	— 2 17	3 31a	— 2 35	3 14a	— 2 48	2 57a	— 2 57	2 41a	— 3 2
⚴	5 34	—21 57	5 16	—21 10	5 28	—20 20	4 41	—19 29	4 24	—18 36
♃	9 18	+10 51	8 53	+10 43	8 28	+10 39	8 3	+10 36	7 39	+10 37
♄	4 25	—17 40	4 3	—17 32	3 42	—17 23	3 20	—17 13	2 59	—17 3
♅	7 42	+ 1 54	7 18	+ 1 53	6 53	+ 1 52	6 31	+ 1 53	6 8	+ 1 54

Days of Month.	Moon Souths. Mean Time. h. m.	Moon rises or sets. Mean Time. — Boston, &c. h. m.	N. York, &c. h. m.	Wash'ton, &c. h. m.	Cha'ston, &c. h. m.	N. Orl's, &c. h. m.	PHENOMENA AND OBSERVATIONS. *Sundays and Holidays.* Washington Mean Time. d. h. m.
		sets.	*sets.*	*sets.*	*sets.*	*sets.*	
1	2 6a	7 8a	7 13a	7 18a	7 31a	7 39a	1 4 14a. ⚶ ☍ ⊙ intens. of lt. 0.619
2	3 6	8 19	8 23	8 28	8 39	8 45	3 10 30a. ☌ ♄ ☾ ♄ 6 36 S.
3	4 2	9 32	9 35	9 39	9 46	9 51	6 1 32a. ☌ ♂ ☾ ♂ 5 21 S.
4	4 56	10 43	10 45	10 47	10 52	10 54	7 4 46a. ☌ ♅ ☾ ♅ 4 18 S.
5	5 46	11 52	11 53	11 54	11 56	11 58	9 1 36a. ☌ ♃ ☾ ♃ 2 40 S.
6	6 35	. . .	. . .	. . .	. . .	. . .	10 3 4m. ☿ gr. elon. 20 36 E.
S.	7 23a	0 58m	0 58m	0 58m	0 56m	0 57m	*2d Sunday in Advent.*
8	8 11	2 4	2 3	2 2	1 56	1 57	11 7 0m. ⚶ in Aphelion.
9	8 59	3 8	3 6	3 4	2 56	2 54	12 6 42m. ☌ ♀ ⚴ ⚴ 17 52 N.
10	9 48	4 10	4 7	4 4	3 54	3 51	15 11 54m. ☌ ♀ η ♑ ✱ 0 54 S.
11	10 37	5 11	5 7	5 3	4 50	4 47	15 9 24a. ♅ stationary.
12	11 27	*rises.*	*rises.*	*rises.*	*rises.*	*rises.*	18 1 7m. ☿ stationary.
13	☍	4 43a	4 47a	4 53a	5 8a	5 15a	19 7 0m. ⚴ gr. Hel. Lat. S.
S.	0 16m	5 35a	5 41a	5 45a	6 0a	6 6a	*3d Sunday in Advent.*
15	1 4	6 29	6 34	6 38	6 52	6 59	19 2 11a. ☿ in ☊
16	1 51	7 25	7 29	7 33	7 44	7 50	19 7 25a. ☌ ♀ ♄ ♀ 0 49 S.
17	2 37	8 23	8 27	8 30	8 39	8 43	19 8 38a. ☌ ♀ ι ♑ ✱ 0 32 N.
18	3 21	9 21	9 23	9 26	9 32	9 35	20 8 58m. ☌ ♃ τ ♑ ✱ 0 17 S.
19	4 4	10 19	10 21	10 22	10 25	10 28	20 10 52a. ♀ gr. elon. 47 16 E.
20	4 47	11 19	11 19	11 19	11 20	11 20	21 11 18m. □ ♂ ⊙
S.	5 30m	. . .	. . .	. . .	. . .	. . .	*4th Sunday in Advent.*
22	6 14	0 19m	0 18m	0 18m	0 15m	0 15m	21 5 19a. ⊙ ent. ♑ Win. beg.
23	7 1	1 21	1 20	1 18	1 13	1 13	24 3 47m. ☿ in Perihelion.
24	7 51	2 27	2 24	2 22	2 14	2 11	26 1 22a. ♃ stationary.
25	8 45	3 34	3 31	3 28	3 16	3 14	Christmas Day.
26	9 32	4 42	4 38	4 35	4 21	4 17	27 11 58m. ☿ in Inf. ☌ ⊙
27	10 43	*sets.*	*sets.*	*sets.*	*sets.*	*sets.*	28 0 15m. □ ♅ ⊙
S.	11 46m	4 44a	4 48a	4 53a	5 8a	5 16a	*1st Sunday after Christmas.*
29	0 48a	5 55	6 0	6 5	6 18	6 24	28 1 33a. ☌ ☿ ☾ ☿ 1 10 S.
30	1 48	7 10	7 14	7 17	7 27	7 33	31 11 21m. ☌ ♄ ☾ ♄ 6 28 S.
31	2 45	8 23	8 25	8 28	8 36	8 39	31 4 50a. ☌ ♀ ι ♒ ✱ 1 17 S.

THE

AMERICAN ALMANAC,

FOR THE YEAR

1846,

Being the latter part of the 70th, and the beginning of the 71st, year of the Independence of the United States of America;

" the 6559th year of the Julian Period;

" the latter part of the 5606th and the beginning of the 5607th, year since the creation of the world, according to the Jews;

" the 2599th year (according to Varro) since the foundation of Rome;

" the 2593d year since the era of Nabonassar, which has been assigned to Wednesday, the 26th of February of the 3967th year of the Julian Period, which corresponds, according to the chronologists, to the 747th, and, according to the astronomers, to the 746th year, before the birth of Christ;

" the 2622d year of the Olympiads, or the second year of the 656th Olympiad, beginning in July, 1846, if we fix the era of the Olympiads at 775½ years before Christ, or at or about the beginning of July of the year 3938 of the Julian Period;

" the latter part of the 1262nd, and the beginning of the 1263d year (of twelve lunations) since the Hegira, or flight of Mahomet, which, as is generally supposed, took place on the 16th of July, in the year 622 of the Christian era.

I. THE CALENDAR AND CELESTIAL PHENOMENA FOR THE YEAR.

SIGNS OF THE PLANETS, &c.

☉ The Sun.	♂ Mars.	⚳ Ceres.
⊕ The Earth.	⚶ Vesta.	♃ Jupiter.
● ☽ ○ ☾ The Moon.	⚵ Juno.	♄ Saturn.
☿ Mercury.	⚴ Pallas.	♅ Herschel or Uranus.
♀ Venus.		✱ A fixed star.

☌ Conjunction, or having the same Longitude or Right Ascension.
□ Quadrature, or differing 90° in " " "
☍ Opposition, or " 180° in " " "
☊ The ascending, ☋ the descending node.

The sign + is prefixed to the latitude, or declination, of the Sun, or other heavenly body, when *north*, and the sign — when *south*; but the former prefixed to the hourly motion of the Moon in latitude, indicates that she is approaching, and the latter that she is receding from, the *north* pole of the ecliptic.

The letters *M. A.*, *m. a.*, denote *Morning* and *Afternoon*.

CHRONOLOGICAL CYCLES.

Dominical Letter, .	D.	Solar Cycle, ...	7
Epact	3	Roman Indiction, . . .	4
Lunar Cycle, or Golden Number,	4	Julian Period, . . .	6559

SIGNS OF THE ZODIAC.

Spring signs.	1. ♈ Aries. 2. ♉ Taurus. 3. ♊ Gemini.	Autumn signs.	7. ♎ Libra. 8. ♏ Scorpio. 9. ♐ Sagittarius.
Summer signs.	4. ♋ Cancer. 5. ♌ Leo. 6. ♍ Virgo.	Winter signs.	10. ♑ Capricornus. 11. ♒ Aquarius. 12. ♓ Pisces.

BEGINNING AND LENGTH OF THE SEASONS.

				h.	m.	s.	
Sun enters ♑	(Winter begins)	1845,	Dec. 21st,	5	18	54 A.	M. Time at Wash'ton.
" " ♈	(Spring "	1846,	March 20th,	6	37	49 A.	
" " ♋	(Summer "	"	June 21st,	3	22	35 A.	
" " ♎	(Autumn "	"	Sept. 23d,	5	23	22 M.	
" " ♑	(Winter "	"	Dec. 21st,	11	4	30 A.	

	d.	h.	m.	s.
Sun in the Winter Signs	89	1	18	55
" " Spring	92	20	44	46
" " Summer	93	14	0	47
" " Autumn	89	17	41	8
" north of Equator, (Spring and Summer)	186	10	45	33
" south of " (Winter and Autumn)	178	19	0	3
Length of the tropical year, commencing at the winter solstice, 1845, and terminating at the winter solstice, 1846,	365	5	45	36
Mean or average length of the tropical year,	365	5	48	48

Left Page

DARKNESS OF THE NIGHTS DURING THE YEAR 1846.

For Boston, New York, Philadelphia, Washington, &c.

The number of hours at the top of the page denotes the average time for the month from the end of evening twilight to the beginning of morning twilight.

The dots in the table denote the hours of entire darkness, when there is neither sun, moon, nor twilight; and their disposition denotes the hours before or after midnight.

Days of Month.	January 12 h.	Feb'y 11 h.	March 9 h.	April 8 h.	May 7 h.	Jun. 5 h.	July 6 h.	Aug. 7 h.	Sept. 8 h.	Oct. 9 h.	Nov. 11 h.	Dec. 12 h.
1												
2												
3												
4												
5												
6												
7												
8												
9												
10												
11												
12												
13												
14												
15												
16												
17												
18												
19												
20												
21												
22												
23												
24												
25												
26												
27												
28												
29												
30												
31												

(Harvest Moon. — Hunter's Moon.)

Right Page

of his opposition to the Sun, being then also nearest to the Earth, in which position he will not be this year.

1846.	Venus.	Mars.	1846.	Venus.	Mars.
January 15	0.351	0.880	July 15	0.761	0.990
February 14	0.087	0.899	August 15	0.851	0.998
March 15	0.055	0.920	September 15	0.919	1.000
April 15	0.326	0.942	October 15	0.966	0.996
May 15	0.514	0.962	November 15	0.992	0.986
June 15	0.653	0.978	December 15	1.000	0.971

Position and Magnitude of the Rings of Saturn, according to Bessel and Struve, for every fortieth day in the year, at 7 hours in the morning.

M. Time at Washington. 7h. M.	a.	b.	p.	l.	l'.
1846 January 1	35.23	+ 9.07	+ 7 12.1	+ 14 55.5	+ 13 34.1
February 10	34.58	7.76	6 55.1	12 58.3	13 4.1
March 22	35.24	6.72	42.3	10 59.3	12 33.8
May 1	37.08	6.13	29.5	9 31.2	12 3.0
June 10	39.64	6.22	24.3	9 2.0	11 32.0
July 20	41.93	7.06	25.9	9 41.7	11 0.6
August 29	42.58	8.15	39.6	11 2.2	10 28.8
October 8	41.08	8.59	48.0	12 3.9	9 56.8
November 17	38.50	8.02	48.1	12 1.6	9 24.4
December 27	36.22	6.81	38.9	10 5.5	8 51.7
" 31	36.04	6.67	37.5	10 40.3	8 48.5

a denotes the semitransverse axis of the rings.

b " " semiconjugate axis of the rings, positive when their northern surface is visible, negative when their southern.

p denotes the inclination of the Northern semiconjugate axis of the rings to the circle of declination; + when East, — when West.

l " " angle of elevation of the Earth above the plane of the rings, as seen from Saturn; + when North, — when South.

l' " " elevation of the Sun above the plane of the rings, as seen from Saturn; + when North, — when South.

The Conjunction of Saturn will take place on the 9th of February, and the Opposition on the 20th of August. The Right Ascension of this planet will not during the year differ much from 22h., and its declination will not be less than 12° South, so that it will not rise to a great height even when in the meridian.

10 *January, First Month, begins on Thursday.* [1846.

Twilight begins and ends. Mean time.

	1st day. Begins.	1st day. Ends.	7th day. Begins.	7th day. Ends.	13th day. Begins.	13th day. Ends.	19th day. Begins.	19th day. Ends.	25th day. Begins.	25th day. Ends.
	h. m.	h. m.	h. m.	h. m.	h. m.	h. m.	h. m.	h. m.	h. m.	h. m.
Boston,	5 48m	6 20a	5 48m	6 24a	5 48m	6 29a	5 47m	6 35a	5 44m	6 42a
N. York,	5 46	6 22	5 46	6 26	5 46	6 31	5 45	6 37	5 42	6 44
Wash.	5 43	6 25	5 44	6 29	5 44	6 34	5 43	6 39	5 41	6 45
Charles.	5 35	6 33	5 36	6 37	5 37	6 41	5 36	6 46	5 35	6 51
N. Orl's,	5 31	6 37	5 33	6 40	5 34	6 44	5 33	6 49	5 32	6 54

APOGEE AND PERIGEE OF THE MOON.

Apogee, 13th day, 2h. M. | Perigee, 26th day, 10h. A.

PHASES OF THE MOON.

First Quarter, 4th day, 9h. 17.2m M. | Last Quarter, 20th day, 10h. 43.8m. M.
Full Moon, 12th " 8 53.4 M. | New Moon, 27th " 4 14.9 M.

Days of Month.	Days of Week.	Sun's *upper* limb rises and sets, (corr. for refract.) M. T. Boston, &c. rises.	Boston, &c. sets.	New York, &c. rises.	New York, &c. sets.	Wash'ton, &c. rises.	Wash'ton, &c. sets.	Charleston, &c. rises.	Charleston, &c. sets.	N. Orleans, &c. rises.	N. Orleans, &c. sets.	High Water. M. Time. Boston, &c.	New York, &c.	Charleston, &c.
		h. m.	h. m.	h. m.	h. m.	h. m.	h. m.	h. m.	h. m.	h. m.	h. m.	h. m.	h. m.	h. m.
1	Th.	7 30	4 38	7 25	4 43	7 19	4 49	7 3	5 5	6 56	5 12	2 1a	11 41m	10 1m
2	F.	30	39	25	44	19	50	3	6	56	13	2 49	0 29a	10 49
3	S.	30	40	25	45	19	51	3	7	57	13	3 37	1 17	11 37
4	*Su.*	7 30	4 41	7 25	4 46	7 19	4 52	7 3	5 7	6 57	5 14	4 23a	2 3a	0 23a
5	M.	30	42	25	47	19	52	3	8	57	15	5 16	2 56	1 16
6	Tu.	29	43	25	48	19	53	4	9	57	15	6 23	4 3	2 23
7	W.	29	44	25	49	19	54	4	10	57	16	7 33	5 13	3 33
8	Th.	29	45	24	50	19	55	4	11	57	17	8 51	6 31	4 51
9	F.	29	46	24	51	19	56	4	12	57	18	9 52	7 32	5 52
10	S.	29	47	24	52	19	57	4	12	57	19	10 41	8 21	6 41
11	*Su.*	7 29	4 48	7 24	4 53	7 19	4 58	7 3	5 13	6 57	5 19	11 23a	9 3a	7 23a
12	M.	28	50	23	54	18	59	3	14	57	20	. . .	9 40	8 0
13	Tu.	28	51	23	55	18	5 0	3	15	57	21	0 0m	10 15	8 35
14	W.	28	52	23	56	18	1	3	16	57	22	0 35	10 46	9 6
15	Th.	27	53	22	57	18	2	3	17	57	23	1 6	11 18	9 38
16	F.	27	54	22	59	17	3	3	18	57	24	1 38	11 50	10 10
17	S.	26	55	21	5 0	17	5	2	19	57	25	2 10	. . .	10 43
18	*Su.*	7 26	4 56	7 21	5 1	7 16	5 6	7 2	5 20	6 56	5 25	2 43m	0 23m	11 16a
19	M.	25	58	21	2	16	7	2	21	56	26	3 16	0 56	11 54
20	Tu.	24	59	20	3	15	8	2	21	56	27	3 54	1 34	. . .
21	W.	24	5 0	19	4	15	9	1	22	56	28	4 39	2 19	0 39m
22	Th.	23	1	19	5	14	10	1	23	55	29	5 36	3 16	1 36
23	F.	22	3	18	7	14	11	0	24	55	30	6 53	4 33	2 53
24	S.	22	4	17	8	13	12	0	25	55	31	8 13	5 53	4 13
25	*Su.*	7 21	5 5	7 17	5 9	7 12	5 13	7 0	5 26	6 54	5 31	9 29m	7 9m	5 29m
26	M.	20	6	16	10	12	15	6 59	27	54	32	10 29	8 9	6 29
27	Tu.	19	8	15	11	11	16	58	28	53	33	11 21	9 1	7 21
28	W.	18	9	14	13	10	17	58	29	53	34	0 11a	9 51	8 11
29	Th.	17	10	13	14	9	18	57	30	52	35	0 59	10 39	8 59
30	F.	16	12	12	15	8	19	57	31	52	36	1 43	11 23	9 43
31	S.	15	13	12	16	8	20	56	32	51	37	2 27	0 7a	10 27

1846.] *January has Thirty-one Days.* 11

Passage of the Meridian (mean time) and Declination of the Planets.

	1st day. Souths.	1st day. Dec.	7th day. Souths.	7th day. Dec.	13th day. Souths.	13th day. Dec.	19th day. Souths.	19th day. Dec.	25th day. Souths.	25th day. Dec.
	h. m.	° ′	h. m.	° ′	h. m.	° ′	h. m.	° ′	h. m.	° ′
☿	11 15m	—20 14	10 41m	—20 28	10 28m	—21 20	10 27m	—22 13	10 34m	—22 41
♀	3 17a	—12 57	3 13a	—10 24	3 6a	— 7 51	2 57a	— 5 23	2 45a	— 3 3
♂	5 40	+ 2 40	5 30	+ 4 16	5 20	+ 5 52	5 11	+ 7 26	5 1	+ 8 59
⚶	9 22	+16 3	8 56	+16 17	8 31	+16 35	8 6	+16 55	7 43	+17 17
⚵	7 54m	— 8 32	7 36m	— 8 42	7 18m	— 8 49	7 0m	— 8 52	6 42m	— 8 52
⚳	2 22a	— 3 4	2 6a	— 3 2	1 50a	— 2 57	1 34a	— 2 49	1 18a	— 2 38
⚴	4 5	—17 33	3 48	—16 37	3 32	—15 40	3 16	—14 42	3 0	—13 43
♃	7 12	+10 40	6 49	+10 46	6 27	+10 55	6 5	+11 5	5 43	+11 18
♄	2 34	—16 50	2 13	—16 38	1 52	—16 26	1 31	—16 14	1 11	—16 1
♅	5 40	+ 1 56	5 17	+ 1 59	4 54	+ 2 2	4 31	+ 2 6	4 8	+ 2 11

Days of Month.	Moon Souths. Mean Time.	Moon rises or sets. Mean time. Boston, &c.	N. York, &c.	Wash'tn, &c.	Cha'ston, &c.	N. Orl's, &c.
		sets.	sets.	sets.	sets.	sets.
	h. m.	h. m.	h. m.	h. m.	h. m.	h. m.
1	3 39a	9 36a	9 37a	9 39a	9 42a	9 45a
2	4 31	10 53	10 53	10 52	10 53	10 54
3	5 21	11 56	11 54	11 53	11 49	11 50
S.	6 9a	. . .	. . .	. . .	. . .	. . .
5	6 57	1 1m	0 59m	0 58m	0 51m	0 49m
6	7 46	2 3	2 0	1 58	1 49	1 46
7	8 34	3 5	3 2	2 58	2 46	2 42
8	9 23	4 1	3 57	3 54	3 39	3 36
9	10 12	4 56	4 51	4 47	4 33	4 29
10	11 1	5 45	5 40	5 36	5 21	5 18
S.	11 48a	rises.	rises.	rises.	rises.	rises.
12	☍	5 19a	5 23a	5 28a	5 39a	5 46a
13	0 34m	6 16	6 20	6 23	6 33	6 38
14	1 19	7 14	7 16	7 19	7 26	7 30
15	2 2	8 12	8 14	8 16	8 20	8 23
16	2 45	9 11	9 11	9 11	9 14	9 15
17	3 27	10 9	10 9	10 10	10 8	10 8
S.	4 10m	11 9a	11 9a	11 8a	11 3a	11 3a
19	4 55	. . .	. . .	. . .	. . .	11 59
20	5 42	0 12m	0 9m	0 7m	0 1m	. . .
21	6 33	1 16	1 13	1 11	1 1	0 58m
22	7 27	2 22	2 18	2 14	2 2	1 59
23	8 24	3 26	3 22	3 18	3 5	3 0
24	9 24	4 29	4 24	4 21	4 6	4 2
S.	10 25m	5 27m	5 23m	5 19m	5 6m	5 1m
26	11 27	sets.	sets.	sets.	sets.	sets.
27	0 27a	5 55a	5 59a	6 2a	6 10a	6 15a
28	1 24	7 12	7 13	7 16	7 21	7 24
29	2 18	8 26	8 28	8 28	8 29	8 31
30	3 11	9 38	9 37	9 38	9 35	9 35
31	4 2	10 46	10 46	10 44	10 38	10 38

PHENOMENA AND OBSERVATIONS.

Sundays and Holidays.

Washington Mean Time.

d. h. m. ° ′
1 2 45a. ♂ in ☊
1 5 36a. ☉ in Perigee.
1 7 11a. ☌ ♂ ♅, ♅ 0 46 S.
2d Sunday after Christmas.
3 11 40m. ☿ gr. Hel. Lat. N.
Epiphany.
3 10 50a. ☌ ♅ ☾, ♅ 4 4 S.
4 1 11m. ☌ ♂ ☾, ♂ 3 9 S.
5 6 28a. ☌ ♃ ☾, ♃ 2 28 S.
7 4 18m. ☿ stationary.
1st Sund. after Epiphany.
8 4 57m. ♀ in ☊
8 5 33m. ☌ ♀ σ ♒ ✱ 1 18 S.
12 6 35a. ☌ ☿ ξ^2 ♎ ✱ 1 59 S.
14 8 45a. ☌ ♂ ε ♓, ✱ 0 53 N.
15 5 43m. ☌ ☿ μ^1 ♐ ✱ 0 32 N.
16 6 52m. ☌ ♀ λ ♒, ✱ 1 39 S.
2d Sunday after Epiphany.
16 3 52a. ☌ ♀ ♄, ♀ 13 27 N.
17 4 50m. ☌ ♂ e ♓, ✱ 1 57 S.
17 0 21a. ☌ ☿ δ ♎, ✱ 0 58 N.
18 9 44m. ☿ gr. elong. 24 12 W.
20 11 9m. ⚶ Stationary.
22 5 11m. □ ♃ ☉
3d Sunday after Epiphany.
25 1 56a. ☌ ☿ ☾, ☿ 4 9 S.
26 11 57m. ♀ at greatest brill.
26 11 42a. ☿ in ☋
28 3 18m. ☌ ♄ ☾, ♄ 6 21 S
29 9 17a. ☌ ♀ ☾, ♀ 0 31 S.
31 8 8m. ☌ ♅ ☾, ♅ 3 44 S.

12 *February, Second Month, begins on Sunday.* [1846.

Twilight begins and ends. Mean time.

	1st day.		7th day.		13th day.		19th day.		25th day.	
	Begins. h. m.	Ends. h. m.	Begins. h. m.	Ends. h. m.	Begins. h. m.	Ends. h. m.	Begins. h. m.	Ends. h. m.	Begins. h. m.	Ends. h. m.
Boston,	5 38m.	6 50a.	5 32m.	6 56a.	5 26m.	7 3a.	5 18m.	7 10a.	5 9m.	7 17a.
N. York,	5 37	6 51	5 31	6 57	5 25	7 4	5 18	7 10	5 10	7 16
Wash.	5 36	6 52	5 31	6 58	5 25	7 4	5 18	7 10	5 10	7 16
Charles.	5 31	6 57	5 27	7 1	5 23	7 6	5 17	7 11	5 10	7 16
N. Orl's	5 29	6 59	5 25	7 3	5 21	7 8	5 16	7 12	5 11	7 15

APOGEE AND PERIGEE OF THE MOON.

Apogee, 9th day, 4h. M. | Perigee, 24th day, 9h. M.

PHASES OF THE MOON.

First Quarter, 3d day, 0h. 3.1m. M. | Last Quarter, 19th day, 11h. 35 6m. A.
Full Moon, 11th " 4h. 4.0m. M. | New Moon, 25th " 2 23.8 A.

Days of Month.	Days of Week.	Sun's *upper* limb rises and sets, (corr. for refract.) M. T. Boston, &c. rises. h. m.	Boston, &c. sets. h. m.	New York, &c. rises. h. m.	New York, &c. sets. h. m.	Wash'ton, &c. rises. h. m.	Wash'ton, &c. sets. h. m.	Charleston, &c. rises. h. m.	Charleston, &c. sets. h. m.	N. Orleans, &c. rises. h. m.	N. Orleans, &c. sets. h. m.	High Water. M. Time. Boston, &c. h. m.	New York, &c. h. m.	Charleston, &c. h. m.
1	*Su.*	7 14	5 14	7 11	5 18	7 7	5 21	6 55	5 33	6 51	5 38	3 9a	0 49a	11 9m
2	M.	13	15	10	19	6	23	55	34	50	38	3 53	1 33	11 53
3	Tu.	12	17	9	20	5	24	54	34	49	39	4 38	2 18	0 38a
4	W.	11	18	7	21	4	25	53	35	49	40	5 31	3 11	1 31
5	Th.	10	19	6	22	3	26	52	36	48	41	6 47	4 27	2 47
6	F.	9	21	5	23	2	27	52	37	47	41	8 9	5 49	4 9
7	S.	8	22	4	25	1	28	51	38	47	42	9 26	7 6	5 27
8	*Su.*	7 6	5 23	7 3	5 26	7 0	5 29	6 50	5 39	6 46	5 43	10 23a	8 3a	6 23a
9	M.	5	24	2	27	6 59	30	49	40	45	44	11 5	8 45	7 5
10	Tu.	4	25	1	28	58	32	48	41	44	45	11 43	9 23	7 43
11	W.	2	26	0	30	57	33	47	42	44	46	. . .	9 54	8 14
12	Th.	1	28	6 58	31	55	34	47	43	43	46	0 14m	10 26	8 46
13	F.	0	29	57	32	54	35	46	44	42	47	0 46	10 55	9 15
14	S.	6 59	30	56	34	53	36	45	45	41	48	1 15	11 26	9 36
15	*Su.*	6 57	5 32	6 55	5 35	6 52	5 38	6 44	5 46	6 40	5 49	1 36m	11 57a	10 17a
16	M.	56	33	53	36	51	39	43	47	39	50	2 17	. . .	10 50
17	Tu.	54	35	52	37	49	40	42	48	38	51	2 50	0 30m	11 26
18	W.	53	36	51	39	48	41	41	48	38	52	3 26	1 6	. . .
19	Th.	52	38	49	40	47	42	40	49	37	52	4 9	1 49	0 9m
20	F.	50	39	48	41	46	44	39	50	36	53	5 1	2 41	1 1
21	S.	48	40	46	43	44	45	37	51	35	54	6 19	3 59	2 19
22	*Su.*	6 47	5 42	6 45	5 44	6 43	5 46	6 36	5 52	6 34	5 55	7 47m	5 27m	3 47m
23	M.	46	43	44	45	42	47	35	53	33	56	9 12	6 52	5 12
24	Tu.	44	45	42	46	40	48	34	54	32	57	10 16	7 56	6 16
25	W.	42	46	41	48	38	49	33	55	31	57	11 7	8 47	7 7
26	Th.	41	47	39	49	37	51	32	56	30	58	11 54	9 34	7 54
27	F.	39	49	38	50	36	52	31	57	28	59	0 39a	10 19	8 39
28	S.	38	50	37	51	34	53	30	58	27	6 0	1 21	11 1	9 21

1846.] *February has Twenty-eight Days.* 13

Passage of the Meridian (mean time) and Declination of the Planets.

	1st day. Souths. h. m.	Dec. ° ′	7th day. Souths. h. m.	Dec. ° ′	13th day. Souths. h. m.	Dec. ° ′	19th day. Souths. h. m.	Dec. ° ′	25th day. Souths. h. m.	Dec. ° ′
☿	10 48m	—22 26	11 1m	—21 26	11 17m	—19 38	11 33m	—17 1	11 49m	—13 35
♀	2 26a	— 0 39	2 5a	+ 0 59	1 39a	+ 2 4	1 7a	+ 2 26	0 31a	+ 2 1
♂	4 51	+10 45	4 42	+12 12	4 33	+13 37	4 24	+14 58	4 16	+16 15
⚶	7 17	+17 45	6 56	+18 10	6 36	+18 37	6 17	+19 4	5 59	+19 32
⚵	6 20m	— 8 47	6 0m	— 8 39	5 40m	— 8 26	5 19m	— 8 10	6 57m	— 7 49
⚳	0 59a	— 2 21	0 44a	— 2 6	0 28a	— 1 47	0 12a	— 1 28	11 56m	— 1 6
⚴	2 42	—12 33	2 26	—11 33	2 11	—10 32	1 55	— 9 31	1 40a	— 8 29
♃	5 18	+11 36	4 58	+11 53	4 37	+12 11	4 17	+12 31	3 57	+12 52
♄	0 46	—15 45	0 26	—15 31	0 5	—15 18	11 44m	—15 4	11 23m	—14 51
♅	3 41	+ 2 17	3 19	+ 2 23	2 56	+ 2 29	2 34a	+ 2 36	2 11a	+ 2 43

Days of Month.	Moon Souths. Mean Time. h. m.	Moon rises or sets. Mean time. Boston, &c. h. m.	N. York, &c. h. m.	Wash'n, &c. h. m.	Cha'ston, &c. h. m.	N. Orl's, &c. h. m.	PHENOMENA AND OBSERVATIONS. Sundays and Holidays. Washington Mean Time. d. h. m. ° ′
		sets.	sets.	sets	sets.	sets.	
S.	4 52a	11 52a	11 50a	11 48a	11 40a	11 37a	*4th Sunday after Epiphany.*
2	5 42	. . .	. . .	. . .	. . .	.	1 4 2a. ☌ ♂ ☾ ♂ 0 48 S.
3	6 31	0 55m	0 53m	0 49m	0 38m	0 35m	2 5 2m. ☌ ♃ ☾ ♃ 1 51 S.
4	7 20	1 55	1 51	1 47	1 34	1 31	4 4 54a. ♀ gr. Hel. Lat. N.
5	8 9	2 51	2 46	2 43	2 28	2 24	5 1 4a. □ ⚶ ☉
6	8 58	3 41	3 37	3 33	3 18	3 14	6 3 21m. ☿ in Aphelion.
7	9 45	4 27	4 22	4 18	4 4	4 1	7 10 56m. ♀ stationary.
S.	10 32a	5 7m	5 3m	4 59m	4 47m	4 43m	*Septuagesima Sunday.*
9	11 16	5 43	5 41	5 37	5 26	5 23	7 2 52a. ☌ ⚶ β♎ ✱ 0 11 S.
10	☍	rises.	rises.	rises	rises.	rises.	10 6 22m. ☌ ♄ ☉
11	0 1m	6 5a	6 7a	5 9a	6 14a	6 17a	10 2 52a. ♀ in Perihelion.
12	0 44	7 3	7 5	7 6	7 9	7 11	16 0 2m. ☌ ♂ ♃ ♂ 1 50 N.
13	1 27	8 3	8 3	8 4	8 3	8 4	19 0 52m. ☌ ⚶ δ¹♉ ✱ 1 49 S.
14	2 10	9 3	9 3	9 1	8 58	8 58	21 6 50m. ☌ ☿ ♄ ☿ 1 4 S.
S.	2 54m	10 4a	10 2a	10 0a	9 54a	9 53a	*Sexagesima Sunday.*
16	3 40	11 7	11 4	11 2	10 53	10 50	22 3 52m. ☌ ⚶ δ³♉ ✱ 1 40 S.
17	4 28	. . .	. . .	. . .	11 52	11 49	24 0 52m. ☌ ☿ ☉
18	5 19	0 9m	0 6m	0 3m	. . .	. . .	24 7 56a. ☌ ♄ ☾ ♄ 6 20 S.
19	6 13	1 12	1 8	1 4	0 51m	0 48m	25 0 5m. □ ⚶ ☉
20	7 10	2 14	2 10	2 6	1 52	1 48	25 6 26m. ☌ ☿ ☾ ☿ 7 14 S.
21	8 8	3 12	3 7	3 4	2 50	2 45	25 5 8a. ☌ ⚶ ε♉ ✱ 0 41 S.
S.	9 8m	4 5m	4 1m	3 57m	3 44m	3 41m	*Shrove Sun.* Wash'n b. 1732.
23	10 7	4 51	4 49	4 45	4 35	4 32	26 0 12m. ☌ ♀ ☾ ♀ 4 45 N.
24	11 5	sets.	sets.	sets	sets.	sets.	26 1 50a. ☿ gr. Hel. Lat. S.
25	0 1a	5 59a	6 0a	6 1a	6 4a	6 8a	*Ash Wednesday.*
26	0 55	7 12	7 13	7 13	7 13	7 14	26 6 1a. ☌ ☿ ♀ ☿ 11 41 S.
27	1 48	8 24	8 23	8 23	8 19	8 20	27 0 57m. ☌ ♂ π♈ ✱ 0 18 N
28	2 40	9 33	9 31	9 29	9 23	9 21	27 8 17a. ☌ ♅ ☾ ♅ 3 25 S.

2

14	March, Third Month, begins on Sunday.										[1846.
	Twilight begins and ends. Mean Time.										
	1st day.		7th day.		13th day.		19th day.		25th day.		
	Begins. h. m.	Ends. h m.	Begins. h. m.	Ends. h. m.	Begins. h. m.	Ends. h. m.	Begins. h. m.	Ends. h. m.	Begins. h. m.	Ends. h. m.	
Boston,	5 3m	7 23a	4 53m	7 29a	4 43m	7 37a	4 32m	7 45a	4 20m	7 52a	
N. York,	5 4	7 22	4 54	7 28	4 44	7 35	4 34	7 42	4 23	7 49	
Wash.	5 5	7 21	4 55	7 27	4 46	7 34	4 36	7 40	4 26	7 46	
Charles.	5 7	7 19	4 59	7 24	4 51	7 29	4 43	7 33	4 34	7 38	
N. Orl's.	5 7	7 19	5 0	7 23	4 53	7 27	4 45	7 31	4 37	7 35	

APOGEE AND PERIGEE OF THE MOON.

Apogee, 8th day, 2h. A. | Perigee, 24th day, 2h. A.

PHASES OF THE MOON.

First Quarter, 4th day, 5h. 23.8m. A. | Last Quarter, 20th day, 8h. 49.8m. M.
Full Moon, 12th " 9h. 40.9m. A. | New Moon, 27th " 0h. 42.4m. M.

Days of Month.	Days of Week.	Sun's *upper* limb rises and sets, (corr. for refract.) M. T.										High Water. M. Time.		
		Boston, &c.		New York, &c.		Wash'ton, &c.		Charleston, &c.		N. Orleans, &c.		Boston, &c	New York, &c.	Charleston, &c
		rises. h. m.	*sets.* h. m.	*rises.* h. m.	*sets.* h. m.	*rises.* h. m.	*sets.* h. m.	*rises.* h. m.	*sets.* h. m.	*rises.* h. m.	*sets.* h. m.	h. m.	h. m.	h. m.
1	*Su.*	6 36	5 51	6 35	5 53	6 33	5 54	6 28	5 59	6 26	6 1	2 3a	11 43m	10 3m
2	M.	35	52	34	53	32	55	27	59	25	1	2 41	0 21a	10 41
3	Tu.	33	53	32	54	30	56	26	6 0	24	2	3 19	0 59	11 19
4	W.	31	54	30	55	29	57	25	0	23	2	4 3	1 43	0 3a
5	Th.	30	55	29	56	27	57	23	1	22	3	4 51	2 31	0 51
6	F.	28	56	27	57	26	58	22	1	21	3	6 1	3 41	2 1
7	S.	26	57	25	57	24	59	21	2	20	4	7 25	5 5	3 25
8	*Su.*	6 25	5 58	6 24	5 59	6 23	6 0	6 20	6 3	6 19	6 4	8 46a	6 26a	4 46a
9	M.	23	59	22	6 0	21	1	19	3	17	4	9 52	7 32	5 52
10	Tu.	21	6 0	20	1	20	2	17	4	16	5	10 35	8 15	6 35
11	W.	20	2	19	2	18	3	16	5	15	6	11 15	8 55	7 15
12	Th.	18	3	17	3	17	4	15	6	14	6	11 47	9 27	7 47
13	F.	16	4	16	4	15	5	13	6	13	7	· · ·	9 58	8 18
14	S.	14	5	14	5	13	6	12	7	12	8	0 18m	10 27	8 47
15	*Su.*	6 13	6 6	6 12	6 7	6 12	6 7	6 11	6 8	6 10	6 8	0 47m	10 59a	9 19a
16	M.	11	7	11	8	10	8	10	9	9	9	1 19	11 32	9 52
17	Tu.	9	9	9	9	9	9	8	9	8	10	1 52	· · ·	10 27
18	W.	7	10	7	10	7	10	7	10	7	10	2 27	0 7m	11 5
19	Th.	6	11	6	11	6	11	6	11	6	11	3 5	0 45	11 50
20	F.	4	12	4	12	4	12	4	12	4	11	3 50	1 30	· · ·
21	S.	2	13	2	13	3	13	3	12	3	12	4 45	2 25	0 45m
22	*Su.*	6 0	6 14	6 1	6 14	6 1	6 14	6 1	6 13	6 2	6 13	6 0m	3 40m	2 0m
23	M.	5 59	15	5 59	15	5 59	15	5 59	14	1	13	7 32	5 12	3 32
24	Tu.	57	17	58	16	58	16	58	14	5 59	14	8 55	6 35	4 55
25	W.	55	18	56	17	56	17	57	15	58	14	9 59	7 39	5 59
26	Th.	53	19	54	18	54	18	56	16	57	15	10 50	8 30	6 50
27	F.	52	20	52	19	53	19	55	16	56	16	11 33	9 13	7 33
28	S.	50	21	51	20	51	19	54	17	55	16	0 16a	9 56	8 16
29	*Su.*	5 48	6 22	5 49	6 21	5 50	6 20	5 52	6 18	5 53	6 17	0 57a	10 37m	8 57m
30	M.	46	23	47	22	48	21	51	19	52	17	1 37	11 17	9 37
31	Tu	45	24	46	23	47	22	50	19	51	18	2 15	11 55	10 15

1846.]	March has Thirty-one Days.									15
	Passage of the Meridian (mean time) and Declination of the Planets.									
	1st day.		7th day.		13th day.		19th day.		25th day.	
	Souths. h. m.	Dec. ° ′	*Souths.* h. m.	Dec. ° ′	*Souths.* h. m.	Dec. ° ′	*Souths.* h. m.	Dec. ° ′	*Souths.* h. m.	Dec. ° ′
☿	0 1a	—10 48	0 19a	— 6 0	0 38a	— 0 35	0 55a	+ 5 2	1 8a	+10 6
♀	0 7	+ 1 20	11 29m	— 0 9	10 56m	— 1 49	10 28m	— 3 22	10 5m	— 4 33
♂	4 10	+17 4	4 2a	+18 13	3 54a	+19 19	3 47a	+20 18	3 39a	+21 12
⚶	5 46	+19 50	5 29	+20 19	5 12	+20 46	4 56	+21 12	4 40	+21 37
⚵	4 43m	— 7 35	4 20m	— 7 9	3 56m	— 6 38	3 32m	— 6 5	3 7m	— 5 28
⚳	11 46	— 0 52	11 30	— 0 28	11 15	— 0 4	10 59	+ 0 20	10 43	+ 0 46
⚴	1 30a	— 7 49	1 15a	— 6 49	0 59a	— 5 48	0 45a	— 4 48	0 30a	— 3 48
♃	3 45	+13 6	3 25	+13 29	3 6	+13 52	2 47	+14 15	2 28	+14 39
♄	11 9m	—14 42	10 49m	—14 28	10 28m	—14 15	10 7m	—14 3	9 46m	—13 51
♅	1 56a	+ 2 48	1 34a	+ 2 55	1 11a	+ 3 3	0 49a	+ 3 11	0 27a	+ 3 19

Days of Month.	Moon Souths. Mean Time.	Moon rises or sets. Mean Time. Boston, &c.	N. York, &c.	Wash'tn, &c.	Cha'ston, &c.	N. Orl'ns, &c.	PHENOMENA AND OBSERVATIONS. *Sundays and Holidays.*
		sets.	*sets.*	*sets.*	*sets.*	*sets.*	Washington Mean Time.
	h. m.	h. m.	h. m.	h. m.	h. m.	h. m.	d. h. m.
S.	3 32a	10 40a	10 38a	10 35a	10 25a	10 22a	1st *Sund. in Lent.* *St. David.*
2	4 23	11 43	11 40	11 36	11 24	11 20	1 9 3a. ☌ ♃ ☾ ♃ 1 5 S.
3	5 14	· · ·	· · ·	· · ·	· · ·	· · ·	2 1 0m. ☌ ☿ ♀ ☿ 11 36 S.
4	6 4	0 41m	0 37m	0 32m	0 19m	0 16m	2 9 31m. ☌ ♂ ☾ ♂ 1 28 N.
5	6 53	1 34	1 31	1 26	1 11	1 8	2 4 4a. ♀ in inf. ☌ ☉
6	7 41	2 22	2 18	2 13	2 0	1 56	5 7 38a. sup. ☌ ☿ ☉
7	8 28	3 5	3 1	2 57	2 44	2 40	7 5 27m. ☌ ♀ ⚴ ⚴ 0 25 S.
S.	9 13a	3 43m	3 39m	3 36m	3 24m	3 21m	2d *Sunday in Lent.*
9	9 58	4 16	4 13	4 11	4 2	3 59	7 2 12a. ☌ ♂ δ ♈ ✱ 0 56 N.
10	10 41	4 47	4 45	4 42	4 36	4 34	10 3 56a. ⚵ stationary.
11	11 25	*rises.*	*rises.*	*rises.*	*rises.*	*rises.*	17 0 45a. ☌ ☿ ⚳ ☿ 8 18 N.
12	☋	5 56a	5 56a	5 56a	5 57a	5 59a	17 1 27a. ☿ in ☊
13	0 8m	6 55	6 54	6 54	6 52	6 52	18 11 44m. ☌ ☿ ♅ ☿ 0 55 N.
14	0 53	7 57	7 56	7 54	7 49	7 49	21 1 39a. ♀ stationary.
S.	1 38m	9 0a	8 57a	8 56a	8 48a	8 45a	3d *Sunday in Lent.*
16	2 26	10 3	10 0	9 57	9 47	9 43	22 3 2m. ☿ in Perihelion.
17	3 16	11 6	11 2	10 58	10 46	10 43	*St. Patrick.*
18	4 9	· · ·	· · ·	11 59	11 44	11 41	22 4 52a. ☌ ⚳ ♅ ⚳ 7 31 S.
19	5 4	0 6m	0 2m	· · ·	· · ·	· · ·	24 10 42m. ☌ ♄ ☾ ♄ 6 24 S.
20	6 1	1 5	1 0	0 57m	0 43m	0 38m	20 6 36a. ☉ ent. ♈. *Spr'g bg's.*
21	6 58	1 57	1 53	1 50	1 36	1 33	24 7 1a. ☌ ♀ ☾ ♀ 1 25 N.
S.	7 55m	2 44m	2 41m	2 38m	2 26m	2 24m	4th *Sund. in Lent.*
23	8 51	3 28	3 25	3 23	3 14	3 11	27 8 35m. ☌ ⚶ i ♉ ✱ 0 21 S.
24	9 46	4 5	4 4	4 2	3 57	3 56	27 9 14m. ☌ ♅ ☾ ♅ 3 13 S.
25	10 40	4 41	4 40	4 41	4 38	4 38	Lady Day.
26	11 33	*sets.*	*sets.*	*sets.*	*sets.*	*sets.*	27 10 24m. ☌ ♂ A[1] ♉ ✱ 0 12 N.
27	0 26a	7 11a	7 9a	7 7a	7 2a	7 2a	28 9 44m. ☌ ☿ ☾ ☿ 1 10 N.
28	1 18	8 19	8 16	8 14	8 6	8 4	29 4 30a. ☌ ♃ ☾ ♃ 0 21 S.
S.	2 10a	9 25a	9 22a	9 19a	9 8a	9 5a	5th *Sunday in Lent.*
30	3 3	10 27	10 23	10 19	10 7	10 4	30 6 21a. ☌ ♄ ι ♒ ✱ 0 56 S.
31	3 54	11 23	11 19	11 16	11 1	10 58	30 10 38a. ☌ ♀ ☉

16 *April, Fourth Month, begins on Wednesday.* [1846.

Twilight begins and ends. Mean time.

	1st day.		7th day.		13th day.		19th day.		25th day.	
	Begins. h. m.	Ends. h. m.	Begins. h. m.	Ends. h. m.	Begins. h. m.	Ends. h. m.	Begins. h. m.	Ends. h. m.	Begins. h. m.	Ends. h. m.
Boston,	4 7m.	8 1a.	3 55m.	8 9a.	3 43m.	8 18a.	3 31m.	8 27a.	3 19m.	8 37a
N. York,	4 11	7 57	3 59	8 5	3 48	8 14	3 37	8 22	3 26	8 30
Wash.	4 15	7 53	4 4	8 1	3 53	8 9	3 43	8 17	3 33	8 25
Charles.	4 25	7 43	4 16	7 49	4 7	7 55	3 59	8 0	3 51	8 5
N. Orl's.	4 29	7 39	4 21	7 44	4 13	7 49	4 5	7 53	3 58	7 58

APOGEE AND PERIGEE OF THE MOON.

Apogee, 5th day, 8h. M. | Perigee, 20th day, 6 h. A.

PHASES OF THE MOON.

First Quarter, 3d day, 0h. 3.6m. A. | Last Quarter, 18th day, 3h. 16.3m. A.
Full Moon, 11th day, 0h. 46.8m. A. | New Moon, 25th day, 11h. 40.2m. M.

Days of Month.	Days of Week.	Sun's *upper* limb rises and sets, (corr. for refract.) M. T. Boston, &c. rises. h. m.	Boston, &c. sets. h. m.	New York, &c. rises. h. m.	New York, &c. sets. h. m.	Wash'ton, &c. rises. h. m.	Wash'ton, &c. sets. h. m.	Charleston, &c. rises. h. m.	Charleston, &c. sets. h. m.	N. Oleans, &c. rises. h. m.	N. Oleans, &c. sets. h. m.	High Water. M. Time. Boston, &c. h. m.	New York, &c. h. m.	Charleston, &c. h. m.
1	W.	5 43	6 25	5 44	6 24	5 46	6 23	5 48	6 20	5 50	6 19	2 52a	0 32a	10 52m
2	Th.	41	27	42	26	44	24	47	21	49	19	3 34	1 14	11 24
3	F.	40	28	41	27	42	25	46	21	47	20	4 21	2 1	0 21a
4	S.	38	29	39	28	41	26	45	22	46	20	5 17	2 57	1 17
5	*Su.*	5 36	6 30	5 37	6 29	5 39	6 27	5 43	6 23	5 45	6 21	6 39a	4 19a	2 39a
6	M.	35	31	36	30	37	28	42	23	44	22	7 58	5 38	3 58
7	Tu	33	32	34	31	36	29	41	24	43	22	9 6	6 46	5 6
8	W.	31	33	33	32	34	30	39	25	41	23	9 59	7 39	5 59
9	Th.	30	34	31	33	33	31	38	26	40	23	10 36	8 16	6 36
10	F.	28	36	30	34	31	32	37	26	39	24	11 11	8 51	7 11
11	S.	26	37	28	35	30	33	36	27	38	25	11 44	9 24	7 44
12	*Su.*	5 25	6 38	5 26	6 36	5 28	6 34	5 34	6 28	5 37	6 25	. . .	10 0a	8 20a
13	M.	23	39	25	37	27	35	33	28	36	26	0 20m	10 34	8 54
14	Tu.	21	40	23	38	25	36	32	29	35	26	0 54	11 10	9 30
15	W.	20	41	22	39	24	37	31	30	34	27	1 30	11 47	10 7
16	Th.	18	42	20	40	23	38	30	31	32	28	2 7	. . .	10 49
17	F.	16	43	19	41	21	39	28	31	31	28	2 49	0 29m	11 38
18	S.	15	45	17	42	20	40	27	32	30	29	3 38	1 18	. . .
19	*Su.*	5 13	6 46	5 16	6 43	5 18	6 41	5 26	6 33	5 29	6 29	4 39m	2 19m	0 39m
20	M.	12	47	15	44	17	42	25	33	28	30	5 54	3 34	1 54
21	Tu.	10	48	13	45	16	42	24	34	27	31	7 16	4 56	3 16
22	W.	9	49	11	46	14	43	23	35	26	31	8 33	6 13	4 33
23	Th.	7	50	10	47	13	44	21	36	25	32	9 34	7 14	5 34
24	F.	6	51	8	48	11	45	20	36	24	33	10 27	8 7	6 27
25	S.	4	52	7	49	10	46	19	37	23	33	11 12	8 52	7 12
26	*Su.*	5 3	6 53	5 6	6 50	5 9	6 47	5 18	6 38	5 22	6 34	11 55m	9 35m	7 55m
27	M.	1	55	4	51	8	48	17	38	21	34	0 34a	10 14	8 34
28	Tu.	0	56	3	52	6	49	16	39	20	35	1 13	10 53	9 13
29	W.	4 58	57	2	54	5	50	15	40	19	36	1 51	11 31	9 51
30	Th.	57	58	0	55	4	51	14	41	18	36	2 29	0 9a	10 29

1846.] *April has Thirty Days.* 17

Passage of the Meridian (mean time) and Declination of the Planets.

	1st day.		7th day.		13th day.		19th day.		25th day.	
	Souths. h. m.	Dec. ° ′	*Souths.* h. m.	Dec. ° ′	*Souths.* h. m.	Dec. ° ′	*Souths.* h. m.	Dec. ° ′	*Souths.* h. m.	Dec. ° ′
☿	1 10a	+14 13	0 57a	+15 36	0 31a	+14 52	11 55m	+12 27	11 19m	+ 9 30
♀	9 45m	— 5 21	9 32m	— 5 30	9 22m	— 5 12	9 15	— 4 30	9 10	— 3 27
♂	3 31a	+22 8	3 24a	+22 50	3 16a	+23 25	3 9a	+23 53	3 2a	+24 15
⚶	4 22	+22 4	4 7	+22 25	3 53	+22 46	3 39	+23 3	3 25	+23 18
⚵	2 37m	— 4 45	2 10m	— 4 4	1 43m	— 3 25	1 15m	— 2 45	0 47m	— 2 7
⚴	10 24	+ 1 14	10 8	+ 1 40	9 52	+ 2 6	9 36	+ 2 31	9 19	+ 2 55
⚳	0 12a	— 2 39	11 57	— 1 40	11 42	— 0 43	11 27	+ 0 13	11 12	+ 1 9
♃	2 7	+15 8	1 48a	+15 32	1 30a	+15 56	1 12a	+16 20	0 54a	+16 44
♄	9 21m	—13 37	8 50m	—13 26	8 38m	—13 16	8 16m	—13 7	7 54m	—12 58
♅	0 0 a	+ 3 29	11 38	+ 3 37	11 16	+ 3 45	10 54	+ 3 53	10 31	+ 4 0

Days of Month.	Moon Souths. Mean Time. h. m.	Moon rises or sets. Mean time. Boston, &c. sets. h. m.	N. York, &c. sets. h. m.	Wash'tn, &c. sets. h. m.	Cha'ston, &c. sets. h. m.	N. Orl's, &c. sets. h. m.	PHENOMENA AND OBSERVATIONS. *Sundays and Holidays.* Washington Mean Time. d. h. m. ° ′
1	4 45a	. . .	. . .	. . .	11 52a	11 48a	1 10 54m. ☿ gr. Hel. Lat. N.
2	5 34	0 14m	0 10m	0 6m	. . .	. . .	4 7 45m. ☌ ♂ υ¹ ♉ ✱ 0 0
3	6 22	1 0	0 51	0 51	0 38m	0 35m	7 4 23a. ♀ at gr. brilliancy.
4	7 8	1 40	1 36	1 32	1 20	1 16	8 11 9a. ☿ stationary.
S.	7 53a	2 15m	2 13m	2 9m	1 59m	1 56m	*Palm Sunday.*
6	8 37	2 48	2 45	2 43	2 36	2 34	
7	9 20	3 17	3 16	3 14	3 9	3 8	10 2 47m. ☌ ♂ τ ♉ ✱ 0 25 S.
8	10 4	3 46	3 45	3 45	3 42	3 42	12 11 5a. ☌ ⚶ o ♉ ✱ 0 56 S.
9	10 48	4 13	4 13	4 13	4 14	4 15	19 4 8m. Inf. ☌ ☿ ☉
10	11 34	*rises.*	*rises.*	*rises.*	*rises.*	*rises.*	Good Friday.
11	☍	6 49a	6 47a	6 45a	6 39a	6 37a	19 8 18m. ☌ ⚶ ζ ♉ ✱ 1 59 S.
S.	0 21m	7 53a	7 50a	7 48a	7 39a	7 36a	*Easter Sunday.*
13	1 12	8 58	8 54	8 50	8 38	8 36	20 10 10a. ☌ ♄ ☾ ♄ 6 29 S.
14	2 4	10 0	9 56	9 52	9 39	9 35	22 4 3m. ☌ ♀ ☾ ♀ 3 15 S.
15	3 0	10 59	10 55	10 51	10 38	10 33	23 8 49a. ☌ ♅ ☾ ♅ 3 6 S.
16	3 56	11 54	11 49	11 45	11 32	11 29	24 7 4a. ☌ ☿ ☾ ☿ 1 5 S.
17	4 53	. . .	. . .	. . .	. . .	. . .	24 10 59a. ☿ in ☋
18	5 50	0 43m	0 39m	0 35m	0 23m	0 21m	25 6 52m. ☌ ♀ ι ♓ ✱ 1 52 N.
S.	6 45m	1 26m	1 23m	1 21m	1 11m	1 8m	*Low Sunday.*
20	7 39	2 5	2 3	2 0	1 53	1 53	
21	8 32	2 40	2 39	2 38	2 35	2 34	26 3 14m. ☌ ⚶ B ♉ ✱ 1 12 N.
22	9 23	3 13	3 13	3 13	3 13	3 14	26 1 3a. ☌ ♃ ☾ ♃ 0 19 N.
23	10 15	3 47	3 48	3 49	3 52	3 55	St. George.
24	11 6	*sets.*	*sets.*	*sets.*	*sets.*	*sets.*	27 11 11a. ☌ ☿ ♀ ☿ 6 57 N.
25	11 58	7 6a	7 4a	7 1a	6 51a	6 48a	Eclip. of Sun, vis. in U. S.
S.	0 50a	8 10a	8 7a	8 3a	7 51a	7 48a	*2d Sunday after Easter.*
27	1 42	9 11	9 6	9 2	8 49	8 46	28 10 17m. ⚶ in ☊
28	2 34	10 4	10 0	9 56	9 42	9 38	29 2 4m. ☌ ♂ ☾ ♂ 4 55 N.
29	3 25	10 53	10 48	10 44	10 30	10 27	29 6 28a. ♀ in ☋
30	4 14	11 36	11 32	11 28	11 16	11 12	29 7 57a. ☌ ♀ ♀ ♀ 5 42 N.

18 *May, Fifth Month, begins on Friday.* [1846.

Twilight begins and ends. Mean time.

	1st day.		7th day.		13th day.		19th day.		25th day.	
	Begins. h. m.	Ends. h. m.	Begins. h. m.	Ends. h. m.	Begins. h. m.	Ends. h. m.	Begins. h. m.	Ends. h. m.	Begins. h. m.	Ends. h. m.
Boston,	3 7m	8 47a	2 56m	8 57a	2 45m	9 7a	2 35m	9 17a	2 25m	9 28a
N. York,	3 14	8 40	3 4	8 49	2 54	8 58	2 45	9 8	2 36	9 18
Wash.	3 22	8 32	3 13	8 40	3 4	8 48	2 55	8 57	2 47	9 7
Charles.	3 43	8 11	3 36	8 17	3 28	8 24	3 22	8 30	3 17	8 37
N. Orl's.	3 51	8 3	3 45	8 8	3 38	8 14	3 33	8 20	3 28	8 26

APOGEE AND PERIGEE OF THE MOON.

Apogee, 3d day, 3h. M. | Perigee, 15th day, 2h. A. | Apogee, 30th day, 10h. A.

PHASES OF THE MOON.

First Quarter,	3d day,	6h. 43.6m. M.		Last Quarter,	17th day,	8h. 18.5m. A.
Full Moon,	11th "	0h. 58.1m. M.		New Moon,	24th "	11h. 36.1m. A.

Sun's upper limb rises and sets, (corr. for refract.) M. T. — High Water. M. Time.

Days of Month.	Days of Week.	Boston, &c. rises. h. m.	Boston, &c. sets. h. m.	New York, &c. rises. h. m.	New York, &c. sets. h. m.	Wash'ton, &c. rises. h. m.	Wash'ton, &c. sets. h. m.	Charleston, &c. rises. h. m.	Charleston, &c. sets. h. m.	N. Orleans, &c. rises. h. m.	N. Orleans, &c. sets. h. m.	High Water Boston, &c. h. m.	High Water New York, &c. h. m.	High Water Charleston, &c. h. m.
1	F.	4 56	7 0	4 50	6 56	5 2	6 52	5 13	6 42	5 17	6 37	3 7a	0 47a	11 7m
2	S.	54	1	58	57	1	53	12	43	16	38	3 52	1 32	11 52
3	*Su.*	4 53	7 2	4 56	6 58	5 0	6 54	5 11	6 43	5 16	6 38	4 41a	2 21a	0 41a
4	M.	52	3	55	59	4 59	55	10	44	15	39	5 47	3 27	1 47
5	Tu.	50	4	54	7 0	58	56	9	45	14	40	7 0	4 40	3 0
6	W.	49	5	53	1	57	57	8	45	13	40	8 8	5 48	4 8
7	Th.	48	6	52	2	55	58	7	46	12	41	9 8	6 48	5 8
8	F.	47	7	51	3	54	59	7	47	12	42	9 54	7 34	5 54
9	S.	46	8	49	4	53	7 0	6	47	11	42	10 34	8 14	6 34
10	*Su.*	4 44	7 9	4 48	7 5	4 52	7 1	5 5	6 48	5 10	6 43	11 15a	8 55a	7 15a
11	M.	43	10	47	6	51	2	4	49	9	44	11 54	9 34	7 54
12	Tu.	42	11	46	7	50	2	3	49	9	44	· · ·	10 11	8 31
13	W.	41	12	45	8	49	3	2	50	8	45	0 31m	10 52	9 12
14	Th.	40	13	44	9	49	4	2	51	7	46	1 12	11 34	9 54
15	F.	39	14	43	10	48	5	1	51	7	46	1 54	· · ·	10 42
16	S.	38	15	42	11	47	6	0	52	6	47	2 42	0 22m	11 34
17	*Su.*	4 37	7 16	4 41	7 12	4 46	7 7	5 0	6 53	5 5	6 47	3 34m	1 14m	· · ·
18	M.	36	17	40	13	45	8	4 50	54	5	48	4 34	2 14	0 34m
19	Tu.	35	18	39	14	44	9	58	54	4	48	5 43	3 23	1 43
20	W.	34	19	39	15	43	10	58	55	4	49	6 56	4 36	2 56
21	Th.	33	20	38	16	43	10	57	55	3	50	8 5	5 45	4 5
22	F.	32	21	37	17	42	11	57	56	3	50	9 7	6 47	5 7
23	S.	31	22	36	18	41	12	56	57	2	51	10 2	7 42	6 2
24	*Su.*	4 31	7 23	4 36	7 19	4 41	7 13	4 56	6 57	5 2	6 51	10 53m	8 33m	6 53m
25	M.	30	24	35	20	40	14	55	58	1	52	11 37	9 17	7 37
26	Tu.	29	25	34	20	39	14	55	59	1	53	0 17a	9 57	8 17
27	W.	29	25	34	21	39	15	54	7 0	1	53	0 55	10 35	8 55
28	Th.	28	26	33	22	38	16	54	0	0	54	1 30	11 10	9 30
29	F.	27	27	32	23	38	17	54	1	0	54	2 8	11 48	10 8
30	S.	27	28	32	23	37	17	53	1	0	55	2 44	0 24a	10 44
31	*Su.*	4 26	7 29	4 31	7 24	4 37	7 18	4 53	7 2	4 59	6 55	3 25a	1 5a	11 25m

1846.] *May has Thirty-one Days.* 19

Passage of the Meridian (mean time) and Declination of the Planets.

	1st day.		7th day.		13th day.		19th day.		25th day.	
	Souths. h. m.	Dec. ° ′	*Souths.* h. m.	Dec. ° ′	*Souths.* h. m.	Dec. ° ′	*Souths.* h. m.	Dec. ° ′	*Souths.* h. m.	Dec. ° ′
☿	10 51m	+ 7 23	10 32m	+ 6 42	10 22m	+ 7 27	10 20m	+ 9 21	10 24m	+12 6
♀	9 6	— 2 5	9 3	— 0 28	9 2	+ 1 21	9 1	+ 3 20	9 0	+ 5 25
♂	2 56a	+24 30	2 49a	+24 38	2 42a	+24 39	2 35a	+24 34	2 28a	+24 22
⚶	3 11	+23 31	2 58	+23 41	2 45	+23 48	2 32	+23 52	2 19	+23 53
⚵	0 19m	— 1 32	11 46	— 0 54	11 18	— 0 27	10 49	— 0 5	10 22	+ 0 12
⚴	9 3	+ 3 19	8 46m	+ 3 40	8 29m	+ 4 0	8 12m	+ 4 18	7 55m	+ 4 34
⚳	10 57	+ 2 1	10 42	+ 2 54	10 27	+ 3 45	10 12	+ 4 34	9 57	+ 5 21
♃	0 36a	+17 7	0 21a	+17 30	0 0a	+17 52	11 43	+18 13	11 25	+18 34
♄	7 32m	—12 51	7 10m	—12 44	6 48m	—12 39	6 25	—12 35	6 2	—12 32
♅	10 8	+ 4 7	9 46	+ 4 14	9 23	+ 4 21	9 1	+ 4 27	8 38	+ 4 33

Moon rises or sets. Mean time.

Days of Month.	Moon Souths. Mean Time. h. m.	Boston, &c. h. m.	N. York, &c. h. m.	Wash'n, &c. h. m.	Cha'ston, &c. h. m.	N. Orl's, &c. h. m.	PHENOMENA AND OBSERVATIONS. *Sundays and Holidays.* Washington Mean Time. d. h. m.
		sets.	*sets.*	*sets.*	*sets.*	*sets.*	
1	5 1a	· · ·	· · ·	· · ·	11 56a	11 53a	1 11 43m. ☿ stationary.
2	5 47	0 13m	0 10m	0 7m	· · ·	· · ·	1 9 56a. ☍ ☿ ☉ intens. of lt. 0.330
S.	6 31a	0 47m	0 44m	0 42m	0 33m	0 31m	*3d Sunday after Easter.*
4	7 15	1 18	1 16	1 14	1 9	1 7	3 11 52a. ☌ ♂ B♉ ✱ 0 3 S
5	7 58	1 49	1 49	1 47	1 42	1 42	5 1 18m. ☌ ⚶ H♊ ✱ 0 21 S.
6	8 41	2 14	2 14	2 14	2 13	2 14	5 2 37m. ☿ in Aphelion.
7	9 26	2 41	2 43	2 43	2 46	2 48	9 10 9m. ☌ ♂ H♊ ✱ 1 23 S.
8	10 13	3 11	3 13	3 15	3 20	3 22	11 6 12m. ☌ ⚶ η♊ ✱ 1 12 S.
9	11 2	*rises.*	*rises.*	*rises.*	*rises.*	*rises.*	11 11 11m. ♀ gr. elon. 46 1 W.
S.	11 55a	6 43a	6 41a	6 37a	6 26a	6 23a	*4th Sunday after Easter.*
11	☍	7 49	7 45	7 41	7 28	7 25	14 2 55a. ☌ ♃ ☉
12	0 51m	8 51	8 17	8 43	8 29	8 25	16 10 0m. ☌ ☿ ⚵ ☿ 4 7 N.
13	1 48	9 49	9 45	9 41	9 28	9 23	16 6 52a. ☌ ♂ ⚶ ⚶ 0 47 S.
14	2 47	10 41	10 37	10 33	10 21	10 18	16 8 28a. ☿ gr. elon. 25 29 W.
15	3 45	11 26	11 24	11 20	11 10	11 7	18 6 26m. ☌ ♄ ☾ ♄ 6 29 S.
16	4 41	· · ·	· · ·	· · ·	11 55	11 53	19 9 54m. ☌ ♀ ♅ ♅ 1 7 N.
S.	5 36m	0 7m	0 4m	0 2m	· · ·	· · ·	*Rogation Sunday.*
18	6 28	0 42	0 42	0 40	0 36m	0 35m	21 5 55m. ☌ ♅ ☾ ♅ 2 58 S.
19	7 19	1 16	1 16	1 15	1 14	1 14	21 9 15m. ☌ ♀ ☾ ♀ 4 1 S.
20	8 10	1 48	1 48	1 50	1 51	1 53	21 0 54a. □ ♄ ☉
21	9 0	2 20	2 23	2 24	2 29	2 32	Ascension Day.
22	9 50	2 55	2 58	3 1	3 9	3 13	22 2 11a. ☌ ♀ e♓ ✱ 0 24 N.
23	10 41	3 32	3 36	3 39	3 50	3 56	23 1 2m. ☌ ☿ ☾ ☿ 3 14 S.
S.	11 33m	*sets.*	*sets.*	*sets.*	*sets.*	*sets.*	*Sund. after Ascension.* Q. Victoria born 1819.
25	0 25a	7 55a	7 51a	7 47a	7 32a	7 29a	23 3 12a. ☌ ♂ ε♊ ✱ 0 50 N.
26	1 16	8 46	8 42	8 38	8 24	8 20	24 8 56m. ☌ ♃ ☾ ♃ 0 56 N.
27	2 6	9 31	9 27	9 23	9 10	9 6	25 1 9a. ☿ gr. Hel. Lat. S.
28	2 54	10 11	10 8	10 4	9 52	9 48	27 1 37a. ☌ ♂ ☾ ♂ 5 55 N.
29	3 41	10 46	10 44	10 41	10 31	10 28	28 2 25m. ☌ ♀ μ♓ ✱ 1 2 S.
30	4 26	11 18	11 15	11 13	11 6	11 4	31 9 0a. ☌ ♀ o♓ ✱ 0 39 N.
S.	5 9a	11 47a	11 45a	11 44a	11 39a	11 39a	*Whit Sunday. Pentecost.*

Twilight begins and ends. Mean Time.

	1st day. Begins. h. m.	1st day. Ends. h. m.	7th day. Begins. h. m.	7th day. Ends. h. m.	13th day. Begins. h. m.	13th day. Ends. h. m.	19th day. Begins. h. m.	19th day. Ends. h. m.	25th day. Begins. h. m.	25th day. Ends. h. m.
Boston,	2 17m	9 37m	2 12m	9 44 a	2 9m	9 50 a	2 8m	9 54a	2 9m	9 55a
N. York,	2 29	9 25	2 25	9 31	2 23	9 37	2 22	9 40	2 23	9 41
Wash.	2 41	9 13	2 37	9 19	2 36	9 24	2 35	9 27	2 36	9 28
Charles.	3 13	8 41	3 10	8 46	3 10	8 50	3 10	8 52	3 11	8 53
N. Orl's.	3 24	8 30	3 22	8 34	3 22	8 38	3 22	8 34	3 23	8 41

PERIGEE AND APOGEE OF THE MOON.

Perigee, 11th day, 8h. A. | Apogee, 27th day, 3h. A.

PHASES OF THE MOON

First Quarter, 2d day, 0h. 22.0m. M. | Last Quarter, 16th day, 1h. 29.8m. M.
Full Moon, 9th " 10h. 27.8m. M. | New Moon, 23d " 0h. 39.6m. A.

Sun's *upper* limb rises and sets, (corr. for refract.) M. T. — High Water. M. Time.

Days of Month.	Days of Week.	Boston, &c. rises. h. m.	Boston, &c. sets. h. m.	New York, &c. rises. h. m.	New York, &c. sets. h. m.	Wash'ton, &c. rises. h. m.	Wash'ton, &c. sets. h. m.	Charleston, &c. rises. h. m.	Charleston, &c. sets. h. m.	N. Orleans, &c. rises. h. m.	N. Orleans, &c. sets. h. m.	High Water Boston, &c. h. m.	High Water New York, &c. h. m.	High Water Charleston, &c. h. m.
1	M.	4 25	7 30	4 31	7 24	4 36	7 19	4 52	7 3	4 59	6 56	4 10a	1 50a	0 10a
2	Tu.	25	30	30	25	36	19	52	3	59	56	4 59	2 39	0 59
3	W.	25	31	30	26	36	20	52	4	59	57	6 2	3 42	2 2
4	Th.	24	32	30	26	35	21	52	4	59	57	7 6	4 46	3 6
5	F.	24	32	29	27	35	21	52	5	58	58	8 6	5 46	4 6
6	S.	24	33	29	28	35	22	51	5	58	58	9 8	6 48	5 8
7	*Su.*	4 23	7 34	4 29	7 28	4 34	7 23	4 51	7 6	4 58	6 59	9 58a	7 38a	5 58a
8	M.	23	34	29	29	34	23	51	6	58	59	10 45	8 25	6 45
9	Tu.	23	35	28	30	34	24	51	7	58	7 0	11 31	9 11	7 31
10	W.	23	36	28	30	34	24	51	7	58	0	. . .	9 57	8 17
11	Th.	22	36	28	31	34	25	51	8	58	1	0 17m	10 40	9 0
12	F.	22	37	28	31	34	25	51	8	58	1	1 0	11 25	9 45
13	S.	22	37	28	32	34	26	51	8	58	1	1 45	. . .	10 35
14	*Su.*	4 22	7 38	4 28	7 32	4 34	7 26	4 51	7 9	4 58	7 2	2 35m	0 15m	11 25a
15	M.	22	38	28	32	34	26	51	9	58	2	3 25	1 5	. . .
16	Tu.	22	38	28	33	34	27	51	9	58	2	4 20	2 0	0 20m
17	W.	22	39	28	33	34	27	51	10	58	3	5 21	3 1	1 21
18	Th.	22	39	28	33	34	28	51	10	58	3	6 28	4 8	2 28
19	F.	22	39	28	34	34	28	52	10	59	3	7 33	5 13	3 33
20	S.	23	40	28	34	34	28	52	11	59	3	8 42	6 22	4 42
21	*Su.*	4 23	7 40	4 29	7 34	4 34	7 28	4 52	7 11	4 59	7 4	9 43m	7 23m	5 43m
22	M.	23	40	29	34	35	28	52	11	59	4	10 33	8 13	6 33
23	Tu.	23	40	29	34	35	29	52	11	5 0	4	11 18	8 58	7 18
24	W.	23	40	29	35	35	29	53	11	0	4	0 2a	9 42	8 2
25	Th.	24	41	29	35	35	29	53	11	0	4	0 39	10 19	8 39
26	F.	24	41	30	35	36	29	53	12	0	4	1 15	10 55	9 15
27	S.	25	41	30	35	36	29	54	12	1	4	1 49	11 29	9 49
28	*Su.*	4 25	7 40	4 31	7 35	4 37	7 29	4 54	7 12	5 1	7 5	2 23a	0 3a	10 23m
29	M.	25	40	31	35	37	29	54	12	1	5	2 59	0 39	10 59
30	Tu	26	40	31	35	37	29	55	12	2	5	3 36	1 16	11 36

Passage of the Meridian (mean time) and Declination of the Planets.

	1st day. Souths. h. m.	1st day. Dec. ° ′	7th day. Souths. h. m.	7th day. Dec. ° ′	13th day. Souths. h. m.	13th day. Dec. ° ′	19th day. Souths. h. m.	19th day. Dec. ° ′	25th day. Souths. h. m.	25th day. Dec. ° ′
☿	10 38m	+15 58	10 57m	+19 25	11 23m	+22 30	11 56m	+24 25	0 30a	+24 44
♀	9 1	+ 7 55	9 2	+10 4	9 3	+12 10	9 6	+14 12	9 9m	+16 5
♂	2 20a	+23 50	2 12a	+23 33	2 5a	+23 0	1 58a	+22 22	1 50a	+21 38
⚶	2 5	+23 50	1 52	+23 44	1 40	+23 34	1 28	+23 23	1 15	+23 7
⚵	9 50	+ 0 23	9 24	+ 0 28	8 58	+ 0 28	8 34	+ 0 24	8 10	+ 0 13
⚳	7 35m	+ 4 49	7 17m	+ 4 58	6 59m	+ 5 4	6 41m	+ 5 6	6 23m	+ 5 3
⚴	9 40	+ 6 14	9 25	+ 6 56	9 9	+ 7 37	8 53	+ 8 16	8 38	+ 9 5
♃	11 4	+18 56	10 46	+19 15	10 28	+19 33	10 10	+19 49	9 52	+20 5
♄	5 35	−12 30	5 12	−12 30	4 49	−12 31	4 25	−12 33	4 1	−12 37
♅	8 12	+ 4 39	7 49	+ 4 44	7 26	+ 4 48	7 3	+ 4 52	6 40	+ 4 55

Moon rises or sets. Mean Time. — PHENOMENA AND OBSERVATIONS. *Sundays and Holidays.*

Days of Month	Moon Souths. Mean Time. h. m.	Boston, &c. h. m.	N. York, &c. h. m.	Wash'tn, &c. h. m.	Cha'ston, &c. h. m.	N. Orl's, &c. h. m.	Washington Mean Time. d. h. m.
		sets.	*sets.*	*sets.*	*sets.*	*sets.*	
1	5 52a	. . .	. . .	. . .	. . .	. . .	2 0 4a. ☌ ⚵ ξ² Ceti ✱ 1 24 N.
2	6 34	0 15m	0 14m	0 14m	0 12m	0 12m	2 7 54a. ♀ in Aphelion.
3	7 18	0 43	0 43	0 43	0 44	0 45	
4	8 3	1 11	1 12	1 14	1 16	1 20	5 6 55a. ☌ ☿ ♃ ☿ 0 41 S.
5	8 51	1 40	1 43	1 45	1 52	1 55	5 7 48a. ☌ ♂ δ ♊ ✱ 1 26 S.
6	9 42	2 15	2 18	2 21	2 30	2 35	
S.	10 37a	*rises.*	*rises.*	*rises.*	*rises.*	*rises.*	*Trinity Sunday.*
8	11 34	6 35a	6 31a	6 28a	6 13a	6 10a	11 7 30a. ♄ stationary.
9	☍	7 37	7 33	7 30	7 16	7 11	13 0 44a. ☿ in ☊
10	0 34m	8 33	8 28	8 24	8 11	8 8	14 10 20m ☌ ⚵ μ Ceti ✱ 1 44 N.
11	1 33	9 23	9 19	9 16	9 4	9 2	*Corpus Christi. Fête Dieu.*
12	2 33	10 5	10 2	10 0	9 52	9 49	14 0 54a. ☌ ♄ ☾ ♄ 6 26 S.
13	3 30	10 43	10 42	10 40	10 35	10 34	14 5 14a. ☌ ♂ × ♊ ✱ 1 52 N.
S.	4 24m	11 19a	11 18a	11 18a	11 16a	11 15a	*1st Sunday after Trinity.*
15	5 17	11 51	11 53	11 53	11 54	11 55	15 9 21m. ☌ ♀ ⚵ ⚵ 5 0 S.
16	6 8	. . .	. . .	. . .	. . .	. . .	17 0 55m. ☌ ♅ ☾ ♅ 2 45 S.
17	6 57	0 24m	0 26m	0 28m	0 31m	0 34m	18 2 17m. ☿ in Perihelion.
18	7 47	0 57	1 0	1 2	1 10	1 13	19 10 35a. ☌ ♀ ☾ ♀ 1 33 S.
19	8 37	1 33	1 36	1 40	1 49	1 54	20 6 52m. Sup. ☌ ☿ ☉
20	9 28	2 10	2 15	2 18	2 30	2 37	21 3 17m. ☌ ♃ ☾ ♃ 1 31 N.
S.	10 19m	2 53m	2 57m	3 2m	3 16m	3 22m	*2d Sunday after Trinity.*
22	11 9	*sets.*	*sets.*	*sets.*	*sets.*	*sets.*	21 3 23a. ☉ ent. ♋ Sum. beg.
23	0 0a	7 27a	7 23a	7 18a	7 5a	7 2a	23 10 47a. ☌ ☿ ☾ ☿ 5 59 N.
24	0 49	8 10	8 6	8 2	7 50	7 46	St. John Baptist.
25	1 36	8 46	8 44	8 40	8 29	8 26	25 3 1a. ♀ great. Hel. Lat. S.
26	2 21	9 19	9 16	9 14	9 6	9 4	25 8 51a. ☌ ♂ ☾ ♂ 6 24 N.
27	3 5	9 50	9 48	9 46	9 40	9 39	28 10 7m. ☿ gr. Hel. Lat. N.
S.	3 48a	10 17a	10 17a	10 16a	10 12a	10 12a	*3d Sunday after Trinity.*
29	4 30	10 45	10 44	10 45	10 45	10 45	
30	5 13	11 12	11 13	11 13	11 16	11 18	30 9 9a. ☿ stationary.

22 *July, Seventh Month, begins on Wednesday.* [1846.

Twilight begins and ends. Mean Time.

	1st day.		7th day.		13th day.		19th day.		25th day.	
	Begins. h. m.	Ends. h. m.	Begins. h. m.	Ends. h. m.	Begins. h. m.	Ends. h. m.	Begins. h. m.	Ends. h. m.	Begins. h. m.	Ends. h. m.
Boston,	2 12m	9 54a	2 19m	9 49a	2 26m	9 44a	2 35m	9 37a	2 44m	9 28a
N. York,	2 26	9 40	2 32	9 36	2 39	9 31	2 46	9 25	2 54	9 18
Wash.	2 39	9 27	2 44	9 24	2 51	9 19	2 58	9 14	3 5	9 7
Charles.	3 13	8 53	3 17	8 51	3 22	8 48	3 27	8 45	3 32	8 40
N. Orl's.	3 25	8 41	3 29	8 39	3 33	8 37	3 37	8 34	3 42	8 30

PERIGEE AND APOGEE OF THE MOON.

Perigee, 9th day, 11h. A. | Apogee, 25th day, 2h. M.

PHASES OF THE MOON.

First Quarter,	1st day,	4h. 15.4m. A.	New Moon,	23d day,	2h. 54.7m. M.
Full Moon,	8th "	6h. 2.7m. A.	First Quarter,	31st "	5h. 54.8m. M.
Last Quarter,	15th "	8h. 15.7m. M.			

Sun's *upper* limb rises and sets, (corr. for refract.) M. T. — High Water. M. Time

Days of Month.	Days of Week.	Boston, &c. rises. h. m.	Boston, &c. sets. h. m.	New York, &c. rises. h. m.	New York, &c. sets. h. m.	Wash'ton, &c. rises. h. m.	Wash'ton, &c. sets. h. m.	Charleston, &c. rises. h. m.	Charleston, &c. sets. h. m.	N. Orleans, &c. rises. h. m.	N. Orleans, &c. sets. h. m.	High Water Boston, &c. h. m.	High Water New York, &c. h. m.	High Water Charleston, &c. h. m.
1	W.	4 26	7 40	4 32	7 35	4 38	7 29	4 55	7 12	5 2	7 5	4 19a	1 59a	0 19a
2	Th.	27	40	32	35	38	29	55	12	2	5	5 6	2 46	1 6
3	F.	27	40	33	34	39	29	56	12	3	5	6 9	3 49	2 9
4	S.	28	40	34	34	39	28	56	11	3	5	7 13	4 53	3 13
5	*Su.*	4 29	7 39	4 34	7 34	4 40	7 28	4 57	7 11	5 4	7 4	8 20a	6 0a	4 20a
6	M.	29	39	35	34	41	28	57	11	4	4	9 24	7 4	5 24
7	Tu.	30	39	35	33	41	28	58	11	5	4	10 19	7 59	6 19
8	W.	30	38	36	33	42	27	58	11	5	4	11 10	8 50	7 10
9	Th.	31	38	37	33	42	27	59	11	6	4	. . .	9 41	8 1
10	F.	32	38	37	32	43	27	59	10	6	4	0 1m	10 31	8 51
11	S.	33	37	38	32	44	26	5 0	10	7	3	0 51	11 16	9 36
12	*Su.*	4 33	7 37	4 39	7 31	4 44	7 26	5 0	7 10	5 7	7 3	1 36m	. . .	10 24a
13	M.	34	36	39	31	45	26	1	9	8	3	2 24	0 4m	11 13
14	Tu.	35	36	40	30	46	25	2	9	8	3	3 13	0 53	. . .
15	W.	36	35	41	30	46	24	2	9	9	2	4 0	1 40	0 0m
16	Th.	37	34	42	29	47	24	3	8	9	2	4 53	2 33	0 53
17	F.	37	34	43	29	48	23	3	8	10	1	5 51	3 31	1 51
18	S.	38	33	43	28	49	23	4	7	10	1	7 3	4 43	3 3
19	*Su.*	4 39	7 32	4 44	7 27	4 49	7 22	5 5	7 7	5 11	7 1	8 13m	5 53m	4 13m
20	M.	40	31	45	26	50	21	5	6	11	0	9 24	7 4	5 24
21	Tu.	41	30	46	26	51	21	6	6	12	0	10 19	7 59	6 19
22	W.	42	30	47	25	52	20	6	5	12	6 59	11 5	8 45	7 5
23	Th.	43	29	48	24	52	19	7	5	13	59	11 44	9 24	7 44
24	F.	44	28	48	23	53	18	8	4	14	58	0 21a	10 1	8 21
25	S.	45	27	49	23	54	18	8	4	14	58	0 55	10 35	8 55
26	*Su.*	4 46	7 26	4 50	7 22	4 55	7 17	5 9	7 3	5 15	6 57	1 26a	11 6m	9 26m
27	M.	47	25	51	21	56	16	10	2	15	56	1 57	11 37	9 57
28	Tu.	48	24	52	20	57	15	10	1	16	56	2 30	0 10a	10 30
29	W.	49	23	53	19	58	14	11	1	17	55	3 3	0 43	11 3
30	Th.	50	22	54	18	58	13	12	0	17	54	3 41	1 21	11 41
31	F.	51	21	55	17	59	12	12	6 59	18	54	4 24	2 4	0 24a

1846.] *July has Thirty-one Days.* 23

Passage of the Meridian (mean time) and declination of the Planets.

	1st day.		7th day.		13th day.		19th day.		25th day.	
	Souths. h. m.	Dec. ° ′	*Souths.* h. m.	Dec. ° ′	*Souths.* h. m.	Dec. ° ′	*Souths.* h. m.	Dec. ° ′	*Souths.* h. m.	Dec. ° ′
☿	1 0a	+23 29	1 23a	+21 5	1 39a	+17 59	1 49a	+14 33	1 53a	+11 7
♀	9 13m	+17 47	9 17m	+19 19	9 22m	+20 31	9 28m	+21 28	9 35m	+22 6
♂	1 42a	+20 47	1 34a	+19 53	1 26a	+18 53	1 18a	+17 49	1 9a	+16 41
⚶	1 3	+22 49	0 51	+22 26	0 39	+22 4	0 26	+21 34	0 14	+21 5
⚵	7 44	−0 3	7 22	−0 21	6 59	−0 44	6 38	−1 9	6 15	−1 37
⚳	6 4m	+4 57	5 44m	+4 45	5 24m	+4 27	5 4m	+4 5	4 43m	+3 31
⚴	8 23	+9 26	8 7	+9 59	7 51	+10 27	7 34	+10 55	7 18	+11 19
♃	9 34	+20 19	9 15	+20 33	8 57	+20 45	8 38	+20 57	8 19	+21 7
♄	3 37	−12 41	3 12	−12 47	2 48	−12 54	2 23	−13 1	1 58	−13 10
♅	6 17	+4 57	5 54	+4 58	5 30	+4 59	5 7	+5 0	4 43	+4 59

Moon rises or sets. Mean Time. — PHENOMENA AND OBSERVATIONS. *Sundays and Holidays.*

Days of Month.	Moon Souths. Mean Time. h. m.	Boston, &c. h. m.	N. York, &c. h. m.	Wash'ton, &c. h. m.	Cha'ston, &c. h. m.	N. Orl's, &c. h. m.	Washington Mean Time. d. h. m.
		sets.	*sets.*	*sets.*	*sets.*	*sets.*	
1	5 57a	11 41a	11 43a	11 45a	11 50a	11 52a	1 3 37m. ☉ in Apogee.
2	6 42	. . .	. . .	. . .	. . .	. . .	2 0 52m. ☌☿⚶ ☿ 0 31 N.
3	7 30	0 11m	0 15m	0 17m	0 25m	0 29m	3 4 22a. □♀☉
4	8 22	0 46	0 50	0 53	1 4	1 10	Independence declared 1776.
S.	9 17a	1 28m	1 32m	1 37m	1 49m	1 55m	*4th Sunday after Trinity.*
6	10 16	2 15	2 20	2 25	2 39	2 46	6 0 52m. ♂ gr. Hel. Lat. N.
7	11 16	*rises.*	*rises.*	*rises.*	*rises.*	*rises.*	6 0 41a. □♅☉
8	☍	7 11a	7 7a	7 3a	6 51a	6 48a	6 9 11a. ☌♀♃ ♀ 1 22 S.
9	0 17m	7 59	7 56	7 54	7 44	7 41	7 5 48m. ☿ in ♉
10	1 17	8 42	8 39	8 37	8 31	8 29	8 6 52a. ☌♃ν¹♉ ✱ 1 52 N.
11	2 14	9 19	9 17	9 17	9 13	9 13	10 3 17m. ☌☿♂ ☿ 0 20 N.
S.	3 9m	9 53a	9 54a	9 54a	9 54a	9 54a	*5th Sunday after Trinity.*
13	4 2	10 27	10 27	10 29	10 31	10 34	11 7 16a. ☌♄☾ ♄ 6 21 S.
14	4 54	11 0	11 3	11 4	11 11	11 14	14 7 15a. ☌♅☾ ♅ 2 30 S.
15	5 45	11 35	11 37	11 41	11 49	11 54	18 7 50a. ☌♃☾ ♃ 2 6 N.
16	6 35	. . .	. . .	. . .	. . .	. . .	19 6 50a. ☌♀ο♉ ✱ 0 17 N.
17	7 25	0 12m	0 16m	0 20m	0 31m	0 37m	19 8 7a. ☌♀☾ ♀ 2 5 N.
18	8 16	0 53	0 57	1 1	1 14	1 22	20 5 31m. ♅ stationary.
S.	9 6m	1 38m	1 42m	1 47m	2 2m	2 8m	*6th Sunday after Trinity.*
20	9 56	2 26	2 30	2 36	2 50	2 57	21 10 13a. ☿ in ♉
21	10 45	3 17	3 23	3 27	3 41	3 48	24 0 52a. ☌♀♅ ♀ 1 24 S.
22	11 33	*sets.*	*sets.*	*sets.*	*sets.*	*sets.*	24 5 9a. ☌♂☾ ♂ 6 15 N.
23	0 19a	7 21a	7 18a	7 16a	7 7a	7 5a	25 5 15a. ☌☿☾ ☿ 4 0 N.
24	1 3	7 53	7 51	7 48	7 43	7 41	28 6 52m. ☿ in Aphelion.
25	1 46	8 21	8 21	8 20	8 15	8 14	28 9 1m. ☌♃τ♉ ✱ 1 27 N.
S.	2 28a	8 49a	8 48a	8 49a	8 47a	8 47a	*7th Sunday after Trinity.*
27	3 11	9 16	9 16	9 17	9 18	9 20	28 1 50a. ☌⚶☉
28	3 54	9 43	9 46	9 47	9 50	9 53	28 8 38a. ☿ gr. elon. 27 12 E.
29	4 38	10 14	10 16	10 18	10 25	10 28	29 1 35m. □☿☉
30	5 23	10 46	10 48	10 52	11 2	11 6	29 3 7m. ☌♀η♊ ✱ 0 15 N.
31	6 12	11 22	11 27	11 30	11 42	11 48	30 5 1a. ☌♀μ♊ ✱ 0 14 N.

24 *August, Eighth Month, begins on Saturday.* [1846.

Twilight begins and ends. Mean Time.

	1st day. Begins. h. m.	1st day. Ends. h. m.	7th day. Begins. h. m.	7th day. Ends. h. m.	13th day. Begins. h. m.	13th day. Ends. h. m.	19th day. Begins. h. m.	19th day. Ends. h. m.	25th day. Begins. h. m.	25th day. Ends. h. m.
Boston,	2 55m	9 17a	3 5m	9 5a	3 15m	8 53 a	3 24m	8 42a	3 34m	8 30a
N. York,	3 4	9 8	3 14	8 56	3 23	8 45	3 32	8 34	3 40	8 24
Wash.	3 14	8 58	3 22	8 48	3 30	8 38	3 38	8 28	3 46	8 18
Charles.	3 39	8 33	3 45	8 25	3 50	8 18	3 56	8 10	4 2	8 2
N. Orl's.	3 48	6 24	3 54	8 16	3 59	8 9	4 4	8 2	4 8	7 56

PERIGEE AND APOGEE OF THE MOON.

Perigee, 7th day, 8h. M. | Apogee, 21st day, 5h. M.

PHASES OF THE MOON.

Full Moon, 7th day, 0h. 31.4m. M. | New Moon, 21st day, 6h. 17.2m. A.
Last Quarter, 13th " 5h. 43.3m. A. | First Quarter, 29th " 5h. 10.4m. A.

Sun's *upper* limb rises and sets, (corr. for refract.) M. T. — High Water. M. Time.

Days of Month.	Days of Week.	Boston, &c. rises. h. m.	Boston, &c. sets. h. m.	New York, &c. rises. h. m.	New York, &c. sets. h. m.	Wash'ton, &c. rises. h. m.	Wash'ton, &c. sets. h. m.	Charleston, &c. rises. h. m.	Charleston, &c. sets. h. m.	N. Orleans, &c. rises. h. m.	N. Orleans, &c. sets. h. m.	High Water Boston, &c. h. m.	High Water New York, &c. h. m.	High Water Charleston, &c. h. m.
1	S.	4 52	7 20	4 56	7 16	5 0	7 11	5 13	6 58	5 18	6 53	5 17a	2 57a	1 17a
2	*Su.*	4 53	7 18	4 57	7 14	5 1	7 10	5 14	6 58	5 19	6 52	6 28a	4 8a	2 28a
3	M.	54	17	58	13	2	9	15	57	20	52	7 43	5 23	3 43
4	Tu.	55	16	59	12	3	8	15	56	20	51	9 0	6 40	5 0
5	W.	56	15	5 0	11	4	7	16	55	21	50	10 2	7 42	6 2
6	Th.	57	14	1	10	5	6	17	54	21	49	10 57	8 37	6 57
7	F.	58	12	2	9	6	5	17	53	22	48	11 46	9 26	7 46
8	S.	59	11	3	7	6	4	18	52	23	48	. . .	10 14	8 34
9	*Su.*	5 0	7 10	5 4	7 6	5 7	7 2	5 19	6 51	5 23	6 47	0 34m	10 58a	9 18a
10	M.	1	8	5	5	8	1	19	50	24	46	1 18	11 44	10 4
11	Tu.	2	7	6	4	9	0	20	49	25	45	2 4	. . .	10 47
12	W.	3	6	7	2	10	6 59	21	48	25	44	2 47	0 27m	11 33
13	Th.	4	4	8	1	11	58	21	47	26	43	3 33	1 13	. . .
14	F.	5	3	9	0	12	55	22	46	26	42	4 20	2 0	0 20m
15	S.	6	1	10	6 58	13	54	23	45	27	41	5 15	2 56	1 15
16	*Su.*	5 7	7 0	5 11	6 57	5 14	6 53	5 23	6 44	5 27	6 40	6 27m	4 7m	2 27m
17	M.	8	6 58	12	55	15	52	24	43	28	39	7 45	5 25	3 45
18	Tu.	10	57	13	54	16	51	25	42	29	38	9 2	6 42	5 2
19	W.	11	55	14	53	17	50	25	41	29	37	10 1	7 41	6 1
20	Th.	12	54	15	51	17	48	26	40	30	36	10 47	8 27	6 47
21	F.	13	52	16	50	18	47	27	38	30	35	11 25	9 5	7 25
22	S.	14	51	17	48	19	45	28	37	31	34	11 59	9 39	7 59
23	*Su.*	5 15	6 49	5 17	6 47	5 20	6 44	5 28	6 36	5 32	6 33	0 30a	10 10m	8 30m
24	M.	16	48	18	45	21	43	29	35	32	32	1 0	10 40	9 0
25	Tu.	17	46	19	44	22	41	30	34	33	31	1 30	11 10	9 30
26	W.	18	44	20	42	23	40	30	32	33	30	2 1	11 41	10 1
27	Th.	19	43	21	41	24	38	31	31	34	28	2 33	0 13a	10 33
28	F.	20	41	22	39	25	37	32	30	34	27	3 8	0 48	11 8
29	S.	21	39	23	37	26	35	32	29	35	26	3 49	1 29	11 49
30	*Su.*	5 22	6 38	5 24	6 36	5 26	6 34	5 33	6 28	5 35	6 25	4 41a	2 21a	0 41a
31	M.	23	36	25	34	27	32	33	26	36	24	5 50	3 30	1 50

1846.] *August has Thirty-one Days.* 25

Passage of the Meridian (mean time) and Declination of the Planets.

	1st day. Souths. h. m.	1st day. Dec. ° ′	7th day. Souths. h. m.	7th day. Dec. ° ′	13th day. Souths. h. m.	13th day. Dec. ° ′	19th day. Souths. h. m.	19th day. Dec. ° ′	25th day. Souths. h. m.	25th day. Dec. ° ′
☿	1 48a	+ 7 31	1 38a	+ 5 9	1 17a	+ 3 57	0 45a	— 4 26	11 58m	— 6 41
♀	9 42m	+22 22	9 49m	+22 13	9 57m	+21 41	10 4m	+20 46	10 11	+19 30
♂	0 59a	+15 16	0 50a	+14 0	0 41a	+12 39	0 32a	+11 17	0 23a	+ 9 51
⚶	0 0	+20 27	11 48m	+19 51	11 35m	+19 13	11 23m	+18 32	11 11m	+17 49
⚵	5 51	— 2 12	5 31a	— 2 43	5 11a	— 3 17	4 52a	— 3 50	4 33a	— 4 25
⚴	4 18m	+ 2 47	3 56m	+ 1 59	3 33m	+ 1 5	3 9m	+ 0 0	2 45m	— 1 11
⚳	6 58	+11 44	6 41	+12 4	6 23	+12 21	6 5	+12 35	5 57	+12 48
♃	7 57	+21 18	7 38	+21 26	7 18	+21 33	6 58	+21 40	6 38	+21 45
♄	1 29	—13 20	1 3	—13 30	0 38	—13 39	0 13	—13 49	11 43a	—14 1
♅	4 15	+ 4 58	3 51	+ 4 56	3 27	+ 4 54	3 3	+ 4 51	2 39m	+ 4 47

Moon rises or sets. Mean time. — PHENOMENA AND OBSERVATIONS. *Sundays and Holidays.*

Days of Month.	Moon Souths. Mean Time. h. m.	Boston, &c. h. m.	N. York, &c. h. m.	Wash'ton, &c. h. m.	Cha'ston, &c. h. m.	N. Orl's, &c. h. m.	Washington Mean Time. d. h. m.
		sets.	*sets.*	*sets.*	*sets.*	*sets.*	
1	7 4a	. . .	. . .	. . .	. . .	. . .	1 1 52m. ☿ in Aphelion.
S.	7 59a	0 8m	0 12m	0 17m	0 30m	0 36m	*8th Sunday after Trinity.*
3	8 58	0 57	1 2	1 6	1 21	1 28	
4	9 57	1 55	1 59	2 4	2 19	2 26	
5	10 58	*rises.*	*rises.*	*rises.*	*rises.*	*rises.*	
6	11 57	6 33a	6 30a	6 28a	6 19a	6 16a	7 6 34a. ☌ ♀ ζ ♊ ✱ 1 24 S.
7	☍	7 13	7 12	7 10	7 4	7 4	8 2 25m. ☌ ♄ ☾ ♄ 6 22 S.
8	0 55m	7 51	7 50	7 49	7 48	7 48	9 2 15m. ♂ in Aphelion.
S.	1 50m	8 26a	8 27a	8 28a	8 29a	8 31a	*9th Sunday after Trinity.*
10	2 45	9 0	9 3	9 4	9 9	9 11	10 9 4a. ☌ ♀ δ ♊ ✱ 0 19 N.
11	3 37	9 36	9 38	9 42	9 49	9 53	11 2 26m. ☌ ♅ ☾ ♅ 2 16 S.
12	4 30	10 12	10 16	10 19	10 30	10 35	11 2 55m. ☿ stationary. Meteoric Period
13	5 21	10 53	10 58	11 2	11 14	11 21	15 6 52m. ♀ stationary.
14	6 12	11 37	11 41	11 46	. . .	. . .	15 10 33m. ☌ ♃ ☾ ♃ 2 38 N.
15	7 3	. . .	. . .	. .	0 0m	0 6m	16 5 37m. ☌ ♀ λ ♉ ✱ 0 25 S.
S.	7 53m	0 24m	0 28m	0 34m	0 48m	0 55m	*10th Sunday after Trinity.*
17	8 43	1 15	1 20	1 25	1 39	1 45	19 3 15m. ☌ ♀ ☾ ♀ 5 2 N.
18	9 31	2 8	2 13	2 17	2 30	2 37	20 4 58a. ☍ ♄ ☉
19	10 17	3 3	3 7	3 11	3 22	3 29	20 7 22a. ☌ ☿ ♂ ☿ 6 11 S.
20	11 2	*sets.*	*sets.*	*sets.*	*sets.*	*sets.*	20 9 50a. ♀ in ☊
21	11 45	6 25a	6 23a	6 22a	6 16a	6 16a	21 0 50a. ☿ gr. Hel. Lat. S.
22	0 28a	6 53	6 53	6 52	6 49	6 49	22 7 43m. ☌ ☿ ☾ ☿ 0 30 S.
S.	1 10a	7 21a	7 21a	7 20a	7 21a	7 22a	*11th Sunday after Trinity.*
24	1 52	7 48	7 49	7 50	7 53	7 56	22 0 18a. ☌ ♂ ☾ ♂ 5 29 N.
25	2 36	8 18	8 19	8 22	8 27	8 30	23 0 44a. □ ♀ ☉
26	3 21	8 48	8 51	8 54	9 2	9 6	25 4 27a. Inf. ☌ ☿ ☉
27	4 8	9 23	9 26	9 31	9 40	9 46	
28	4 57	10 3	10 8	10 12	10 24	10 31	
29	5 49	10 48	10 53	10 59	11 13	11 19	30 1 14m. ☌ ♄ ι ♒ ✱ 0 29 S.
S.	6 45a	11 41a	11 46a	11 51a	. . .	. . .	*12th Sunday aft. Trinity.*
31	7 42	. . .	. . .	. . .	0 5m	0 13m	31 1 44m. ☌ ♃ ι ♉ ✱ 0 27 S.

26 *September, Ninth Month, begins on Tuesday.* [1846.

Twilight begins and ends. Mean time.

	1st day.		7th day.		13th day.		19th day.		25th day.	
	Begins. h. m.	Ends. h. m.	Begins. h. m.	Ends. h. m.	Begins. h. m.	Ends. h. m.	Begins. h. m.	Ends. h. m.	Begins. h. m.	Ends. h. m.
Boston,	3 44m	8 16a	3 51m	8 4a	3 59m	7 52a	4 7m	7 40a	4 16m	7 28a
N. York,	3 49	8 11	3 56	8 0	4 3	7 49	4 10	7 37	4 18	7 26
Wash.	3 54	8 6	4 0	7 56	4 7	7 45	4 14	7 34	4 21	7 23
Charles.	4 8	7 52	4 12	7 43	4 17	7 34	4 22	7 25	4 28	7 16
N. Orl's.	4 14	7 46	4 17	7 39	4 21	7 31	4 25	7 22	4 30	7 14

PERIGEE AND APOGEE OF THE MOON.

Perigee, 4th day, 6h. A. | Apogee, 17th day, 10 h. M.

PHASES OF THE MOON.

Full Moon, 5th day, 8h. 8.3m. M. | New Moon, 20th day, 10h. 25.6m. M.
Last Quarter, 12th " 6h. 34.0m. M. | First Quarter, 28th " 2h. 18.4m. M.

Days of Month.	Days of Week.	Sun's *upper* limb rises and sets, (corr. for refract.) M. T. Boston, &c. rises. h. m.	Boston, &c. sets. h. m.	New York, &c. rises. h. m.	New York, &c. sets. h. m.	Wash'ton, &c. rises. h. m.	Wash'ton, &c. sets. h. m.	Charleston, &c. rises. h. m.	Charleston, &c. sets. h. m.	N. Orleans, &c. rises. h. m.	N. Orleans, &c. sets. h. m.	High Water. M. Time. Boston, &c. h. m.	New York, &c. h. m.	Charleston, &c. h. m.
1	Tu.	5 24	6 35	5 26	6 33	5 28	6 31	5 34	6 25	5 37	6 23	7 16a	4 56a	3 16a
2	W.	26	33	27	31	29	29	35	24	37	21	8 40	6 20	4 40
3	Th.	27	31	28	29	30	28	35	22	38	20	9 45	7 25	5 45
4	F.	28	29	29	28	31	26	36	21	38	19	10 41	8 21	6 41
5	S.	29	28	30	26	32	25	37	20	39	18	11 28	9 8	7 28
6	*Su.*	5 30	6 26	5 31	6 25	5 33	6 23	5 37	6 19	5 39	6 17	. . .	9 52a	8 12a
7	M.	31	24	32	23	34	21	38	17	40	15	0 12m	10 38	8 58
8	Tu.	32	22	33	21	35	20	39	16	40	14	0 58	11 20	9 40
9	W.	33	21	34	20	35	18	39	15	41	13	1 40	. . .	10 21
10	Th.	34	19	35	18	36	17	40	13	41	12	2 21	0 1m	11 3
11	F.	35	17	36	16	37	15	41	12	42	11	3 3	0 43	11 48
12	S.	36	15	37	15	38	14	41	11	42	9	3 48	1 28	. . .
13	*Su.*	5 37	6 14	5 38	6 13	5 39	6 12	5 42	6 9	5 43	6 8	4 40m	2 20m	0 40m
14	M.	38	12	39	11	40	10	43	8	44	7	5 48	3 28	1 48
15	Tu.	39	10	40	9	41	9	43	7	44	6	7 11	4 51	3 11
16	W.	40	8	41	8	42	7	44	5	45	4	8 29	6 9	4 29
17	Th.	41	7	42	6	43	6	45	4	45	3	9 35	7 15	5 35
18	F.	43	5	43	4	44	4	45	2	46	2	10 20	8 0	6 20
19	S.	44	3	44	3	44	2	46	1	46	1	10 58	8 38	6 58
20	*Su.*	5 45	6 1	5 45	6 1	5 45	6 1	5 46	6 0	5 47	5 59	11 30m	9 10m	7 30m
21	M.	46	0	46	5 59	46	5 59	47	5 58	47	58	0 2a	9 42	8 2
22	Tu.	47	5 58	47	58	47	58	48	57	48	57	0 31	10 11	8 31
23	W.	48	56	48	56	48	56	48	56	49	56	1 2	10 42	9 2
24	Th.	49	54	49	54	49	54	49	54	49	54	1 33	11 13	9 33
25	F.	50	53	50	53	50	53	50	53	50	53	2 7	11 47	10 7
26	S.	51	51	51	51	51	51	50	52	50	52	2 44	0 24a	10 44
27	*Su.*	5 52	5 49	5 52	5 50	5 52	5 50	5 51	5 50	5 51	5 51	3 26a	1 6a	11 26m
28	M.	53	47	53	48	53	48	52	49	51	49	4 19	1 59	0 19a
29	Tu	54	46	54	46	54	46	52	48	52	48	5 30	3 10	1 30
30	W.	56	44	55	44	55	45	53	46	53	47	6 58	4 38	2 58

1846.] *September has Thirty Days.* 27

Passage of the Meridian (mean time) and Declination of the Planets.

	1st day. Souths. h. m.	Dec. ° '	7th day. Souths. h. m.	Dec. ° '	13th day. Souths. h. m.	Dec. ° '	19th day. Souths. h. m.	Dec. ° '	25th day. Souths. h. m.	Dec. ° '
☿	11 13m	+10 6	10 53m	+11 47	10 51m	+11 43	11 2m	+ 9 47	11 18m	+ 6 11
♀	10 18	+17 37	10 24	+15 39	10 29	+13 26	10 34	+10 59	10 39	+ 8 21
♂	0 12a	+ 8 9	0 3a	+ 6 39	11 53	+ 5 7	11 44	+ 3 35	11 34	+ 2 1
⚶	10 56m	+16 58	10 43m	+16 12	10 31	+15 23	10 18	+14 34	10 5	+13 44
⚵	4 11a	— 5 4	3 53a	— 5 40	3 36a	— 6 15	3 19a	— 6 51	3 2a	— 7 25
⚴	2 15m	— 2 43	1 49m	— 4 10	1 22m	— 5 41	0 55m	— 7 15	0 27m	— 8 50
⚳	5 24	+13 0	5 4	+13 7	4 44	+13 12	4 23	+13 16	4 0	+13 19
♃	6 14	+21 50	5 52	+21 54	5 31	+21 57	5 9	+21 59	4 46	+22 0
♄	11 14a	—14 11	10 48a	—14 20	10 23a	—14 29	9 58a	—14 36	9 33a	—14 42
♅	2 11m	+ 4 42	1 47m	+ 4 38	1 22m	+ 4 33	0 58m	+ 4 27	0 33m	+ 4 22

Days of Month.	Moon Souths. Mean Time. h. m.	Moon rises or sets. Mean Time. Boston, &c. sets. h. m.	N. York, &c. sets. h. m.	Wash'ton, &c. sets. h. m.	Cha'ston, &c. sets. h. m.	N. Orl's, &c. sets. h. m.	PHENOMENA AND OBSERVATIONS. *Sundays and Holidays.* Washington Mean Time. d. h. m.
1	8 40a	0 43m	0 47m	0 52m	1 6m	1 13m	3 11 35m. ☿ stationary.
2	9 39	1 49	1 53	1 58	2 10	2 16	4 10 7m. ☌ ♄ ☾ ♄ 6 28 S.
3	10 37	3 2	3 6	3 9	3 19	3 24	
4	11 33	*rises.*	*rises.*	*rises.*	*rises.*	*rises.*	
5	☍	6 19a	6 20a	6 19a	6 19a	6 20a	7 10 58m. ☌ ♅ ☾ ♅ 2 11 S.
S.	0 29m	6 56a	6 56a	6 58a	7 0a	7 3a	13*th Sunday after Trinity.*
7	1 24	7 31	7 33	7 36	7 42	7 46	8 5 1m. ☌ ☿ α♌ ✱ 0 52 N.
8	2 18	8 8	8 12	8 16	8 24	8 29	8 8 34m. □ ♃ ⊙
9	3 11	8 50	8 54	8 58	9 9	9 16	9 0 0a. ☿ in ☊
10	4 5	9 33	9 37	9 42	9 55	10 1	10 3 58m. ☌ ♂ ⊙
11	4 57	10 19	10 24	10 30	10 44	10 50	11 3 22m. ☿ gr. elon. 17 55 W.
12	5 48	11 9	11 14	11 20	11 34	11 40	11 11 15a. ☌ ♃ ☾ ♃ 3 1 N.
S.	6 39m	. . .	. . .	. . .	. . .	. . .	14*th Sunday after Trinity.*
14	7 27	0 3m	0 8m	0 12a	0 26m	0 33m	12 0 52a. ☌ ♀ ♅ ♀ 10 6 S.
15	8 14	0 58	1 1	1 6	1 17	1 24	13 6 5a ☌ ♀ ⚶ ⚶ 2 2 N.
16	8 59	1 54	1 58	2 1	2 11	2 16	13 7 5a. ☌ ♀ α♌ ✱ 0 34 S.
17	9 43	2 51	2 53	2 56	3 4	3 8	14 1 33m. ☿ in Perihelion.
18	10 26	3 47	3 49	3 51	3 56	3 59	18 2 41a. ☌ ♀ ☾ ♀ 5 41 N.
19	11 9	*sets.*	*sets.*	*sets.*	*sets.*	*sets.*	19 7 13m. ☌ ☿ ☾ ☿ 5 46 N.
S.	11 51m	5 53a	5 53a	5 54a	5 56a	5 58a	15*th Sunday after Trinity.*
21	0 35a	6 21	6 22	6 25	6 29	6 33	Jewish year 5607 begins.
22	1 20	6 51	6 56	6 57	7 4	7 8	20 6 39m. ☌ ♂ ☾ ♂ 4 8 N.
23	2 6	7 22	7 25	7 29	7 39	7 45	23 2 52m. ♀ in Perihelion.
24	2 54	8 3	8 7	8 11	8 23	8 29	23 5 23m. ⊙ ent. ♎ Aut. beg.
25	3 46	8 47	8 51	8 56	9 9	9 16	24 9 23m. ☿ gr. Hel. Lat. N.
26	4 38	9 36	9 41	9 46	10 1	10 7	
S.	5 34a	10 32a	10 37a	10 42a	10 56a	11 3a	16*th Sunday after Trinity.*
28	6 30	11 34	11 39	11 44	11 57	. . .	28 8 30m. ☍ ♀ ⊙ intens. of lt. 0.793
29	7 26	. . .	. . .	. . .	. . .	0 3m	St. Michael.
30	8 22	0 42m	0 45m	0 50m	1 1m	1 7	29 5 17m. ☌ ☿ ♂ ☿ 0 54 N.

28 *October, Tenth Month, begins on Thursday.* [1846.

Twilight begins and ends. Mean Time.

	1st day.		7th day.		13th day.		19th day.		25th day.	
	Begins. h. m.	Ends. h. m.	Begins. h. m.	Ends. h. m.	Begins. h. m.	Ends. h. m.	Begins. h. m.	Ends. h. m.	Begins. h. m.	Ends. h. m.
Boston,	4 23m	7 17a	4 30m	7 6a	4 37m	6 55a	4 44m	6 46a	4 50m	6 38a
N. York,	4 25	7 15	4 32	7 4	4 38	6 54	4 44	6 46	4 50	6 38
Wash'ton,	4 27	7 13	4 33	7 3	4 38	6 54	4 44	6 46	4 50	6 38
Cha'ston,	4 32	7 8	4 36	7 0	4 40	6 52	4 45	6 45	4 49	6 39
N. Orl's,	4 34	7 6	4 37	6 58	4 41	6 51	4 45	6 45	4 48	6 40

PERIGEE AND APOGEE OF THE MOON.

Perigee, 3d day, 2h. M. | Apogee, 15th day, 1h. M. | Perigee, 30th day, 11h. A.

PHASES OF THE MOON.

Full Moon,	4th day, 4h. 58.1m A.	New Moon,	20th day, 2h. 35.6m. M.
Last Quarter,	11th " 10h. 59.8m. A.	First Quarter,	27th " 10h. 1.8m. M

Days of Month.	Days of Week.	Sun's *upper* limb rises and sets, (corr. for refract.) M. T. Boston, &c. rises.	Boston, &c. sets.	New York, &c. rises.	New York, &c. sets.	Wash'ton, &c. rises.	Wash'ton, &c. sets.	Charleston, &c. rises.	Charleston, &c. sets.	N. Orleans, &c. rises.	N. Orleans, &c. sets.	High Water. M. Time. Boston, &c.	New York, &c.	Charleston, &c.
		h. m.	h. m.	h. m.	h. m	h. m.	h. m.	h. m.	h. m.	h. m.	h. m.	h. m.	h. m.	h. m.
1	Th.	5 57	5 42	5 56	5 43	5 55	5 43	5 54	5 45	5 53	5 46	8 22a	6 2a	4 22a
2	F.	58	40	57	41	56	42	54	44	54	45	9 26	7 6	5 26
3	S.	59	39	58	39	57	40	55	42	54	43	10 19	7 59	6 19
4	*Su.*	6 0	5 37	5 59	5 38	5 58	5 39	5 56	5 41	5 55	5 42	11 6a	8 46a	7 6a
5	M.	1	35	6 0	36	59	37	57	40	55	41	11 50	9 30	7 50
6	Tu.	2	33	1	35	6 0	35	57	39	56	40	. . .	10 14	8 34
7	W.	3	32	2	33	1	34	58	37	57	39	0 34m	10 56	9 16
8	Th.	4	30	3	31	2	32	59	36	57	37	1 16	11 36	9 56
9	F.	6	28	4	30	3	31	6 0	35	58	36	1 56	. . .	10 36
10	S.	7	27	5	28	4	29	0	33	59	35	2 36	0 16m	11 20
11	*Su.*	6 8	5 25	6 7	5 27	6 5	5 28	6 1	5 32	5 59	5 34	3 20m	1 0m	. . .
12	M.	9	23	8	25	6	26	2	31	6 0	33	4 10	1 50	0 10m
13	Tu.	10	22	9	23	7	25	2	30	0	32	5 9	2 49	1 9
14	W.	11	20	10	22	8	23	3	29	1	31	6 29	4 9	2 29
15	Th.	13	19	11	20	9	22	4	27	2	30	7 48	5 28	3 48
16	F.	14	17	12	19	10	21	5	26	2	29	8 56	6 36	4 56
17	S.	15	15	13	17	11	19	5	25	3	27	9 45	7 25	5 45
18	*Su.*	6 16	5 14	6 14	5 16	6 12	5 18	6 6	5 24	6 4	5 26	10 23m	8 3m	6 23m
19	M.	17	12	15	14	13	16	7	23	4	25	10 57	8 37	6 57
20	Tu.	18	11	16	13	14	15	8	22	5	24	11 28	9 8	7 28
21	W.	20	9	18	12	15	14	9	21	6	23	0 4a	9 44	8 4
22	Th.	21	8	19	10	16	13	9	19	6	22	0 38	10 18	8 38
23	F.	22	6	20	9	17	11	10	18	7	21	1 10	10 50	9 10
24	S.	23	5	21	7	19	10	11	17	8	20	1 46	11 26	9 46
25	*Su.*	6 24	5 3	6 22	5 6	6 20	5 9	6 12	5 16	6 9	5 19	2 26a	0 6a	10 26m
26	M.	26	2	23	4	21	8	13	15	9	19	3 10	0 50	11 10
27	Tu.	27	1	24	3	22	6	13	14	10	18	4 5	1 45	0 5a
28	W.	28	4 59	26	2	23	5	14	13	11	17	5 16	2 56	1 16
29	Th.	29	58	27	1	24	4	15	12	12	16	6 40	4 20	2 40
30	F.	31	57	28	4 59	25	2	16	11	12	15	8 0	5 40	4 0
31	S.	32	55	29	58	26	1	17	10	13	14	9 5	6 45	5 5

1846.] *October has Thirty-one Days.* 29

Passage of the Meridian (mean time) and Declination of the Planets.

	1st day. Souths. h. m.	Dec. ° ′	7th day. Souths. h. m.	Dec. ° ′	13th day. Souths. h. m.	Dec. ° ′	19th day. Souths. h. m.	Dec. ° ′	25th day. Souths. h. m.	Dec. ° ′
☿	11 34m	+ 0 12	11 49m	− 4 26	0 2a	− 8 52	0 15a	−12 58	0 27a	−16 38
♀	10 43	+ 5 33	10 47	+ 2 39	10 51m	− 0 18	10 54m	− 3 16	10 58m	− 6 12
♂	11 25	+ 0 27	11 15	− 1 7	11 6	− 2 42	10 57	− 4 16	10 48	− 5 49
⚶	9 52	+12 53	9 38	+12 3	9 25	+11 11	9 12	+10 21	8 58	+ 9 29
⚵	2 44a	− 8 07	2 28a	− 8 31	2 11a	− 9 2	1 55a	− 9 32	1 39a	−10 1
⚴	11 54	−10 39	11 26	−12 8	10 58	−13 30	10 30	−14 44	10 2	−15 48
⚳	3 37m	+13 20	3 13m	+13 20	2 49m	+13 19	2 23m	+13 17	1 56m	+13 16
♃	4 23	+22 0	4 0	+22 0	3 36	+22 0	3 11	+21 58	2 46	+21 56
♄	9 9a	−14 48	8 44a	−14 52	8 20a	−14 56	7 56a	−14 58	7 32a	−14 58
♅	0 9m	+ 4 16	11 40	+ 4 10	11 16	+ 4 4	10 51	+ 3 59	10 27	+ 3 54

Days of Month.	Moon Souths. Mean Time	Moon rises or sets. Mean Time. Boston, &c.	N. York, &c.	Wash'ton, &c.	Cha'ston, &c.	N. Orl's, &c.	PHENOMENA AND OBSERVATIONS. *Sundays and Holidays.*
		rises.	*rises.*	*rises.*	*rises.*	*rises.*	Washington Mean Time.
	h. m.	h. m.	h. m.	h. m.	h. m.	h. m.	d. h. m.
1	9 17a	3 36a	3 35a	3 33a	3 27a	3 27a	1 5 29a. ☌ ♄ ☾ ♄ 6 36 S.
2	10 12	4 12	4 12	4 11	4 10	4 10	2 6 52m. ☿ stationary.
3	11 7	4 49	4 49	4 50	4 51	4 53	2 9 0m. ☌ ☿ f¹ ♎ ✱ 1 30 S.
S.	☍	5 24a	5 26a	5 27a	5 32a	5 35a	17*th Sunday after Trinity.*
5	0 2m	6 3	6 5	6 8	6 15	6 20	4 8 4a. ☌ ♅ ☾ ♅ 2 15 S.
6	0 56	6 41	6 45	6 48	6 59	7 5	5 7 43m. ♃ stationary.
7	1 51	7 25	7 29	7 34	7 46	7 52	5 4 50a. ☍ ♅ ☉
8	2 45	8 11	8 15	8 21	8 34	8 41	7 5 50a. sup. ☌ ☿ ☉
9	3 38	9 2	9 6	9 12	9 26	9 32	9 9 21m. ☌ ♃ ☾ ♃ 3 10 N.
10	4 30	9 55	10 0	10 5	10 18	10 25	
S.	5 21m	10 49a	10 54a	10 58a	11 11a	11 18a	18*th Sunday after Trinity.*
12	6 9	11 46	11 49	11 54	. . .	. . .	
13	6 55	. . .	. . .	. . .	0 5m	0 10m	
14	7 40	0 43m	0 45m	0 48m	0 57	1 1	15 9 33m. ♀ gr. Hel. Lat. N.
15	8 23	1 39	1 41	1 44	1 50	1 53	17 9 26a. ☿ in ☋
16	9 6	2 36	2 38	2 39	2 42	2 46	
17	9 48	3 34	3 34	3 34	3 36	3 37	18 11 2a. ☌ ♀ ☾ ♀ 3 10 N.
S.	10 32m	4 31m	4 31m	4 31m	4 29m	4 29m	19*th Sunday after Trinity.*
19	11 16	*sets.*	*sets.*	*sets.*	*sets.*	*sets.*	Solar Eclipse, invis. in U. S.
20	0 2a	5 27a	5 29a	5 33a	5 42a	5 47a	19 0 58m. ☌ ♂ ☾ ♂ 2 21 N.
21	0 51	6 3	6 7	6 11	6 22	6 28	20 2 37a. ☌ ♀ ♂ ♀ 0 43 N.
22	1 42	6 45	6 49	6 54	7 7	7 13	20 7 43a. ☌ ☿ ☾ ☿ 1 5 S.
23	2 35	7 33	7 38	7 43	7 57	8 4	21 4 40m. ☌ ☿ γ ♉ ✱ 1 58 N.
24	3 30	8 27	8 33	8 37	8 52	8 59	
S.	4 25a	9 27a	9 32a	9 37a	9 50a	9 57a	20*th Sunday after Trinity.*
26	5 20	10 32	10 36	10 40	10 52	10 58	
27	6 15	11 39	11 43	11 47	11 55	. . .	
28	7 9	. . .	. . .	. . .	. . .	0 1m	28 1 9m. ☿ in Aphelion.
29	8 2	0 50m	0 53m	0 55m	1 1m	1 4	28 11 59a. ☌ ♄ ☾ ♄ 6 36 S.
30	8 54	2 1	2 2	2 4	2 6	2 9	29 2 40m. ♄ stationary.
31	9 46	3 12	3 13	3 12	3 12	3 13	

30 *November, Eleventh Month, begins on Sunday.* [1846.

Twilight begins and ends. Mean Time.

	1st day.		7th day.		13th day.		19th day.		25th day.	
	Begins.	Ends.	Begins.	Ends.	Begins.	Ends.	Begins.	Ends.	Begins.	Ends.
	h. m.	h. m.	h. m.	h. m.	h. m.	h. m.	h. m.	h. m.	h. m.	h. m.
Boston,	4 58m	6 30a	5 5m	6 23a	5 11m	6 18a	5 17m	6 14a	5 23m	6 11a
N. York,	4 57	6 31	5 4	6 24	5 10	6 19	5 15	6 16	5 21	6 13
Wash.	4 57	6 31	5 3	6 25	5 8	6 21	5 13	6 18	5 19	6 15
Charles.	4 54	6 34	4 59	6 29	5 3	6 25	5 7	6 23	5 12	6 22
N. Orl's.	4 53	6 35	4 55	6 31	5 1	6 28	5 5	6 26	5 9	6 25

APOGEE AND PERIGEE OF THE MOON.

Apogee, 11th day, 9h. A. | Perigee, 25th day, 5h. A.

PHASES OF THE MOON.

Full Moon, 3d day, 4h. 3.2m. M. | New Moon, 18th day, 5h. 51.8m. A.
Last Quarter, 10th " 6h. 35.8m. A. | First Quarter, 25th " 5h. 22.9m. A.

Days of Month.	Days of Week.	Sun's *upper* limb rises and sets, (corr. for refract.) M. T. Boston, &c. rises.	Boston, &c. sets.	New York, &c. rises.	New York, &c. sets.	Wash'ton, &c. rises.	Wash'ton, &c. sets.	Charleston, &c. rises.	Charleston, &c. sets.	N. Orleans, &c. rises.	N. Orleans, &c. sets.	High Water. M. Time. Boston, &c.	New York, &c.	Charleston, &c.
		h. m.	h. m.	h. m.	h. m.	h. m.	h. m.	h. m.	h. m.	h. m.	h. m.	h. m.	h. m.	h. m.
1	*Su.*	6 33	4 54	6 30	4 57	6 27	5 0	6 18	5 9	6 14	5 13	9 33a	7 13a	5 33a
2	M.	34	53	31	56	28	4 59	19	9	15	13	10 23	8 3	6 23
3	Tu.	36	51	32	54	29	58	19	8	15	12	11 8	8 48	7 8
4	W.	37	50	34	53	31	57	20	7	16	11	11 52	9 32	7 52
5	Th.	38	49	35	52	32	56	21	6	17	10	. . .	10 14	8 34
6	F.	39	48	36	51	33	55	22	5	18	10	0 34m	10 54	9 14
7	S.	41	47	37	50	34	54	23	4	18	9	1 14	11 33	9 53
8	*Su.*	6 42	4 45	6 38	4 49	6 35	4 53	6 24	5 4	6 19	5 8	1 53m	. . .	10 34a
9	M.	43	44	40	48	36	52	25	3	20	8	2 34	0 14m	11 14
10	Tu.	44	43	41	47	37	51	26	2	21	7	3 14	0 54	. . .
11	W.	46	42	42	46	38	50	27	2	22	6	4 1	1 41	0 1m
12	Th.	47	41	43	45	39	49	27	1	23	6	4 59	2 39	0 59
13	F.	48	40	44	44	40	48	28	0	23	5	6 12	3 52	2 12
14	S.	49	39	46	43	41	47	29	0	24	5	7 22	5 2	3 22
15	*Su.*	6 51	4 39	6 47	4 43	6 43	4 47	6 30	4 59	6 25	5 4	8 27m	6 7m	4 27m
16	M.	52	38	48	42	44	46	31	59	26	4	9 22	7 2	5 22
17	Tu.	53	37	49	41	45	45	32	58	27	3	10 4	7 44	6 4
18	W.	54	36	50	40	46	44	33	58	27	3	10 44	8 24	6 44
19	Th.	56	35	51	39	47	44	34	57	28	3	11 19	8 59	7 19
20	F.	57	34	53	39	48	43	35	57	29	2	11 57	9 37	7 57
21	S.	58	34	54	38	49	43	36	56	30	2	0 35a	10 15	8 35
22	*Su.*	6 59	4 33	6 55	4 38	6 50	4 42	6 37	4 56	6 31	5 2	1 13a	10 53m	9 13m
23	M.	7 0	32	56	37	51	42	37	56	32	1	1 54	11 34	9 54
24	Tu.	2	32	57	36	52	41	38	55	33	1	2 30	0 10a	10 30
25	W.	3	31	58	36	54	41	39	55	33	1	3 29	1 9	11 29
26	Th.	4	31	59	35	55	40	40	55	34	1	4 27	2 7	0 27a
27	F.	5	30	7 0	35	56	40	41	55	35	1	5 36	3 16	1 36
28	S.	6	30	2	35	57	40	42	54	36	0	6 52	4 32	2 52
29	*Su.*	7 7	4 30	7 3	4 34	6 58	4 39	6 43	4 54	6 37	5 0	8 4a	5 44a	4 4a
30	M.	8	29	4	34	59	39	44	54	38	0	9 8	6 48	5 8

1846. *November has Thirty Days.* 31

Passage of the Meridian (mean time) and Declination of the Planets.

	1st day. Souths.	Dec.	7th day. Souths.	Dec.	13th day. Souths.	Dec.	19th day. Souths.	Dec.	25th day. Souths.	Dec.
	h. m.	° ′	h. m.	° ′	h. m.	° ′	h. m.	° ′	h. m.	° ′
☿	0 41a	—20 16	0 54a	—22 45	1 6a	—24 31	1 15a	—25 31	1 19a	—25 37
♀	11 4m	— 9 32	11 8m	—12 16	11 14m	—14 49	11 20m	—17 8	11 27m	—19 11
♂	10 37	— 7 36	10 28	— 9 6	10 20	—10 34	10 11	—12 0	10 3	—13 23
⚶	8 42	+ 8 31	8 28	+ 7 41	8 15	+ 6 53	8 0	+ 6 7	7 46	+ 5 22
⚵	1 20a	—10 32	1 5a	—10 57	0 49a	—11 20	0 34a	—11 41	0 18a	—12 1
⚴	9 31	—16 49	9 6	—17 26	8 41	—18 3	8 16	—18 25	7 53	—18 38
⚳	1 24m	+13 13	0 55m	+13 11	0 26m	+13 10	11 52	+13 11	11 22	+13 13
♃	2 17	+21 53	1 51	+21 49	1 24	+21 45	0 58m	+21 41	0 31m	+21 35
♄	7 4a	—14 58	6 41a	—14 56	6 18a	—14 52	5 55a	—14 48	5 33a	—14 42
♅	9 59	+ 3 48	9 34	+ 3 43	9 10	+ 3 39	8 46	+ 3 36	8 22	+ 3 33

Days of Month.	Moon Souths. Mean Time.	Moon rises or sets. Mean Time. Boston, &c.	N. York, &c.	Wash'ton, &c.	Cha'ston, &c.	N. Orl's, &c.	PHENOMENA AND OBSERVATIONS. *Sundays and Holidays.* Washington Mean Time.
	h. m.	rises. h. m.	rises. h. m.	rises. h. m.	rises. h. m.	rises. h. m.	d. h. m. ° ′
S.	10 41a	3 56a	3 58a	4 0a	4 6a	4 9a	21*st Sunday after Trinity.*
2	11 35	4 33	4 36	4 39	4 49	4 54	1 4 11m. ☌ ♅ ☾ ♅ 2 21 S.
3	☍	5 14	5 18	5 22	5 34	5 40	
4	0 30m	6 0	6 4	6 9	6 23	6 28	5 4 4a. ☌ ♃ ☾ ♃ 3 4 N.
5	1 24	6 49	6 54	6 59	7 13	7 20	9 6 0m. ☌ ♃ ι ♉ ✱ 0 26 S.
6	2 18	7 43	7 47	7 52	8 6	8 13	9 9 52m. ☌ ⚶ ξ¹ ♍ ✱ 1 43 N.
7	3 10	8 37	8 42	8 46	9 0	9 7	9 6 52a. ☌ ⚶ ν ♍ ✱ 0 2 N.
S.	4 0m	9 35a	9 39a	9 43a	9 54a	10 1a	22*d Sunday after Trinity.*
9	4 49	10 32	10 36	10 39	10 49	10 53	9 8 25a. ☌ ☿ ⚵ ☿ 12 24 S.
10	5 34	11 29	11 31	11 34	11 41	11 45	
11	6 18	. . .	. . .	. . .	. . .	. . .	
12	7 1	0 26m	0 28m	0 30m	0 34m	0 38m	Olmsted's Meteoric Shower.
13	7 43	1 23	1 23	1 24	1 27	1 28	
14	8 26	2 20	2 20	2 20	2 20	2 21	14 6 12a. ☌ ⚳ λ ♉ ✱ 1 8 S.
S.	9 10m	3 18m	3 18m	3 17m	3 13m	3 18m	23*d Sunday after Trinity.*
16	9 56	4 20	4 18	4 16	4 9	4 9	16 8 2a. ☌ ♂ ☾ ♂ 0 19 N.
17	10 44	sets.	sets.	sets.	sets.	sets.	16 10 12a. □ ♄ ☉
18	11 34	4 41a	4 45a	4 50a	5 2a	5 9a	17 11 43m. ☿ gr. Hel. Lat. S.
19	0 28a	5 28	5 32	5 38	5 51	5 57	18 3 59m. ☌ ♀ ☾ ♀ 1 3 S.
20	1 23	6 21	6 26	6 31	6 45	6 52	19 6 52m. ☌ ⚶ π ♍ ✱ 1 21 N.
21	2 20	7 20	7 25	7 29	7 44	7 50	19 11 13a. ☍ ⚳ ☉ intens. of lt. 1.011
S.	3 16a	8 25a	8 28a	8 33a	8 46a	8 51a	24*th Sunday after Trinity.*
23	4 11	9 32	9 36	9 39	9 49	9 55	20 4 37m. ☌ ☿ θ Oph. ✱ 0 44 N.
24	5 5	10 42	10 44	10 47	10 54	10 58	20 10 25m. ☌ ☿ ☾ ☿ 6 38 S.
25	5 58	11 51	11 52	11 53	11 58	. . .	21 6 52m. ♀ stationary.
26	6 49	. . .	. . .	. . .	. . .	0 1m	22 9 57a. ☿ gr. elon. 21 47 E.
27	7 41	1 0m	1 1m	1 1m	1 2m	1 3	25 6 32m. ☌ ♄ ☾ ♄ 6 26 S.
28	8 32	2 10	2 9	2 9	2 6	2 6	28 10 17m. ☌ ♅ ☾ ♅ 2 20 S.
S.	9 24m	3 18m	3 17m	3 15m	3 9m	3 9m	*Advent Sunday.*
30	10 18	4 26	4 24	4 22	4 13	4 11	St. Andrew.

32 *December, Twelfth Month, begins on Tuesday.* [1846.

Twilight begins and ends. Mean Time.

	1st day.		7th day.		13th day.		19th day.		25th day.	
	Begins. h. m.	Ends. h. m.	Begins. h. m.	Ends. h. m.	Begins. h. m.	Ends. h. m.	Begins. h. m.	Ends. h. m.	Begins. h. m.	Ends. h. m.
Boston,	5 29m	6 9a	5 35m	6 9a	5 40m	6 8a	5 43m	6 10a	5 46m	6 14a
N. York,	5 27	6 11	5 33	6 11	5 37	6 11	5 41	6 13	5 44	6 16
Wash.	5 25	6 13	5 30	6 14	5 34	6 14	5 38	6 16	5 41	6 19
Charles.	5 17	6 21	5 22	6 22	5 26	6 23	5 29	6 25	5 32	6 28
N. Orl's.	5 13	6 25	5 18	6 26	5 24	6 17	5 25	6 29	5 28	6 32

APOGEE AND PERIGEE OF THE MOON.

Apogee, 9th day, 6h. A. | Perigee, 21st day, 11h. M.

PHASES OF THE MOON.

Full Moon, 2d day, 5h. 38.3m. A. | New Moon, 18th day, 7h. 34.2m M.
Last Quarter, 10th " 4h. 8.0m. A. | First Quarter, 25th " 1h. 28.2m. M.

Days of Month.	Days of Week.	Sun's *upper* limb rises and sets, (corr. for refract.) M. T. Boston, &c. rises. h. m.	Boston, &c. sets. h. m.	New York, &c. rises. h. m.	New York, &c. sets. h. m.	Wash'ton, &c. rises. h. m.	Wash'ton, &c. sets. h. m.	Charleston, &c. rises. h. m.	Charleston, &c. sets. h. m.	N. Orleans, &c. rises. h. m.	N. Orleans, &c. sets. h. m.	High Water. M. Time. Boston, &c. h. m.	New York, &c. h. m.	Charleston, &c. h. m.
1	Tu.	7 10	4 29	7 5	4 34	7 0	4 39	6 45	4 54	6 38	5 0	10 2a	7 42a	6 2a
2	W.	11	29	6	33	1	39	45	54	39	0	10 54	8 34	6 54
3	Th.	12	28	7	33	2	38	46	54	40	0	11 37	9 17	7 37
4	F.	13	28	8	33	2	38	47	54	41	0	. . .	9 59	8 19
5	S.	14	28	9	32	3	38	48	54	41	0	0 19m	10 39	8 59
6	*Su.*	7 15	4 28	7 10	4 32	7 4	4 38	6 49	4 54	6 42	5 0	0 59m	11 16a	9 36a
7	M.	16	28	11	32	5	38	49	54	43	0	1 36	11 53	10 13
8	Tu.	17	28	12	32	6	38	50	54	44	1	2 13	. . .	10 52
9	W.	17	28	13	32	7	38	51	54	44	1	2 52	0 32m	11 30
10	Th.	18	28	14	32	8	38	52	54	45	1	3 30	1 10	. . .
11	F.	19	29	15	32	9	38	53	55	46	1	4 14	1 54	0 14m
12	S.	20	28	15	32	9	39	54	55	46	2	5 6	2 46	1 6
13	*Su.*	7 21	4 28	7 16	4 32	7 10	4 30	6 54	4 55	6 47	5 2	6 12m	3 52m	2 12m
14	M.	22	28	16	33	11	30	55	55	48	2	7 18	4 58	3 18
15	Tu.	22	20	17	33	12	30	56	56	48	2	8 22	6 2	4 22
16	W.	23	20	18	33	12	40	56	56	49	3	9 23	7 3	5 23
17	Th.	24	29	18	33	13	40	57	56	50	3	10 6	7 46	6 6
18	F.	24	29	19	34	14	40	58	57	50	4	10 53	8 33	6 53
19	S.	25	30	20	34	14	41	58	57	51	4	11 36	9 16	7 36
20	*Su.*	7 26	4 30	7 20	4 35	7 15	4 41	6 59	4 58	6 51	5 4	0 20a	10 0m	8 20m
21	M.	26	31	21	35	15	42	59	58	52	5	1 3	10 43	9 3
22	Tu.	26	31	21	36	16	42	7 0	59	52	5	1 47	11 27	9 47
23	W.	27	32	22	36	16	43	0	59	53	6	2 32	0 12a	10 32
24	Th.	27	32	22	37	17	43	1	5 0	53	7	3 22	1 2	11 12
25	F.	28	33	23	37	17	44	1	0	54	7	4 13	1 53	0 13a
26	S.	28	34	23	38	17	44	1	1	54	8	5 11	2 51	1 11
27	*Su.*	7 28	4 34	7 23	4 39	7 18	4 45	7 2	5 2	6 55	5 8	6 21a	4 1a	2 21a
28	M.	29	35	23	39	18	46	2	2	55	9	7 31	5 11	3 31
29	Tu.	29	36	24	40	18	47	2	3	55	10	8 45	6 25	4 45
30	W.	29	37	21	41	19	47	2	4	56	10	9 47	7 27	5 47
31	Th.	30	37	24	42	19	48	3	4	56	11	10 38	8 18	6 38

1846.] *December has Thirty-one Days.* 33

Passage of the Meridian (mean time) and Declination of the Planets.

	1st day. Souths. h. m.	Dec. ° ′	7th day. Souths. h. m.	Dec. ° ′	13th day. Souths. h. m.	Dec. ° ′	19th day. Souths. h. m.	Dec. ° ′	25th day. Souths. h. m.	Dec. ° ′
☿	1 9a	—24 48	0 34a	—23 1	11 38m	—20 40	10 52m	—19 16	10 30m	—19 38
♀	11 35m	—21 5	11 43m	—22 17	11 52	—23 16	0 1a	—23 48	0 10a	—23 54
♂	9 55	—14 42	9 47	—15 58	9 40	—17 10	9 33m	—18 17	9 26m	—19 19
⚶	7 31	+ 4 40	7 17	+ 4 0	7 1	+ 3 23	6 46	+ 2 50	6 30	+ 2 21
⚵	0 3a	—12 17	11 48	—12 31	11 33	—12 43	11 18	—12 52	11 3	—12 59
⚴	7 31	—18 41	7 9a	—18 37	6 48a	—18 29	6 28a	—18 12	6 8a	—18 50
⚳	10 53	+13 18	10 24	+13 25	9 56	+13 35	9 28	+13 48	9 2	+14 4
♃	[0 4m / 11 59a]	+[21 30 / 21 29]	11 32	+21 23	11 5	+21 17	10 38	+21 11	10 12	+21 6
♄	5 10	—14 35	4 48	—14 28	4 26	—14 19	4 4	—14 9	3 42	—13 58
♅	7 58	+ 3 31	7 34	+ 3 29	7 10	+ 3 28	6 47	+ 3 28	6 23	+ 3 29

Days of Month.	Moon Souths. Mean Time. h. m.	Moon rises or sets. Mean Time. Boston, &c. rises. h. m.	N. York, &c. rises. h. m.	Wash'ton, &c. rises. h. m.	Cha'ston, &c. rises. h. m.	N. Orl's, &c. rises. h. m.
1	11 12a	3 51a	3 54a	4 0a	4 12a	4 17a
2	☍	4 38	4 42	4 47	5 1	5 7
3	0 5m	5 30	5 34	5 39	5 54	6 0
4	0 59	6 25	6 29	6 34	6 48	6 54
5	1 50	7 21	7 24	7 29	7 42	7 49
S.	2 40m	8 19a	8 22a	8 26a	8 37a	8 42a
7	3 27	9 16	9 19	9 22	9 31	9 35
8	4 12	10 13	10 15	10 18	10 23	10 26
9	4 55	11 10	11 12	11 13	11 17	11 19
10	5 37	. . .	. . .	. . .	. . .	. . .
11	6 20	0 8m	0 8m	0 8m	0 9m	0 10m
12	7 3	1 5	1 5	1 5	1 3	1 3
S.	7 47m	2 4m	2 3m	2 2m	1 57m	1 57m
14	8 34	3 4	3 2	2 59	2 53	2 51
15	9 23	4 6	4 4	4 0	3 50	3 47
16	10 15	*sets.*	*sets.*	*sets.*	*sets.*	*sets.*
17	11 10	4 8a	4 13a	4 18a	4 32a	4 39a
18	0 8a	5 7	5 12	5 16	5 30	5 38
19	1 6	6 11	6 15	6 21	6 34	6 39
S.	2 4a	7 19a	7 22a	7 27a	7 38a	7 44a
21	3 0	8 29	8 33	8 36	8 44	8 49
22	3 54	9 41	9 43	9 45	9 50	9 53
23	4 47	10 51	10 51	10 53	10 55	10 57
24	5 38	. . .	. . .	. . .	11 59	. . .
25	6 29	0 1m	0 1m	0 0m	. . .	0 0m
26	7 21	1 9	1 8	1 7	1 2m	1 2
S.	8 12a	2 17m	2 15m	2 12m	2 6m	2 4m
28	9 5	3 22	3 20	3 16	3 6	3 3
29	9 57	4 25	4 22	4 18	4 6	4 3
30	10 50	5 25	5 21	5 16	5 3	5 0
31	11 41	6 18	6 14	6 10	5 56	5 53

PHENOMENA AND OBSERVATIONS.

Sundays and Holidays.

Washington Mean Time.

d. h. m. ° ′
2 2 8m. ☿ stationary.
2 7 16a. ☌ ♃ ☾ ♃ 2 51 N.
3 8 21a. ☍ ♃ ☉
4 10 28m. ☌ ⚶ ☉
6 11 14m. ☿ in ☊
2d Sunday in Advent.
8 5 4a. ☌ ♀ ⚶ ⚶ 9 57 N.
10 11 12m. ♀ in ☋
11 0 50m. ☿ in Perihelion.
11 6 51a. Inf. ☌ ☿ ☉
12 5 14m. ☌ ☿ ♀ ☿ 1 57 N.
14 5 27m. ☌ ☿ ⚶ ☿ 7 38 S.
3d Sunday in Advent.
15 4 22a. ☌ ♂ ☾ ♂ 1 45 S.
15 7 33a. sup. ☌ ♀ ☉
17 8 45m. ☌ ☿ ☾ ☿ 0 50 S
18 8 29m. ☌ ♀ ☾ ♀ 4 44 S.
19 0 45m. □ ♀ ☉
20 1 11m. ♅ stationary.
4th Sund. in Advent. Mahom's year 1263 begins.
St. Thomas.
21 8 37m. ☿ gr. Hel. Lat. N.
21 8 47a. ☿ stationary.
21 11 4a. ☉ ent. ♑ Win. beg.
Christmas Day.
22 3 17a. ☌ ♄ ☾ ♄ 6 7 S.
1st Sunday after Christmas.
25 3 18a. ☌ ♅ ☾ ♅ 2 7 S.
29 8 27a. ☌ ♃ ☾ ♃ 2 46 N.
31 9 40m. ☌ ♂ ω¹ ♏ ✱ 0 1 N.
31 9 41a. ☿ gr. elon. 22 41 W.

ECLIPSES IN 1846.

In the year 1846, there will be only two eclipses; both of the Sun, one of which will be visible in the United States, and the other invisible.

I. Saturday, April 25th. An annular and total Eclipse of the Sun, partially visible in the United States.

Beginning of the general eclipse at 8h. 54.3m. M. [Mean Time at Washington,] in latitude 6° 15′ South, and longitude 119° 40′ West of Greenwich.

Beginning of the annular eclipse at 9h. 55.2m. M. in latitude 2° 11′ S. and longitude 135° 51′ W. of Greenwich.

† Beginning of the total eclipse at 10h. 8.9m. M. in latitude 2° 0′ N. and longitude 113° 9′ West of Greenwich.

Central eclipse at Noon, at 11h. 47.8m. M. in latitude 25° 21′ N. and longitude 74° 31′ West of Greenwich.

† End of the total eclipse at 1h. 12.5m. A. in latitude 30° 32′ N. and longitude 34° 14′ West of Greenwich.

End of the annular eclipse at 1h. 29.5m. A. in latitude 24° 56′ N. and longitude 3° 43′ West of Greenwich.

End of the general eclipse at 2h. 30.4m. A. in latitude 20° 52′ N., and longitude 20° 4′ West of Greenwich.

This eclipse will be visible throughout Mexico, Texas, the United States, Canada, New Brunswick, Nova Scotia, Newfoundland, Central America, the regions of South America north of the Equator, the West India Islands, the south of Greenland, Iceland, Great Britain, France, Spain, Holland, the Netherlands, and the north-western portion of Africa. Being a large eclipse in both Europe and America, *it will be exceedingly valuable for determining the relative longitudes of places upon the two continents.*

The total eclipse will pass over the north of Guatemala, and across the island of Cuba; and the central line will pass over the following points on the earth's surface:

Latitude.	Longitude W. from Greenw'h.	Latitude.	Longitude W. from Greenw'h.
2 11 S.	135 51	29 25 N.	61 3
1 19 N.	123 26	30 52	46 37
5 38	112 7	30 4	31 37
11 18	100 36	27 58	17 48
17 37	89 33	24 56	3 43
25 21	74 31		

† The change of the central eclipse from the annular to the total phase is not distinctly mentioned in the Nautical Almanac; but the marks upon the chart in that work show that this most obvious fact was not overlooked by the computers of that Almanac.

The phases of the eclipse for all places in the United States may be determined from the following tables. The Sun's semi-diameter and horizontal parallax are the same as at conjunction:

The following table of elements will serve to calculate the eclipse for any place in the United States.

Greenw'h. M. Time.	D's Hour angle for Greenw.	☉'s R. A. less ☾'s R. A.	☉'s Dec. North.	☾'s Dec. North.	Rel. hourly motion in R. A.	Rel. hourly motion in Dec.	☾'s Hor. Par.	For Interval of	D's hour angle.	Change in Relat. R. A.
h. m.	° ′ ″	″	13° ° ′ ″	13° ° ′ ″	′	″	″	m.s.	° ′ ″	″
3 0	46 32 56	−3657.3	11 46.8	8 57.8	1893.0	464 1	3476.7	0 10	2 25	5.3
5	47 45 19	−3499.6	50.9	9 40.5	.0	463.7	.6	0 20	4 50	10.5
10	48 57 41	−3341.9	54.9	10 23.2	.1	.3	.4	0 30	7 14	15.8
15	50 10 4	−3184.1	59.0	11 5.9	.1	462.9	.3	0 40	9 39	21.0
20	51 22 27	−3026.4	12 3.1	11 48.5	.1	.5	.2	0 50	12 4	26.3
25	52 34 50	−2868.6	7.2	12 31.2	.2	.1	.0	1 0	14 29	31.5
30	53 47 13	−2710.8	11.3	13 13.7	.2	461.7	3475.9	1 10	16 54	36.8
35	54 59 36	−2553.0	15.4	13 56.2	.2	.3	.8	1 20	19 18	42.1
40	56 11 58	−2395.2	19.4	14 38.7	.3	460.9	.7	1 30	21 43	47.3
45	57 24 21	−2237.5	23.5	15 21.1	.4	.5	.6	1 40	24 8	52.6
50	58 36 44	−2079.9	27.6	16 3.6	.4	.1	.5	1 50	26 33	57.9
55	59 49 7	−1921.9	31.6	16 46.0	.4	459.7	.3	2 0	28 56	63.1
4 0	61 1 30	−1764.1	35.7	17 28.4	.5	.3	.2	2 10	31 22	68.4
5	62 13 53	−1606.3	39.8	18 10.7	.5	458.9	.1	2 20	33 47	73.6
10	63 26 15	−1448.5	43.9	18 53.0	.6	.5	3474.9	2 30	36 12	78.9
15	64 38 38	−1290.7	47.9	19 35.3	.6	.1	.8	2 40	38 37	84.2
20	65 51 1	−1132 9	52.0	20 17.5	.6	457.7	.7	2 50	41 2	89.4
25	67 3 24	− 975.1	56.0	20 59.7	.7	.3	.5	3 0	43 25	94.7
30	68 15 47	− 817 3	13 0.1	21 41.9	.7	456.9	.4	3 10	45 50	99.9
35	69 28 10	− 659.5	4.1	22 24.0	.7	.5	.3	3 20	48 15	105.2
40	70 40 32	− 501.6	8.1	23 6.1	.7	.0	.1	3 30	50 40	110.5
45	71 52 55	− 343.8	12.2	23 48.2	.8	455.6	.0	3 40	53 5	115.7
50	73 5 18	− 186.0	16.3	24 30.2	.8	2	3473.9	3 50	55 29	121.0
55	74 17 40	− 28.2	20.3	25 12.1	.8	454.8	.8	4 0	57 54	126.2
5 0	75 30 3	+ 129.6	24.4	25 54.1	.8	.4	.7	4 10	60 19	131.5
5	76 42 26	287.4	28.5	26 36.0	.9	.0	.6	4 20	62 44	136.8
10	77 54 49	445.2	32.5	27 17.9	.9	453.6	.4	4 30	65 9	142.0
15	79 7 12	603.1	36.6	27 59.7	.9	2	.3	4 40	67 33	147.3
20	80 19 35	760.9	40.7	28 41.5	1894.0	452.8	.2	4 50	69 58	152.5
25	81 31 58	918.7	44.7	29 23.3	.0	.4	.1	5 0	72 23	157.8
30	82 44 20	1076.6	48.8	30 5.1	.0	.0	.0			
35	83 56 43	1234.4	52.9	30 46.8	.0	451.5	3472.9			
40	85 9 6	1392.2	56.9	31 28.5	.1	.1	.7			
45	86 21 28	1550.1	14 1.0	32 10.2	.1	450.7	.7			
50	87 33 51	1707.9	5.1	32 51.8	.1	.3	.5			
55	88 46 14	1865.7	9.2	33 33.4	.2	449.9	.3			
6. 0	89 58 36	2023.6	13.3	34 14.9	.2	.5	.2			
5	91 10 59	2181.5	17.4	34 56.4	.2	.0	.1			
10	92 23 22	2339 4	21.4	35 37.9	.2	448.7	3471.9			
15	93 35 44	2497.2	25.5	36 19.3	.2	.2	.9			
20	94 48 7	2655.1	29.6	37 0.7	.3	447.8	.7			
25	96 0 30	2813.0	33.6	37 42.1	.3	.4	.6			
30	97 12 52	2970.7	37.7	38 23.4	.3	446.9	.5			
35	98 25 15	3128 6	41.8	39 4.6	.3	.5	.4			
40	99 37 38	3286 5	45.8	39 45.8	.4	1	.3			
45	100 50 0	3444.3	49.9	40 27.1	.4	445.6	.1			
50	102 2 23	3602.2	51.0	41 8.2	.4	.2	.0			
55	103 14 46	3760.1	58.1	41 49.4	.5	444.8	3470.8			
7 0	104 27 8	3917.9	15 2.3	42 36.6	.5	.3	.7			

OCCULTATIONS.

Elements for facilitating the calculation of Occultations which may be visible in the United States, in 1846.

Day of the Month.	Star's Name.	Magnitude.	Washington, Mean Time of apparent conjunction in R. A. of Moon and Star.	At the time of Conjunction.			Limiting Parallels between which the occult. is visible.
				Apparent R. A. of Moon and Star.	Apparent Declination of Star.	Star N. or S. of Moon.	
			h. m. s.	h. m. s.			
Jan. 10	E² Orion.	5.6	3 9 19 A.	6 5 49.83	19 12 13.5 N.	53 27 N.	82 N. 15 N.
13	A² ♋	6	6 10 55	8 38 30.92	12 40 9.6	38 41	90 9
	a¹ ♋	6	10 48 38	8 47 32.81	12 12 26.7	29 51	73 1 S.
14	a³ ♋	5	0 7 13 M.	8 50 5.68	12 26 49.7	4 55	41 26
16	p⁴ ♌	5.6	11 30 42 A.	11 5 54.20	0 45 56.1	29 48	72 6
22	x ♎	5	7 44 42 M.	15 33 5.69	19 10 22.1 S.	66 36	71 37 N.
29	VENUS		9 16 35 A.	9 37.06	1 31 23.6	31 7	70 7 S.
Feb. 4	y ♉	4	7 14 50 A.	4 19 39.44	18 50 0.3 N.	28 59 N.	72 N. 9 N.
6	E² Orion.	5.6	9 9 43	6 5 49.72	19 12 13.3	24 37	66 6
10	A² ♋	6	0 20 6 M.	8 38 31.16	12 40 7.9	39 7	90 10
	a³ ♋	5	6 15 18	8 50 5.95	12 26 47.9	6 10	42 24 S.
15	58 ♍	5	8 26 50 A.	13 9 25.37	9 44 4.6 S.	27 26	64 9
16	α ♍	1	0 13 43 M.	13 17 7.26	10 21 29.6	29 3	65 7
19	s¹ ♏	4	0 47 11	15 56 30.79	19 22 42.7	48 40	71 13 N.
	γ ♏	4	3 33 11	16 3 4.54	19 3 14.8	18 5	39 18 S.
20	ρ Ophi.	4.5	7 45 27	17 11 47.39	20 56 19.1	68 1	69 41 N.
22	o¹ ♐	5	7 30 33	19 12 44.79	18 7 44.8	26 16	50 11 S.
23	β ♑	3.4	7 1 45	20 12 21.38	15 15 40.3	24 41	52 13
Mar. 1	JUPITER		9 2 33 A.	2 21 38.88	13 7 7.7 N.	65 31 N.	90 N. 41 N.
4	y ♉	4	7 29 6 M.	4 19 38.97	18 49 59.4	13 15	50 7 S.
7	k ♋	5	6 4 56 A.	7 24 51.00	16 9 0.1	58 37	90 41 N.
9	x ♋	5.6	5 45 53	8 59 26.38	11 16 49.6	31 18	75 1
11	n Sext.	6	8 37 19	10 37 15.47	3 17 34.4	42 27	90 8
14	50 ♍	6	10 19 16	13 1 44.56	9 30 42.7 S.	59 4	80 27
15	α ♍	1	5 49 19 M.	13 17 7.80	10 21 33.2	38 18	79 2
16	a² ♎	3	9 45 25 A.	14 42 24.56	15 24 0.1	7 6	34 28 S.
17	s¹ ♏	2	6 18 42	15 56 31.60	19 22 45.2	61 42	71 1
29	JUPITER		4 29 53	2 43 18.67	14 56 15.0 N.	21 1	59 7 S.
Apr. 3	λ □	4.5	6 2 42 A.	7 9 15.94	16 48 38.4 N.	45 36 N.	90 N. 24 N.
4	k □	5	1 39 15 M.	7 24 50.09	16 9 0.6	48 47	90 27
8	p⁴ ♌	5.6	7 8 28 A.	11 5 54.94	0 45 49.2	38 57	90 4
13	a² ♎	3	4 3 0 M.	14 42 25.06	15 24 2.1 S.	10 58	38 25 S.
May 8	α ♍	1	9 18 39 A.	13 17 8.13	10 21 35.6 S.	39 14 N.	79 N. 3 N.
11	s¹ ♏	4	2 6 36 12	15 56 32.75	19 22 47.4	66 31	71 38
	γ ♏	4	10 18 17	16 3 6.54	19 3 19.3	36 3	62 0
12	ψ Ophi.	5	3 14 7 M.	16 15 9.25	19 40 15.9	55 5	70 21
15	o¹ ♐	5	2 24 57	19 12 47.15	18 7 39.8	42 43	72 6
16	β² ♑	3.4	2 53 49	20 12 23.60	15 15 32.9	38 41	71 1
	γ ♒	5	11 34 7 A.	21 1 14.11	11 59 16.2	27 5	59 10 S.

Day of the Month.	Star's Name.	Magnitude.	Washington, Mean Time of apparent conjunction in R. A. of Moon and Star.	At the time of Conjunction.			Limiting Parallels between which the occult. is visible.
				Apparent R. A. of Moon and Star.	Apparent Declination of Star.	Star N. or S. of Moon.	
			h. m. s.	h. m. s.			
May 21	δ ♓	5	2 20 13 M.	0 40 42.77	6 44 51.4 N.	3 41 N.	39 N. 30 S.
June 6	a² ♎	3	9 37 3 A.	14 42 25.41	15 24 2.8 S.	12 59 N.	40 N. 23 S.
8	β¹ ♏	2	4 55 22 M.	15 56 33. 1	19 22 47.6	66 52	71 38 N.
16	λ ♓	5	1 7 12	23 34 13.71	0 56 15.5 N.	0 1	35 35 S.
July 5	↓ Ophi.	5	10 31 40 A.	16 15 9.60	19 40 15.7 S.	60 30 N.	70 N. 28 N.
8	♐	5	7 45 19	19 12 48.31	18 7 36.0	34 25	59 3 S.
	a² ♐	5.6	7 48 25	19 12 56.25	18 34 55.2	62 1	71 27 N.
Aug. 2	y ♏	4	2 48 13 M.	16 3 6.60	19 3 18.4 S.	54 53 N.	71 N. 22 N.
5	ζ¹ ♐	5	6 24 58	19 12 48.45	18 7 35.4	37 47	64 0
6	β² ♑	3.4	5 34 48	20 12 25.23	15 15 25.6	25 28	53 12 S.
	z¹ ♒	6	8 58 41 A.	20 51 31.36	13 38 18.8	67 48	76 33 N.
7	γ ♒	5	0 51 8 M.	21 1 15.96	11 59 6.3	7 12	37 29 S.
9	21 ♓	6	7 21 15 A.	23 41 37.85	7 3 53.7	17 11	52 18 S.
11	ε ♓	4	3 21 17 M.	0 55 0.75	7 3 53.7	17 11	52 18 S.
18	λ □	4.5	5 44 34	7 9 16.07	16 48 24.5	45 34	90 25 N.
27	a² ♎	3	9 38 14 A.	14 42 24.58	15 23 59.2 S.	51 46	75 19
Sep. 10	A.S.C. 454	6	8 51 22 A.	3 59 13.78	16 55 30.8 N.	47 10 N.	90 N. 25 N.
11	β¹ ♉	4	3 25 45 M.	4 14 6.83	17 10 39.8	56 41	90 38
	β² ♉	5	4 32 49	4 16 38.33	17 34 15.8	36 47	85 15
	δ □	5	11 10 35 A.	5 34 24.46	18 25 56.7	28 45	70 11
29	♐	5	0 5 57 M.	19 12 47.81	18 7 36.0 S.	55 21	72 21
30	β² ♑	3.4	0 42 16	20 12 24.81	15 15 26.0	38 56	71 2
	γ ♒	5	8 58 0 A.	21 1 15.74	11 59 6.1	16 36	46 20 S.
Oct. 3	21 ♓	6	4 32 26 A.	23 41 38.38	0 13 44.6 N.	48 50 N.	90 N. 10 N.
4	ε ♓	4	11 43 35	0 55 1.63	7 3 59.6	4 31	39 29 S.
5	54 Ceti.	6	7 58 29	1 42 45.40	10 17 2.9	24 14	60 9
7	δ □	5	7 39 52	5 34 25.07	18 25 57.6	21 36	59 4 N.
12	k □	5	2 46 20 M.	7 24 51.97	16 9 0.8	35 2	83 12
Nov. 4	A.S.C.454	6	4 3 54 A.	3 59 15.05	16 55 33.1 N.	40 38 N.	90 N. 17 N.
	β¹ ♉	6	10 23 5	4 14 8.16	17 10 41.8	50 4	90 29
	β² ♉	4.5	10 52 45	4 15 17.93	17 5 2.5	57 27	90 38
	β³ ♉	5	11 27 30	4 16 39.67	17 34 20.8	30 9	71 8
5	m ♉	5	5 19 44	4 58 25.94	18 25 57.6	22 1	60 4
8	□	4.5	3 51 8 M.	7 48 38.6	18 46 36.6	29 44	72 7
9	A² ♋	6	11 12 20 A.	8 38 32.15	12 40 5.4	27 57	69 1 S.
10	a² ♋	5	5 3 35 M.	8 50 6.85	12 26 45.2	1 18 S.	33 31
28	♓	5	5 4 29 A.	0 55 1.55	7 3 59.2	0 47 N.	36 32
	ζ¹ ♓	6	9 51 4	1 5 45.52	6 45 58.5	69 8	90 41 N.
Dec. 2	δ¹ ♉	4	7 38 42 A.	4 14 8.54	17 10 41.5 N.	51 45 N.	90 N. 31 N.
2	δ² ♉	4.5	8 8 35 A.	4 15 18.31	17 5 2.2	59 11	90 40
2	δ³ ♉	5	8 43 36 A.	4 16 40.06	17 34 20.6	31 55	74 10
3	m ♉	5	7 39 49 M.	4 58 26.42	18 25 57.1	25 5	64 7
4	μ □	5	8 26 11 A.	6 33 31.16	17 47 16.5	35 21	83 15
5	k □	5	8 1 37 A.	7 24 53.60	16 8 55.6	43 37	90 7
9	16 Sext.	6	2 3 14 M.	10 11 13.66	6 55 6.2	37 26	57 5
11	β¹ ♌	4.5	0 52 29 M.	11 29 7.16	0 1 14.1	12 3	48 23 S.
25	α ♎	3	10 28 58 A.	0 55 1.28	7 3 57.5	11 44 S.	24 45
30	119 ♉	5.6	9 10 59	5 23 16.18	18 28 24.2	32 9 N.	79 16 N.
30	120 ♉	6	9 45 50	5 24 35.27	18 25 29.7	35 19	83 19

Selected Bibliography

Books

Anderson, Charles R. *Melville in the South Seas.* New York: Dover Publications, Inc., 1966.

Beaglehold, J. C., ed. *The Journals of Captain James Cook on His Voyages of Discovery, 1776–1780,* III, Parts I and II. Cambridge, England: Hakluyt Society, 1967.

Beller, E. A., and M. du P. Lee, Jr., eds. *Selections from Bayle's Dictionary.* Westport, Conn.: Greenwood Press, Inc., 1969.

Berry, Arthur. *A Short History of Astronomy from Earliest Times Through the Nineteenth Century.* New York: Dover Publications, Inc., 1961.

Bowen, Merlin. *The Long Encounter: Self and Experience in the Writings of Herman Melville.* Chicago: University of Chicago Press, 1960.

Braswell, William. *Melville's Religious Thought.* Durham, N.C.: Duke University Press, 1943.

Browne, Ray B. *Melville's Drive to Humanism.* Lafayette, Ind.: Purdue University Studies, 1971.

Burton, Robert. *The Anatomy of Melancholy.* New York: Empire State Book Co., 1924.

Chase, Richard. *Herman Melville: A Critical Study.* New York: MacMillan Co., 1949.

Davis, Merrell R. *Melville's* Mardi: *A Chartless Voyage.* New Haven: Yale University Press, 1952.

Dillingham, William B. *An Artist in the Rigging: The Early Work of Herman Melville.* Athens: University of Georgia Press, 1972.

Dixon, Roland B. *Oceanic,* Vol. IX. Cooper Square Publishers, Inc., 1964.

Eichler, Lillian. *The Customs of Mankind; with Notes on Modern Etiquette and the Newest Trend in Entertainment.* Garden City: Nelson Doubleday, Inc., 1924.

Ellis, William. *Polynesian Researches.* London: Dawsons of Pall Mall, 1967.

Feidelson, Charles N., Jr. *Symbolism and American Literature.* Chicago: University of Chicago Press, 1953.

Fiedler, Leslie A. *Love and Death in the American Novel.* Rev. ed. New York: Stein & Day Publishers, 1966.

Fowler, Alastair. *Spenser and the Numbers of Time.* New York: Barnes & Noble, Inc., 1954.

Franklin, H. Bruce. *The Wake of the Gods: Melville's Mythology.* Stanford: Stanford University Press, 1963.

Goldman, Irving. *Ancient Polynesian Society.* Chicago: University of Chicago Press, 1970.

Golson, Jack, ed. *Polynesian Navigation: A Symposium on Andrew Sharpe's Theory of Accidental Voyages.* Wellington, N.Z.: The Polynesian Society (Incorporated), 1963.

Grimal, Pierre, ed. *Larousse World Mythology.* New York: G. P. Putnam's Sons, 1965.

Hargrave, Catherine Perry. *A History of Playing Cards and a Bibliography of Cards and Gaming.* New York: Dover Publications, Inc., 1966.

Hawthorne, Nathaniel. *The American Notebooks.* Edited by Randall Stewart. New Haven: Yale University Press, 1932.

Hetherington, Hugh W. *Melville's Reviewers, British and American: 1846–1891.* Chapel Hill: University of North Carolina Press, 1961.

Jobes, Gertrude, and James Jobes. *Outer Space: Myths, Name Meanings, Calendars; From the Emergence of History to the Present Day.* New York: Scarecrow Press, Inc., 1964.

Levin, Harry. *The Power of Blackness: Hawthorne, Poe, Melville.* New York: Alfred A. Knopf, Inc., 1958.

Lewis, Richard W. B. *The American Adam: Innocence, Tragedy, and Tradition in the 19th Century.* Chicago: University of Chicago Press, 1955.

Leyda, Jay. *The Melville Log: A Documentary Life of Herman Melville, 1819–1891.* In 2 vols. with a new supplementary chapter. New York: Gordian Press, Inc., 1968.

Matthiessen, F. O. *American Renaissance, Art and Expression in the Age of Emerson and Whitman.* New York: Oxford University Press, 1941.

Melville, Herman. *The Complete Stories of Herman Melville.* Edited by Jay Leyda. New York: Random House, Inc., 1949.

————. *Journal of a Visit to London and the Continent, by Herman Melville, 1849–1850.* Edited by Eleanor Melville Metcalf. Cambridge: Harvard University Press, 1948.

Miller, James E., Jr. *A Reader's Guide to Herman Melville.* New York: Farrar, Straus & Giroux, Inc., 1962.

Minningerode, Meade. *Some Personal Letters of Herman Melville and a Bibliography.* New York, New Haven, Princeton: The Brick Row Book Shop, Inc., 1922.

Moxon, Joseph. *A Tutor to Astronomy and Geography.* London, 1969.

Olson, Charles. *Call Me Ishmael.* New York: Regnal & Hitchcock, 1947.

Parker, Hershel, ed. *The Recognition of Herman Melville: Selected Criticism Since 1846.* Ann Arbor: The University of Michigan Press, 1970.

Parr, Johnstone. *"Tamburlaine's Malady" and Other Essays on Astrology in Elizabethan Drama.* Westport, Conn.: Greenwood Press, Inc., 1971.

Rafinesque, Constantine Samuel. *Celestial Wonders and Philosophy.* Philadelphia, 1838.

Reddall, Henry Frederic. *Fact, Fancy, and Fable.* Detroit: Gale Research Co., 1968.

Richman, John. *Journal of Captain Cook's Last Voyage to the Pacific Ocean.* Ann Arbor: University Microfilms, Inc., 1966.

Sealts, Merton M., Jr. *Melville as a Lecturer.* Cambridge, Mass.: Harvard University Press, 1957.

_____. *Melville's Reading: A Check-list of Books Owned and Borrowed.* Madison: University of Wisconsin Press, 1966.

Seelye, John. *Melville: The Ironic Diagram.* Evanston: Northwestern University Press, 1970.

Stern, Milton R. *The Fine Hammered Steel of Herman Melville.* Urbana: University of Illinois Press, 1957.

Tallant, Robert. *Mardi Gras.* Garden City, N. Y.: Doubleday & Co., Inc., 1948.

Thompson, Lawrance. *Melville's Quarrel with God.* Princeton: Princeton University Press, 1952.

Walsh, William S. *Curiosities of Popular Customs and of Rites, Ceremonies, Observances and Miscellaneous Antiquities.* Philadelphia: J. B. Lippincott, 1898.

Waterman, Philip F. *The Story of Superstition.* New York: Alfred A. Knopf, Inc., 1929.

Weaver, Raymond M. *Herman Melville, Mariner and Mystic.* New York: George H. Doran & Company, 1921.

Wright, Nathalia. *Melville's Use of the Bible.* Durham, N. C.: Duke University Press, 1949.

Periodicals

The American Almanac. Boston, 1844 and 1845.

Bell, Millicent. "Pierre Bayle and Moby-Dick." *PMLA,* LXIV (Sept. 1951), 626–48.

Davis, Merrell R. "The Flower Symbolism in Mardi." *Modern Language Quarterly,* 2 (1941), 625–38.

Graham, Philip. "The Riddle of Melville's *Mardi:* A Reinterpretation." *Texas Studies in English,* 36 (1957), 93–99.

Herbert, T. Walter, Jr. "Calvinism and Cosmic Evil in Moby Dick." *PMLA,* 84 (October 1969), 1613–19.

Hillway, Tyrus. "Taji's Abdication in Herman Melville's *Mardi." American Literature,* 16 (November 1944), 205–7.

———. "Taji's Quest for Certainty." *American Literature,* 18 (March 1946), 27–34.

Jaffe, David. "Some Sources of Melville's *Mardi." American Literature,* 9 (March 1937), 56–59.

Levine, Stuart. "Melville's 'Voyage Thither.' " *The Midwest Quarterly,* 3 (1962), 341–53.

Miller, James E., Jr. "The Complex Figures in Melville's Carpet." *The Arizona Quarterly,* 15 (1959), 197–210.

Mills, Gordon. "The Significance of 'Arcturus' in *Mardi." American Literature,* 14 (May 1942), 158–61.

Monthly Notices of the Royal Astronomical Society containing Abstracts of Papers, and Reports of the Proceedings of the Society, from November 1845, to June 1847, with one Supplement. Vol. 3. London, 1847.

Schulman, Robert. "The Serious Functions of Melville's Phallic Jokes." *American Literature,* 33 (May 1961), 179–94.

The Sidereal Messenger. July 1846 through October 1848. Cincinnati, 1848.

Thomas, Robert B. *The Farmer's Almanac* (for 1846). 54 (1845).

Travis, Mildred. "Mardi: Melville's Allegory of Love." *Emerson Society Quarterly,* 43 (1966), 88–94.

Wright, Nathalia. "The Head and Heart in Melville's *Mardi." PMLA,* 66 (1951), 351–62.

———. "A Note on Melville's Use of Spenser: Hautia and the Bower of Bliss." *American Literature,* 24 (March 1952), 83–85.

Index

Y

Yillah, 14, 39, 40-41, 48, 58, 60-62,
64-65, 75, 80-81, 140, 143-46, 148,
152, 158-60, 181, 187, 189-90, 223,
232, 237-38, 245; as card figure, 58, 65,
75; as cup or Grail, 65, 81, 145-46, 160,
181, 187; as Luna, 41, 143, 159

Yoky, King, 215
Yom Kippur, 81
Yoomy, 34, 40, 162, 167-68, 174-76, 184,
190-91, 195-96, 212, 215, 224, 232,
241; as errant interpreter, 167-68,
175-76, 184, 190-91, 215, 224

Z

Zero Trump, 68-70
Zeus, 178
Zodiac, 2, 17, 30, 35, 38, 53, 83, 115-16,
140, 150, 156, 177, 179, 182, 227; as
calendar, 38; quest through, 38; Sol
through, 35; use in art metaphor, 17, 30,
83, 150